Six-pack:
Plays for Scotland

John McGrath

Polygon
Edinburgh

This volume is published by
Polygon
22 George Square
Edinburgh

Set in Meridien

Typeset by Bibliocraft, Dundee

Printed and bound in Great Britain

A CIP record is available

ISBN 07486 6201 4

The Publisher acknowledges subsidy from the

towards the publication of this volume

Contents

Preface

These plays have not been polished for reading. The innocent reader must bring to them all the colour and clarity that great theatre design and subtle lighting brings, must hear the most thrilling music and beautiful singing voices, must conjure up the emotional depth of great performances, must sense the weight and power given in production to each individual line, must feel the warmth of the conspiracy between the stage and the audience. This is, of course, to demand a great deal of the innocent reader, no less than a recreation, or a new creation of each play. But a playscript alone is only what is left behind after the performance is over. How else to bring it to life again than let the individual imagination play the director, the composer, the designer and the company? And why settle for less than the best?

Yet, at the end of the day, as they say, what drives the imagination is the word. No playwright can completely pass on responsibility for the words on the page. In an age in which the growth of the 'visual' languages of film, television, advertising, and computer iconography is the excuse for vapid imprecision; in which political and financial and industrial powers have one very exact internal language of expansion and profit, but when called upon to speak to the world they hire Public Relations advisers to teach them to speak a rather different language designed to deceive, or even to appear to speak while in fact saying nothing; in which, in short, public language is in danger of losing its ability to tell the truth of the world in all its complexity, then perhaps at least some writers should refuse complicity with this failure by declining to indulge in smart post-modern games-playing, and rather struggle to create recognisable images of a world in transition, and even to dare to ask: transition to what? To answer, we must have words, that mean, and people who say what they mean: otherwise the world becomes one big Waco, with plutonium. I recognise this as hopelessly unfashionable, but have always claimed more affinity with the Pre-modern than the Post. I can't say fashion has ever done much for me, so why should I worry about fashion?

This trusting, perhaps primitive approach to language, may, I suppose, be linked by perceptive critics of my plays to a certain stubborn optimism about the core of their moral and political values, which was, and is, that humanity is capable of two things: co-operation, and change for the better. I feel that fewer and fewer people believe either of these two to be realistic or even possible. There is much in recent history to justify such cynicism. But recent history has been very confusing. Many things have been called what they are not, and many lies have been told about anything that opposes the interests of the larger corporations. But even if you are a fool you cannot believe that the only possible form of social co-operation is Soviet communism, or that the only possible form of socialism in Britain must be James Callaghan's Labourism — the kind that left such a nasty taste in the mouth which the New Labour Party is trying to rinse out with carbolic. You could only believe such things in order to discredit the whole idea of anything working other than multi-national investment and production in a world market controlled not by competition but by the biggest corporations, the mighty barons of the multi-nationals, demanding their Magna Carta of every nation, old and new, moving inexorably to their Utopia: the whole world as their fief.

Are they really so dreadful? Is world peace and global harmony not in their best interests? Are they not just trying to make satisfied consumers of the whole of humanity? Are they not truly about to usher in The End of History? I am often accused of political naivete, usually by people who think — blinded by their own unquestioning naivete — that the answer to all those questions is Yes. They are wrong. They have been told what, and how, to think by those very corporations and their PR people — the transnational medicine-men.

The answer to all these questions is No. Whatever their egregious apologists may dream up, what the global multi-nationals are actually achieving is a world of well-off, 'contented' consumers with money for consumption and an illusion of choice and power through the political processes of the hollowest form of democracy available, on the one hand, and on the other, a submerged but growing mass of people — J K Galbraith's 'Under Class' — with no illusions, no choices, no power, no role in the political processes, and no money to consume anything but shit — the waste-products of the affluent.

So if the politics of these plays sometimes appears a little strident, the moral tone a little fervent in places, please forgive, for what lies under and behind is an ignited sense of reality.

But in spite of this, I have tried to write plays that will, above all, entertain — and use the forms of popular entertainment to draw them closer to their audiences. Of course there is music, there is comedy, corny and otherwise, there is variety, there is high drama and low drama, there is fun and frolics: the plays aim to make theatre available to everyone, to give people 'A Good Night Out'.

The audiences these plays in particular have in mind in the first instance are audiences of non-theatre-goers in Scotland. Some are primarily for people in their communities in the Highlands and Islands, some more for people in the industrial or post-industrial areas. These audiences are significantly different culturally, but they have been united during the 1980s and 90s by a deep resentment that Scotland is being ruled by a contemptuous, non-representative government in Westminster and a set of inept bureaucratic cliques in Edinburgh.

This will come to an end. But I hope the other qualities that unite them will not. A sense of shared social responsibility, the feeling that we are all in some degree part of each other, has held firm in Scotland as in other nordic nations. The notion still exists that pride in one's country need not be chauvinist or racist. The notion of respect for other people, their homes, their views, their right to happiness, has not entirely gone, or been disfigured by fear into manic possessive individualism. There is plenty wrong with Scotland, but if it can

vii

develop its own place in the world without losing its social morality and its cultural specifics, it will become an even better place to be than it is now.

About the selection. Though the plays chosen touch on four decades, and as many styles of theatre-making, they are neither chronological nor fully representative. There are many others I have written during the last twenty-seven years which are left out with great reluctance, which perhaps may appear in another volume. The earliest, and perhaps most conventional drama, I wrote for Richard Eyre to direct at the Lyceum, Edinburgh: *Random Happenings in the Hebrides, or The Social Democrat and the Stormy Sea*. I was writing it in that sunny May of 1968 when word came of the 'Events' in Paris. I put it aside for a few weeks while I went over there, then came back to finish it. It is about the 1960s, and opposes two realities: the glib Wilsonite political power-games of its well-meaning incomer MP, and the unpalatable realities of life in a raw, marginalised island. The furious banging on the bar counter for a drink that will do no good when it comes is trying to say something about the inadequacies of Labourism, the failure of the compromised hopes of the 60s.

Out of Our Heads comes from the mid-70s, and more banging on the bar, as by this time the articulate in the working class sense defeat and incorporation, and the inarticulate sink into apathy and/or schizophrenia.

Blood Red Roses is a play for the 80s. The wheel of reaction and forthright, unashamed greed turns as Thatcher mounts the tank disguised as a pulpit, moral values are reversed, and old heroes are turned into villains. It is a play about resistance, and the processes that undermine it.

Joe's Drum comes from the time of the very fulcrum of the crowbar that upended the UK: the time, in 1979, of both the negative Devolution vote in the last gasp of Callaghan's disastrous government, and the triumphant election of Thatcher and her dogmatic friends to what became ultimate power — the dictatorship of the majority. In the play, as in life at that time, the very nature of democracy — the way the will of the people is formed, expressed, and carried out — was brought into question. What was representative parliamentary democracy, in itself a dubious variant of the real thing, became penetration of the whole of civil society by a small set of inflexible autocrats, became rule by Cabinet committee, and what little voice was left to the people was confused and humbled into silence and inertia.

Of the two apparently 'historical' plays, *The Cheviot, the Stag and the Black Black Oil* was written for and with the 7:84 Theatre Company (Scotland). I have written at some length elsewhere about the gestation of this piece, particularly in 'The Year of the Cheviot' an article for Plays and Players reproduced in the Methuen edition of this play.

The other, *Border Warfare*, was rejected by my successor at 7:84, and put on at Glasgow's Tramway by Wildcat, with help from Channel 4 via Freeway Films and Glasgow's European City of Culture funds. It raids and loots several other plays of mine trying to tell the huge story of Scotland from the dark Ages up to the 1990s, in terms of her relationship with England.

I have written many plays in between and since these plays — for 7:84 (England) and its audiences, for Jude Kelly's West Yorkshire Playhouse, for Nick Kent at the Tricycle, for schools tours, for a derelict factory in Athens and even one for a Dutch steel-town. But I hope these plays from four decades will give an idea of what we have been up to in Scotland all these years.

Apart from *Random Happenings in the Hebrides*, the first performances of all the other plays were directed by me. I worked in several styles, but all of them encouraged the actors and musicians and indeed the rest of the company to feel free to make creative contributions in all areas. Consequently many thoughts, gags, songs and pieces of information kept popping up during rehearsal. While as writer/director I must take full responsibility for what finally emerged from this process, I must give due credit to, and thank all those who collaborated so generously in the making of these plays.

If I may be forgiven an even more personal note: although these plays are written for Scotland, I am not ethnically Scots, being an itinerant Liverpool-Irish person of Welsh upbringing, Oxford and London training, and Scottish only by marriage, domicile and commitment. So I owe a huge debt to those who taught me what Scotland is, and can be: Elizabeth MacLennan, and several generations of her Highland/Glasgow family; my own children, and their friends; the many theatre-workers I had such joy in making theatre with, in particular my ever-shifting bunch of 'regulars', amongst whom, over the years, David MacLennan, John Bett, Billy Riddoch, Dave Anderson, Elizabeth, Terry Neason, Bill Paterson, Alex Norton, Allan Ross, and the Gaels, Simon Mackenzie, Catherine-Ann MacPhee, Dolina Maclennan, and the many, many others equally magnificent but too numerous to list here; the many writers, thinkers, academics, researchers, historians, journalists, film-makers, and the one Hamish Henderson, not to mention Sorley Maclean and John MacInnes, who will never know how much I have learnt, borrowed or stolen from them; and of course the many people of Scotland in audiences, in dances, in bars, in political meetings, marches, rallies, in countless kitchens and sitting-rooms, who have told and I hope will go on telling me where it's at.

Whether she likes it or not I'm going to thank Marion Sinclair, and Polygon; and Susie Brown and Avril Watt and Chloe Sizer for fundamental support.

Above all I thank Liz, Finn, Danny and Kate, who gave so much and had to put up with so much, and kept me sane.

This book is not about the past, it's about the future, so it's dedicated to Kate, and her friends, and the generation who will make Scotland what it can be.

John McGrath

ix

Acknowledgements

The Cheviot, the Stag and the Black Black Oil was first published by the West Highland Free Press, and is now available in a handsome edition from Methuen, to whom many thanks.

Blood Red Roses and *Joe's Drum* were first published by 7:84 Theatre Company (Scotland), the latter with Aberdeen People's Press. Both are now out of print.

Random Happenings in the Hebrides was first published by Davis-Poynter.

I have in the course of looting various strands of popular entertainment borrowed or stolen from many sources.

Border Warfare

Border Warfare was first presented by Wildcat Stage Productions and Freeway Stage at the Old Museum of Transport (The Tramway Theatre), Glasgow, on 23 February 1989. The cast list:

JOHN McGRATH	Director
PAMELA HOWARD with ANNETTE GILLIES and ANDREW SEMPLE	Design
KRIS MISSELBROOKE	Lighting Design
RAB HANDLEIGH	Music
ARCHIE FISHER	Musical Research
STEWART HAPPS	Movement
ANDREW FISHER	Masks

The Company

Derek Anders
Dave Anderson
Robin Begg
John Bett
Juliet Cadzow
Rab Handleigh
Michael Marra
Maria Miller
John Purcell
Bill Riddoch
John A Sampson
Mike Travis

with

John Cairns
George Drennan
David Dunn
Martin McCardie
Katrina McPherson
Kathleen Wishart

DAVID MacLENNAN, APRIL CHAMBERLAIN	Production and Management for Wildcat
SUSIE BROWN, DAVID BROWN	Production and Management for Freeway

ACT ONE

Prologue

As the audience enter, not more than ten minutes before the start of
the show, they are coming into the Forest of Scotland in the Dark Ages.

Large Scots pines hang over the space, which is lit through green gobbos,
and small clumps of alder and birch (on wheels) are scattered through
the area, and darker corners of forest lurk along the edges. In all of
them, stuffed bears, wolves, otters, pine-martens, foxes, wildcats, red
and roe-deer, twinkle in the darkness, and eagles, ospreys, ravens and
rooks hover or perch overhead. Two 'live' bears, and a wild, shaggy
wolf, move around, trying to hide from the audience, occasionally
jumping out at them from unexpected corners.

MUSIC is playing: on synth, noises suggestive of volcanic bubbling,
emptying marsh-gases, the howl of wind over travelling glacier, the
bellow of stranded whales, the groaning of primeval forest: but above
it all, all the time, the high, lyrical, optimistic sounds of the melody
of life coming into being, of growth and learning. Percussion rumbles
quietly under this, screeches and tears, rattles and pings, but never
thundering or reaching high crescendos, always under.

As the audience comes in, TWO VOICES, a male and a female, greet
them, amplified on echo, slightly distorted, one voice repeating after
the other, somewhere up in the roof-beams:

SOUNDS throughout all this of animal barks, yelps, screams, bellows,
of bird-song and rooks calling, of sudden roars and bellows, of bleats
and dying squeaks.

VOICES: Welcome to the Forest of Scotland . . . (Repeated
often.) . . . Welcome to the Dark Ages, the Cold
Ages, the Age of Brute and Mammoth . . . Welcome
to the Green Forest of Scotland . . . .

                Here are bears, and beaver and otter
Here are wolves that wander at will
Here are pole-cat, pine-marten, wildcat spitting
Here Roe-deer and red-deer and reindeer bellow,
Badgers scuffle and pad along pathways
Hedgehogs trundle and hares leap high . . .
Welcome to the Dark Age of the Forest of Scotland,
Ranging over us, eagle and raven and rook
Swoop to the bone of rabbit and weasel and stoat:
Ferrets flash yellow and orioles flash golden
In shafts of sun under stippling birichen,
Soft the needle-bed under pine and whin,
Snake under braken, snail in her shell.

                Welcome to the Forest of Scotland . . . (Repeat.)

4

Welcome to the Dark Ages, the Cold Ages, the
Age of glacier and murrain, of melting ice-cap and
splitting of rock . . .Welcome to the Green Forest
of Scotland . . .

Here are bog, loch and lochan,
Salmon and seal and sea-trout leaping.
Here lurk toad and serpent and sloe-worm,
Adder and newt, diver and duckling,
Eider and pochard, shell duck and Golden Eagle,
Goose and Goosander, Grey-lag and Barnacle,
Here stand Heron in stilted silence
Or flap like owls in long-armed flying.
Here crumbles undergrowth, trees of the tundra,
Rots into peat-bog, under myrtle and cotton:
Here stand the hills, granite and sandstone,
Grampian, Cairngorm, Ochil and Trossach,
Pentland and Lammermuir, Mountain over Marshland;
All alive with beast and bird,
Boar and bull, heifer and hind,
With rat and squirrel, roach and beetle
And small birds so bright that are quick on the wing.

Welcome to this Forest of Scotland . . . (Repeat).
Welcome to the Dark Ages,
After the Roman had retired defeated . . .
After Calgacus had driven them away . . .
Welcome to the Cold, to the Damp, to the Dark,
                              Dark Ages . . .
Welcome to Scotland, her Forest so Green . . .

As MUSIC modulates, a high boy-ish soprano sings a line of very early,
clear and echoing plainchant, there is a hint of organ in the synth
underneath. After a few seconds a muffled clapper as in a funeral.

Enter, lead by a TIPSTAFF clearing the way by beating on the ground
with his staff, a PROCESSION. After the TIPSTAFF, a coffin decorated
with St Andrews flags, on a rickety old pram, and full of huge thistles
is pushed on by a BEAR, and followed by fourteen hooded figures in
TWOs, the men's VOICES groling deep accompanying burden to the
high soprano.

The birdsong, etc fades almost completely.

As they come in, surreptitious, almost unseen pushing and shoving,
vying for place and standing on cloak tails, and as they reach the centre
of the hall, a more vigorous set of pushes, with one sent flying back,
another thrown forward, a third standing on the tails of the two who
push the coffin, soon VOICES are raised, and a general rammie, with
hoods pulled back and claws out.

The high soprano floats above all this.

Enter then a float with a broken goal-post on it, and a figure who is a cross between the hammer-thrower on Scott's Porage Oats and a pie-eyed member of the Tartan Army, with vest and kilt and hammer, but also a huge Lion Rampant flag flowing out from his shoulders. On his float, he wears a ghetto-blaster, in place of a sporran, from which comes the ever-growing chant: Scotland! Scotland! with a Hampden or Wembley or Murrayfield roar behind it. He swings his great hammer around his head, pausing only to march up and down joining in the chant, and occasionally tear off a few bits of goal-post or dig up some Wembley turf. Now and again he gives us snatches or 'Flower of Scotland', and then spray opens a few cans of lager.

TARTAN ARMY: (sings). Ting-a-ling-a-ling
Jimmy Johnston's on the wing
And it's EA-SY! EA-SY!!

(sings) If you hate the fuckin' English clap your hands!
— Clap Clap Clap —
If you hate the fuckin' English clap your hands!

The mayhem with the monks also continues to develop, soon the body in the coffin rises up through the thistles, a small gaunt figure in white shroud and pale green face and hair. She piercingly blows a whistle.

The fighting pauses, the music and singing halt, the Tartan Army man plugs the jack from his earphones in the ghetto-blaster thus silencing it. All hold.

CORPSE: I was a Pict and slain by a Scot,
An Anglian peasant by an English army,
A Gael by a Gollach,
A Presbyterian tortured by Mary's men,
A Tim shot through the head by an Orangeman,
A Piscy by Cromwell,
A Highlander by Cumberland,
I was a heretic burnt by Knox,
A Comyn stabbed by Bruce,
A crofter's child with cholera on the boat to
   Nova Scotia
I was a soldier on the Somme,
A young wife with TB in the slums of Paisley:
I was a miner when the roof went,
A witch at the stake,
A still-born child,
A baby with AIDS:

(The Soprano and music begin again gently —)

I was the flower of Scotland

6

Broken at the stem,
Eaten by slugs,
Trampled under heavy boots:
I was hit by my husband,
I was strangled by my mother,
I was cast down a well,
I was drowned in the Minch:

Let me now lie in peace.
Put me in the earth with decency and thoughtfulness.

The deep voices join in again. TARTAN ARMY slumps down in a chair,
sucking a huge bottle of whisky with a baby's teat on it.

The PROCESSION reforms — this time in single file.

The CORPSE sings along with the soprano voice — which is her voice
— she stays upright as the pram/coffin is pushed around to exit where
it came in from, more or less. The figures put their hoods on, and as
they follow each other singing holy songs, they all produce daggers,
etc and stab each other in the back rhythmically.

TARTAN ARMY is taken off quietly.

The SOUNDS of the Forest resume, take over —

VOICES: Welcome to the Forest of Scotland . . .
                 Welcome to the Dark Ages
                 After the Romans had retired defeated . . .
                 After Calgacus had driven them away . . .
                 Welcome to the Cold, to the Damp, to the Dark,
                                                       Dark Ages . . .
                 Welcome to Scotland, her Forest so Green . . .

Scene One — Towards One Kingdom

After the sequence fades, a spot on the last figure in the procession,
who turns, throws back his hood, smiles, throws off his cloak to reveal
himself as the LORD of BON ACCORD (or MISRULE). He runs and
jumps up on a convenient high place, drawing the audience round him:

LORD OF   My Lords and Ladies, children too
BON ACCORD: A welcome to one and all of you:
                 For all our Players I speak this word
                 For I am the Lord of Bon Accord —
                 No more I play the dumb-cluck fool,
                 For that they cried me Lord Misrule —
                 But Bon Accord I bring to all
                 Whose minds and hearts are not closed and small:

7

Since on our most legitimate stages
'Relationships' are all the rages —
Then to our illegitimate boards
Relationships may bring rewards,
For we must pander to the private parts
Of the Scottish Council of the Arts,
And try to follow yesterday's trend
(For that is all they understand) —

So gather round and watch and weigh
This story that we tell today:
We don't sell culture, fashion, or soap,
But try to find a cause for hope:
There's not been much, the truth to tell,
The past ten years were close to hell:
Relationships! I've lost the strand — !
Between this spiky Scottish land
And England smooth and strong and bland —
That's our theme, a thousand years long,
We trust you're feeling fit and strong —
Up there lies Scotland, Give her a cheer!

(A short blast of pipe music, a caber tosser rushes over.)

And there lies England's watery beer —

(Two skinhead football hooligans race over beating up an old lady.)

A healthy mix of prejudice and fact,
No high-wire, wobbly 'balancing' act —
Our play with Scotland sets the scene:
And here she comes: the Pictish Queen!

Percussion. Old horns. A great rumbling and bellowing as QUEEN OF PICTS is drawn in on her float. She has a huge and colourful banner with the strange images of the Pict on it. She has flaming red hair and a furious temper, which she is now giving full rein to, storming about, climbing up higher to see something threatening, bellowing at the pitch of her voice. She is tattooed wonderfully over all the parts we can see, and very warlike.

Also on her cart, seated, is her son, one of the thirty King Bruides, who translates for her. He is also quite fearsome, but clearly dominated by his mother.

She utters angrily, like oaths, a selection of the following — which are genuine Pictish words. (Unfortunately no one knows what they mean, so she can feel free!)

PICTISH QUEEN: Ettocahets!
                      Iratedoareus!!

Aheh — ht — tan — nn . . .
Nehtetri! Nehtetri!
Hc-cv-vev-v . . .
Iratodoareus!!
Bes meg-qnanam — movvez —
Meq-Bruide
Meq-Bredei
Meq-Bridei
Meq-Nehtan
Nehtan Diuperr
Bliesblituth!
Usconbuts!
Canutu-lachama!!
Iratodo-areus!!
Uurad — Uurad —

During this the watching LORD OF BON ACCORD yells at her son
BRUIDE —

BON ACCORD: Bruide! Bruide! Oh King of the Picts! TRANSLATE!!
Nobody speaks Pictish any more! Translate or we'll
all go home —

BRUIDE scowls, speaks with thick Inverness accent.

BRUIDE: Are you wise? Are you surprised Us Picts end up
with Nahin —

BOND ACCORD: Nahin? Nahin?
Speak English!

BRUIDE: Nahin!!
Nahin at all — That's what we Picts end up with!

PICTISH QUEEN takes a running kick at him, indicates to go on. She
continues her performance.

BRUIDE: She says her grandmother's son was Bruide 18th
High King of all the Picts, her mother's son was
Bruide 19th, I am her son, I am Bruide 20th, her
daughter's son will be Bruide 22nd and she doesn't
give a damn who their fathers were, there's always
some confusion possible, and the safest way is to
pass the kingdom down through the women —

PICTISH QUEEN holds forth at him — selected from above —

And she'd like to remind you that our kingdom
stretches from Orkney to Argyll, from Ullapool to
Edinburgh, and all the land of Scotland north of
the Clyde and the Forth is divided into smaller

Pictish kingdoms, who all pay tribute to the High King, Bruide her son — that's me, by the way — and she's never been so insulted in her life!

PICTISH QUEEN waves her spear at the South-West —

BRUIDE: She says the bloody Irish are coming over in dribs and drabs to pick the tatties and they're not going home!

BON ACCORD: There were no tatties in Pictland!

BRUIDE: It's a manner of speaking — we Picts have no concept of history!

PICTISH QUEEN: Forcus!! Farcus!! Ipe! Ipe!!

At this a SMALL GROUP of BRITTONS run in, very agitated, jumping up and down, pointing in the same direction as PICTISH QUEEN. They speak with a Cumbrian accent —

BRUIDE and PICTISH QUEEN laugh at them, mocking their jumping up and down, and their fear —

BRUIDE: Oh dear, the poor little Brittons are getting very excited! Hello Brittons! We're coming to eat you all up — Cumberland sausages, lovely!

BRITTONS: (make terrible Melvyn Bragg noises).

BON ACCORD: What! You — little Cumbrian wench — What are all these Melvyn Braggs going on about?

BRITTONIC TRANSLATOR: The bloody Irish are coming — As if we haven't had enough! First of all the bloody Romans come over here, seducing our women, laying waste our fields, and slaughtering us till we had to run for the hills, to Cumbria and the Isle of Man, and Galloway and Ayrshire. That's us, the Strathclyde Brittons, decent people driven north by the English government — and we won't be the last decent people driven North by the English government. You Picts keep taking the piss, now these bloody Micks, swarming over in hordes from Ulster: and I've got news for Bruide — they haven't come to pick the tatties!

PANDEMONIUM, war-horns, bag-pipes, timpani as the SCOTS, the IRISH, sail in on a mighty warship: they are FERGUS, ANGUS and LOARN.

They utter war-cries in Gaelic and in dreadful mock-Irish, brandishing the Tri-colour, spears, their shields covered with the West Highland Free Press, their prow decorated with 'Scottish' as on the STV logo,

10

and the computerised thistle. One of them, with an Armalite, is in a balaclava, the rest more historical.

The PICTS and BRITS swirl around trying to repel them and the noise is deafening — then suddenly they all stop and stare in amazement as another float arrives from the South-East: on it, EADWIN and EADWINA, two tall beautiful blonde people, hand in hand, drinking Skol lager, reading a Danish Love-Making Manual. They play an Abba number on their tape-deck.

EADWIN: Eadwina: shall we attempt page 173?

EADWINA: Not now, Eadwin: Look!

The SCOTS demand, via FERGUS:

FERGUS: And just who in the name of all that's permissive would you be? And from whence did you spring?

EADWIN: I am Eadwin, and this is Eadwina — (GROWLS of male desire from all other areas.) Ve are Angles, from Danemark originally but ve have lived here for a long time now, and ve have occupied all of Northumbria, Lindisfarne, all of the Lammermuirs and ve are peacefully farming the rich and fruitful plains of the Lothians, and ve make love not war! By the way: who are yo?

FERGUS: We are the Scots!

LOUD COMPLAINTS from all OTHERS — along the lines of 'you're Teagues, Micks, Tim Molloys, Left-footers, Fenian Bastards, slitter-slaughter Holy Water Scatter the Papishes every one, etc'.

ANGUS: (Dublin accent). We are three sons of Eric — King of Dalriada in Ireland, and we come to Alba to found here a new Dalriada, called Dalriada Scotland. Loarn here will grab hold of some land and call it Lorne, Fergus will grab Bute, Arran, Cowal and Kintyre, and I myself will hold green Islay and fair Jura; and the Kingship of Dalriada Scotland will pass from generation to generation from family to family in strict rotation. And what you ignorant Picts call Alba, will come to be called Scot-land, after us, and our grandchilder and their grandchilder will rule over this Scotland, from Windermere to Cape Wrath, from The Old Man of Hoy to Whitby.

MUSIC in. LORD OF BON ACCORD appears high on the Scottish stage, resplendent now as King William of Lyon, with banners blowing out from all the contesting parts being placed behind him as he continues the story, on mike, over the music that rises and unites as the four floats — PICTS, SCOTS, ANGLES and BRITTONS, are drawn together below the Scottish stage to make a phalanx, apparently united. However, even as they draw together there are problems, territorial claims, disputes, all contained within the surface harmony and loyalty.

Scene Two — *William The Lyon/The Knights*

WILLIAM THE LYON:	Our Scotland was not rich in corn-growing land or gold or armies: but if Scotland could hold together the sum of her parts, then I, William the Lyon, King of all Scotland, could take her into the community of nations alongside all others, no matter how proud.

And so after St Columba and St Ninian and St Mungo and St Kentigern had done their work, and given all a common creed, then Kenneth son of Alpin, thought of a way to unite the Scots of whom he was King, and the Picts under their Matriarchs. He thought he'd marry the daughter of the Queen — so her son would still be king — and his son would be king: and so they drew slowly together. And the Picts joined with the Angles to fight the Strathclyde Brittons, and eventually a sort of peace was made.

BON ACCORD: Peace! Peace! Ha — in Scotland a peace made is rarely a peace kept. Blood was spilt in every corner of the land as the jealousies and tempers rose like forest fires in the summertime.

Every time a poor farmer scratched the ground to grow his oats or his barley, some great oaf of an Earl or a Norwegian raided and ravaged, burnt the land and killed the cattle — Macbeth was a bit of a problem, but not for long. Then came a bunch called the MacHeths or Mackays who thought they should be kings and that William here should be headless — oh aye: a turbulent, bloodthirsty, venomous history. Something undoubtedly was needed to pull us all together: and there it is, knocking forever knocking on our door:

A TRUMPET: the stage of England is lit, to reveal a bristle of pikes and swords, and a Red Ensign.

WILLIAM OF LYON: We were united, God bless them, by the English! We fought together as Scots to keep them out. And to keep the peace, our kings married their princesses and that's how my grandfather King David when

12

> he was only eight years old went to the English
> Court — which was no more English than Julius
> Caesar.

On English stage, a young DAVID with his back to us is being instructed by FOUR ANGLO-NORMAN KNIGHTS, in various arts, mostly of warfare. The instruction is in French, which DAVID also uses.

Birds sing at the English Court, and a thrush overdoes it.

Over the top of this, WILLIAM continues:

> There he learnt a trick or two: how it's done, how
> to rule, how to keep your subjects under the thumb
> and secure your kingdom: as perfected by the
> Norman Kings of England! it's called Feudalism:
> you simply import a class of ruling noblemen, who
> swear allegiance to you, and you send them out into
> your countryside, grant them land to raise rents,
> to build castles, to raise armies, and to terrorise the
> humble and the mighty into swearing allegiance
> to you as well: what a wonderful system!

BON ACCORD: But where did grandfather David find these feudal
lords to put fear into the Scottish people? Why in
England! Then as now, the Scottish ruling class
came up from London, on the 12th-century shuttle,
the feudal 125!

FOUR great fortified horses proceed from the South grandly to Scotland — and on them a BRUCE, a COMYN, a BALLIOL, and a WALLACE on a smaller horse, behind the others!

MUSIC French 13th-century courtly (or military?) music.

BRUCE, COMYN and BALLIOL discuss the landscape, the weather and the population around them in Anglo-French, pointing at the audience and laughing at them, as they move up the hall.

WILLIAM goes on mike, over all this.

WILLIAM: Up came the adventurers, the mercenary aristocracy,
the planted ruling-class, as if to the Scottish Tory Party
Annual Conference, and with the same intention: to
bring law and order to Scotland. The Lascelles, the
de Soules, the Burnetts and Oliphants, the Giffords
and Lindsays and Grahams and Collevilles, those
who called themselves de Moravia and became the
Murrays, the Somervilles and Avenels, the Martins
and Freskins — up they came to get their fief of
land, and to swear fealty to Grandpa David — and

13

now, of course, to me! And who are these proud knights? Not the Sales Managers of the multinationals, but great-grandfathers of noble Scottish heroes — Robert the Bruce, who held Annandale; the Comyn, whose parcels of land spread far and wide; de Bailleul, whose heir John Balliol became the puppet king of Scotland, and the humble administrator, Richard de Wallis — Richard of Wales, the great-great-grandfather of the Hero of the Scots himself — Sir William Wallace!

BON ACCORD: They arrived. They took land from the king. They penetrated even north of Inverness, to Dingwall, westwards into Argyll, into the heartland of the Gallowegians, as far as Stranraer. And everywhere they built their castles and mottes, like Belfast barracks, holding military power and upholding the rule of the king and the unity of the kingdom . . . And soon the old Scots Earls were knitted into the system, became feudal landowners themselves, and import and native were joined together by marriage and dowry to hold down the people, to quell rebellion, and to grow ever richer and mightier under the protection of the Crown, the Monarch — Him!

By now the FOUR KNIGHTS have occupied the FOUR FLOATS of Scotland, and erected Mottes, of lath and barbed-wire, on them, and spaced them out again.

WILLIAM THE LYON comes on laughing wickedly and buckling on his armour, followed by some SOLDIERS —

Tymps rumble under:

WILLIAM: Before I was King I was Earl of Northumberland, that was then part of Scotland — but Henry of England took Northumberland away from me — Well, now I'm off to get some of it back — to harry Harry! Come on my lads, there's plenty to be had and nobody to stop us —

He leaps or climbs energetically up onto a chariot and is pushed to ALNWICK, the central Tower. Here a Geordie WIFE puts her head over the parapet —

GEORDIE WIFE: Gan awa' Jockies a', Gan awa' Willie,
We'll na let ye in, we're no' so damn silly —

WILLIAM: We'll aye wait till ye're stervit,

14

And beggan for mercie
Then we'll open your doors and your waime,
Betty Percy!

As they argue, WILLIAM quite comfortably, ENGLISH SOLDIERS are moving through the audience with drawn swords, stealthily, asking for complicity . . .

GEORDIE WIFE: Ye wee Scottish hinnies, ye'll nere brak my door in
Gif ye enter my waime, I'll be lyin' back snorin! . . .

WILLIAM: Ye'll sit up and tak notice
When we tak a' your siller
Your auld goose and your kie
And your corn frae the miller . . .

GEORDIE WIFE: Gan awa' Willie noo, as quick as ye'll flee
For your guards they are blind and see
not what I see . . .

The ENGLISH SOLDIERS leap up on WILLIAM, take him by force, and drag him to the English Court. There HENRY II stands, pleased, as he watches WILLIAM approach:

HENRY: William the Lyon, the King of the Scots
I'll teach you a lesson you'll never forget

As WILLIAM is forced to kneel, to be publicly humiliated and then allowed home in subjection, to his mournful people the Treaty of Falaise echoes around the building.

VOICE: (very English, William Waldegrave). This is the treaty and settlement which William, king of Scots, has made with his lord, Henry, king of the English. William, king of Scots, has become the liegeman of the king for Scotland, and for all his other lands, and has sworn fealty to him as his lord. All the bishops, abbots, and clergy of the realm of the king of Scots from whom he wishes to receive it, and their successors, shall swear fealty to the king as liege Lord.

(MUSIC slow air 'Theme of English Conquest'.)

The king of Scots and David his brother, and the barons, and his other men, have also granted to the king that the church of Scotland shall henceforward owe such subjection to the church of England as it should do, and was accustomed to do in the time of his predecessors as kings of England.

The guarantee to the king, and Henry his son, and

their heirs, that this treaty and settlement will be strictly observed by the king of Scots and his heirs, the king of Scots has delivered to the king the castles of Roxburgh, Berwick, Jedburgh, Edinburgh and Stirling, to be at his complete disposal.

(Fades slowly.)

And for maintaining the castles the king of Scots will assign proportionally from his revenue, as the king may desire.

As the reading of the Treaty fades away, the air played through it rises then finishes.

WILLIAM: And Henry's soldiers sat through our land, from Aberdeen down to Roxburghe, and our hostages wasted themselves in London, until the great day came, and the cruel king Henry, the Second of England, died and was buried in France. Then my dear good companion Richard known as the Lion-Hearted, soon made amends, removed his greedy English soldiers, gave us back our Scottish lands, our hostages and cancelled all Henry's ransoms and claims on us.

We thought we could live together as two nations on the one island in mutual respect and friendship. And so, for a time, we did. For nearly half a century I dedicated my life to the belief that there was such a thing as the Kingdom of Scotland: and that I was in charge of it.

MUSIC funereal beat: discordant harmonies —

WILLIAM folds his arms across his chest, walks slowly off.

BON ACCORD: In 1214, William, the Red-Face, Uilleam Garbh — Harsh William to the Gael, Leo Justitiae — the Lion of Justice — to all, died, with Scotland independent, at peace and standing alongside the other nations of Europe as a sovereign state.

Scene Three — Proud Edward

In England, more trumpets, birdsong and plainchant as a young EDWARD I comes on in a white shift, looking very young and innocent, but with a wicked smile. As he speaks, he is dressed by his SERVANTS in shining armour, with all the accoutrements — his horse, also armoured, etc is lead on during the song for Alexander, and he is lowered onto it:

EDWARD I: I see England as a tortoise — no, a monster turtle,
It's warm heart and soft, rich body secure within,
Pleasuring itself on blackcurrant leaves and raspberries,
Making a solemn progress around the fecund gardens
    of Europe,
Coupling to its satisfaction with turtle princesses —
Its cold lizard eye blinking from prize to prize
Betraying to the world neither joy nor sorrow:
I see England as a great Crustacean
In need of a shell, an uncrackable carapace:
An armour of surrounding lands, hard, and shaped
To England's will.
If those nations about us will not guarantee friendship,
And no nation can guarantee what may not always
    be true —
Then I must take them, and shape them to my shape,
And buckle them about me; and they,
Being of earth, not of horn, or metal, shall feed me,
And feed my armies who keep them in subjection,
Send gold and their brightest jewels to me,
Send their ambitious sons to flatter me,
Offer their daughters like raspberries and currant leaves
To my flickering eye, as I ride inside.
For I will be a great king: my England a great nation.
France is the nearest: I have enough of France —
Normandy of course, Gascony I conquered:
Looking west to Wales, I took her in a week —
My son shall be Prince of Wales, that nation now
A Principality, to decorate a baby's cradle:
Ireland? My armies found the Irish kings
Willing to bend the knee.
But Scotland . . .
They make allegiances with Norway and with
    France,
They trade with Flanders, Denmark, whom they
    please,
Their kings will marry where they choose:
And yet I am their feudal lord,
They owe their fealty to me alone,
To their superior.

(A SAD SONG comes from Scotland: a FUNERAL is taking place: the
funeral of ALEXANDER III.)

        What's this? Is Alexander dead? His neck
broken?
Fell from his horse? Ha — in Fife!?
And which wild Scotsman shot the horse?
Don't make me laugh —

SONG from Scotland, as EDWARD I works out a strategy:

SONG: When Alexander our King was dead
           That lead us all in love and order
           Our young men turned from meat and drink
           From wine and sport and all their pleasure:
           Our gold was turned from gold to lead:
           Oh Christ borne into Virginity —
           Come then to Scotland's aid right soon —
           For she stands in great Perplexity . . .

Change of tune to 'Patrick Spens' melody.

EDWARD I: So Yolande the French bride whose bed in Kinghorn
           The King's horn was seeking when he should have
               stayed in Edinburgh,
           Has finally stopped pretending she is pregnant:
           And the heir to Scotland's throne is a three-year-old girl:
           Margaret of Norway: and they've sent across the sea
           To the court of King Eric: she may never arrive!

Two VERSES of 'Patrick Spens' — with some of the story acted out.

SINGER: To Noroway, to Noroway,
           To Noroway o'er the faem;
           The King's daughter of Noroway,
           'Tis thou maun bring her hame.

           Make ready make ready, my merrymen a'!
           Our gude ship sails the morn.
           Now ever alake, my master dear,
           I fear a deadly storm!

           I saw the new moon, late yestreen,
           Wi' the auld moon in her arm;
           And, if we gang to sea, master,
           I fear we'll come to harm.

           Half owre, half owre to Aberdour,
           'Tis fifty fathoms deep,
           And there lies gude Sir Patrick Spens,
           Wi' the Scots lord at his feet.

EDWARD I: Oh dear me: she is dead. Died of a sickness,
           In Orkney. Now what will they do?
           They have no heir —

He waits gleefully, on his war-horse.

Enter ROBERT BRUCE THE COMPETITOR, in great agitation swirling his axe — He is, however, 80.

ROBERT BRUCE THE COMPETITOR: I am the King, the Crown was settled on me! I, Robert Bruce, am the oldest grandson of Earl Henry and oldest surviving male heir of King David — let no man deny it!

Enter JOHN BALLIOL with more cunning and skill.

JOHN BALLIOL: It is the custom of the country to inherit, if there is no male heir, through the oldest daughter — and the oldest daughter's oldest daughter is none other than Devorguilla, who is my mother: through her, I, John Balliol inherit the Kingdom of Scotland! Let no man deny it — !

Enter COMYN — chancing his arm:

COMYN: Tanistry is the more ancient custom of the country: to gather together those with close ties to the throne, such as I, Comyn, have: and let our peers choose the wisest, most powerful, and most suitable candidate for the throne, the man to whom they would most readily bend the knee: Myself. There can be no doubt of that — they have already told me as much —

ROBERT BRUCE THE COMPETITOR and BALLIOL laugh at him, duped. They begin to argue as —

LORD OF BON ACCORD now appears on Scots stage, laughing:

LORD OF BON ACCORD: There were fifteen of them! Including King Eric of Norway! Each one more positive than the next, and all ready to fight for it. So what they called the Community of the Realm of Scotland — all the high heid-yins — appointed Six Guardians: And then they had a wonderful idea! In situations like this it was common practice to invite a friendly monarch of another country to adjudicate — to see fair play: and who better, they thought, than nice King Edward of England: oh grandmama, what big teeth you've got —

EDWARD's horse rears up — he rides in glory up to Scotland, sending messengers to the three COMPETITORS, and calling out to BON ACCORD, who has now become BISHOP of ST ANDREWS:

EDWARD I: My Lords, Earls, Bishops and Freemen of Scotland! It is my pleasure to review your Great Causes — First, of course, I shall require a seisin Which makes over Scotland to be my possession — In order, of course, then to dispose of it

19

> To whichever Competitor has most to recommend him.

ROBERT BRUCE THE COMPETITOR has been reading the message
from EDWARD I. He explodes with anger —

ROBERT BRUCE: This is no judge! This is the hangman!
He needs, he writes, to know should I succeed
Would I swear homage, owe fealty, and submit
The king of Scotland to England's Majesty:
   himself!
Edward! This I cannot, I will not do —

EDWARD I: Then clearly inheritance through oldest male
Is not in the best tradition of Scotland:
Robert Bruce, I find your claim invalid.

The MESSENGER comes back from JOHN BALLIOL, with his letter:
EDWARD reads it, smiles.

> John Balliol: grandson of Devorguilla
> Direct descendant from David king of Scots,
> And our most loyal, servile and obsequious friend:
> Your country's crown belongs to you alone,
> You have both surest claim and wisest mind —
> Let all in Scotland hear my judgement:
> John Balliol is your king — Long Live King John!
>
> (Mutters.) So kiss my arse — oops — time I was
>   gone . . .

EDWARD and his men — SURREY, CRESSINGHAM, ORMSBY, possess
Scotland. JOHN BALLIOL'S cart goes to Scots stage. He ascends in
grandeur — MUSIC for a hollow Coronation — and BON ACCORD;
smiling wryly, crowns him at Scone, as EDWARD watches patronisingly.

BON ACCORD: (MUSIC ends). Of all the Kings in Scotland's scabby
   hall of fame,
Toom Tabard, none has brought her greater shame!

EDWARD: The Carapace is now complete:
With Scotland, Ireland, France and Wales
Secure about her, England's might
Can move four-legged, grow and grow:
When I command, who dares say No?

(He re-mounts to return to England.)

JOHN BALLIOL: And be it known that whereas our dear brother
Edward, our superior lord and feudal master, king
of England, is making war upon the king of France,
he earnestly requires us his feuars to prepare a great

20

army to assist him, to present itself ready for battle, with four thousand merks to pay for its victuals, at the port of Dover in eight weeks' time —

SCOTSWOMAN: No!

As large a CROWD of SCOTS as possible emerges all over Scotland, one after another saying: No! It develops into a demonstration.

MUSIC Martial: Tympani:

EDWARD and his THREE ENGLISH WARRIORS — SURREY, CRESSINGHAM, and ORMSBY turn in anger, killing the Scots as they defy them, taking the Stone of Destiny from Scone, occupying once again the Scots Castles, taking terrible vengeance.

In the midst of this carnage, JOHN BALLIOL'S crown is taken from him by EDWARD — he is ceremonially stripped of all the emblems of power, and lead away to England, a prisoner.

EDWARD: It is moments like these which make a pleasure out of duty:
To evacuate such a turd, win a country as mere booty.

The ENGLISH withdraw, and a mourning song for Scotland comes from those laid waste. The land turns green again, becomes ETTRICK FOREST. The animals are there again, and the sounds of the forest. (July 1297.) The trees are moved to Scots stage in new configuration.

SONG: 'Ettrick Forest'
When we first rade doon Ettrick,
The day was dying, the wild birds calling,
The wind was sighing, the leaves were falling,
And silent and weary, but closer thegither,
We urged our steeds thro' the faded heather,
When we first rade doon Ettrick.

Scene Four — Wallace

Feel of song changes, enter WILLIAM WALLACE, with Scots supporters.

SONG: When we next rade doon Ettrick,
Our bridles were ringing, our hearts were dancing,
The waters were singing, the sun was glancing,
And blithely our voices rang out thegither,
And we brushed the dew frae the blooming heather,
When we first rade doon Ettrick.

As verse ends, MUSIC continues under the scene. One of the SCOTS SUPPORTERS is a Borderer, riding with WALLACE.

BORDERER: These folk are wicked — outlaws! This is the Forest of Selkirk, what you call Ettrick Forest, even though it has not many trees —

Aye, outlaws: and for why? The king of England now rules Scotland, and he put his English sheriff into Lanark to keep us down: William Heselrig. D'ye see this man William Wallace — aye, weel he comes from a big family, but he had for his mistress a woman called Marion Braidfute in Lanark, and Marion bore him a couple of bairns, bonnie wee bairns: but Heselrig didnae like William the Wallace, for he stood up against the English — so Heselrig sets fire to the hoose, and Marion and the two bonnie bairns were burnt to death! It was a' because she was going with him. Onywiy, he kills the sheriff! And he's ta'en a terrible dislike to the English. Is that no' right?

WALLACE SOLDIER: Aye, but we're no' outlaws, we're soldiers. I'm in an army, noo. The English were for sending me to fight for them in France: I thocht I'd raither fight against them at home. There's hunners of us. Soon there'll be thoosans. We're going to Scone the noo, to murder the English justiciar, Ormsby — another bastard. Then we're to join with Andrew Murray's men frae the North, him that was there when the English sacked Borthwick: terrible massacre, innocent people, old people, children. Andrew Murray hates the English too. We're tae join wi' him and make a plan. We're to rid Scotland of English.

WALLACE's army sets off. STIRLING BRIDGE is set up —

WALLACE addresses his army.

WALLACE: When we strike, we kill.
Then we're nowhere to be seen.
Until we strike again —

BORDERER: 'Guerilla warfare', invented in Scotland in 1297 by this man here, William Wallace. And Murray frae the Highlands.

He runs off after WALLACE and his CREW. They climb up as high as they can, to the top of Abbey Craig, above Stirling Bridge. As they go:

SINGER: 'Scots Wha Hae'
Scots wha hae wi' Wallace bled
Scots wha hae Bruce has often led,

22

Welcome to your gory bed, or to victory.
Now's the day and now's the hour,
See the front o' battle lour,
See approach proud Edward's power, chains and
    slavery.

BORDERER: King Edward got wind that Murray and Wallace
and the likes of myself were looking fit to drive
out his Englishmen altogether — more and more
Scotsmen were running to join us, more and more
bastard English getting red collars: so he woke up
his Duke of Surrey and sent him up to squash us flat.

The ENGLISH ARMY now approach the other side of the bridge, with
drums going: they are on huge medieval knight's hobby horses.

Nae chance, man! We're up on the Abbey Craig at
Stirling, waiting and watching, waiting and watching.
Doon below us, the old Stirling Brig over the Forth
— a wee narrow thing, they can only get over two
at a time — and once they're over, they're up to
their knees in bog. Oho — here they come, here
they come!

MUSIC as the ENGLISH approach the Brig, and stop.

WALLACE: Tell your commander that we are not here to make
peace but to do battle to defend ourselves and
liberate our kingdom. Let them come on, and we
shall prove this in their very beards —

SCOTS ARMY sings the second verse of 'Scots Wha Hae': —

Wha would be a traitor knave,
Wha can fill a coward's grave,
Wha sae base as be a slave, let him turn and flee.
Wha for Scotland's king and law,
Freedom's sword will strongly draw,
Freeman stand or freeman fa', let him follow me.

During SONG, the English KNIGHTS with their bulking hobby-horses,
cross the narrow Brig again, and flounder and sink in the bog:

At the end of the verse, and through the THIRD VERSE, the SCOTS
charge down from Abbey Craig and massacre them.

ALL: By oppressions woes and pains,
By your sons in servile claims,
We will drain our dearest veins, but they shall
    be free.
Lay the proud usurpers low,

> Tyrants fall in every foe,
> Liberty's in every blow, let us do or dee!

End of SONG, end of sequence of Stirling Brig.

MUSIC of English anger and menace.

ACTION moves to English Court.

EDWARD I: Cressingham slaughtered. Good.
              His body mutilated. Good.

              Half my army lead into a bog, Good good —
              With no way to advance, no way to retreat
              And no way to send them help? Good Good Good!
              Now this Wallace and his army of outlaws
              Roam triumphant over Scotland, my sheriffs,
              My justices driven out, my Majesty a mockery.
              And not content, he rides with his brigands
              Into England, Northumberland, Durham,
              Down the West by Carlisle and Cockermouth,
              Plundering and burning, with a cold cruel malice:
              He has not yet seen the half of my malice, my
                  cruelty,
              The coldness of an Englishman with vengeance in
                  his heart.

              Ha, he has united every man in England against him —
              They will pay taxes till they can pay no more
              To rid us of this murderous Scotsman:
              I will go as a pilgrim to the shrine of Walsingham,
              To St John of Beverley, to St Cuthbert of Durham,
              And with their saintly banners urge my army on
                  in Holy War —
              We shall take this womanising upstart Scot,
              And tear his limbs from his body while he is still
                  alive —

Enter ROBERT THE BRUCE, later KING —

ROBERT: Wallace was a brutal man, third son of a small
              estate in Ayrshire, a wild man with little finesse
              but effective. His brutality was done in the fury
              of battle when his blood ran high and killing was
              every man's imperative.

              But the torments inflicted on Wallace himself by
              Edward of England were the cold cruelty of an evil
              man: torments performed on his prisoner, with the
              implacability of the surgeon's knife.

              Edward sent up all of England's strength to crack

24

the nut of Scotland, and at Falkirk, Wallace and
his men were overrun.

Then Edward set about dividing Scotland up among
his English lords: fifty-one of them were granted
huge areas of Scotland — Aymer de Valence, the Earl
of Lincoln, John de St John, the Earl of Warwick,
William Latimer. John de Segrave, Robert Clifford,
Robert Fitzroger . . . They garrisoned all the castles,
they handed down justice.

MUSIC — quiet Wallace music.

The Wallace was once again a fugitive, with an ever-
dwindling band, harrying not only the English, but
also those who collaborated with them.

Thousands of English soldiers hunted him through
the land, but while they were searching Ettrick
Forest he was in Drumalban, and while they beat
over the hills of Speyside he was in Fife, or ejecting
the Bishop of Reading's men from the Castle of
May on the coast of Caithness.

WALLACE moves very fast around the playing areas.

And Edward forced the Scots to go hunt for him,
on pain of losing land or life — but whenever we
came near him, he ambushed and escaped with
our corn and our silver.

WALLACE now blends into the audience.

It was the common people of Scotland who were
for Wallace, who fed him, concealed him and lead
him through the wild country. The reward was
more than any poor man could dream of: but not
one of them sold him.

It was when he was in Glasgow he was betrayed
— as usual by one of the great ones — the Earl
of Menteith. They say he was taken in bed with a
woman, and conveyed straight away to England
and the tender mercy of Edward. No-one tried to
rescue him. Not one of us raised a finger. But we
knew what was to come.

If the Scots abandoned Wallace, the English couldn't
wait to lay hands on him!

(Very quiet last verse 'Ettrick Forest'.)

SINGER: When I last rade doon Ettrick,
                 The winds were shifting, the storm was waking,
                 The snow was drifting, my heart was breaking,
                 For never again will we ride thegither,
                 In sun or storm on the mountain heather,
                 When I last rade doon Ettrick.

ROBERT BRUCE: He was tried in Westminster Hall, and taken to
                 Smithfield to be hanged. He was cut down before he
                 was dead, his belly slit open, his bowels removed,
                 and his penis cut off while he was still alive. His
                 heart, liver, lungs and entrails were torn from his
                 body and thrown on a fire. Then his head was cut off.

                 On Edward's order, his body was then hacked into
                 four pieces: one quarter was sent to Newcastle and
                 put on show above the common sewer; a second
                 quarter went to Berwick, a third to Perth, and the
                 fourth to Stirling, scene of his greatest victory. His
                 head was stuck on a pole on London Bridge, where
                 it remained gazing up the Thames towards the City
                 of London.

Enter ROBERT THE BRUCE to Scots stage.

Scene Five — The Bruce

                 In order to live to fight another day, we Scots had
                 to swear loyalty to Edward. I am Robert the Bruce,
                 my grandfather was that Robert whose rightful
                 claim to the throne of Scotland was thrown out
                 by Edward, and I am the rightful king of Scotland,
                 but I was forced to swear obedience to him. Even
                 as I swore, I knew I would have justice, and that
                 Scotland would have its freedom.

                 Within a year, I, Robert the Bruce, decided I could
                 collaborate no longer. I would make myself king of
                 Scotland, and drive out the English from my land.

                 One man stood in my way to the crown: Comyn.
                 He also claimed the throne of Scotland. I met him
                 in a churchyard in Dumfries. I decided to resolve
                 the question.

The float he is on moves rapidly over to where COMYN stands, and,
in a violent gesture, ROBERT runs him through with his sword, and
raises it triumphant. Immediately, deafening church bells ring out,
ambivalent — neither joy for ROBERT nor sorrow for COMYN

EDWARD I, now older and sicker, runs on to stare in disbelief at
ROBERT.

The SCOTS emerge from holes, also are amazed at ROBERT THE BRUCE.
They move about arguing.

Then ISABEL of Fife comes on, very reminiscent of the Pictish Queen,
bringing with her the royal accoutrements, to the centre of the Scots
stage, where the Stone of Destiny had been.

The bells stop. EDWARD watches, still calculating.

ISABEL: What happened to those men who are supposed
to be Scotsmen?

My blessed husband calls himself the Earl of Buchan,
but he's so far in with the English, he's taken to
living in Leicestershire —

My nephew who calls himself Earl of Fife is so far
in Edward's servitude I dare not call him here to
Scone to put the crown on bold Robert's head.

So I'll do it myself.

Come out from your hidey-holes, your little warren
of guilt, you noble bunnies of Scotland! Leave off
tugging at your Mammy's dug, and stand up for
Scotland!

You have seen what this Edward has done to Ireland.
You've seen what he's done to Wales! You've heard
his 'Ordinance' for bending Scotland to his will! If
you don't want to end up the servants of England's
needs, the serfs of the master-race, step out into
the sunshine and make your way to Scone, and
declare for King Robert, the First of Scots!

As the music of a HIGH MASS breaks out, the LORDS of SCOTLAND
move reluctantly towards Scone. ROBERT THE BRUCE waits, while
EDWARD rages —

BRUCE: I was not idle before my Coronation:
With my band I took Dumfries —
Dalswinton
Tibbers
Ayr
My companion Robert Boyd took Rothesay Castle,
then Inverkip —
I made sure of Dunaverty
My special place at the tip of Kintyre

>   Which I stocked well, for I had an eye on the
>   future —
>   I controlled the Clyde —
>   I would have Menteith out of Dumbarton
>   I went to Glasgow —
>   Bishop Wishart gave his blessing,
>   He exhorted his flock to follow me
>   He prayed for Scotland
>   He gave me the robes and vestments of the old
>   Scots king
>   And the banner of Alexander III —
>   As fast as their podgy legs would carry them
>   My enemies in Scotland were fast becoming my
>   friends.
>   In six weeks, I was ready:
>   I would be crowned King at Scone —
>   Edward had stolen our Stone of Destiny:
>   But he could not break the granite of my resolution:
>   I would be crowned King —
>   And Scotland would be mine, and its own —
>   A Free Nation in the world once more —

High Mass soars up as ISABEL crowns ROBERT.

ROBERT is King of Scots.

EDWARD does a huge, very fast and dangerous run on his horse, from behind England to the Scottish stage, and smashes his hammer/axe onto the stage. He climbs up on to it in a mighty rage, and drives BRUCE away.

EDWARD's men now take up defensive positions on floats, horses, etc all over Scotland, with the main stage, after EDWARD leaves it, turning into Edinburgh castle, as EDWARD 'lays waste' — and ISABEL watches scornfully.

BRUCE, after the 'Battle', vanishes into the AUDIENCE — or far corners of the hall, or up trees and lighting towers, or behind float/castles.

EDWARD: Bruce! Bruce! Die like your Wallace!
            Die like a spider, Die like a slug!
            Valence! Take my army, revenge —
            It was your brother he killed in Dumfries
            Your revenge will be my revenge on Scotland's
            treachery —
            You will burn, and slay, and raise the Dragon,

(VALENCE sweeps on with the fearsome Dragon banner.)

            You will show no mercy to man or beast,

28

> You will kill those you capture, burn corn and cattle
> And you will bring to me this Bruce called King:
> I have a coronation ready in Smithfield
> That will make Wallace's death an act of kindness!

(He gets back on his horse, old now, and tired.)

> I have brought law and order to England,
> I have brought power, and safety and domination:
> Now I am old: I will not see my life's work
> Undone by a rampant Scottish Earl:
> I have plans for Scotland: for her own good
> She should hear what I say: For her own good . . .

He rides off in silence, slowly, for a few seconds, then a 'Japanese' sequence begins: all his men on their vantage points perform a fierce ritual slaughter dance — Music, Tympanum, Screams; Fire, and Blood down the Walls, and Carnage.

It stops abruptly. BRUCE is up a high and distant place.

BRUCE: The English took Scotland and crushed her. We
            were not ready for them. Within three months of
            my crowning at Scone, my people were routed, at
            Methven, and no prisoner spared. I was on the wing
            through the heather, down to Dunaverty on the tip
            of Kintyre, with traitorous MacDougalls hunting
            me to the north, and the MacDonalds and McCans
            to the south. I made my way quietly to the coast
            of Antrim, where the odd wandering King aroused
            little comment being a not uncommon sight, and if
            ever I needed to look at a spider it would be there
            on Rathlin Island, at that time.

            It was there I realised the full beauty of the way
            Wallace fought. We would never defeat the English
            in open battle, nor would we resist them in great
            castles: our strength was not in our numeric might,
            nor in costly machinery of seige, nor in cannon and
            great war-horses. Our strength was that we were
            in our own country —

(MUSIC quietly in: a subtle, but still insistent, version of 'Japanese' music.)

> We would move faster and surer — We knew the
> hills, we travelled unburdened —
>
> We were invisible, for we could melt away like
>   snow off a dyke —
> We would strike fiercely and hard — for we had
>   bitter anger in our hearts.

29

> We could strike fiercely and well — for they were
>   occupying our land,
> And we were experiencing a new emotion,
> That was more than self-interest,
> More than the greed of a clutch of ruling families,
> More than the simple reaction of the peasant
>   to terror:
> We were feeling desire for the freedom of our
>   nation:
> It travelled through the land, like fire in a thatch,
> And the Scots were aflame —
> And many an Englishman too came to join us at
>   that time of times.
> And our strength above all else and the reason
> We could not fail was the people of Scotland,
> And the inextinguishable flame of their desire for
>   freedom.

The music has been moving through this. Now it increases:

A sequence as follows:

(i)   EDWARD reads his letter to Valence — (this is interspersed with (ii):

> Since we have not found in Sir Michael Wemyss'
> either good word or service, and he has now shown
> in deed that he is a traitor and our enemy, we
> command you to burn his manor where we stayed,
> and all his other manors, to destroy his lands and
> goods and to strip his gardens clean so that nothing
> is left, for an example to others like him.

(ii)   Night in Scotland — owls hoot — BRUCE and a FEW SCOTS
raid and capture a series of castles and strongholds. As each
one is taken, its name is announced, interspersed with BRUCE's
comments:

VOICE: Turnberry Castle

BRUCE: We move through the hills of Carrick and Galloway —

(The next engagement is an ambush.)

VOICE: Glen Trool.

BRUCE: We ambushed and routed them. We moved north
                    beyond Ayr.

VOICE: Loudun Hill.

BRUCE: We chased them to Bothwell, we scattered them
                    back to Ayr —

EDWARD: And as for Sir Gilbert de la Hay, to whom we showed much courtesy when he stayed with us in London recently, and in whom we thought we could place our trust, but whom we now find to be a traitor and our enemy, we order you to burn down all his manors and houses, destroy all his lands and goods, and strip all his gardens so that nothing is left, and if possible do worse to him than to Sir Michael Wemyss.

VOICE: Despite the fearful vengeance inflicted upon the Scots who adhered to Bruce, his numbers increased daily —

BRUCE: My poor brother John was captured, and hanged, and drawn, and beheaded —

VOICE: Douglasdale, upper Clydesdale, the Ettrick Forest —

BRUCE: James Douglas with one army took the Borders — I went to the highlands, gathering another army as I went, moving more men on galleys up the coast to Loch Linnhe.

VOICE: Inverlochy —

BRUCE: John Comyn of Badenoch surrendered — I let him live: he joined me. We stormed up the Great Glen —

VOICE: Castle Urquhart, Inverness, Nairn —

BRUCE: The earl of Ross supported Edward   but he was glad to make a truce: we moved on —

VOICE: Elgin, Banff —

BRUCE: I had Comyn of Buchan, another collaborator, within my grasp: but I fell ill. They thought I would die. I had no intention of dying. Another army rose up to support me in Sutherland under William Wiseman:

VOICE: Skelbo Castle, Tarradale —

BRUCE: I recovered and met Buchan on the road from Inverurie to Oldmeldrum: we chased them: the whole of the North was ours — the Borders were ours —

VOICE: The Pass of Brandes, Dunstaffnage Castle —

BRUCE: We took on the traitorous MacDougalls in Argyle: they waited to ambush us on the slopes of Ben Cruachan above Loch Awe: James Douglas climbed

31

higher up the hill and as they attacked us, James attacked them: they ran for their lives —

VOICE: Galloway —

BRUCE: My wee brother Edward took another army to the MacDonalds and hunted them to Ulster . . .

VOICE: Aberdeen —

BRUCE: Aberdeen Castle finally gave in.

ISABEL: (Lines 225–75 in original.)
Ah! Freedom is a noble thing!
Great happiness does freedom bring.
All solace to a man it gives;
He lives at ease that freely lives.
A noble heart can have no ease,
Nor anything that well can please
If freedom fail; the right of choice
Is sought above all other joys.

But he that has been always free
Can never know the reality,
The anguish and the wretched fate
That is a part of slavery's state.
A thing, when we experience it,
Makes evident its opposite.
If bondage he has ever known,
Then freedom's blessings he will own,
And reckon freedom worth in gold
More than the world will ever hold!

He that is thrall has nothing his;
All he possesses subject is
To his overlord, whoe'er he be.
He is not even this much free:
To choose to do, or not to do,
That which his heart inclines him to.

By far is slavery worse than death!
For even while a slave draws breath
It will destroy him, body and bones;
But death will trouble him but once.
To say no more, can none relate
The hardness of the slave's estate.

Thus lived they in a state of thrall,
Both lords and poor men, one and all.
For of their leaders some they slew,
And some they hanged, and some they drew.

BRUCE: The English still held the castles in the South — isolated, afraid and unprovisioned: we didn't need battering rams, seige engines: we used darkness, skill, rope-ladders with iron grappling-hooks, and the courage of the finest men Scotland to slip in, open the doors, and take them.

VOICE: Perth.

ROBERT: One dark night, we waded the moat, the water at one point was up to my chin. We threw up the ladders, over the wall — I was the second man over — in with us, out with the English, to heaven or to hell with a couple of burgers and Perth was ours —

VOICE: Roxburghe —

BRUCE: Not to be outdone, Jamie Douglas tackled Roxburghe — Pitch dark night — up with the ropes, up with the rope-ladders, over goes Jamie, Roxburghe's ours —

This scene is acted out on the 'mobile' fortress —

VOICE: Edinburgh

The next scenes happens on the 'Scots' stage, the highest point being scaled from the floor —

ROBERT: We send a few men to the East Gate, the top of the High Street — to make a noise: the guards all run to defend it. Tom Randolph goes over the loch with a scaling party, and with him goes William Francis: now this Willie used to slip in and out of the castle at night to lie with his girlfriend, so he leads them up the North face, the rock that looks onto Princes Street in your day, up they go, like flies up a wall — over go the ladders, and in — they took the guard from behind, opened the East Gate — Edinburgh Castle was ours.

VOICE: Stirling —

ROBERT: Ah, Stirling. Aye — my brother Edward tackled Stirling. He couldn't get in. He made a deal with Sir William Mowbray, the English commander: if no-one came to relieve the castle within twelve months, it would be ours. I gave my wee brother a kick in the pants: he had lead us into a trap. Up to this point, we had not fought one pitched battle against England's mighty army. Now we would be forced to — my best hope was that they would not

> be well lead. Edward the First was dead: Edward
> the Second was King of England —

LIGHTS up on English stage: EDWARD II is kissing his favourite,
GAVESTON, in a fond farewell — his QUEEN, ISABELLA, watches:

EDWARD II: Go, Gaveston: they will not dare to harm you. They
are jealous, nothing more —

GAVESTON: I think they will kill me —

EDWARD II: They cannot — I am their king.

GAVESTON goes from EDWARD's embrace, and off.

EDWARD II: (to audience). Don't think, because I love Piers
    that I lack courage:
That I will not fight: Irish, French, or barbarous Scot.
Don't think because I love Piers, I am not a good
    husband:
We do our duty, Isabella and I: we have children —
Don't think, because I love Piers, that I am stone-deaf
To the challenge to our dignity and might
Of this news from Stirling Castle: I shall act!
I shall assemble the greatest army England ever saw,
I shall lead them myself into battle with this Bruce,
And rid the world of his arrogance forever —
The greatest army England ever saw . . .

He goes.

ISABELLA: The greatest idiot England ever saw —
Your Piers is prisoner of the earls of England:
Tomorrow he will die a hideous death:
Go, my little droopy King: and may the Scots make
mincemeat of you —

ACTION switches now down the centre of the hall — ROBERT is on
a float with trees on it, in front of Stirling Castle — the Scots stage —
which flies the English flag. In front of him, the SCOTS have formed two
'schiltroms' circles of spearmen, their spears bristling out, which move
slowly forward. The ENGLISH are mounted on great armour-plated
war-horses.

ROBERT: The day dawned I had never wished to see. Over
20,000 English, Welsh, Irish, French, Flemish,
German soldiers, in ten brigades, with their massive
war-horses, thousands of archers, against 6,000
Scots, with spears, axes and broadswords. Last night
could have ended it all — I was out scouting around
with a few men when Sir Geoffrey de Bohun and a

squadron of English cavalry caught us: he levels his
lance, thunders his war-horse at me, and thought
to finish me, there and then. Poor Geoffrey. He
missed. As he went by, I raised my axe, split him
wide open like a log for the fire: later Randolph's
men routed an English brigade trying to go round
behind us. The English had a sleepless night. They
were worried. So was I — I broke my axe on Bohun's
skull. It was a good axe. I asked my captains: Do
you want to fight this battle? They all said they did.
So we will fight. Today is June the 24th, 1314. This
is the land above the Bannock Burn. You may not
enjoy learning about dates and battles any more
than I enjoy fighting them: but learn this: that if
we lose this battle today, Scotland will cease to
exist, and the English rule us for ever more. But if
we win, Scotland will have her freedom, until the
English find other means of taking it away —

THE BATTLE begins. The Scots Schiltrom holds, the war-horses are
killed or driven back, the Scots win the day.

At the end, with the SCOTS triumphant and the ENGLISH in flight,
the SCOTS flag goes up on the castle.

ROBERT: Edward rode off back to the South-East of England
as fast as his horse would gallop, where, a few years
later Isabella and Mortimer deposed and murdered
him: they made a bold face of it, but the English
had been thrown out. A month before I died, they
ratified the Treaty of Edinburgh, which left Scotland
independent, and at peace.

                       Even the Pope at Avignon gave us his approval —
after Bernard of Linton wrote to him, on behalf of
all Scots, living and still to be born, a letter which
will stand long after I am forgotten —

BERNARD OF LINTON reads from Arbroath Abbey — the Declaration:

BERNARD: Most Holy Father and Lord: The Most Holy Fathers
your predecessors bestowed many favours and
numerous privileges on this kingdom and people
of Scotland, as being the special charge of the
Blessed Peter's brother. Thus our nation under their
protection did indeed live in freedom and peace
up to the time when that mighty prince the King
of the English, Edward, the father of the one who
reigns today, when our kingdom had no head and
our people harboured no malice or treachery and

35

were then unused to wars or invasions, came in the guise of a friend and ally to harass them as an enemy. The deeds of cruelty, massacre, violence, pillage, arson, imprisoning prelates, burning down monasteries, robbing and killing monks and nuns, and yet other outrages without number which he committed against our people, sparing neither age nor sex, religion nor rank, no one could describe nor fully imagine unless he had seen them with his own eyes.

But from these countless evils we have been set free, by the help of Him Who though He afflicts yet heals and restores, by our most tireless Prince, King and Lord, the Lord Robert. He, that his people and his heritage might be delivered out of the hands of our enemies, met toil and fatigue, hunger and peril, like another Maccabaeus or Joshua and bore them cheerfully. Him, too, divine providence, his right of succession according to our laws and customs which we shall maintain to the death, and the due consent and assent of us all have made our Prince and King. To him, as to the man by whom salvation has been wrought unto our people, we are bound both by law and by his merits that our freedom may be still maintained, and by him, come what way, we mean to stand.

Yet if he should give up what he has begun, and agree to make us or our kingdom subject to the King of England or the English, we should exert ourselves at once to drive him out as our enemy and a subverter of his own rights and ours, and make some other man who was well able to defend us our King; for, as long as but a hundred of us remain alive, never will we on any conditions be brought under English rule. It is in truth not for glory, nor riches, nor honours that we are fighting, but for freedom — for that alone, which no honest man gives up but with life itself.

AT end of reading, MUSIC: ROBERT is on his death-bed.

ROBERT: By the Treaty of Edinburgh, my five-year-old son David was to marry Edward's five-year-old daughter Joan, at Berwick.

Two Processions bearing doll-models in golden capes set out, one from England, one from Scotland, with incense and plainchant —

I was dying. And my one regret was that I had

36

> never been on a crusade. So I ordered that after
> my death, my heart be taken by Jamie Douglas to
> fight the Moor and defend Christianity.

He steps or slides out of his death-bed as surgeons approach with saws,
and proceed to hack through bones, while the wedding goes on with
sweet ceremony — at the castle in the centre: then the two dolls are
brought to Scotland and set up on thrones, side by side — and ROBERT's
body is taken off, and the heart put in a casket, and given to JAMES
DOUGLAS who goes off to fight the Infidel.

Scene Six — The Death of Kings

BON ACCORD appears from behind the thrones.

BON ACCORD: Let us sit upon the ground and tell sad tales —
not of the deaths, but of the lives of kings. The
Scottish kings: here they come, each one more
disastrous than the next, falling over themselves
with incompetence, stupidity, mismanagement and
terrible bad luck . . . not to mention their Guardians
and advisers —

The four floats are drawn up in line down the centre out from the
Scottish stage, the audience sitting and standing on either side, the
succession of kings parades slowly but non-stop down this aisle, while
BON ACCORD tells their stories, occasional scenes take place, and
occasional interruptions come from England. There is suitable music
throughout. The style must be a sort of Commedia del Arte parade,
with masks —

The crown is set up on a stand.

BON ACCORD: Here comes David, son of the Bruce —
All his father had won he proceeded to lose:
At seven years old he put the crown on his head —
In two years for his life to Paris he fled:

(DAVID II hides. On comes EDWARD BALLIOL, seizes crown.)

     John Balliol's son Edward rode back for the crown —
With promise to England to lay Scotland down
Like a pipe of port for their later ingestion —
But Edward's foul treason upset Scots digestion:
We drove him away like a wasp in the sun
Like a wasp he came back: to sting and to run.
To Edward of England he gave half our nation:
The border then ran from the Don to Dumbarton.
Then out went the English to fight against France —

> And out went King Balliol, with a kick in the pants:

(EDWARD BALLIOL runs off and a seventeen-year-old DAVID II comes out again.)

> And stout young and jolly King David returned,
> Lead his troops into England and harried and
>   burned —

(ROBERT THE STEWARD joins him.)

> But the Englishmen caught him, threw him in the
>   Tower:
> For eleven long years he was in Edward's power —

(DAVID II is taken to England put in 'the Tower'. ROBERT THE STEWARD sees him go, assumes power in Scotland —)

> Now as Regent came Robert, yes, defeat has its
>   uses! —
> The first of the Stewarts, the last of the Bruces —
> Eleven long years Robert ruled like a king —
> He could not find the ransom — he said — that
>   would bring
> David back to his throne: but he came once again
> To find plague on his doorstep: Black Death held
>   the rein —
> When David was gone Robert rose in his pride,
> He was old he was sick — but would not be denied —
> While his lords fought the English, he stayed in
>   his bed,
> While his sons fought and feuded, poor Robert
>   lay dead:
> But who's this? Why his eldest son, Robert of
>   course —
> A little bit daft with a kick from a horse:
> Sicker and older, he let all slip and slide,
> The law went unnoticed, the criminal untried —
> His brother proud Albany thought he'd make a
>   good king —
> So he did in young David, and told them to bring
> Him Prince James, the next son: but James took
>   no chance,
> He jumped on a boat and sailed off to France —

> But the luck of this sad row of Kings did not fail:
> He was caught by the English and thrown into jail.
> Proud Albany proved himself loyal and handsome:
> For eighteen long years he would not pay the
>   ransom!

When James came to Scotland he seized tight
    the helm,
And made laws for the firm and sure peace of the
    realm —
But again the Scots lords showed their loyalty's
    worth —
They murdered poor James — in a convent —
    in Perth,
Now his son James the Second was then seven
    years old,
But grew to be ruthless, cunning and bold —
The Douglas were troublesome, claiming the crown:
So he asked them to dinner and cut them all down;
He found cannon intriguing, he loved a good bang —
He laid seige to Roxburghe, some English to hang:
The cannon ball stuck, burst the cannon asunder
And James was despatched by ballistical blunder —
James the Third was just eight when his father
    exploded,
So his power these kind nobles very quickly eroded:
Boyd put him in prison to show him who's master,
And told him his chums were a national disaster —
A fresh Albany rose up, with a fat English purse
To claim Scotland was his --and was England's of
    course!
James went out to meet him with his trusty Scots
    Lords —
At Lauder they hanged all his chums with stout cords,
And surrendered to Albany, without drawing their
    swords:
But the king soon recovered and drove the
    traitors out —
But at Sauchieburn they fought him: and put him
    to rout.
James fell from his horse, and sent for a priest —
Who shrived him then knifed him: his troubles had
    ceased.

Oh God help the people with such men for their
    master —
What is hard for the Lord, for the poor man: disaster.

A final coda as a PEASANT crouches on the ground, and the kings
come back to take their bows standing on his back —

A lute is played on the Scottish stage, and a quiet song sung as at the
Court of JAMES IV.

Enter WILLIAM DUNBAR, a young poet, looking quite modern and
trendy.

DUNBAR:

I'd hate you to think we did nothing else in Scotland
but worry about the English: we'd lives of our own
to get on with, so let's get this straight, the English
were no more important than a cloud of cleggies
to a war-horse, or a flea to a pair of lovers in bed.
My name's William Dunbar, by the way, poet.

James the Fourth was my boss, and no finer king
in Europe: he'd the likes of myself writing poetry
for him, and Robert Henryson and Gavin Dunbar
as well, with David Lindsay coming on quite well
too. Aye, and he started up a Royal College of
Surgeons, new colleges in Aberdeen and St Andrews,
and compulsory education for the sons of those
who could pay. We'd a proper Court of Session set
up and some due respect for the law inflicted on
the Highlanders — so what need did we have for
boring old wars with England? We were building a
civilisation here fit to live alongside the Parisians,
the Florentines, the Sevillians: we needed peace
to put the economy back on its feet, and peace to
develop our own contribution to the world. Peace.

So James took a deep breath and married the daughter
of Henry VII of England — Margaret Tudor — aye,
a strong-looking woman — on 8th of August 1503,
as part of a Treaty of Perpetual Peace with England.
The marriage, if you're interested, is given suitably
loyal garnish in my wee poem 'The Thistle and the
Rose', price two marks from any good bookseller.
Aye: a perpetual peace with England. Just what we
all needed. And perpetual it was: for ten years.

Then England teamed up with the Pope and made war
on France, and we'd an old-established friendship
with France, so to help them out . . . ach, it makes
me sick, it was nothing to do with us, that age of
chivalry and heroism was over, we'd better things
to do — but no, our good King James leads the army
himself, an army that had in its ranks the whole
of our tender, budding civilisation, the youth of
our literature, the springtime of our nation: James
leads the army — to help out the French — to do
battle with the English at Flodden Field. They were
massacred, all the finest men we had, and the king
himself, James IV, the finest flower of Scotland's
history . . .

SONG:

'Flowers of the Forest'.

40

SINGER: Dule and wae for the order sent our lads tae the
                   Border,
               The English for aince by guile won the day;
               The flooers o' the forest, that focht aye the foremost,
               The prime o' oor land, now lie cauld in the clay.

               We hear nae mair lilting at out yowe-milking,
               Women and bairns are heartless and wae;
               Sighin' and moanin' on ilka green loanin'
               The flooers o' the forest are a' wede away.

Scene Seven — Henry's Rough Wooing

At end of song, enter to England: Henry VIII, who is delighted at the
Scots' tragedy —

Henry VIII does a dance to 'Greensleeves', goes as if to exit, smirks,
but he swings back on the audience.

HENRY VIII: I did not spend my whole life's energy on the writing
of silly melodies! — Ah, not even on the bedding
of ugly Duchesses, plain Janes or Yuppie Annies,
as history would have you imagine. No. More than
on the music, more than on the women, I spent my
forces on two things: on acquiring money, and on
war! I was ready to fight every dukedom, kingdom
and empire in Europe: England, my England, the
England I was to leave for my son, and for his sons,
would dominate Europe; and all the rest of them.
Snapping up the crumbs and the gnawed carcases
we tossed behind us —

But first (by now he has mounted his horse) —
First, I must have Scotland! There should be no
great problem — my sister Margaret Tudor was
James's Queen, she and the Earl of Arran whom I
have bought at great expense are the guardians of
my nephew little King James V, and I have declared
myself: Protector of Scotland!

(Enter DACRE.)

               Yes, Dacre, what is it?

DACRE: The Scots Council will not have Arran as Guardian
of their King —

HENRY VIII: They were massacred at Flodden by our second
team! Do we have to send our first team to obliterate
the entire nation?

DACRE: There are plenty of treacherous nobles in Scotland
              willing to take English gold — I have 400 of them
              working for me, spying, intriguing, murdering the
              enemies of the English: it has become an old Scottish
              tradition . . .

              (Laughs.)

              Leave them alone, Your Majesty, and the Scots
              will massacre each other — when James called a
              Parliament, the Douglases and the Hamiltons set
              about each other in Edinburgh High Street, leaving
              nearly 100 dead on the roadway! What a nation!
              Cleansing the Causeway, they called it —

HENRY VIII: Here's what I wrote about Scotland, Dacre: 'The
              inhabitants of the North are a wild, barbaric people,
              living on a great field of stone and ice, where
              nothing will grow, and the birds do not lay eggs,
              but drop their fledglings from the branch of a tree,
              where it is dark all winter long, where they say the
              Devil himself holds his earthly court — As for the
              South, it's a poor, unproductive land, where the
              towns are like English villages, and the soil barren;
              where they can afford no trained Army, but cry
              out for men at the town cross, and the Treasury is
              too empty to pay for modern weapons of war . . .
              where they set one noble family with writs of fire
              and slaughter to burn down villages and, to stamp
              out entirely whole other families of wild men, like
              savages.
              And where coins are worthless.'

              That's what I wrote about Scotland, Dacre — And I
              will not have my ambitions for a great country such
              as England thwarted by its miserable inhabitants!

JAMES V: (comes on quietly to Scottish end). Scotland is now
              a nation with no power, a pawn to be sacrificed to
              some great king or Emperor, an item of international
              barter — Only one thing is consistent in these terrible
              times — the Parliament of the Thrie Estaites will
              tolerate no man, faction or treaty that threatens
              the sovereignty of Scotland — oh there are those
              who point out how, for the love of France, Scotland
              suffers great pain, how useful would be 'amity'
              with England. But the Parliament will not submit.

              In the end, in spite of all my fears, it came to
              war with England again: we met them at Solway

Moss; they destroyed our poor, out-dated army.
We were so few, so badly equipped. The great
lords, the Douglasses, the mighty Border barons,
the fierce Highlander, the Argylls and the crafty
Hamiltons were so busy fighting one another, they
let Scotland herself be walked over by the Auld
Enemy, the English. Within a few weeks of that
shameful defeat, I was dead — my daughter Mary
was the Queen of the land torn apart by the greed
of its own nobility, unable to defend itself against
the diplomacy of France, or the anger of Henry of
England. And she was six days old.

MARY OF GUISE carries on infant MARY QUEEN OF SCOTS to
domestic stage.

MARY OF GUISE: She is my daughter, so she is Queen of Scotland.
She is heir to Margaret Tudor, and so will one day
be Queen of England. She will marry the Dauphin,
and so become Queen of France. She will found
a dynasty that will draw our countries together
into one mighty force to withstand the Spaniards,
the Netherlanders, the Infidel or whoever may
oppose us.

HENRY VIII: I have my own ideas as to the way to unify the
French with England, and my army is preparing
to try them out — this woman is a French spy, a
schemer from the house of Guise, and an adherent
to the Pope: she must have no power over my
grand-niece!

MARY OF GUISE: She is my daughter, she is a Catholic, and she is
a Frenchwoman!

HENRY VIII: My Lord Arran: my Lord Angus!

(ANGUS enters in chains. ARRAN comes from Scotland.)

Arran — I appoint you Guardian of my grand-niece
Mary and Regent of Scotland. To assist you, I shall
send home my Lord Angus and all those Lords taken
prisoner at Solway Moss who have now foresworn
the Pope: they are set to bring about a revolution
in your pagan, Papist Scotland: go, Lord Angus —
you are set free: use your freedom well, and don't
forget who gave it to you.

The sound of crackling fires from Scotland, flames flickering over the
whole land —

ENTER CARDINAL BEATON on the Scottish stage, a stake and a bonfire below it, with a PROTESTANT being tied to the stake.

BEATON: Scotland knows well how to use heretics: your English Lollard Resby, your Minister, your Bohemian Paul Crow, and our noble, learned and much-travelled Patrick Hamilton: burnt in the fire. My dear uncle took great pleasure in making Hamilton's exit as unpleasant as his religion was dangerous.

ARRAN: You are a great man with torture, my Lord Cardinal — and with cruelty, and with burning: but your uncle was told then, as he tortured Patrick Hamilton, he was as well to burn the others in deep cellars, for the reek of Maister Hamilton has infected as many as it blew upon! Scotland is seeking new loanings, Beaton: you should start to beg forgiveness now from those you have sinned against —

HENRY VIII: Seize the child, Arran — You are her Protector — Protect her well!

(ANGUS suddenly appears on the domestic stage, threatens MARY of GUISE.

ARRAN and ANGUS drive out MARY OF GUISE and seize the infant MARY.

MARY OF GUISE forms up with BEATON but both are driven off. The fires die down. HENRY moves on a float towards Scotland.)

Good! Now we have Treaties to ratify — a Treaty of Allegiance between our two countries, a Treaty of marriage between my son Edward and your little Queen Mary. As Regent of Scotland, Arran, you must ratify these Treaties.

ARRAN: You must know, your Majesty, that I am a Hamilton, and we of the House of Hamilton are of royal descent, indeed our claim on Scotland's crown is second only to that of the House of Stewart, indeed some in my family would say our claim is the greater —

HENRY VIII: Arran, what do you want?

ARRAN: A fair hearing for my claim, and perhaps prospects for its advancement — loyal to you and to England as we are —

HENRY VIII: At this moment! Well, Arran — I have a daughter, Elizabeth . . .

ARRAN: Yes, your Majesty —

HENRY VIII: And you have a son, do you not?

ARRAN: Yes, your Majesty —

HENRY VIII: Ratify the Treaties, Arran —

ANGUS: Other of the Scots nobles, Assured to you as they
                may be, your Majesty, would prefer some more
                tangible evidence of your Majesty's appreciation
                of their loyalty to your cause and the difficulty of
                their position in a Scots Parliament very jealous of
                its sovereignty and independence —

HENRY VIII: You should be languishing at the bottom of an
                English oubliette, or paying a great ransom —

ANGUS: But we are here, in Scotland, loyal and devious
                servants.

HENRY VIII: I am angry —

ANGUS: A little recognition, is all we ask — we have secured
                already that the English Bible will be current in
                Scotland, Protestant services held in our native
                tongue: perhaps a few expenses — ?

HENRY VIII is furious.

DACRE: I assure your Majesty, that this Scottish nation
                is of such malicious nature towards Englishmen,
                that they cannot abide, nor suffer to hear, that
                Englishmen should have any manner of superiority
                or dominion over them.

ARRAN: I have ratified the Treaties Majesty —

BEATON and MARY OF GUISE emerge menacingly behind him.

HENRY VIII: Good — very good —

ARRAN: But I'm afraid I must give way to the greater powers,
                who also command the respect of the people of
                Scotland —

HENRY VIII: You treacherous idiot!

ANGUS: And I must confess I can no longer hold back the
                sentiments of the Scots parliament, which are for
                the Auld Alliance which respects our sovereignty,
                and against allegiance with an Auld Enemie, who
                seeks to eat us up!

HENRY VIII: This country is impossible! These people are slippery eels, ungraspable snakes rather! My Lord Hertford, my kindness, and subtle goodwill have not been appreciated by these barbarous Scots — we can no longer have them threatening our Northern border making alliances with our enemies, and demanding bigger bribes — under the sun live not more beasts and unreasonable people than be there of all degrees!

MUSIC, as lights go grey, sounds of massacre, rape, looting, and burning HERTFORD/SOMERSET and ENGLISH KNIGHTS bear down on their horses on Scotland, swinging swords and axes.

Put Scotland to sword and fire! Burn Edinburgh town, so rased and defaced when you have sacked and gotten what you can of it, as there may remain forever a perpetual memory of the vengeance of God lightened upon them for their falsehood and disloyalty!

MUSIC breaks while: HENRY continues his ranting orders:

Beate down and over the castle, sack Holyrood house, and as many townes and villaiges about Edinborough as ye may conveniently sack Lythe and burne and subverte it and all the rest, putting man, woman, and childe to fyre and swoorde without exception where any resistance shalbe made agaynst you, and this done, passe over to the Fyfelande and extende like extremityes and destructions in all townes and villaiges whereunto ye may reche convenyently, not forgetting among all the rest so to spoyle and turne upset downe the Cardinalles town of St Andrews, as thupper stone may be the nether, and not one stick stande by an other, sparing no creature alyve within the same, specially such as either in frendeship or blood be alyed to the Cardinall. And so this journey shall succede moost this wayes to his majestes honour.

BON ACCORD: These were the most savage and devastating of all England's invasions of Scotland. Almost every single town in Scotland was looted, butchered and burnt to the ground. The elegant abbeys of the Borders, churches and monasteries, all over Scotland were destroyed, their contents stolen away. And once again the poor peasants and farmers saw their crops burnt, their buildings set on fire; the women raped and the little children tossed from sword to sword —

46

MUSIC in again: ANGUS enters, very angry — driving out the English.

HENRY VIII: Lord Angus — what does this mean? You are in
my debt, my Lord —

ANGUS: Your ravaging army has brought terror, not only
to your enemies but also to the lands and families
of your former friends, that we are 'Assured' no
more —

SOMERSET: (as he fights against TWO SCOTS swordsmen).
Scotsmen! Can you not understand the advantage
to both countries of a union between our two
countries! Let Scot and Englishman merge under
the old indifferent name of Briton — in the one
empire of Great Britain which would then be able
to defy the mightiest Powers in Europe!

The TWO SCOTS overpower SOMERSET, disarm him. He turns to
ARRAN.

ARRAN: After a wooing as rough as that Scotland received
at the point of your sword, we could not expect a
peaceful or an equal marriage. We have suffered too
much at the hands of England — we look, as ever,
to France. By our new treaty our young Queen is
now in France, and will marry the Dauphin. The
French army will protect Scotland. We are united
as never before with our old allies.

SOMERSET retreats down the hall.

        You have put us to fire and the sword once too often.
Now your vain England is surrounded by troubles
— from Ireland; from those of the old religion in
Devon and Cornwall; from the Spaniards and the
Castilians to the South; from the North — Scotland:
and from Henry of France, who will drive you out
of his country, as we drove you from ours:

Henri II of France appears in the distance.

HENRY II: (to SOMERSET). You will by this Treaty remove
yourselves for all time to come from the town of
Boulogne, and from all French soil with the exception
of the town of Calais. You will furthermore remove
your English troops for all time from the territories
of Scotland, never to return —

HENRY VIII: (now very old and sick). Where now can I look
for men to take Scotland for God, then deliver her

to me? Where is the man with the two-handed
sword, where is this John Knox? I will have him
released from the galleys and speak to him: if he will
serve England's purpose, I shall take him into my
protection. I fear I may not be long for this world
— the pox is eating my innards and my brain is
softening in its pan — a word from John Knox to
the Almighty may not come amiss:

KNOX enters on his mobile pulpit, at the English end, swinging his sword.

KNOX: I have suffered for the Lord, I have endured torments
                  for the Lord — I will kill for the Lord!

HENRY VIII: Master Knox, I will provide you with English gold
                  and English arms to assist you in ridding your
                  country of the Whore of Babylon — the Pope of
                  Rome, and all his servants!

KNOX: I need only God and his servants —

A great crackling fire burns all over Scotland, CROWD burns heretics.

HENRY VIII: See where your fellow Protestants are burning,
                  where stakes and fires consume God's Elect all over
                  Scotland.

KNOX: I go, in God's name.

HENRY VIII: I die a happier man . . .

He does a ghostly exit.

Scene Eight — Knox and Mary

KNOX moves in his pulpit towards Scotland. He thunders over the
crackle of the fire —

KNOX: The tyrauntes of this earth have learned, by long
                  experience, that they are never able to prevaile
                  against Godde's truth; yet, because they are bounde
                  slaves to their maister the Devil and his lieutenant the
                  Pope they can not ceasse to persecute the membres
                  of Christ, when the Devel blowes his wynde in
                  the darknesse of the night; that is, when the light
                  of Christe's Gospel is taken away, and the Devil
                  raigneth by idolatory, supersticion, and tyranny.

                  This I wryt, that you shall not wonder to see the
                  poysoned Papistes nowe so to rage and triumphe

48

against the eternal truth of God. Wonder not that the tyrantes of this worlde are so obedient, and redye to folowe the cruel counsels of suche disguysed monsters; for they are subjecte to obey the Devel, their prince and father, as the unstable sea is to lyft up the waves when the vehement wynde bloweth upon it.

He is called the Prince of Darknes, that hath power in the ayre. It is said, that he worketh in the children of unbelefe, because he styrreth them to trouble Godde's elect; as he entered into the herte of Judas, and moved him to betray his Maister. He is called Prince over the sonnes of pride, and Father of al those that are lyers and enemies to Goddes truthe; over whom he hath no less power this day, for this is their houre and power graunted to them; they can not ceasse nor asswage their furious fumes, for the Devil, their sire, stirreth, moveth, and carieth them, even at his wyl. But in this that I declare the power of the Devell workinge in cruel tyrauntes, think you that I gyve to them power at their pleasure? No, not so, Brethern, not so: worldlye tyrauntes have no power at al to trouble the saintes of God, but as their bridle shal be lowsed by Godde's handes.

'O Lorde! those cruel tyrauntes are loused by thy hande, to punish our former ingratitude, whom, we trust, thou wilt not suffer to prevail for ever; but when thou haste corrected us a lytle, and has declared unto the worlde the tyrannye that lurked in their boldened breastes, then wilt thou breake their jawe-bones, and wilt shut them up in their caves againe, that the generation an posteritie folowynge may prayse thyne holy name before thy congregacion. Amen.'

A great fanfare in England, and and a procession lead by the pulpit and KNOX finds its way to the Scottish stage. The burnings stop — as KNOX reaches the 'Scots' stage, everything stops — he looks at MARY, Queen of Scots.

KNOX: Who are you?

MARY: I am your Queen.

KNOX: You may be Queen of Scotland, but God himself rules in the hearts of your people: God is your king. From this time forward, the story of our people will not be the story of kings and queens, but of God and his subjects!

Go — you have sinned, you are a wanton, you are a harlot guilty of murdering your husband — go:

MARY: And who will be your King?

KNOX: Leave your son James: we will be ruled by him — so long as he, in turn, is ruled by us. Go: your cousin Elizabeth of England will make you most welcome . . .

(SONG — for Mary: She goes to England: ELIZABETH will not see her: she is lead to Fotheringhay — ie the mobile tower, and imprisoned in it.

The SCOTS, lead by KNOX, sing another hymn, as ELIZABETH signs her death warrant —

As hymn ends:)

KNOX: The Kingdom of God has come.

ELIZABETH: My grandfather Henry Tudor said once, of this divided island of Britain: 'the greater shall draw the lesser' — so it has proved to be. The infant James is ruled by Scots nobles whom I and my dear Lord Cecil see fit to approve of, the Scots are bound to England by the Protestant faith, by the greater force of our arms, by the similarity of our tongues, by commerce and by mutual need. It is England's desire which dictates her foreign alliances and enmities. Scotland will cease to exist — at least as an opponent of England's will — the greater has drawn the lesser: let the Spaniards send ten thousand Armadas, this island now stands firm, united in purpose, and ready to reach out over the oceans to the lands, which my great mariners bring fresh news of month by month: I may despise my Puritans at home, but Knox and his Presbyterians in Scotland, and the colluding noblemen of that compromised country have together brought to me what every monarch of England since Edward I has been denied — power over Scotland. It is not yet complete, not yet total — *that* only a complete incorporating union will bring — but power . . . . If only I had an heir on whom I could settle this great power, my joy would be complete —

A mocking fanfare from Scotland — playing it — James VI & I. He laughs at her.

JAMES VI: And when she died, so I, the powerless child of Mary, James VI, the impotent King of Scotland,

whose father was murdered by his mother's lover,
who was a token in the hands of so many great
men, so many mighty powers, whose person was
owned and controlled by so many and venal Lords
and purchased Earls — oh and when she died — so
the lesser, I, James, and my people, the Stewards,
and my country, Scotland, oh so the lesser drew
the greater: and England fell to me. In Scotland
I had erected around me a fence of new Scottish
nobles, who owed everything they had to me, I
built up my Privy Councillors, my Lords of the
Articles, to govern my Scots parliament, I ruled
Scotland by my little quill pen: so when Elizabeth
who murdered my mother died with no heir from
her diseased womb, then it was I who inherited
England: you were proud, Elizabeth, of what had
fallen in your lap: but you were merely paving the
way for myself — God's annointed, the Absolute
Monarch of Scotland and England —

He moves in procession to England and the throne, with music slowly
modulating from mockery to 'God Save the Queen'.

I am the Husband and the whole Isle is my lawful
wife; I am the Head, and it is my Body; I am the
shepherd and it is my Flocke; I hope therefore that
no man will be so unreasonable as to think that I that
am a Christian King under the Gospel should be a
polygamist, and husband to two wives; that I being
the Head should have a divided and monstrous Body.

(Reaches throne.)

I that am James VI of Scotland and James I of England
do hereby proclaim myself James, King of Great
Britain, France and Ireland — And I hereby order
my Commissioners from the Scots parliament to
meet with my Commissioners from the parliaments
of England and Wales, to draw up such acts as may
be needful for this union. Let Scotland be as Wales
was — united to England as to the principal, that
they shall ever acknowledge one Church and one
king, and be joined in a perpetual marriage, for the
peace and prosperity of both nations, and for the
honour of their king.

MUSIC ends.

How says my English parliament?

QUIET VOICE: No.

51

JAMES VI:	How say the Estaites of Scotland?
SEVERAL QUIET VOICES:	No.
JAMES VI:	It will come — it must come —

JAMES VI goes, gleeful, mocking.

SONG:
> 'The Moss Trooper's Lament'
> O' all the gallant Borders ilk water, moss and fell,
> Oh all ye weel kent neuks and cleauchs, forever
> oh farewell.
>
> Chorus:
> For we'll gang nae mair arovin, arovin through
> the nicht,
> We'll gang nae mair arovin, tho' the moon shine
> oh sae bricht.
>
> For the king has o'er the Border gane in London
> town to dwell,
> And we must friens wi' England be since he bides
> there himsel'.
>
> Chorus:
> For we'll gang nae mair arovin, arovin' through
> the nicht,
> We'll gan nae mair arovin, tho' the moon shine oh
> sae bricht.
>
> For when the harvest moon shone bricht, what
> blythe times did we see,
> On ilka nicht we' splent and spauld we rade richt
> merrilie.
>
> For when a' the gallant Borders hae lost their
> riders gay,
> The Scots will miss their hardy lads and cry 'alas
> the day'.
>
> Chorus:
> For we'll gang nae mair arovin, arovin through
> the nicht,
> We'll gang nae mair arovin, tho' the moon shine
> oh sae bricht.

<u>END ACT ONE</u>

ACT TWO

Scene One — Animal Crackers

The trees are cleared, the forest pushed back behind the Scottish stage area.

As the audience return, they are entertained by some ANIMALS — but by now the animals are city and circus animals, exotic, or freakish, or doing dances or aping human behaviour — wearing clothes, etc. The bears are chained, wear clothes and do dances, the dogs pull little carts, there are three-headed ponies and twin-bodied sheep, there are orcs and hippogriffes, half-bird, half-animals, there are camels.

Most of this action is now at the English end, where also a small consort plays early 17th-century court music — with a high counter tenor solo of great virtuosity as a feature of it.

Enter to English Court, JAMES I & VI, by now a strange, neurotic, haunted figure, very clever and politically astute, but riven with anxieties and superstitions. As he writes and broods, a proclamation is heard.

PROCLAIMER: We thairfoir, the Lordis spirituall and temporall of this realme, being heir assembled, unitid and assisted with those of hir lait Majesteis Previe Counsall and with the Lord Maior, alderman, and citizens of Londone, and a multitude of utheris of this realme, do now heirby, with ane full voice and consent of toung and hart, publiche and proclame that the heich and michtie Prince JAMES THE SEXT, King of Scotland, is now, by the diath of our lait Soverane Quene of Ingland, of famous memorie, become also our onlie lawfull, lineall and ryghtfull leige Lord, JAMES THE FIRST, King of Ingland, France and Irland, Defendar of the Faith.

The Proclamation continues under this — During this also a dance of the WEIRD ANIMALS.

JAMES: Just as the good food which is pure and wholesome that we eat is by deep mystery alchemised in our entrails into noxious stinking substances of which our bodies must be rid, so in the bowels of the body politic and the body spiritual there are transformations of God's creatures into those foul, sulphurous creatures of Satan that will do great harm and put in great danger all those around them if they be not purged out by instruments. I speak here of demons, devils and hobgoblins, of elvish creatures and incubus and succubus. I speak of things that rear their monstrosity in dream and nightmare, and I speak of persons that do walk

54

amongst us — witches, warlocks, wizards and other
such toads of human flesh.

(The ANIMALS act out the Gunpowder Plot — but are arrested by
OTHER ANIMALS.)

> Deep in the bowels of our parliament went such
> creatures with gunpowder and fuse plotting in such
> a way to create a mighty explosion within these
> entrails and spread their poisonous doctrines over
> the whole of our kingdom. Praise be to God such
> intestinal explosions were muted and put down.

> But this Guy Fawkes and his Popish crew while they
> may not have spattered our person over the walls
> of our chamber have nonetheless thrown my great
> plan for the union of England and Scotland into
> doubt and confusion: for the English parliament
> was to debate this very Act as drawn up by my
> Commissioners for Union, and press it on through
> into acceptance in England, whereupon I have
> little doubt my parliament in Scotland would have
> ratified such a union or any kind of union which I as
> their King proposed — for I have proclaimed myself
> King of Great Britain, and am in danger of finding
> there is no such nation! But this Fawkes, causing
> such delay, and the English being so stubbornly
> set against my other desires, and being so turned
> in their minds against the Scots will now find time
> for idle tongues to wag and flicker with venom —
> But I will have this Union!

> Let it be as Wales was, united to England, as the
> principal; and let all at last be compounded and
> united into one kingdom. And since the crown, and
> the law, is resident in England, England can have
> no fear, for they shall ever acknowledge one church
> and one king, and be joined in a perpetual marriage
> for the peace and prosperity of both nations, and
> for the honour of their king!

A huge outcry from both ends:

PAMPHLETEERS and BALLADEERS some of them still half-animals,
set up among the crowd and deliver a series of scurrilous invectives
against this Union, and bellow songs of abuse at each other.

SCOTS   This Union must never be! To unite Scotland to
PAMPHLETEER 1:   England would be as the coupling of a hippopotamus
                 with a capercailie — impossible to achieve with

55

much dignity, and if it were achieved, productive
of an altogether unnatural issue!

ENGLISH
PAMPHLETEER 1:
Scotland, to unite with Scotland! 'Tis a contry too
good for those that inhabit it, but not good enough
for anyone else to be bothered with conquering it!

SCOTS
PAMPHLETEER 2:
The English are a race that murder with a cold heart,
that smile as they slit your throat, and even as they
steal your purse will be shaking you by the hand!

ENGLISH
PAMPHLETEER 2:
The ayre of Scotland might indeed be wholesome
and health-giving but for the stinking people that
live there!

SCOTS
PAMPHLETEER 3:
The English would rule us by the work of a
Commissioner, a Secretary, a Viceroy, sitting in
solitary dignity in Edinburgh, where now our own
parliament sits, issuing edicts on behalf of England,
where once we made our own laws!

ENGLISH
PAMPHLETEER 3:
Their beasts in Scotland be generally thin and small
— except for their women, of which sort there are
none greater in the world!

SCOTS
PAMPHLETEER 3:
A Curse on the Sassenach, bringer of sorrow!
A Curse on the Sassenach, vainglorious and proud!

A Curse on the Sassenach, crowing like a cock on
a dunghill!
We'll pluck your feathers —
And slit your throat —
And Roast ye, and Eat ye — stuffed!

JAMES:
I hereby do threaten with the most severest penalties
and pains and torments all those of my subjects
who cause to utter such Pasquillis, libells, Rhymes,
Cockalanies, comedies and occasions whereby they
do slander, malign and revile the estate and country
of England and the worthy subjects of his Majesty's
kingdom!

(Reluctantly, they draw back, and become Members of both Parliaments
— JAMES continues:)

Let it not be said that I cannot manage the Scots
parliament! If Scotland should refuse, I will compel
their assets, for I have a stronger party in my debt
than the party of the mutineers; through the Lords
of the Articles, who are appointed by myself I rule
them, and through my Divine Right as King from

whom all Law descends, I rule them — Let the
Parliaments proceed . . .

The ENGLISH PARLIAMENT floats across in front of the English stage,
in mock wigs, some on animals:

ENGLISH
PARLIAMENT 1:
And whereas, Mr Speaker, we in England are blessed
with a certain discipline, courtesy and deference
to those above them from our lower orders, the
Scots rabble are renowned throughout the world
for their drunkenness, their lewdness and their
rank insubordination! It would be most detrimental
to the English race to allow their society to be
infected and their blood debased by this nation
of importunate Beggars, Thieves, Drunkards and
Upstart Murderers.

The SCOTTISH PARLIAMENT, also some animals, cross below the Scots
stage, in full session.

They stop as JAMES tries out a series of flags for the union.

SCOTS
PARLIAMENT 1:
It is no little grief to us to hear, Your Majesty, what
discontentments there will be at meetings to enforce
this Union, so greatly hated by the English, and so
little pleasing to us — except in that obedience we
owe unto your Majesty!

SCOTS
PARLIAMENT 2:
These flags, Your Majesty! They are breeding some
heat and miscontent between Majesty's subjects!
Our seafaring men cannot be induced to receive
any of these flags, Your Majesty!

JAMES:
Not one of them! See! We have more! My loyal
seafaring subjects will delight to set out upon the
turbulent ocean with such proud banners to proclaim
their new Nationhood!

SCOTS
PARLIAMENT 3:
In every one, Your Majesty, the English cross of
Saint George remains whole and is drawn over and
obscures the Cross of Saint Andrew — Pray God
bless Your Most Sacred Majesty with a long and
prosperous reign and enternal felicity!

ENGLISH
PARLIAMENT 2:
So, Mister Speaker, if this union is to be, and I
would pray it is *not* to be, then we are agreed it
must be a full, incorporating union as desired by our
late Queen, wherein our English law, our English
parliament and our English Church remain intact
and reign supreme over every citizen in this union,
for there is no other way, no other solution!

SCOTS PARLIAMENT 1:	This cannot be! This will not be! Our Lord and King now residing in London has seen fit to force upon us these measures which will turn our Scots Kirk into but a diocese of Canterbury, and Anglican bishopric: these Articles of Perth have indeed given great offence not only to Scotland, but even unto God our Supreme Law-Giver, who hath spoken unto John Knox, the breath of the Lord, and to Melville, the founder of our true religion, and hath said Let there be in your holy land of Scotland neither the trappings of Romishness, nor the pomp of prelates, nor the puffed-up pride of any mortal man who would set himself up as the bailiff of the Lord, who would come between a righteous Scotsman and his Maker! Let us sing together the Old Hundredth, Praise the Lord!
ALL SCOTS PARLIAMENT:	Praise the Lord!

A fanfare from England. ANNE of Denmark has been sitting waiting for James.

SOMERSET comes in with JAMES, and as JAMES sits, kneels to take his leave, and to kiss James's hand. JAMES falls on his neck, kisses his cheeks warmly, gazes into his eyes —

JAMES:	For God's sake, when shall I see thee againe? On my soul, I shall neither eat nor sleep until you come again —
SOMERSET:	This being Friday, your Majesty, I shall come on Monday —
JAMES:	For God's sake, let me — shall I? Shall I?
	(He holds him very tight and kisses his neck.)
SOMERSET:	I must go, Your Majesty —
JAMES:	Then for God's sake, give thy lady this kiss for me —

JAMES kisses him, follows him down to the float, kisses him again, then again as he goes. The COVENANTING BODY sings louder than ever. JAMES returns to his throne, turns suddenly, vicious. A silence.

JAMES:	I shall never see his face again. (SOMERSET screams off stage.) He who cannot dissimulate, cannot be a king.

ANNE looks hopefully to him, smiles. He smiles to her. Then VILLIERS,

very young and beautiful appears behind the QUEEN. JAMES smiles
even more on him —

JAMES: Ah Villiers — I declare you to be the handsomest
        bodied man in all England. And they say your
        intellectuals are very great —

They go closer together. ANNE stands. She is pregnant again. She goes
slowly as the COVENANTERS resume their singing. JAMES turns on
them. They stop. JAMES in tight spot.

JAMES: I have been king of Scotland for fifty-eight years.
        When I came to the throne Scotland was awash
        with blood, faction tore at faction, Englishman
        harried Scotsman, Highlander murdered Highlander,
        Borderer plundered, killed and raped, and the
        land of Scotland could not be governed. Now, as
        I approach my end, Scotland is at peace, with the
        world and within itself. She has a strong, stable
        government whose laws are obeyed, and a church
        at peace also. And she has come into the unity of
        nations. Her language is now, for the main part,
        English: no longer when a Scottish boat puts in at
        Tilbury must we send interpreters to fathom their
        words. No longer is Irish spoken except in the wider
        regions, and all men of substance in the Highlands
        and the Hebrides send their sons to learn in the
        English language, and speak it themselves. The
        entire lawless men, such as those of Clan MacGregor,
        whose very name will vanish from the earth, are
        outlaw and hunted. The wicked men Grahams and
        Armstrongs, Elliotts and Musgraves of the Marches
        are settled now in Ireland, or removed entirely to
        the Carolinas.

        I have failed to unite my two kingdoms: but I have
        left them in unity of purpose.

        When my dear son Charles succeeds to the throne
        of England and to the throne of Scotland, he
        will stand firm on the foundations of a secure
        government, peace within and ever-expanding
        prosperity without as our industries flourish and
        our trade grows greater yet.

Scene Two — Lucifer and Laud

He goes, as if to die. From Scotland a great clatter of snare-drums and
war-drums, and voices of PRESBYTERIANS raised in anger.

From amongst them arises the dread figure of Archibald JOHNSTON of

Warriston, a lawyer and religious fanatic, who 'roared, yowled pitifully and skirled' in his devotional torments — a man 'walking on the dizzy edge of madness'.

WARRISTON: Oh brethren, where is there the man amongst you that can deny that he has sinned? You have sinned, and you have sinned and you have sinned, and I — Oh Lord, yeah verily I, even I Archibald Johnston of Warriston, yeah I have sinned! But whence comes this cleansing our spirits crave? Whence comes this divine light without which we enter into the pit of eternal darkness?

Ah brethren, this divine light shines not on us for the purchasing of indulgences and other such Papish errors and blasphemies! No brethren, no, nor will this divine light shine on us until Charles our King in England be parted from his Scarlet whore, the Archbishop Laud.

The COVENANTERS join in the frenzy — Enter above on Scots stage on one side BISHOP OF GALLOWAY and A LORD OF THE ARTICLES, (bearing a throne), and on the other side, the awesome figure of the 'Gley'd Argyll' — Archibald Campbell, 8th Earl and 1st Marquis of ARYGLL: who waits and watches ominously. As WARRISTON ends:

A fanfare (very English-sounding) at the other end. CHARLES I comes in, very vain and arrogant; a huge silk swathe is laid over his throne. He sits on it, gazing worried at Scotland. With him comes his ARCHBISHOP, LAUD.

CHARLES I: Good Lord!

LAUD: Yes, Your Majesty — ?

CHARLES I: Not you, Laud — What is happening in my Northern Kingdom? There appears to be a certain fanaticism catching fire there — against our Bishops and against our appointed government, the Lords of the Articles — I think perhaps the time has come for me to visit my other kingdom and indeed to be crowned Charles I, King of Scots, with full ceremony, at Sconn —

LAUD: Scoon —

CHARLES I: Soon? Immediately Archbishop, and you will come with me, and we shall set these Presbyterian bigots to obeying the law of the land, and you will terrify them into accepting my Bishops — remember my dear father: 'No bishops, no king, no nobility!' And

they will say their Prayers My Way, according to
my Prayer Book —

He and LAUD step onto a float, CHARLES I puts the silk drape around
his shoulders, and it flies out behind him as he and LAUD move at
some speed up to Scotland — CHARLES I continues:

And I shall revoke all the gifts of Church lands
made by my predecessors to these fat noblemen,
and these lands will be restored to me! And I shall
provide with their rents benefices for my Anglican
clergy and my Scottish bishops —

BALMERINO in Scotland is outraged, yells No Revocation! The MOB
— who are beginning a large-scale rumble and ascending mutter as
CHARLES I and LAUD approach.

BALMERINO: Your Majesty, in all loyalty, we the nobles and
commons, the Community of the Realm of Scotland,
do present this humble petition, this 'Supplication'
to Your Majesty —

CHARLES I: What man is this?

BALMERINO: Lord Balmerino, may it please Your Majesty —

CHARLES I: You would oppose the will of your sovereign Lord:
your king whose power derives from God alone,
whose will therefore is God's will, whose authority
overrides the authority of man, of Church Assembly,
of Parliament and of all other such frail human
baubles!?

BALMERINO: My Lord, you should know the will of your people —

CHARLES I: Should? You tell me what I should — ?

Arrest him, try him for his life, for treason, for insult
to the king, lese-majeste . . .
(To LAUD.)
Laud, on our return you shall be Archbishop of
Canterbury and you shall prescribe a new Book of
Canons for both our Churches wherein my supreme
authority and the power of my bishops is written
into the law of both our Churches! I will not have
these Balmerinos telling me Should!

As the float resumes its procession to Scotland, a woman, JENNY GEDDES,
leaps out from the crowd of COVENANTERS, brandishing a stool.

JENNY GEDDES: Deil colic the waime o' thee!

CHARLES I: What does she say?

LAUD: She wishes the Evil One to rot your guts, my Lord —

JENNY GEDDES: You that call yourself King know this, that you are not my king, nor our king, for our king is the King of Heaven who lives in our hearts and in our souls and in our own sharp intellects — and no Man for such is what you be, will usurp the place of that King, nor will your words speak louder to us than the words of Him who dwelleth within us. Nor, oh proud and vainglorious prince of men, will the power of your Bishops be upheld over the free voice of the true believers, nor will they in their arrogance hand down translations of God's meaning to God's people who must search each one within herself for what the Almighty has intended, nor will these carnal men, these Bishops, appropriate unto themselves the lands, the harvests, the beasts, the nourishment, the flesh of the women, the necessary possessions of the people of Scotland — for it is below the dignity of a child of God either to be robbed as we are by them, or to rob, as they do in order to sustain themselves in idleness and puffed-up emptiness . . .

A single figure, PYM, appears on the English stage, and now applauds her speech. CHARLES I and LAUD turn round in a panic, see him —

LAUD: John Pym!

JENNY GEDDES: (becoming agitated). And I say unto you, proud man, I that am no-one, I, Jenny Geddes of Embro, I, less than nothing in the eyes of Your Majesty, I, to be known henceforth as a Madwoman, a Witch, a screaming Harpie from below the pit of Hell, I say unto you that before the poor people of Scotland will bend the knee to you or to your Bishops, we will raise a riot in this country that will spread beyond the seas like the roaring of the Gales and by it you and your breed of tyrants will be swept away and toss'd up to the clouds and hurled over mountain-tops in the mighty blustering wind that is blown from the Mouths of the people of this land —

She hurls the three-legged stool at him.

By now the agitation of JENNY has been matched by the rising mutterings (of agreement) of the CROWD and the activities of CHARLES'S PUSHERS, who are also SOLDIERS, beating their way through the

CROWD, who move back still protesting and rioting until CHARLES I and LAUD reach the Scots stage, and step up onto it; hastily CHARLES seats himself upon the throne, and the SCOTS BISHOP who has been anxiously waiting there raises the crown and with a few perfunctory phrases, lays it on his head.

BISHOP: In the name of all those here Assembled (looks around — no-one) er — in the name of Almighty God — I do hereby crown you Charles the First, King of Scots —

CHARLES I: Summon a Parliament. Laud, take this crown from me — it weighs heavily on my head —

(PARLIAMENT assembles)

Thank you. Now, Parliament, I only have one day to spare for Scotland, I really must get back to my desk in London — you do understand I'm sure — so would you mind if I just read through the Titles of these Bills which I require you, my Parliament of Scotland, to approve before I make them law: I'll be fairly quick, as we only have a few hours, and there are 168 of them:

Bill anent levying of taxes for the supply of the king —

Any dissent?

(An MP stands.) (To LAUD.)

Take his name. Sit! (He sits.)

Law Anent the Introduction of the new Prayer Book — Dissent?

(Three stand.) Take their names — Sit! (They sit.)

Law Anent the Revocation of all gifts of church land to subjects of the king since year 1540 — Dissent?

(BALMERINO stands.) Balmerino! Write it down! Sit!

(BALMERINO stands.)

BALMERINO: I will speak on this matter, Your Majesty!

CHARLES I: Sit, Balmerino, or you will hang for treason!

BALMERINO: Majesty, this House —

CHARLES I: Your king orders you to sit . . .

(He sits. CHARLES I rushes gobbledegook through ending:)

Number 168, Law Anent the Suppression of the
Profession of Bard in our wilder territories, such
Bards having the temerity to put the population in
mind of unfortunate events which occurred in years
gone by, thus inciting them to angry reflection and
to precipitate action in their own time, such Bards
shall be either forced to take up some less harmful
profession or be banished this land —

Dissent? Ah — no dissent: Thank you. Having
concluded my Scottish business for the day, indeed
the year, I must announce to you my intention to
appoint a new body to be known as the Court of
High Commission, which will arrange the business
of this part of Great Britain while I am away on
other duties, in the other part.

(A growl of protest from the PARLIAMENT.)

This parliament may of course meet during my
necessarily long absences, and my Court of High
Commission will order its business, its Acts and
Proclamations in accordance with my wishes as
your king, and further as Head of your Church,
which I already am, but which I will cause to be
enunciated once more for all to understand —

As such, I shall take a great personal interest and pride
in the long overdue revision of your ecclesiastical
liturgy, which I shall have sent to you post-haste
from London whenever this most holy work is
completed —

(A growing DIN of rumblings and screechings, vocal and percussive
have been greeting this speech. CHARLES feels himself in danger,
gathers his long cloak about him, and steps onto the royal float —)

Laud, deliver us —

LAUD: As your Majesty wishes —

Scene Three — The Fiery Cross

They whisk off at speed to London and out. The NOISE rises to a
crescendo, then the COVENANT is announced — the Fiery Cross is carried
through the hall, ends up on the Scottish stage behind WARRISTON,
who preaches:

WARRISTON: Oh Scotland, whom our Lord took off the dunghill

64

and out of hell and made a fair bride to himself!
Oh Scotland, this day of thy glorious Covenant
which is the glorious marriage day of this kingdom
with God, Scotland thou art now as Israel, the
only two sworn Nations to the Lord. The Lord
who will embrace both us the little younger sister,
and the elder sister, the Church of the Jews! Oh
Scotland, this Covenant is a marriage Covenant
to Jesus Christ, never to be forgotten . . . . For in
this sacred Covenant which on this day, the 28th
day of February the year of our Lord 1638 is being
signed in Greyfriars Church Edinburgh by all our
nobility and barons, will tomorrow be signed by all
our ministers and burgesses, and will from that day
be signed by every true Scotsman, save heretics,
in this Covenant, say I, we the Nation of Scotland
demand no less than that our parliament make our
laws and no King shall break them, that we shall
have security from any king or person in our lands,
livings, rights, offices, liberties and dignities.

This Covenant binds all who sign to disregard all
the changes made of recent years by our King, until
they had been tried, judged and allowed in free
assemblies of the Church and free parliaments of
the people of Scotland!

Oh ye saints, oh ye sinners, join with your brethern
of righteousness, and sign . . . sign. SIGN . . .

A hymn — maybe the 'Covenanting Hymn' — is sung as signatures
are sought from the audience. Then lights down and slowly up on
ARGYLL, who has remained a still figure through all this.

ARGYLL: I am the Campbell. I am Archibald Campbell, eighth
Earl of Argyll, and I do extend my properties and
increase my rents through the Western parts of
Scotland by squashing flat the unruly and malevolent
class of the West on behalf of the King, and seizing
what pertains to them for myself. At this time,
I can summon to my army some five thousand
swordsmen, and mounted men beyond that. Over all
in my domains I have jurisdiction of life and death,
and though not a brave man in military conflict, I
can be cruel in cold blood. I have suppressed the
MacIans, and hunt down the MacGregors. I am the
MacCailein Mor.

And I am a strict Presbyterian.

I will not sign this Covenant, for a signature will

remain on a document long after it is politic to change allegiances, and forthrightness is far from my nature, though I am a simple man. They have said I am a man of plots, poisonous counsels, wayside ambushings, and craft: but I am merely a deep statesman, a subtle politician, and bring skills and devotion to this great cause of which it has much need . . . they have summoned a free Assembly of the Church in Glasgow Cathedral; the king sends his servile Lord Hamilton running here from London to call us to obedience. I will go to it.

Lights go up on England: CHARLES comes on with HAMILTON:

CHARLES: Flatter them with what hopes you please, Lord Hamilton until I be ready to suppress them.

HAMILTON runs down in a flurry to Scotland, where lights go up on the General Assembly.

WARRISTON: . . . and it is here, written in the registers of our Assemblies that bishops be condemned as contrary to God's Law and to man's freedom, which must clear all our minds that episcopacy has no place in the Church of Scotland —

HAMILTON: My Lord Moderator, this is no free Assembly, here is no shadow or footstep of freedom —

WARRISTON: This Assembly, is free, my Lord the king's servant Hamilton, to judge of its own freedom —

HAMILTON: You cannot be free to judge your superiors, the Bishops set above you by God and King Charles —

WARRISTON: We shall decide whether we are free to do so or not to do so in a vote —

HAMILTON: My Lord Moderator, I order you to dissolve this Assembly at this minute —

WARRISTON: My Lord Moderator, upon your own honour and safety, it is beyond your powers to dissolve this freely gathered Assembly without the consent in a vote of those here met — which we shall not give — nor be ordered to give by a hireling London Scotsman —

HAMILTON: I shall leave this house. Without the King's Commissioner you may vote what you will, it will have no substance: rest assured, His Majesty shall hear of this!

WARRISTON: We are at war. We are at war with the Kingdom
of Satan, and Anti-Christ!

Percussion. ARGYLL turns, steps forward.

ARGYLL: I am but an elder of the Kirk at Inveraray: I beg
your permission to attend your Assembly, and to
speak. I beg you not to misunderstand my delay
in declaring myself. From the start, I have been set
your way. Now it behoves me to join myself openly
to your society, except I should prove a knave.

Let us work, but let us in God's name I entreat you
consider what has brought these Bishops to ruin
— Pride, and Avarice. If we would ourselves avoid
shipwreck, let us shun these two rocks . . .

Therefore let us in all humility cast aside and declare
of no consequence the decisions of the last six
Assemblies of the Church of Scotland.

(CHEERS and VOTE.)

Let us set aside for all time the Service Book, and the
Book of Canons, and annul the abhorrent Articles
of Perth.

(More CHEERS and VOTE.)

Let us denounce and deny this Court of High
Commission which usurps the place in our nation
of our own parliament.

(UPROAR and VOTE.)

Let us abjure and abolish herewith the rule of bishops
in Scotland, and send them forth never to return
within our Kirk, wherein they have no place.

(TUMULT and VOTE.)

But let us abstain from criticism injurious to our
king, and let us make no unnecessary provocation
of the powers that be . . . (He turns away.)

WARRISTON: My Lord Argyll, no one thing doth confirm us
so much as your presence: for you are the most
powerful subject in the land.

My Lord, I have in mind the scurrilous broadsheets
that of late have attacked our Covenant and mocked
us, its authors, and I would that we might resolve

under my direction to demand that all things published should be brought first to our attention and should not be published without our approbation, on pain of seizure and arrest of their author . . . . Those in favour — (VOTE.) Good. And now to the question of salmon-fishing on the Sabbath: this papish and most ungodly activity must no longer be permitted within our sacred nation — etc.

Percussion as lights fade on Assembly, or it is moved off. ARGYLL, in spots, moves to centre stage. He calls to John PYM, who appears on the English stage:

ARGYLL: John Pym!

PYM: Lord Argyll —

ARGYLL: Our brethren in England have much to learn from us in Scotland. We too need your help and your friendship in God, for there are many among you who value the meaning of presbytery, who would govern yourselves, not be governed by king or prelate, who would therefore come to our aid — for there will be war: with your king, but not with your people.

PYM: What we can do, we will. But know this, and tell your friends in Scotland this: we are not united as you appear to be, nor are we free to call parliaments as you are. We are many against the king — but these many turn also one against the other —

ARGYLL: Scotland prepares for war. Our old, little crooked soldier, General Leslie has returned from the German wars to lead us, arms are brought in daily from Holland, Committees of war established in every county, entrenchments dug, a cannon foundry under way at Potterow, and fresh levies trained to swell our Army. To our brethren in England we intend no harm: but the force of our own king we shall resist and overcome.

PYM: May God be with you. You give us courage to do what must be done . . .

More percussion: PYM goes. ARGYLL stays, in a low light.

Scene Four — To Help The English Out

A GROUP of Scots Covenantors in black sing a song of going to aid the English Puritans —

'General Leslie's March'

68

> March, march, why the deil dinna ye march?
> Stand to your arms my lads, fight in good order;
> Front about ye musketeers all,
> 'Til you come to the English border.
> Stand Till't and fight like men,
> True gospel to maintain,
> The Parliament's blyth tae see us a' comin'.
> When tae the kirk we come, we'll purge it every room,
> Frae Papish relicks, and a' sic innovations.
> That a' the world may see, there's none in the right
>   but we,
> Of the auld Scottish nation.
> Jenny shall wear the hood, Jocky the sark of God,
> And the kist fu' o' whistles, that mak sic a cleiro,
> Our pipers braw, shall hae them a',
> What e'er come on it,
> Busk up your plaids my lads,
> Cock up your bonnets . . .
> March, march, why the deil dinna ye march?

They carry on singing as they put on armour and take up weapons.

SCOTS ARMY move quietly singing towards England. TAMMY appears on top of tower, watching —

TAMMY: Scotland was united and spoke with one voice, the voice of the Covenant: we had Argyll in our parliament, Wariston in the Kirk, and Leslie our general of the Army: we had discipline and courage, we had strength. The king — our king — sent his English army and his English navy against us, but we drove them back where they came from, — then they tried again, and this time we cut them to pieces and for good measure we took occupation of Northumberland, Cumberland, Westmoreland, Durham, Yorkshire and Lancashire, we ruled England as far down as Hull and Warrington — Then we offered to lend our Army to those we thought our friends in London: We made a solemn League and Covenant with the English, to uphold each the other's freedoms, and to establish the presbyterian way in England. But not for the last time our friends in London bickered among themselves, split into factions, and allowed our oppressors to rule by their division.

Enter to English end in great agitation a warring mob of ENGLISH REVOLUTIONARIES — PYM, A LEVELLER, A DIGGER, AN INDEPENDENT, TAMMY an unwilling Presbyterian — CHARLES I stands high up watching, amused, as they abuse each other mightily —

69

TAMMY: We decided to push further: for equality with England.
For now the king was in arms even in England,
and the English parliament was at last taken by the
men of God, and we seized the moment to advance
both our causes. First we made a solemn League
and Covenant with the English, to uphold each the
other's freedoms, and to establish the presbyterian
way in England: then our Commissioners went
to London to treat for a union: not what they call
a 'perfect' union whereby they would eat us up,
but a federation of equal nations, each with its
own parliament, but united in trade, in dealings
with other nations, in our king — to become an
orderly, covenanted king — and of course in one
true religion of presbytery.

The Scots, under ARGYLL, have marched during this down to London,
and taken up a commanding position.

ARGYLL: Brothers in Christ, we do beseech you to consider
well your position: while you dispute amongst
yourselves, Satan and Anti-Christ, prelate and
papist merrily mock you, and their advocate —
your king and ours — moves unchecked towards
your overthrow, from which will follow all that we
in Scotland dread most heartily: therefore let our
mighty army already within your land join with
you to defeat the king, and let us work together for
an equal, just and peaceable union between us and
the unity of our lands in the way of presbytery . . .

Scene Five — Cromwell's Union

A figure appears higher than him, in armour, with a quiet power and
determination that compels respect: OLIVER CROMWELL.

CROMWELL: That will not be necessary.
There are other ways than Presbytery.
We in England need not Scotch instruction in
   divinity.
We have our own ways that better fit our purposes.
We have our own, New Model Army to fight the
   good fight.
And we have me, Oliver Cromwell, to unite and lead
our warring factions to victory over the king.
If you seek union with us, it will be on our terms:
And they may not be to your liking.

ARGYLL: We are brethern in Christ, we can bring victory —

CROMWELL: Your most helpful Army was not necessary to our
       most complete victory at Naseby —
       And besides, you have to look to your own defences:
       Look — Montrose, I believe, who once signed your
       Covenant —

High up in Scotland, MONTROSE, a slim dashing figure, laughs at
ARGYLL —

MONTROSE: Campbell: you have made too many enemies
       To sit comfortable in Scotland:
       The king has promised the young MacDonald,
       Kalkitto's son, the whole Kintyre if he gives his
       support —
       He is even now sailing over from Antrim to claim it.
       Huntly and the entire Gordons are under arms
       And the whole of the North-East belongs to them:
       While I myself am marching over the Border
       To remind you that our king is still our king,
       And not to be denied —

CROMWELL: So you must go back to Scotland to pursue him
       through the hills and leave us to our English devices,
       for we will defeat the king, and he will bend to our
       wishes, for we owe our allegiance first to God, and
       next to king: and if king impede our duty to God,
       why king must — why king must bend the knee.

ARGYLL turns with SCOTS ARMY and moves reluctantly back to
Scotland, as the ENGLISH REVOLUTIONARIES now muster under
Cromwell, dressed in Roundhead armour and helmets.

TAMMY leans over the parapet of the tower and watches ARGYLL
return.

TAMMY: Did this mean God was not on our side?
       Back came our Army from England with nothing won.
       Back came the Campbell with no union, nor
       presbytery in England —
       (MUSIC in.)

As they go, a great military drum-rattling from England. CROMWELL
watches as CHARLES I is lead across to his execution — A final roll
and the sound of the axe. In silence, the three ROUNDHEADS line
up with CROMWELL. They glower, half-defiant, half-guilty. Drum
continues —

In Scotland, ARGYLL and the ARMY and TAMMY watch in horror,
climb up on to the stage.

A HIGHLAND WOMAN from a high place in Scotland hurls an invective
against Cromwell

HIGHLAND WOMAN:	Oh Cromwell
	Thou has killed thy king!
	Oh Cromwell
	Now brother will kill brother!
	Oh Cromwell
	Thou has slain the father to us,
	Oh Cromwell
	Now son will be free to murder father, mother!
	Oh Cromwell
	Man of cruelty, man of iron, man with no heart,
	Know that thou has torn family asunder,
	Torn loyalty asunder
	Torn obedience asunder
	Oh Cromwell —
	Know that thy murder of God's anointed
	Tears God from our hearts,
	And leaves us naked
	Men and women,
	Eve and Adam
	Leaves poor naked humanity
	To wander the world in solitude:
	For the law of God is gone
	And the law of man is come: which says:
	Whosoever has the greatest strength
	Shall be the most righteous,
	And he who has no strength
	Shall be wicked and wrong!
	Oh Cromwell:
	Thou hast killed thy king!

During a pause in this, FAIRFAX, a civilised Yorkshire Roundhead General, approaches the Cromwellian military machine:

FAIRFAX:	My Lords, I think it doubtful whether we have just cause to make an invasion upon Scotland. We are joined with that Nation in the National League and Covenant, and now to make war on them I cannot see the justice of.
CROMWELL:	They have invaded us since the National Covenant, in that action of Duke Hamilton, which broke the League, and now they give suspicion they intend another invasion — joining with the late king's son, whom they have recognised as their king — we shall requite their hostility and free our country of the great misery and calamity of having an army of Scots within our country: it is better to have war in the bowels of another country than our own.
FAIRFAX:	My Lord, their Parliament has disowned this adventure

of Lord Hamilton, and punished the promoters of it. Those who are satisfied in the justice of this war may cheerfully proceed in it.

CROMWELL: The League is broken by them, and so no longer binding on us!

FAIRFAX: My conscience however is not satisfied, and I willingly lay down my commission as General and Commander of the parliamentary army. I desire to be excused.

CROMWELL: Then I myself shall command our Army — we advance on Scotland.

FAIRFAX watches the machine mount their horses and plod remorselessly toward Scotland.

CROMWELL's men stop: one, BRET, reads from a Declaration:

BRET: To the people of Scotland:
Know that we undertake this business in the fear of God, with bowels full of love, yea, full of pity to the inhabitants of this country. If it shall please God to make Scotland give to the Commonwealth of England a satisfying security against future injuries, we shall rejoice; if not, we dare say that which moves us to this great undertaking is that our cause is just and righteous in the sight of God.

WARRISTON: The Lord Jehovah is with us even as he was with Joshua and Gideon. The army of saints will drive the English sectaries before them even as Joshua smote the enemies of Israel!

CROMWELL'S troops form themselves into a defensive formation. As they do so:

WARRISTON: But know that our army is tainted with those that are impure, men upon whom we must not rest for our support and strength —

ARGYLL: My Lord Wariston, we need *all* our troops!

WARRISTON: God will not be mocked. I have removed over one thousand sinners from our ranks — Now, Good general, let us sweep down from this great hill above Dunbar and attack them —

ARGYLL: My Lord we must not lose our advantage!

WARRISTON: Advantage! Jehovah is our advantage — besides we are sixteen thousand, they are but ten thousand!

Come let us not tarry — attack, attack!

The SCOTS attack and are ritually massacred.

WARRISTON: Howl! Howl! For why has Jehovah deserted his children? What uncleanliness has caused our fall from grace? This son of the king has polluted our cause . . . there are those amongst us who do not observe the Sabbath, or family prayers!!

ARGYLL: Wariston, go your ways! I am away back to Inveraray — I've seen too much — three thousand of our men dead, seven thousand prisoners planted in Ireland — Scotland — at last — defeated.

CROMWELL rides to Edinburgh Castle, and strides about it. His men stand on floats spread out over Scotland.

CROMWELL: So the Scots want a Union? Well now they shall have one. My army occupies the whole of this land. Their parliament is removed. They may send thirty-one representatives to our parliament, but these will be my military commanders, or other Englishmen, or a few very secure Scots. Union? With England? We shall never be prevayled to suffer Scotland to be a kingdom. No, nor a Commonwealth apart. She shall be, like unto Wales, a part of England.

As CROMWELL rides back, a Declaration is made by BRET, to the SCOTS:

BRET: The parliament of the Commonwealth of England do hereby declare for its own security that Scotland shall be incorporated into and become one Commonwealth with that of England; whereby the government enjoyed by the good people of the English Nation, as now settled, without King or House of Lords, may be derived and communicated unto the people of Scotland, the year of our Lord, 1651.

TAMMY: We are to be incorporated as the little bird is incorporated into the body of the great hawk that has eaten it up.

Scene Six — *Quite Restored*

After which a huge celebration is brought in in which Church bells ringing, French court music playing, swathes of rich reds and golds and blues over the black and white that preceded, brilliant costumes and wigs of Restoration fullness and splendour, and CHARLES II and COURTIERS juggling with NELL GWYNNE'S oranges —

CHARLES II: I feel quite restored — I shall have myself crowned Charles the Second of England right away. Since I am already King of Scotland, I shall have no further need to visit the place. My memories of it are most unpleasant, Lord Lauderdale —

LAUDERDALE: Your Majesty, everything you desire shall be done, (a Scots Lord) Scotland is on its knees before you —

CHARLES II: In England they limit my powers, the Parliament must approve every little thing I do —

LAUDERDALE: Oh no, not in Scotland, you need only call the parliament to meet every say six or seven years: you may rule through me, and your bishops now happily restored to us, and your Lords of the Articles, with us again — don't even think of coming to Scotland —

CHARLES II: My dear Lauderdale, I thank you. Perhaps I shall set up a small committee of trusted ministers in London to advise me on Scottish matters: I am so relieved never to have to go there. However in spite of all the little Fitzes I have fathered on several ladies around my Court, my wife and I have failed to produce our own son and heir — and it appears that my strange little brother James may one day become king —

But James has secretly been converted to the Popish religion, why on earth or in heaven I know not, and as he is very likely to cause some concern if he stays in London, and I know not what to do with him, perhaps James could go to Scotland: what a good idea . . .

Now they have their own parliament restored to them, he can sit there in my place, and practice being a king in a quiet out-of-the-way place that no-one cares about. It may bring him to his senses: but I doubt it.

I, however, have serious matters to, er, take in hand — affairs of state, you know — of which I must explore every delicious nook and cranny . . .

CHARLES II goes off pursuing NELL GWYNNE.

Enter on a float JAMES II, in his final exile in St Germain, with a collection of dolls.

JAMES II: Oh yes. My big brother, Charles, was quite restored: and when he died, so I, another James, the Second of England, and the Seventh of Scotland, and the last Stewart king of either — oh when he died so I, yes, James his unfortunate younger brother, came to the throne of both. After three years, I had fled to France — to a pleasant enough palace, St Germain-en-laye, lent to me by King Louis — for life. And here I sit and amuse my children with the story of my days, — for the story of my life is both sad and comical, and not at all as your history books tell it.

My father was a king — his people made war on him, and chopped off his head — I loved my father: They put me in prison. When I was eleven I escaped to France. I became a soldier, and an admiral; And when Charles came back to be king, I was the gallant Duke of York. Then I fell in love — ah love, my downfall! I married her: Maria Beatrice d'Este: a beautiful woman but a Catholic. I myself had become convinced of the truth of the church of Rome, but privately. Now there was no hiding it: they sent me to Scotland. When Charles died, they tried to stop me, but I became king. Now know this: my crime was not that I was going to hand these countries over to the Pope, or stuff incense up their noses, no! My crime was that I would have Tolerance for all creeds. I revoked the ban on Jews living here, I was willing for Anglican, Presbyterian, any belief to be enjoyed by those who wished to embrace it.

For that, and for that alone, I was threatened with death. So the magnates of England sought out my sickly daughter Mary, — in Holland — see, and her husband King William of Orange — there he is, there's King Billy on his horse — for they knew William would never tolerate Toleration! They knew that He would massacre Catholic and Jew in the way they panted for. So when King William came to England, I left again for France, because he had the smell of Cromwell on him.

And here I sit, in this pleasant enough place. And magnates of England took King William of Orange as their king. But they forgot to ask the Scots. Would they take him as their king?

76

Scene Seven — Bring on the Benches

Enter FLETCHER OF SALTOUN.

FLETCHER: I'll tell you what the Scots parliament did — we
seized the chance with both hands — for William
could no more have James king of Scotland than
we could have Louis of France king of England.

We took him — but on our own terms: the English
had made a Bill of Rights and negotiated: we made
a Claim of Rights, and gave not one inch: if William
was to be our king and Mary our Queen, then we
in the Scots parliament would get what so many
in our country desired, and had been denied for so
long — to be rid of the bishops for ever;

To be rid of the Lords of the Articles who rule
Scotland's parliament on behalf of an absent king,
and to be rid of the parliamentary committee that
rules Scotland from London, like a puppet master;
no more soldiers running all over the land, quartered
on the innocent population — and no more Oaths
of Allegiance or Tests of loyalty like the one which
lately drove me into exile and away from my beloved
Scotland for three miserable years —

These made up our Claim: our Grievances — and our
new Majesties were obliged to accept. So with no
bishops, nor Lairds owning benefices, our Church-
goers were free to choose who they would to be
their ministers, and to pray in the way they desired,
the Scots way;

And with no Lords of the Articles, no committees
in London, and regular sittings, our own Scots
parliament became at last what it should always
be — the ruler of Scotland.

Oh I know I showed interest in a union with
England at this time — for such was proposed: it
would have maybe brought us benefits: but there
was then no danger of the English accepting it, so
I was quite safe —

(A crowd of beggars comes now through the audience, importuning,
threatening, cajoling, shoving children, etc.)

And had our parliament not a great deal to attend
to? For there were at this day in Scotland — besides

a great many poor families meanly provided for by
the church-boxes — two hundred thousand people
begging from door to door. These vagabonds are a
very grievous burden to so poor a country. They
live without any regard to the laws of the land,
or even those of God and nature. No magistrate
could ever be informed, or discover, which way
one in a hundred of these wretches died, or that
ever they were baptised. Many murders have been
discovered among them; they are a most unspeakable
oppression to poor tenants — who, if they give not
bread, or some kind of provision, to perhaps forty
such villains in one day, are sure to be insulted
by them. They rob many poor people who live in
houses distant from any neighbourhood. In years of
plenty, many thousands of them meet together in
the mountains, where they feast and riot for many
days; and at country weddings, markets, burials,
and the like public occasions, they are to be seen,
both men and women, perpetually drunk, cursing,
blaspheming, and fighting together. These are such
outrageous disorders, that it were better for the
nation they were sold to the galleys or West Indies,
than that they should continue any longer to be a
burden and curse upon us.

As FLETCHER is drawing to an end, they meet up, a fiddle is raised,
and a great drunken reel is danced, drawing in the audience —

FLETCHER watches. TAMMY comes in. As the dance ends, the BEGGARS
listen as —

TAMMY: The Nobility and Gentry Lord it over their poor
Tennants, and use them worse than Gally-Slaves;
they are all bound to serve them, Men, Women and
Children; the first Fruits is always the Landlord's
due, he is the Man that must first board all the young
Married Women within his Lairdship, and their
Sons are all his Slaves, so that any mean Laird will
have Six or Ten, or more Followers; besides those
of his own Name, that are Inferior to him, must all
Attend him (as he himself must do his Superior,
of the same Name), and all of them attend the
Chief . . . Every Laird (of note) hath a Gibet near
his House, and has Power to Condemn and Hang
any of his Vassals.

A final burst of drunken reel takes them off as MUSIC of 'Darien Song'
begins:

CAPTAIN
DRUMMOND:

Let me explain — You see, we thought the only
way to be upsides with England was to get some
colonies and some foreign trade of our own. So
in 1696 our Parliament established the Company
of Scotland trading to Africa and the Indies — My
God, what a commotion! You'd think by the crying
out and complaining that went on in England, that
we'd declared war on them —

The English king that we thought was also our
king tried to stop us raising money! In Holland,
in Hamburg, in the City of London. So we set to,
and raised it ourselves, in Scotland: four hundred
thousand pounds — nearly a quarter of all the
money circulating in Scotland. Every Duke, Earl,
merchant, burgess gave all they had. Every village
collected its gold and sent it in to Edinburgh — it
was a question of Scotland's future you see. Ships
were bought, stores loaded, and off we set — but
not for Africa or the Indies: the English would have
blown us out of the sea. We went to the isthmus
of Panama. It *was* full of hope. There, we built
New Edinburgh — we thought it would rival New
York: it was to be the keystone of the universe
— a pivot point for trade between the Old world
and the untold wealth of the South Seas — at the
narrowest point between the two great oceans —
the Atlantic and the Pacific. The Spanish, claimed
that the Pope of Rome had 'awarded' it to them.
We could deal with the Spaniards, no bother at
all. And we did. Twice they sent troops to flush us
out — twice we ambushed them and drove them
off. The one thing we could not overcome was the
work of our own king, William. He and the English
Parliament condemned us, and forbade the English
colonies in the West Indies to sell us food, or gunpowder, or anything at all. What a trick. We starved;
it was pitiful. Then eleven Spanish gunboats came
to blockade us, and that was the end of it. All that
hope — all that money — wasted away.

But I say again, Spain was not the problem. It was
the whisperings in the King's ear of the merchants
of the English East India Company, who would
destroy all competition in trade wherever in the
world they found it. They were the people who
sent Scotland back to ruin, and ever increasing
poverty. Scots folk have long memories, and when
every person in Scotland has lost some money, or

a friend, or some pride, that memory will be bitter, as well as long.

The London merchants eat us up, as royal carp will snap up minnows. We are growing impatient, we are growing senselessly violent — I can never forget what we did to those English sailors who put in to Leith — we wanted English blood, and we got it.

A wild rumour had gone around about them attacking a Scottish ship off Malabsar — So we hanged them. The next day, we discovered they were innocent — but not many were daunted: it was enough that they were English. Not that we hated foreigners — No! Just the English.

FLETCHER: I believe the English have used the presence of our monarch in London to rule Scotland — there's no question of that, and it's been to our detriment. But we have not been exactly a colony, like Ireland: it is our great part of the blame, that we have behaved as if we were. But don't think I'm just 'against the English'. The Court, and London, I heartily detest — and their habit of imagining the world revolves around them: yes! But they can't help that, they're just ignorant. No I am against this newly-proposed union, and as a member of our Parliament, I shall speak against it. They say: we shall be part of a new nation: I say, we shall always be two, and if we sell our independence for a few hogshead of sugar and some stinking tobacco, the world will have lost what Scotland can, and will, give to it. And we shall have lost our soul.

Enter his sister MARGARET to Scottish stage.

MARGARET: That was my brother-in-law, Andrew Fletcher of Saltoun, and one of the best Scotland was served by — And boy did he tell that old Parliament of Scotland a thing or two —

Will ye see how it was done? Will ye see how Scotland's great men voted our parliament out of existence? Ye will? Right, well you can join in the parliament yourselves, just to see what it felt like — and at the end of it all, you'll get to vote as well!

Bring on the benches! On you go — Build the Parliament of the Three Estates — and let's see what fools they made of themselves!

80

Aye, this is the moment ye've all been waiting for
— ye get to sit down!

Clear the way for the benches, if you don't mind —
on they come, you can give them a hand — Some
down here as well — etc, etc.

Enter a young Edinburgh clerk with a piece of paper, ALISDAIR.

ALISDAIR: Twenty-thousand, five hundred and forty pounds,
seventeen shillings and seven pence.

MARGARET: What are you saying Alisdair?

ALISDAIR: Money. From the Treasury of England — with a
special request that the whole transaction be kept
secret, and no security insisted on.

MARGARET: And what was it for?

ALISDAIR: For what was called arrears of pay and pensions
to be distributed to members of our Parliament —
but I know fine what happened to it — I took the
trouble to carry away with me a list I was obliged
to copy out. Many of those gentlemen have no
arrears of pay or pensions due to them: the Duke
of Montrose, Duke of Roxburgh, Lord Frazer, Lord
Banff, why, I myself saw all their honest claims met
in full, some months before this. They are being
paid for supporting the union.

MARGARET: There is quite a variety of prices on their votes —
Duke of Roxburgh, £500, Lord Balcarras £500, Lord
Frazer £100, Lord Elibanks £50 —

FLETCHER has come in and listens to this —

ALISDAIR: Aye, and my Lord Banff sold his vote and his country
for eleven pounds, two shillings —

MARGARET: But surely some of these people *are* owed money?

ALISDAIR: Aye — and so are many more — but only those
who needed bringing over to the Union, or who had
done service for the Union, received anything —

FLETCHER comes over and takes the list —

FLETCHER: 'Lord Tweedale' — the leader of the Squadrone
Volante, the Centre Party — '£1,000'. Perhaps that
explains their support for Queensberry. Provost of
Wigton, Provost of Ayr, Lord Cesnock, now Lord

Polwarth, £50, Earl of Cromarty, £300, Earl of Marchmont, £1,150 15 shillings and sevenpence, the Lord Justice Clerk, Lord Ormiston £200, Lord Seafield, £490 —' Wait, wait — The Duke of Queensberry! — £12,325 . . . for equipage . . . but surely these are simple payments of arrears?

ALISDAIR: For which no receipts have been requested, nor no indication in the public ledger that they have been paid — within six months, sir, these sums will be paid *again* — when the true arrears money arrives.

FLETCHER: I see — they are just . . . gifts?

ALISDAIR: Bribes.

FLETCHER goes, silent.

MARGARET: What was happening was shocking — Fletcher was for once speechless: but the country was in a turmoil — the Cameronians of the South-West were threatening to draw the sword —

Enter severally MAXWELL, a Cameronian Minister; and the Duke of Atholl, on floats reminiscent of Britton and Pict.

MAXWELL: Do they think we are children to be seduced by such foolish snares? We are asked will we submit to this pretended Parliament of Great Britain —

Carstares and the Commissioners of the Church of Scotland are merchants in the temple of the Lord! Until the Lord raises a party that will be more pure, and has not fallen so from first love, we must soak the land in our blood, and the blood of our Enemies. Should they deal with our sister as with an harlot? Should they get leave to sell the once Virgin Church and Nation of Scotland, and we not draw the Lord's sword against them? We come to die for the Lord.

ALL: Die for the Lord!

MARGARET: And the Highlanders were ablaze with love for their Stewart king.

ATHOLL: We will not tolerate the English imposing on us a German princess, when we have our own king, James VIII, a handsome young man, in Paris ready for the call: the clans of the West are under arms, and moving with all speed to Blair Atholl, from

there we shall march to fall in under our leader, the
Duke of Hamilton, and join with the Cameronians
of the South-West in a great march on Edinburgh:

MARGARET: And as for our great leader, the Duke of Hamilton —

Enter HAMILTON.

HAMILTON: No! No, no — stop them all coming here — Mother!

LADY
HAMILTON: (his mother). You are the strangest man I ever met —

HAMILTON: Mother why are they coming here?

LADY
HAMILTON: Because you are the Leader of the Opposition to
this Act — they look to you to unite them, to lead
them on Edinburgh!

HAMILTON: I can't do that — Mother, send some people to
them, send messengers, tell them to turn around
and go back home — they can't do this to me!

LADY
HAMILTON: Very well. You will live to regret it —

HAMILTON: But I will *live* — ah?

MARGARET: That was our leader — and the English? Here's
what the Duke of Marlborough was thinking —

DUKE OF MARLBOROUGH rolls up on float from the English end.

DUKE OF
MARLBOROUGH: Scotland is a threat. The worst. In the past they
have made alliance with France against us. At this
moment, the French are using all their guile to
stir up trouble. Where?   right there, on our own
island — French spies, agitators, half the Scots open
Jacobites, the savage Highlanders ready to fall on
us — When? When our back is turned. How can
I march to the Danube with confidence, when I
know there's a nation at the top of the Pennines
that would welcome the French to their shores, and
join them in a swoop on London. And they have a
King to lead them, young James Stewart, in King
Louis's pocket. England could become a province
of France one fine day if we don't do something
about Scotland.

Buy them. We could even let them into Westminster
— if that's part of the bargain, pay it. Young Argyll's
got them organised at a price. (Laughs.)

This new earl of Argyll wants to be an English Duke — he's a Scotch Duke already, now he wants to be an English one as well. Phew, these Scotch. Pay them, buy them. I've got a fight for Europe on my hands — I can't afford mutineers and traitors in the base-camp kitchen.

As MARLBOROUGH'S float moves off, GODOLPHIN, the English first or Prime Minister appears at the top of the Tower, watching Scottish matters through a spy-glass.

MARGARET: And here is the man who managed the whole affair from his office in Whitehall — the English Prime Minister, Lord Godolphin:

GODOLPHIN: Thank you. Expensive business, buying Scotch. Can you see my man Defoe up there? He's in charge of all our informers and agents — quite a handful too, but very helpful . . . This Union: we've got to have it. A full, incorporating union, with their parliament no longer required, their representatives coming to our parliament, and our army in Scotland: a perfect union. It's the only way to settle it. And we'll call England Great Britain, then they can say they're part of Great Britain but we know they're part of England.

Scene Eight — The Last Scots Parliament

FANFARES, and a procession of SCOTS NOBLES move in to the parliament, take their seats, among the audience, on the benches. As they come in, the Great Door of the Parliament closes behind them.

QUEENSBERRY as Commissioner and SEAFIELD as Chancellor sit on thrones at the top of the Parliament.

LORD SEAFIELD, the Chancellor rises to declare the business of the day.

He Calls for Order:

A silence inside. From outside cries of:

ALL: No Union! Seafield ye're a scabby rat! etc.

LORD SEAFIELD: My Lords, Gentlemen, the business we have before us this day, is firstly to approve or disapprove the Treaty of Union of the two Kingdoms of Scotland and England as contained in the Articles of Union. I therefore narrate the Articles of the Treaty of Union, as amended by this Parliament —

84

MARGARET: The twenty-five articles of the Treaty were drawn up in London by thirty Commissioners from each Parliament — over the past three months many amendments have been proposed. The Duke of Queensberry has made sure that only those amendments acceptable to the English have been accepted by the Scots.

SEAFIELD: Article One: That the two kingdoms of Scotland and England, on the first day of May next, and forever after, be united into one Kingdom, by the name of Great Britain; and that the crosses of St Andrew and St George be conjoined and used in all flags, banners, both at sea and on land.

Article Two: That the succession to the Monarchy of the United Kingdom of Great Britain and of the Dominions there unto belonging continue to the most Excellent Princess Sophia Electoress and Duchess Dowager of Hanover, and the Heirs of her Body, being Protestants, upon whom the Crown of England is settled and that all Papists and persons marrying papists shall forever be excluded from and incapable of enjoying the Crown of Great Britain.

Article Three: That the United Kingdom of Great Britain be represented by one and the same Parliament, to be stiled the Parliament of Great Britain.

(A murmur of growl from several quarters.)

Article Four: That all the subjects of the United Kingdom of Great Britain shall have full freedom of intercourse of Trade and Navigation in this United Kingdom and the Dominions and Plantations thereabouts belonging.

MARGARET: The next thirteen clauses are all bargains driven
(Over next part.) by the Scots Merchants to try to improve the sorry state of the Scots economy. Over the last century we have seen England growing rich and fat on the fruits of Empire — meanwhile we Scots, without benefit of empire, are seeing our living fall dramatically — while that in England keeps rising —

SEAFIELD: Article Five: That all ships or vessels belonging to Her Majesties subjects of Scotland

(Continues under.)

at the time of ratifying this Treaty of Union, though

foreign built, be deemed and pass as ships of the build of Great Britain. SIX: That all parts of the United Kingdom for ever, from and after the Union, shall have the same allowances, encouragements and drawbacks, and be under the same prohibitions, restrictions and regulations of trade, and the customs and duties on import and export; and that the customs and duties on import and export settled in England, shall, from and after the Union, take place throughout the whole United Kingdom . . .

And it is agreed that before the Union of the said Kingdoms, the sum of £398,085 and 10 shillings, being the equivalent to be answered to Scotland, be granted by the Parliament of England to her Majesty for the uses after mentioned.

In the first place, that the capital stock or fund of the African and Indian company of Scotland advanced together with interest of 5 per cent be thereby repaid, and that the said company thereupon cease to trade. That all public debts of Scotland shall be repaid. And that £2,000 per annum be devoted to encouraging and promoting manufactures, fisheries and production of coarse wool in Scotland.

After MARGARET finishes:

SEAFIELD: Clause 22: That by virtue of this Treaty, of the Peers of Scotland, sixteen shall be the number to sit and vote in the House of Lords, and forty-five the number of representatives of Scotland in the House of Commons of the Parliament of Great Britain.

QUEENSBERRY stands to speak.

QUEENSBERRY: (rises and walks forward). As we have now come to this most solemn and portentous debate, I find it my duty to recommend to you the words of Her Gracious Majesty Queen Anne, in her commission to me at the Commencing of this Parliament: (Reads.)

'An Entire and perfect Union will be the foundation of lasting peace: it will secure your religion, liberty and property, and remove the animosities amongst yourselves, and the jealousies and differences between our two Kingdoms: it must increase your strength, riches and trade: this whole island will be enabled to resist all its enemies, support the protestant interest everywhere, and maintain the liberties of Europe.' Such is the commission of our gracious Queen, which I trust we shall carry out, here this day.

SEAFIELD: The debate on this motion is now open.

SETON stands up, is recognised, produces papers.

SETON: My Lord Chancellor: Having had the honour to be one of the Commissioners for the treaty, I think it my duty to give some reasons which moved me to approve it, even though I know there are several members so prejudiced against it that I cannot hope from them a favourable audience — My Lord, here are three different ways proposed for retrieving the languishing condition of this nation. That we continue under the same King in a Federation. That the two Kingdoms be incorporated into one. Or that they be entirely separated. As to the first: In a Federation of two Kingdoms, subject to one sovereign — that sovereign will be obliged to prefer the counsel and interest of the stronger to that of the weaker: Suppose the Parliament of Scotland is vested with the power of making peace and war, of rewarding and punishing persons of all ranks, of levying troops, and even refusing orders of the King. My humble opinion is, that we could not reap any benefit from these conditions of Government, without the assistance of England and the people thereof will never be convinced to promote the interest of Scotland, till both kingdoms are incorporated into one: so I can conceive such a state of Federation to be no better for Scotland, than if it were entirely separated from England.

(Applause and cries of approval from Cavaliers, SETON changes tone.)

Suppose, then, we were entirely separated. This nation being poor, and without force to protect its commerce, cannot reap great advantages by it, till it partake of the trade and protection of some powerful neighbour nation, that can provide both these. But we have no valuable branch of export, which does not interfere with the like commodity, in some more powerful neighbour nation, whose interest it is to suppress or discourage *our* commodity. Can it be expected that Holland will suffer us to improve our fishery, which is to them a livelihood to many families, and an immense treasure to the public? If we are separate from England, our exports to

them of linen cloth, cattle and coals will be even
more discouraged than they now are, and this is
the most important and largest part of our foreign
trade. If we lose our trade with England, and traffic
with Muscovy, Sweden, The Nations of Europe —
the sale of our commodities will be of small value
in those places.

(Cries of Rubbish, Why, Explain, etc.)

Because the Dutch and English, by their increase
of trade, can sell them the same goods cheaper and
better than we can. If we look to any other product,
we find that it is already enhanced by the Dutch,
English, French, Spaniards, and Portuguese: we
must expect opposition, from all of them — and
we have no force to debate with even the most
inconsiderable of them.

LOCKHART stands up and shouts.

LOCKHART: Have ye never heard of Alliances, Sir? There are
              other nations in the world beside England!

LOCKHART: If we make alliance, it must be with Holland, or
              France. With Holland we can have no advantageous
              alliance, because its chief branch of trade is the
              same with ours: and from France few advantages
              can be reaped, till the old league be revived betwixt
              France and Scotland, which would give umbrage
              to the English, and occasion a war betwixt them
              and us. From these considerations, I conceive,
              that this nation, by an entire separation from but
              England, cannot extend its trade, but may be in
              danger of returning to that Gothic constitution of
              government, wherein our forefathers were, which
              was frequently attended with feuds, faction and
              foul deeds.

              My Lord, I am sorry, that, in place of things we
              amuse ourselves with words; Spain was formerly
              divided into several kingdoms, ten whereof are
              incorporated into the one kingdom of Spain. France
              was formerly divided into twelve states, which
              are incorporated into the one kingdom of France.
              England was formerly divided into seven kingdoms,
              which are incorporated into the one kingdom of
              England; Scotland itself was formerly divided into
              two kingdoms, which at present are incorporated
              into the one kingdom of Scotland.

88

For my part, I comprehend no durable union betwixt
Scotland and England, but that expressed in this
article by one kingdom, that is to say, one people,
one civil government, and one interest.

HAMILTON sits full of indecision and discomfort. Loud cries directed
at him from all sides.

MPs: Answer, Answer!

HAMILTON sits wriggling in his seat. Looking blacker and blacker.
Suddenly BELHAVEN stands up.

SEAFIELD: My Lord Belhaven.

Loud groans from some. Cries of Ah! from others. Some walk over
to chat with court officers on dias. BELHAVEN stands to deliver his
speech.

BELHAVEN: My Lord Chancellor, when I consider this affair of
                     a Union betwixt the two Nations, I find my mind
                     crowded with a variety of very melancholy thoughts;
                     and I think it my duty to disburden myself of some
                     of them by laying them before and exposing them to
                     the serious consideration of this honourable house.

                     I think I see our free and independent kingdom
                     delivering up that which all the world hath been
                     fighting for since the . . . days of Nimrod; yea, that
                     for which most of all the empires, kingdoms, states,
                     principalities, and dukedoms of Europe, are at this
                     very time engaged in the most bloody and cruel
                     wars that ever were, to wit, a power to manage
                     their own affairs.

                     My Lord, I think I see the noble and honourable
                     peerage of Scotland, whose valiant predecessors led
                     armies against their enemies, now put upon such
                     an equal foot with their vassals, that a petty English
                     Exciseman receives more homage and respect. I
                     think I see the royal state of boroughs, walking their
                     desolate streets, hanging down their heads under
                     disappointments; wormed out of all the branches
                     of their old trade, uncertain what hand to turn to;
                     necessitated to become prentices to their unkind
                     neighbours. I think I see the laborious plow-man,
                     with his corn spoiling upon his hands for want of sale,
                     cursing the day of his birth, dreading the expense
                     of his burial, and uncertain whether to marry or
                     do worse. I think I see the incurable difficulties of

89

the landed men, fettered under the golden chain of equivalents, their pretty daughters petitioning for want of husbands and their sons for want of employment. But above all, my Lord I think I see our ancient mother, Caledonia, like Caesar, sitting in the midst of our senate, ruefully looking round about her, covering herself with her royal garment, attending the fatal blow, and breathing out her last with a et tu quoque mi fili. Are not these, my Lord, very afflicting thoughts?

(During this speech, the reaction is first, of expectation, then, of puzzlement; then of disappointment; finally of boredom. Over last few sentences see HAMILTON, slowly subsiding lower and lower in his seat, in misery.)

I consider this treaty, I see the English constitution remaining firm, the same two Houses of Parliament, the same taxes, customs, excises, the same trade in companies, the same municipal laws and Courts of Justice — and all ours subject either to regulation or to annihilation. Good God! What, is this an entire surrender? My Lord, I find my heart so full of grief and indignation that I must beg pardon not to finish the last part of my discourse, that I may drop a tear at this sad story —

BELHAVEN sits suddenly, apparently too moved to continue. A silence. SETON jumps up.

SETON: My Lord Chancellor, this moving display has not answered the smallest part of my reasoning —

Cries from several of Sit down.

SEAFIELD: Mr Seton, you have made your reasoning you may not speak twice on this issue.

MARCHMONT stands up slowly.

My Lord Marchmont.

MARCHMONT: My Lord Chancellor — I have heard a long speech from my Lord Belhaven, a very terrible one — it requires a short answer — (Laughter.) — Behold he dreamed. But lo!! When he awoke, he found it was a dream. (Loud laughter and applause).

BELHAVEN looks up from tears, in anger. HAMILTON is furious, at yet another defeat.

MARCHMONT sits. Mild approval. FLETCHER stands.

SEAFIELD: Mr Fletcher.

FLETCHER: My Lord Chancellor, I beg your indulgence for my
late arrival. I have met with an accident on my
journey here. But it is as nothing to the calamity
I find on my arrival. I have a poor memory, my
Lord. Yet even I can recall that but two years ago
there were not ten men to be found in this house,
no — in the whole of Scotland — to support a
complete incorporating union with England. Today
I hear loud indeed overwhelming murmurs of
sanctimonious approval for a hypocritical speech
for just such a union. Have I come into a tailors
shop, where so many coats are turned in so short a
time? What has intervened? Nothing — save that
the English Ministers, that have ruled us by indirect
means since the Union of the Crowns, have now
concluded they must now rule us completely and
directly — in fact, they have concluded Scotland
must be removed from the geography of the world,
and North Britain be the designation of a nation,
a people, a tradition once free, self-governing and
in control of its own destiny. They have decided
that, and — let it come as no surprise — suddenly
that is what our Queen most earnestly desires us
to accept. And her Scottish Ministers who sit here
before us on thrones and carved chairs beseech us
to obey. More, they oblige us to obey, if we will
improve our personal fortunes.

I do not speak, my Lord, as one who desires to replace
one Monarch with another now living in France.
No. If we may live, I little value who is King. It is
indifferent to me, provided this parliament is free,
to name or not name Hanover, Stewart, or who you
will. Therefore, I argue no lost causes, my Lord. I
argue the freedom of the Scots parliament — not
the Ministers, who frequently mistake bad former
practice for good precedent. The parliament is not
perfect. We must improve it, set our constitution
to rights, and restore our trade by reaching some
understanding with England to our mutual benefit.

It was for that purpose, and that alone, that we
despatched our Commissioners to London. Could
we then — not ten months ago — have believed
what they have achieved? Are we not here, by
right of our just demands on the Monarch that we
should make the laws of Scotland, we, the people of

91

> Scotland? If we are to abandon this duty to others,
> do we not cease to be Representatives of Scotland?
> Those commissioners who went to England to make
> a trading settlement, and who came back with a
> plan to end our Parliament and our Nation — are
> they not guilty of High Treason?

(Uproar.)

> Are we not all, merely to consider it, guilty of High
> Treason?

More uproar — cries of leave!

SEAFIELD: Mr Fletcher, that is a most serious accusation —

FLETCHER: I can think of no other words that are adequate . . .

SEAFIELD: I must ask you to apologise, or withdraw from this
              Chamber.

FLETCHER: I must not lose my vote, therefore I must apologise,
              which I do, most humbly, for having caused concern
              in the breasts of so many in this noble parliament,
              which I respect above all other institutions.

SEAFIELD: Your apology is, I think, generally accepted —

FLETCHER: Thank you, my Lord. I have much to say about the
              effects on our trade of abandoning our border and
              our safeguards against the merchants of England, but
              it is well known that my view is this; that we have
              long been held back by our dependence on England
              in this matter, and that were we, in our wisdom,
              to pursue a more, not less, independent policy, we
              should grow in the health of our industries, the
              improvement of our agriculture, and the strength
              of our export to the rest of the world. The remedy
              to our present ills lies in our own hands: in the
              increase of power of this, our own parliament, so
              that our great men are not forever seeking the
              favour and approval of English ministers, by an easy
              compliance with their desires, in place of seeking
              the greater good of Scotland; it is the people of
              Scotland alone, without the meddling of English
              politicians, who should appoint our government.
              It is to them alone that our government should
              look for approval. For so many years have we been
              denied this, that we no longer even recognise our
              true grievance. What other way is there to govern
              a free people, than through its own parliament?

If we are to be protected by forty-five Scottish
members in an House of Commons full of Englishmen,
we may improve; but slowly and always following
lamely behind the greater power of England. The
regret of every wise and good man must needs be
extraordinary were he to see the liberty and happiness
of his own country not only obstructed but utterly
extinguished by the private and transitory interests
of self designing men. If this treaty be approved by
us, I shall know that government is but a puppet
show, to please the onlookers — and I, my Lord
Chancellor, am not for playing the marionette.
But that must not be. My Lord, all nations are
dependent, the one on the many, this we know.
But if the greater must always swallow the lesser
and so become greater yet, such a logic is unleashed
on the world as will end in — I know not what.

We are Scotsmen. Let us set our country in order,
and flourish, and add our own, independent, weight
to the world.

He sits in silence.

ARGYLL rises, undercuts FLETCHER.

ARGYLL: My father's head was chopped off by a Stewart. Why?
Because he would not see a Papist on our throne.
Neither will I. Such privileges and liberties as this
parliament may have would be denied altogether
by a Stewart King — our country would be a sea
of blood once more.

We may dream, as Mr Fletcher dreams, of rejecting
this union and remaining independent of England
and the Stewarts. The English will not accept it,
indeed they could even destroy us. Their Aliens Act
showed how easily they could destroy our trade.
Should it come to arms, they will overwhelm us, and
enforce union on us. We have no other alternative.

VOICE: If parliament ratify this Treaty, the Scottish people
will rise up —

ARGYLL: We keep informed of our enemy's intentions. Should
they revolt against this treaty, my Lord Queensberry
has taken certain steps.

VOICES: Oh! Oh! Which steps?

ARGYLL: There are, at his insistence, large numbers of English troops gathered at the Border, at Berwick and at Carlisle. There are English troops on the alert in the North of Ireland ready to land in the west of Scotland, and a reserve force in Holland ready for action in the East of Scotland. You see we are men of principle.

VOICE: What principle's that one?

ARGYLL: The principle of prosperity. Great Britain must have all her resources united, and be liberated forever from an idolatrous church and an autocratic king that impede the progress of men of science and enterprise. Then our Protestant United Kingdom will go on to command Europe, to expand her colonies and her trade into a mighty Empire, to develop her industries and her agriculture until she is undisputed master of the globe. Why should we here in Scotland cut ourselves off from all that, in the interests of a Pretender who scarcely speaks our language, and who will impose his antiquated philosophies on the mass of the people far more ruthlessly and with far more bloodshed and destruction than we. And as for the people — they fail to understand that their wild emotions will never triumph over this historical necessity.

SEAFIELD: rises. We have heard much reasoning upon this Act. Let us now proceed to the vote: Approve the Act ratifying the Treaty of Union of the two Kingdoms of Scotland and England: Yea or No. Let each man stand in order as his name is announced, and let his vote be recorded Approve or Not Approve. (Calls.) The Duke of Douglas!

HAMILTON rises in a fury.

HAMILTON: My Lord Chancellor! I crave leave to speak —

SEAFIELD: Yes, Your Grace, you have leave —-

MARGARET: At last our noble leader has decided to speak. He may have left it a bit late, but we await with interest —

HAMILTON: My Lord — my lord, I do protest.

SEAFIELD: Yes, Duke Hamilton?

HAMILTON: My Lord — it is my name that should be called first —

He sits. A stunned silence.

SEAFIELD: Then, your Grace, your protest shall be registered.
                      Let us proceed to the vote —

                      Er — His Grace the Duke of Douglas —

VOICES: Minor! The Duke is only nine years old!

SEAFIELD: His Grace the Duke of Hamilton —

HAMILTON: (hesitates, sulking, finally stands). Not approve. (Sits.)

SEAFIELD: Mr Fletcher of Saltoun?

FLETCHER: Not approve.

More names are called out.

MARGARET: There was a great crowd outside, in Parliament
                      Square. The people of Edinburgh were angry. Their
                      anger grew the greater when they heard the result
                      of the voting.

SEAFIELD is given a piece of paper. He rises.

SEAFIELD: The voting on this motion: Approve the Treaty of Union:
                      110. Not Approve the Treaty: 69. Abstentions 41.

                      My Lord High Commissioner, this Parliament
                      having approved this Act to ratify the Treaty of
                      Union between the two Kingdoms of Scotland and
                      England, we request you, as the true representative
                      of the person of Her Majesty Queen Anne, to touch
                      it with the Royal Sceptre and thus make it from
                      this day forward the law of this kingdom to which
                      we all must adhere.

QUEENSBERRY: It gives me great pleasure.

SEAFIELD: The End of an Auld Sang —

Through this the hubbub inside the chamber has been growing. Now
as QUEENSBERRY steps forward in his robes to raise the mace and
touch the Act it turns to near uproar — with more uproar outside. He
touches the Act — satisfied.

A large reaction from the Chamber. SEAFIELD hurriedly lays the Act
on the table. A loud and growing noise from all round the outside of
the building.

MARGARET: The fate of Scotland had been decided by its corrupt
                      nobility, and its merchants so full of greed and
                      so empty of imagination. The people of Scotland,

the Highlanders, the Lowland presbyterians, the
Catholics and Episcopalians of the North-East, the
townsfolk of Dundee, Edinburgh and Glasgow had
neither vote nor representation: but they had a
voice, and they let it be heard.

The noise grows very loud. QUEENSBERRY, SEAFIELD, etc are terrified,
as is HAMILTON. They scurry off out the back door.

Church bells ring in England and GODOLPHIN appears smiling on the
English stage.

The sound of the Parliament doors being broken down in Scotland,
shots, jeers as all run off — FLETCHER stands alone in the parliament.

During the next song, the MOB enters, ragged, forlorn, desolate, no
longer violent. They pile up the pieces of the 'doors' into a sort of
funeral pyre, and leave.

SONG: 'Parcel of Rogues'

SINGER: Fareweel to a' our Scottish fame,
                     Fareweel our ancient glory;
                     Fareweel ev'n to the Scottish name,
                     Sae fam'd in martial story.
                     Now Sark rins over Solway sands,
                     An' Tweed rins to the ocean,
                     To mark where England's province stands —
                     Such a Parcel of Rogues in a nation!

                     What force or guile could not subdue,
                     Thro' many warlike ages,
                     Is wrought now by a coward few,
                     For hireling traitor's wages.
                     The English steel we could disdain,
                     Secure in valour's station,
                     But English gold has been our bane,
                     Such a Parcel of Rogues in a nation!

During the song, over an instrumental verse —

MARGARET: And that is how the Scottish parliament, and
                     nation, abolished itself. Not with forty per cent
                     of the entire population voting for it, but with
                     110 of the crooked nobility and the short-sighted
                     merchants.

                     How would you have voted, if you'd been there —
                     and assuming anybody even asked you?

                     All those voting for the Union, leave by the Ayes
                     — this door here —

All those against — through this door here.

And there will be no Abstentions!

And when you come back — we'll tell you how
                you voted — and show you what happened in the
                years to come.

(Finish the song.)

SINGER: O would, eere I had seen the day,
                   That Treason thus could sell us,
                   My auld grey head had lain in clay,
                   Wi' Brurce and loyal Wallace!
                   But pith and power, till my last hour
                   I'll make this declaration,
                   We're bought and sold for English gold —
                   Such a Parcel of Rogues in a nation!

END ACT TWO

ACT THREE

Scene One — *Floating to England*

The third act begins with a rabble-rousing rattle of side- drums among the audience in the foyer and public places. THREE DRUMMERS, followed by MEMBERS of the MOB, go about calling the audience back to witness the results of the recent Union with England, and to see with their own eyes the burdens it placed on the good people of Edinburgh and of Scotland; they lead the audience into the auditorium.

There, on two platforms pushed together, stands GENERAL JOE SMITH, an Edinburgh cobbler, beating his drum. When all are assembled around him:

JOE SMITH: My friends, you'll need to listen to what I have to say, for I'm the voice of the people of Edinburgh, and so of the commonality of Scotland: Joe Smith's my name, a puir cobbler to trade, but when an injustice arises in this town, and I wheek on my drum and beat it along the Cowgate and up the West Bow, and round the Grassmarket, then I'm General Joe, for I lead an army of folk from the closes and the wynds of three or four thousand — the Edinburgh mob — let nobody mock it — (Points up.) Here's one that mocked it — poor old Jock Porteous, Captain of the Town Guard: once they'd won their union and taken away from Scotland our ancient rights and privileges, they set about breaking every article in the Union Agreement one by one — and they're still up to their tricks in your day too, so I see — oh aye, we were right — No Union, (Drum.) No union (Drum.) — that was the cry before our parliament passed that traitor's charter: and no sooner had they made sikkar of their power over us than English taxes, English Customs duties, and worst of all English excise-men came down on our heads.

First it was their tax on the very malt we need for our beer that they had promised not to levy — the Glasgow folk rose up pretty quick against that one; then they captured a lad called Andra Wilson, the English excisemen with their cold noses and watery eyes, and they said that they must hang him for smuggling under their English law: so out comes the Edinburgh mob, all set to rescue bold Andra — but Jock Porteous who was a proud overweening Captain of the Town Guard failed to appreciate the rights and wrongs of it, and when we went to rescue Andra, Jockie orders his lads to fire on their

99

own uncles and cousins: and they killed eight of
them that day, and hanged Andra. Well, we made
sure he was tried for murder, and so he was, and
convicted and sentenced to hang himself: but we
heard he had a reprieve from England, that they
were plotting to set him free: we were no' going to
stand for that. (Drum.) We marched into the city,
we nailed up the West Port to keep out the soldiers
and the guard (Drum.) we burnt down the door of
the Tolbooth prison (Drum.) we hauled out the bold
Jockie (Drum.) and there's where he ended, on a
dyer's pole in the Grassmarket! (Drum, to end.)

(The tattered corpse of Porteous descends on the end of a rope.)

Aye, the Union with England was no' so good for
Jockie Porteous's health, but there were a few —
oh aye, my friends, quite a few — it brought riches
and power to beyond their wildest dreams of what
they could amass in a Scotland that stood alone:
they were the folk who voted for it, and they were
the folk who gained by it.

A PROCESSION from Scotland to England:

On first float, ARGYLL and ISLAY, resplendent. They travel slowly
but smoothly from Scotland to England, as in a coach. They are not,
however, over-fond of each other, and have very different personalities:

JOE SMITH: Would you look at the Campbell brothers —
between them these two delivered Scotland into
the hands of the English ministers for forty years
— John, second Duke of Argyll, and Archie, Lord
Islay, until he became third Duke of Argyll — and
ruled alone —

JOHN, DUKE OF My Brother, Islay, wants to make all his friends Tools
ARGYLL: to Walpole, because he finds his ends in doing so —

ARCHIBALD, My Brother John is a great man but difficult,
ISLAY: always at odds with the role he chooses to play —
wrong-headed, and Romantic: but still my brother . . .

JOHN: My Brother Islay prefers his 'Places' to all other
considerations; friendship, Honour, Relation, gratitude
and service to his country seem at present to have
no weight with him . . .

ARCHIBALD: A great man, but it is I who do the work, I who
must bustle about London and Edinburgh and who
knows where: since the Union with England, we

in Scotland have only sixteen Peers in the House of Lords, chosen in a most subtle manner: the English Prime Minister sends a list to me, and the Scots Peers vote for all those on that list: my job is to make sure of it!

JOHN: The English Prime Minister only remembers Scotland exists when the Jacobites rise up, or when there is an Election to be rigg'd.

ARCHIBALD: We no longer, thank Goodness, have one hundred and fifty-nine Members of Parliament: only forty-five — and in the whole of Scotland but four thousand voters: by the skillful distribution of favours, jobs and some Secret Service cash, I usually manage most of them to be delivered to the party in power in England: with, of course, due gratitude to myself . . .

JOHN: I do favour the union of the *speech* of our two countries. Quite apart from the work of the Society for the Propagation of Christian Knowledge in ensuring that Highland Gaelic speakers no longer practice this barbarous tongue, equating Godliness and civilisation with the speaking of English, I myself favour a similar effort to eradicate the *Scots* tongue, as it is called — an uncouth, inexpressive muttering that will hold Scotland back in the esteem of our partners the English.

He suddenly crumples and dies.

ARCHIBALD: When John died in 1743, of course, I became Duke of Argyll myself, and in spite of rivalries, petty jealousies and local difficulties, with the English Prime Ministers, and their royal masters' choosing as favourites most unsuitable Scotsmen, nevertheless, I did manage to manage Scotland —

A sudden wild outburst of boran, whistles and fiddle from Scotland, and PRINCE CHARLES STEWART leaps on to the stage and strikes a pose — MUSIC continues:

JOE: Oh, my Goodness, here comes Bonnie Prince Charlie! Aye, it was more than Dukes of Argyll marched down to London — it was thousands of poor, deluded Hielanders, brave men but hungry, trying to make up for a bad harvest with turning out to soldier for their chiefs who couldnae speak their Gaelic language, and they risking everything they had for a Prince who couldnae speak the

101

English language: ach, puir creatures, deceived into
thinking a Stewart would set them to rights, their
rightful King: and he no sooner taking Scotland,
then off to claim England: he thought the English
would rise for him as well, but they were no so
stupid, or so gallant.

(CHARLES goes on his horse down towards England: stops: MUSIC stops:)

It was fine singing all the way to Derby: but when
nobody but a few lads in Manchester joined him,
and they sent one English army from the east, and
another from the west, back they had to come, to
Edinburgh, to Perth, all the way back to Culloden
Moor — and the melody changed then, my friends;
(MELODY begins.) the Duke of Cumberland
slaughtered one thousand starving Highlanders and
the English brought the whole of the Highlands
to heel, like whippit spaniels — Charles got away
— see, there he goes, romantically through the
heather — but the widows and the orphans, the
generations humiliated in years to come, had little
to be thankful for. The young man had courage,
and a taste for adventure: he had neither hope of
winning the crown of England, nor care for what
would happen should he fail . . . A fool, a costly fool —

ARCHIBALD ARGYLL is almost at the English stage.

ARCHIBALD: After that, I had great difficulty persuading the
                 English we were not a nation of brigands and thieves
                 — even more than usual. Even I, a Campbell,
                 was suspected of Jacobite leanings and Highland
                 romanticism — Me! A Jacobite! A Romantic! No,
                 in spite of my difficulties, I earned the respect of
                 our English masters —

                 From 1743 to 1760 I managed Scotland. I passed
                 the job on to my nephew the Marquis of Bute —
                 a clever boy — an insolent, scheming, disobedient
                 boy: but my nephew all the same —

The float goes up to the English stage, they step off onto the stage, and
kiss the hem of the cloak of the Hanoverian statue that now looms
over the English end — larger than life.

BUTE now is moving south on his float, a smart young dandy, with
a cut-glass English accent. With him, his brother JAMES STUART
MACKENZIE, conceited, a political craftsman.

BUTE: Farewell, dear uncle, and farewell the tiresome

102

years of Scotch whingeing! I and James my brother
are true born Scots, I did of course go to Eton
and spend most of my life in London, but I think
I know better than Uncle Archie where the new
generation of Scots wants to go! For fifty long years
Scotland has groaned and complained, yearning
for the unattainable! — its heroic past, its lost
independence, its boring old *Scottishness*. But James,
you and I know well that Scotsmen want to forget
about all that nostalgic nonsense, grasp the realities
of a Britain about to defeat France once and for
all time, all set to become the mightiest Imperial
power in the world, seize the opportunities of every
kind such a prospect offers, throw in our lot with
England with joy and enthusiasm, and demand not
our *independence* from such a future, but *equality* in
fighting for it and exploiting it!

JAMES: We need not to be so frightfully different and
preciously unique: we need to be *more* like the
English, not less, in our manners, our dress, our
education and above all in our speech!

BUTE: What a joy it is to hear that a most talented actor
who even though Irish by birth speaks most elegant
English, is even now giving lectures in Edinburgh
on correct English usage and pronunciation —

The float stops as SHERIDAN, on Scots stage, makes a series of very
English vocal noises —

SHERIDAN: Oh ... Ah ... Ha! ... Tincture ... Pling Cds. Would
you please pronounce after me:

Oh!

(Audience are made to copy him.)

Ah! Etc.

JOE SMITH interrupts — addresses audience:

JOE: Noo say efter me: Get ... tae ...

(SHERIDAN whoops and scatters. JOE indicates to the music to continue,
and the float to move on —)

That's enough of that gadgie — let's be hearin' what
our noble leaders and representatives in London
were doing for us — On your way, Lord Bute!

BUTE: As the young King's Tutor and confidant of his dear mother Queen Charlotte, I am confident that I can secure for Scotland that equality of trust which we now seek from His Majesty, and from that will flow the inclination towards equality in the opportunities for service, for mercantile expansion and for just rewards.

JAMES: Already the enormous losses of men from the Scottish Highland regiments in England's wars have assured our friends in England that we are their willing allies, and reduced the number of disaffected youth in the wilder parts . . .

BUTE: Even as my brother James was settling in to his place as Scotland's apologist to the Westminster parliament, another star was rising, as it were, in the east: young Dundas, the Edinburgh lawyer —

The float arrives behind the ARGYLL'S — BUTE and MACKENZIE walk along both to the English stage and kiss the hem; all FOUR watch as HENRY DUNDAS floats on, leaving nephew ROBERT behind on the Scottish stage:

DUNDAS: I come from a family with a small estate, of the middling ranks of society, and though I may have arisen to the very top, I have never forgotten what the common people need — that is discipline and if possible fear — and what is palatable to my own middling classes — a great figure of authority to respect and look up to, and a sensation of complicity with the powers that God has set above them. Don't forget that Robert . . .

ROBERT: No, Uncle —

DUNDAS: One day Robert I shall rise to control the whole of India as I now govern Scotland — and when I turn to that, then Scotland shall be yours —

ROBERT: Yes, Uncle

DUNDAS: At the last election I was able to deliver forty-one out of the forty-five Scots Members of Parliament to the Government interest. But I only control twelve of them personally — by the next election I intend to control twenty-two. Personally. Edinburgh has only twenty-five voters, surely they can all be bought — or thirteen of them, that's enough! See what you can do Robert —

ROBERT: Yes uncle, Bye uncle —

(SCOTLAND suddenly erupts with Grain Rioters —)

> Help! Uncle Henry! Help!

JOE: (now on SCOTS stage, beats drum).
And while the managers managed, the people went
hungry. The first strike in Scotland, the workers
with-holding their labour, took place in Edinburgh,
in 1734. And from then on, the Edinburgh mob was
the best instrument of democracy Scotland would
hope for: if the grain merchants put their prices up,
we took them down again. If they found a better
price in England and tried to sail away with it, we
were down tae Leith and we'd chopped down the
masts of the grain boats so they couldnae take it
anywhere. If they served us short, we were back
for the rest of the measure:

All this accompanied by dumb-show, with ROBERT as the merchant,
with suitable punctuation from JOE on his drum.

DUNDAS: I shall send four troops of Dragoons and the 53rd Regiment
of Foot to Edinburgh Castle, to quell the people's fire —

The people of Scotland need to know that we shall
be firm, and will stand no nonsense, just as do the
people of India. They love us all the better for it —

He reaches the English stage, kisses the hem: the FIVE SCOTS Managers
stand loyally and sing: 'God Save The King'

> God Save Our Gracious King
> God Save Our Noble King
> God Save The King
> Send him victorious
> Happy and glorious
> Long to reign over us
> God save The King

> Lord, grant that Marshal Wade
> May, by Thy mighty aid,
> Victory bring!
> May he sedition hush,
> And like a torrent rush
> Rebellious Scots to crush,
> God Save The King!

Scene Two — Trees of Liberty

They finish as the heroic figure carrying the flag of Revolution
appears from France, in a tableau on a float, and sings 'La
Carmagnole':

SONG: Madame Véto avait promis
       De faire égorger tout Paris
       (Repeat 1st 2 lines:)

       Mais son coup a marqué
       Dansons la carmagnole

       Vive le son, vive le son,
       Dansons la carmagnole
       Vive le son du canon

The French Revolution float glides away, to cheers from the Scots MOB.

This is greeted by another song from the Scots stage, Burns's 'Tree of Liberty', sung by the members of the MOB.

SONG: *Tree of Liberty*

       Heard ye o' the tree o' France,
       I watna what's the name o't;
       Around it a' the patriots dance,
       Weel Europe kens the fame o't.
       It stands where ance the Bastile stood.
       A prison built by kings, man.
       When Superstition's hellish brood
       Kept France in leading strings, man.

       Upo' this tree there grows sic fruit,
       Its virtues a' can tell, man;
       It raises man aboon the brute,
       It maks him ken himself, man.
       Gif ance the peasant taste a bit,
       He's greater than a lord, man.
       An' wi' the beggar shares a mite
       O' a' he can afford, man.

       Without this tree, alake this life
       Is but a vale o' woe, man;
       A scene o' sorrow mixed wi' strife,
       Nae rael joys we know, man.
       We labour soon, we labour late,
       To feed the titled knave, man,
       And a' the comfort we're to get
       is that ayont the grave, man.

       Wi' plenty o' sic trees, I trow,
       The warld would live in peace, man;
       The sword would help to mak a plough,
       The din o' war wad cease, man.
       Like brethern in a common cause,
       We'd on each other smile, man;

And equal rights and equal laws
Wad gladden every isle, man.

JOE: Aye, the Tree of Liberty was bearing fruit in 1792. The King's birthday, June the Fourth. The Lord Provost o' Edinburgh invites a few o' his cronies tae drink the king's health. Up in the Lawnmarket the toast is ringin' out loud: 'Tae George the third an' last!' And just tae show we didnae care, we chased the soldiers and set their sentry-boxes afire in the High Street. Aye — we had a party a' right. The Home Secretary in London was the very same Henry Dundas who had ruled Scotland on behalf of the English, and his own private fortune, for very nearly forty years. King Harry the Ninth they cried him in Edinburgh. But neither kings nor Henry Dundas were very popular in Scotland in 1792: in May, they burnt his effigy in Fife, and handbills and posters were tae be seen in Edinburgh that were highly uncomplimentary. So he sent four troops of Dragoons, and the 53rd Regiment of Foot to Edinburgh Castle, ta quell the people's fire.

And he sent his wee nephew Robert, the Lord Advocate, to rule the unruly, and in turn tae be ruled by him . . .

Enter ROBERT DUNDAS, with a letter he has written.

ROBERT
DUNDAS: Dear Uncle Henry, The evil spirit of the French Revolution seems to have reached us in Scotland. I was in hopes John Bull would have kept it to himself, but no. There is a lawless force of mob roaming the streets of Edinburgh which even the Dragoons which you so kindly provided cannot dispel.

The present riots began on the King's birthday, with disloyal toasts, and the burning of an effigy of yourself, dear uncle, which I'm told occasioned almost universal happiness.

I was in your mother's house in George Square, with Colonel Francis Dundas, when the mob appeared with yet another effigy of your good self, dear uncle — this time hanging from a scaffold. They tried to smash the windows of your mother's house! Colonel Francis bravely set out to repel them, armed only with Lady Arniston's crutch. But alas the brave warrior was seized and beaten with his own weapon. Thankfully the troops arrived and saved him.

107

We thought the mob had gone away to burn down
the Lord Provost's house in St Andrews Square.
Imagine our chagrin when they returned in even
greater numbers, crowding into George Square as
thick as they could stand. We thought our final hour
had come, when the Dragoons once more came to
our rescue and fired into the crowd. We saw five
or six fall — whether dead or merely wounded I
know not — and the crowd dispersed, but for how
long we dare not say.

The whole of Europe is in the grip of this dreadful
revolutionary fervour, dear uncle, and you Home
Secretary too. Fortunately the mob here do not know
exactly what they want, except a vague desire for
blood — yours, mine and His Majesty's — which
I hope will not be satisfied, alarming as it may be.

There is however another element within Edinburgh
society which does know precisely what it wants. A
young advocate, one Thomas Muir, expelled from
Glasgow University not five years ago, is the prime
mover of a most articulate and cunning organisation
of disaffection known as the Friends of the People.
Now: Alone, they have no strength. And the mob,
alone, have no direction: but should they combine
the one with the other, I fear our days are numbered.
I am resolved to insinuate a spy into the heart of
their counsels, and to set about clapping Mr Muir
into the Tolbooth for High Treason, and thence to
the gallows or at worst Van Dieman's Land, the
very moment I can find a scrap of evidence.

As he goes off another burst of the 'Tree of Liberty'.

SONG: But vicious folks aye hate to see
                        The works o' Virtue thrive, man;
                        The Courtley vermin's banned the tree;
                        And grat to see it thrive, man;
                        Awa' they gaed wi' mock parade,
                        Like beagles hunting game, man,
                        But soon grew weary o' the trade
                        And wished they'd been at hame; man.

                        For freedom, standing by the tree,
                        Her sons did loudly ca', man;
                        She sang a sang o' liberty;
                        Which pleased them ane and a', man.
                        By her inspired, the new-born race
                        Soon drew the avenging steel, man;

> The hirelings ran — her foes gied chase,
> And banged the despot weel, man.

Enter THOMAS MUIR, a young Scots lawyer, a radical Jacobin,
applauding ROBERT.

MUIR: Spoken like a true Lord Advocate, Robert — and
in the short run you'll probably succeed — but no:
sooner or later you and your buying of Scotland cheap
in Edinburgh, and selling it dear in London, will
come crashing to the ground like the might of King
Louis of France: and just as the true representatives
of the people of France rule that great state, so here
the people must rule. That Revolution in France
will resound through the world for years to come,
and the high and mighty in our land will quake
with fear, and tremble, until they give way.

My name, by the way, is Thomas Muir, I'm a
lawyer, I'm a Scotsman and I'm a radical — I see
our friends in England have begun an organisation
for the promotion of the ideals of the French
Revolution among the population, membership fee
two pounds per annum! Well I started The Friends
of the People in Scotland, for a fee of six pence! We
have branches everywhere, fifty-seven of them, all
over Scotland. Tom Paine's *The Rights of Man* they
tried to proscribe, but it was all over Scotland too,
even translated into the Gaelic!

In 1792 we called a National Convention in Blackfriars
Wynd, Edinburgh: the Friends of the People were
going into action —

(The French float, flag flying, comes to Scotland. From the holes and
crannies, bodies appear, lights down to a conspiratorial glow on the
Scots stage. MUIR speaks to the Convention.)

Friends, I have here an address from our brothers
the United Irishmen, praying we should have good
fortune. I shall read it to you . . .

WILSON: Mr Muir, I think it unwise. They are a proscribed
Association, enemies of the British state, and it is
a most inflammatory Address.

MUIR: Mr Wilson, if we cannot even read a letter addressed
to us, how shall we ever bring about those changes
we need?

WILSON: There may be those amongst us who are not what
they seem . . .

MUIR: There may be. Let them crawl to their spymaster Dundas and tell him this: our friends the United Irishmen wish us to succeed (Reads.) 'Not by a calm, contented, secret wish for a reform in Parliament, but by openly, actively and urgently *willing* it, with the unity and energy of an embodied Nation' — embodied, that is, in arms!

TYMPANI, followed by melody of 'A Man's A Man' — MUIR is arrested by TWO SHERIFF'S MEN, placed on the French float, the flax removed, and held while BRAXFIELD's voice resounds through the hall:

BRAXFIELD: There has of late been a spirit of sedition and of revolt against this Constitution.

This cannot be allowed to continue. Was it entirely innocent of the prisoner to talk of 'reform' among ignorant country people, and of preserving their liberty among the lower classes of the towns, who, but for him, would never have known it was in danger. He must know that Parliament will pay no attention to such a rabble.

A Government in every country should be just like a Corporation, and in this country it is made up of the landed interest, which alone has a right to be represented. As for the rabble, who have nothing but personal property, what hold has the nation of them?

Mr Muir, I see little difference between your crime and treason. I feel no punishment for your crime is sufficient now that torture is, er, happily abolished, but fourteen years of transportation to Botany Bay should keep you out of contact with our society while you learn to better your ways. Should you return to any part of Great Britain, you will hang.

As MUIR is lead slowly away towards England, in chains: SONG — 'A Man's A Man' —

Ye see yon birkie ca'd, a lord,
Wha struts, and stares, and a' that,
Though hundreds worship at his word,
He's but a coof for a' that.
For a' that, and a' that,
His ribband, star and a' that,
The man of independent mind,
He looks and laughs and a' that —

Then let us pray that come it may,

110

As come it will for a' that,
That Sense and Worth, o'er a' the earth
Shall bear the gree, and a' that.
For a' that, and a' that,
It's comin yet for a' that,
That Man to Man the warld o'er,
Shall brothers be for a' that —

During this MUIR is lead off, and the fourth float joins the other three in a long line out from the English stage.

JOE: (bangs drum slowly — now on bandstand). And England, as they say, went to war with France — and you can be sure that when they say England goes to war, it means thousands and thousands of Scotsmen will die. And, wondrous to relate, the patriotic fervour of war unites the two nations even closer. But after the war was won, at the glorious battle of Waterloo, then something else was needed to unite the two, for they showed signs of falling apart a little. And that something else was to unite them in the sentimental shallows of the minds of the people for generations to come: for the first time in one hundred and fifty years, a reigning Monarch was to pay Scotland the honour of a Royal Visit!

Scene Three — Revolution becomes Industrial

MUSIC — 'Wee, wee, German Lairdie' —

GEORGE IV now steps on to the English stage, enormously large, with false knees covered in pink tights, and awash with a plethora of tartans
    see various portraits and cartoons — he steps proudly down on to the first float, and dances decorously forward down the line as all four floats roll towards Scotland.

Sounds of cheering crowds, bag-pipes, etc.

The SONG, quite difficult to follow in places, continues through all this:

SONG: 'Wee, Wee German Lairdie'

Wha the deil hae we got for a King,
But a wee, wee German lairdie!
An' whan we gate to bring him hame,
He was delving in his kail-yardie.
Sheughinng kail an' laying leeks,
But the hose and but the breeks,
Up his beggar duds he cleeks,

111

The wee, wee German lairdie.

An' he's clapt down in our gudeman's chair,
Thou wee, wee German lairdie;
An' he's brought fouth o' foreign leeks
An' dibblet them in his yardie.
He's pu'd the rose o' English lowns,
An' brak the harp o' Irish clowns,
But our thistle will jag his thumbs,
The wee, wee German lairdie.

Come up amang the Highland hills,
thou wee, wee German lairdie;
An' see how Charlie's lang Kail thrive,
An' if a stock ye daur to pu'
Or haud the yoking of a pleugh,
We'll break year sceptre o'er yere mou',
Thou wee bit German lairdie!

GEORGE steps off, helped by WALTER SCOTT, and climbs to the highest point in Scotland as the crowd cheer and huzzah!

When it all dies down, he says in various poses:

GEORGE IV: Hoots mon, ock aye,
We are graciously pleased
We are jock ular —
For you'll go no more a-roving
A-roving in the night
You'll go no more a-roving
Let the moon shine so bright,
No! (Suddenly sharp.)
You will go no more a-roving,
Not across my Border.
There will be no more Border Warfare,
Instead you will serve my grand-daughter,
Victoria . . .
You will build her a mighty Empire
On which the sun will never set —
For, Lo, where she comes —
A goddess, an almighty queen,
Whom you will bow down and worship . . .

On the English stage is now unveiled a vision: QUEEN VICTORIA, in her regal pose, but with three pairs of arms reaching out and writhing around her, like Kathakali, the Hindu goddess —

MUSIC — Indian.

VICTORIA: Go Doctor Livingstone from your Scottish bowers —

Make Africa Christian, commercial and ours;
Go Mister Gladstone, send our troops into battle,
For our Empire to grow they must die like cattle,
Go my dear Highlanders, win me more lands,
Though your own has been taken, with pride take
    a stand,
Go MacDonald to Canada, to Australia, Eyre —
Go all to South Africa, and drive out the Boer.
Go Grants to New Zealand, to China go Matheson,
To India, Malaya and Burma go Scottishmen;
In Egypt and Persia swing your kilts, show your knees,
To New Caledonia, to the New Hebrides,
And wherever you go, they obey your command —
For you slaughter and kill for the Queen of England.

On the Scottish stage, a domestic scene, a CHILD recites ROBERT LOUIS
STEVENSON'S 'Lamplighter' poem.

During it, a Lamplighter cycles round the auditorium, stopping to light
gas-lights, all of them under statues of Queen Victoria, but each with
a different continent written above it.

CHILD:

'Lamplighter'
My tea is nearly ready and the sun has left the sky;
It's time to take the window to see Leerie going by;
For every night at tea-time and before you take
    your seat,
With lantern and with ladder he comes posting up
    the street.

Now Tom would be a driver and Maria go to sea,
And my papa's a banker and as rich as he can be;
But I, when I am stronger and can choose what
    I'm to do,
O Leerie, I'll go round at night and light the lamps
    with you!

For we are very lucky, with a lamp before the door,
And Leerie stops to light it as he lights so many more;
And O! before you hurry by with ladder and
    with light,
O Leerie, see a little child and nod to him tonight!

As the poem finishes, and the last gas-light is lit, showing us the Victorian
work-space of the building we are in, a SONG comes in from the BAND,
sung by solo tenor and solo soprano voices with piano accompaniment.
During it, different groups come in and move on floats to the centre
of the playing area, until all four are drawn up in a square, on which
they climb, and join in the chorus, miming their work —

The audience are invited to move all round the square, with some

benches quietly placed along the side-lines. We end up with a raised
Theatre in the Round.

TENOR: From the mountains of Galloway
                          From the shores of Argyll
                          From the green straths of Sutherland
                          It's many a mile —
                          From the Uists and Lewis
                          Lochaber and Skye
                          We are heading for Glasgow
                          With a tear in our eye.

                          For our fields have been stolen
                          Our crofts set on fire
                          And our land given over to sheep:
                          These factories in Glasgow
                          Say it's hands they require,
                          And it's there we must go for our keep.

SOPRANO: From a hungry Connemara
                          From the green hills of Clare
                          From the mountains of Donegal
                          Now empty and bare
                          From Antrim and Leitrim
                          From Cork and Tralee
                          We are sailing to Glasgow
                          Just over the sea —

                          For our fields have been stolen
                          Our crops are destroyed
                          And we're watching our kids starve and die:
                          In the factories in Glasgow
                          We will all be employed —
                          And it's there we must go with a sigh:

They have come in on floats from different directions. Now they meet
and sing together:

BOTH: Now it's black sunless tenements
                          That are packed with disease
                          Where the rats and cockroaches
                          Go chasing the fleas
                          In Greenock and Gorbals
                          In Govan, Townhead,
                          We are working like slaves, we'd
                          Be better off dead.

ALL: And it's WORK — WORK — WORK
                        In coal-mine and dock-side and mill
                        In the yards and the forges we toil and we sweat,

But we're starving and penniless still —

Yes it's WORK — WORK — WORK
For women and children and men
From before the sun rises till after it sets
Will we ever see daylight again. . . .

At the end of the song, the piano continues under the SINGER, as he
speaks to the audience —

SINGER: Building an Empire overseas was not all that Queen
Victoria's Scotsmen got up to. They built their own
little empires at home — their great factories, steel-
mills, coal-mines, chemical works, breweries — and
in them, the natives. The great men of enterprise,
the engineers and shipbuilders — Napier, Elder,
Thomson, Denny, Dubs, Howden, Beardmore,
the magnates of coal and steel — Neilson, Dixon,
Mouldsworth, Dunlop, the Bairds, David Colville;
the Tennants with chemicals, the Coats and the
Monteith cotton empires; the Baxters and Coxes of
Dundee linen and jute; these and many more kept
Scotland upsides with England in scientific research,
and in production. They had their big houses outside
the towns, their estates in the Highlands, and more
and more, their town-house in London. Like the
landed aristocracy before them, the plutocrats of
industry became integrated into the ruling class of
Great Britain, a Kingdom United as it had never
been before.

And in 1832, with the Reform Act the growing
middle and professional classes got the vote — and
joined in the prosperity of their masters, and they
too became Britons, loyal to the Queen.

But what happened to these people — those driven
off their land, forced to look for work in the hell
of the Victorian cities — were they so loyal? Were
they 'British to the core?' What happened to them?

CHORUS comes in again: Work, Work, Work.

ABRAM DUNCAN, a Glasgow woodturner, stands at the end of the
song. He is a young working man. Preferably the actor who played
BON ACCORD.

DUNCAN: No, we may not have been so loyal, so true blue as
our masters, but when a Mr John Collins from the
Birmingham Radicals came up here to ask would

115

we go with them for Reform, for agitation for a
People's Charter of Rights — well, we knew we had
more in common with the folk from Birmingham,
and Feargus O'Connor from Ireland, and Dr Wade
from the London Working Men's Association than
we did with our Scottish Masters or the Scottish
landowners.

And that's how the very first meeting in the whole
of Britain of what they called the Chartists was held
right here in Glasgow: on Glasgow Green: nearly
200,000 people, on a wet Monday 21st May 1838;
they stopped work and came out in a procession
two miles long — seventy trades unions, forty-three
bands of music, 300 banners carried, some from
the Lanarkshire and Renfrewshire villages, and one
Covenanters' flag. And on Glasgow Green, Jimmy
Turner kicked off by telling us how we all had to
behave ourselves, no revolution here, he said, only
correct peaceful behaviour. Then up gets Mr James
Attwood of the Birmingham Political Union — an
Englishman!

ATTWOOD: (Brum accent). For my part, I am no revolutionist. I
ask only Reform. But lined up against us reformers,
who do we see? All the aristocracy. Nine-tenths of
the gentry. All their place-men and their hangers-
on. Just like it was in France. On our side, we have
no strength, except the justness of our cause. And
just it is, for we ask no more than the vote for all
who labour! For our representatives to go to London
for no longer than one year, then to come back
so we can approve or disapprove, and vote again!
For the rights of all who labour to unite in Trades
Unions, so we stand together, rather than fall one
by one!

Up in factory! Up in mill!
Freedom's mighty phalanx swell . . .
Fear ye not your master's power
Men are strong when men unite
And flowers will grow in blooming-time,
When prison-doors their jarring cease:
For liberty will banish crime —
Contentment is the best Police.

From here, from Glasgow, we will send out our great
National Petition! Now that the people of Glasgow
have met, forty-eight other towns will follow suit.

116

Once the forty-nine delegates of these towns have
met in London, I would like to see the House of
Commons that will resist Their Petition! But if God
makes them mad, then another and yet another
petition will be sent. Then we will together unite
in a general strike, such as the ancient Romans
had made on the Aventine Hill, until their wrongs
were removed. I say to you, the people of Glasgow:
your brothers and sisters in Birmingham will not
shrink, in the cause of peace, loyalty and order,
from assisting you, even to the death! Once more,
in your countless masses, come with us! Hearts of
lions, but with the gentleness of lambs, arise! For as
our English poet said; we are many, they are few!

Applause, cheers, etc from the CROWD.

DUNCAN: Aye, Attwood came like the Messiah! Within weeks
the National Petition was adopted in Glasgow,
Edinburgh, Perth, Dundee, in Ayrshire and Fife, by
Working Men's Association, by Radical Associations
all over Scotland.

Our masters had united with the English to exploit
their Empire, and to help them exploit us: so we
united with the English as well, in our own way,
for our own defence!

What happened to the Charter? For a time it was
the burning issue — in one year we had 169 Chartist
organisations in Scotland, we had five newspapers,
we had twenty-three Chartist Churches! But it all
died down after the movement, well — aye well,
aye well — after we had a bit of a split! You see, the
Glasgow Chartists were all for peace, and moderation,
and what they called 'moral force'. Ach, the leaders
were middle-class men with everything to lose: so
they formed something called the Complete Suffrage
Association, and the rest of them withered away.
The same 'moral force' crowd ran the Edinburgh
Chartists — it wasn't till ten years later, in 1848
the Year of Revolutions, that a mild-looking man
called Robert Hamilton went to a huge meeting
on the Calton Hill there, and he stands up and he
speaks to the fifteen thousand of them —

ROBERT   Fellow democrats, friends, for fourteen years I have
HAMILTON: preached moral force. And I am tired of it. I urge
every man here tonight to purchase a musket or a
pike. To join one of the excellent arms societies —

117

like the Muir Club, the Baird and Hardie Cub, or the Burns Club — in order to learn how to use his musket. And to join a National Guard to defend the People's Convention, and the Charter. This is not the time for speeches — the time has come for action: While a revolution will not be for the benefit of any class, still we must show our hard task-masters that we are determined to be slaves no longer. If perish we must, let it be by the sword rather than by hunger.

The Government's new Security of the Community Act would put every man who speaks at a public meeting into a dungeon. Well, fellow-democrats, I intend to speak, and I intend to speak sedition. Let every one of you ten thousand make the same stand as I do, and this base, bloody and tyrannical government will soon discover the jails will not be sufficient to hold us all. They can never put down the united force of the working classes!

DUNCAN: And they threw him into jail, and that was the end of physical force as well — and the end of our great Union with the English working-class: from then on, it was Divide and Rule! In the eyes of the English, Scotsmen stopped being savages and became a thousand Music Hall jokes — and a hundred funny songs . . .

Scene Four — The People's Flag

A huge procession — Trades Union banners etc — singing 'The Red Flag'.

SIX SCOTS WORKERS (men and women) come running on at speed toward the centre platform from six directions, carrying high banners which float out behind them. They use the poles to vault on to the platform, and raise the banners round the stage; they are of the late 19th/early 20th century 'William Morris' kind, with high-sounding mottoes and fine images of the aspirations of the Labour movement of that time.

MUSIC — massed choir sing:

SONG: 'The Red Flag'

ALL: The people's flag is deepest red,
It shrouded oft our martyred dead,
And ere their limbs grew stiff and cold,
Their hearts' blood dyed its ev'ry fold.

Chorus:

Then raise the scarlet standard high!
Within its shade we'll live or die,
Though cowards flinch and traitors jeer,
We'll keep the red flag flying here.

It suits today the weak and base,
Whose minds are fixed on pelf and place;
To cringe before the rich man's frown,
And haul the sacred emblem down.

Then raise the scarlet standard high!
Within its shade we'll live or die,
Though cowards flinch and traitors jeer,
We'll keep the red flag flying here.

With heads uncovered swear we all,
To bear it onward till we fall;
Come dungeon dark or gallows grim,
This song shall be our parting hymn.

Then raise the scarlet standard high!
Within its shade we'll live or die,
Though cowards flinch and traitors jeer,
We'll keep the red flag flying here.

At the same time a small procession of Scots workers carry a huge Red
Flag round the outside of the crowd, then move in to the stage in the
centre, climb up steps on to it, and place the red flag in the centre.

Carrying the flag has been Keir Hardie — as a young man. He now
gets up to speak:

KEIR HARDIE: Come now, Men and Women, I plead with you, for
your own sake and that of your children, for the sake
of the downtrodden poor, the weary, sorehearted
mothers, the outcast, unemployed fathers, — for
their sakes, and for the sake of our beloved socialism,
the hope of peace and humanity throughout the
world — Men and Women, I appeal to you, come
and join us and fight with us in the fight wherein
none shall fail!

For what are we fighting? For the spirit of Robert
Burns, for the ideals of Carlyle, Ruskin and Mill,
for the deep truths of the Holy Bible, and for that
instinct for democracy that beats in the hearts of every
decent working man or woman! We are not fighting
in bitterness against our masters, but confident in
the morality of our claim that every factory, mill

119

and pit should be managed by representatives of its workers! We are fighting for a better world, and a fairer world, where no man is worth more than any other man, and no Nation more than any other Nation!

It is a central policy of the Scottish Labour party, and of the ILP, as it will be of the British Labour party, that Scotland shall no longer be denied Home Rule! Every conference of our party has voted overwhelmingly in favour of this basic right of the Scottish Nation!

Cheers from the WORKERS.

YOUNG
ORANGEMAN:
Nay! No! Never! — We in the Orange Order in Scotland will not allow the working people of Scotland to be deceived! To be duped by those whose only interest is the indulgence of the Pope of Rome, whose only strategy is to turn Ireland into a Papist pig-sty, whose only weapons are lies and duplicity! For what is this Home Rule being preached by that whore of Romish Priests — Gladstone, and these green-eyed rats of socialism in the Scottish Labour Party? It is no more than a scheme to break up the union of Great Britain and Ireland! Why? — In order to further the godless ambitions of Parnell, and the Fenian cut-throats, and deliver Ireland into the hands of the whore of Babylon, the Scarlet Woman, and his Cardinals, Archbishops, Bishops and Priests! It is not enough that our headless set of politicians in London has seen fit to allow the triumphant re-entry into Scotland of Catholic bishops, the hierarchy of Beelzebub? No — now another set wants to break up our union with their cries of Home Rule! They will not succeed! The workers of Scotland will unite to defend Protestantism and the Union, and the true voice of the Church of Scotland and the British Constitution — the Conservative and Unionist Party of Great Britain! Every sound Orangeman is and will remain a *Conservative*!

During this a MIXED GROUP of Socialist Bicyclists cycle round the outside of the audience, singing the last verse and two choruses of 'The Red Flag'.

ALL:
With heads uncovered swear we all,
To bear it onward till we fall;
Come dungeon dark or gallows grim,
This song shall be our parting hymn.

120

Then raise the scarlet standard high!
Within its shade we'll live or die,
Though cowards flinch and traitors jeer,
We'll keep the red flag flying here.

Then raise the scarlet standard high!
Within its shade we'll live or die,
Though cowards flinch and traitors jeer,
We'll keep the red flag flying here.

The YOUNG ORANGEMAN from the stage hurls abuse at them — calling them Godless, Atheists, Harlots, No better than Common Prostitutes! Friends of the Pope not the People, Traitors to Britain, Enemies of the Queen, etc, etc.

Then MAY, a young Socialist schoolteacher rides her bike at speed up a ramp and onto the platform and drives him off with her umbrella. She turns to the audience:

MAY: Good riddance to bad rubbish! Now I'm May Keaney, and I want you all to sit upon the ground as we do in our great Open-Air Socialist Sunday Schools — we have a great many of them in Scotland, and many Labour Churches as well — when we all sing our Socialist hymns, like the one I am going to teach you now . . . It's NOT the one our Socialist Cycling Club were singing as we cycled healthily round the Campsies, but I'm sure you already know the melody! 'The Internationale'! Let's try the words, all together, line by line — Don't be shy — if we sing loud enough we can bring capitalism if not to its knees, at least to its senses! Piano please!

Now a sequence in which as she tries to get the audience to sing 'The Internationale' together, a series of LABOUR MEN get up amongst the audience and try to lead breakaways and splits —

Some of the SPLITTERS as follows:

SPLITTER 1:   Brothers, since Mr Hyndman did us the dreadful honour of visiting us here in Scotland, a highly significant event has occurred — his co-founder of the Social Democrat Federation Mr William Morris, a man of the highest probity, has revealed Mr Hyndman for what he is — an autocrat worse than the Czar — therefore Mr Morris has formed the Socialist League, the only truly democratic organisation for Socialists — which I urge you all to join!

SPLITTER 2:   Now Now Now! The Socialist League's nothing

121

> but a bunch of middle-class dabblers, daubers and scribblers! It's full of University Professors of Greek, school inspectors, Mr Pittendrigh MacGillivray the so-called sculptor, an art dealer and a crew of businessmen!

SPLITTER 3:   We in the Scottish Labour Party can no longer go it alone! We must merge with the ILP and play our part in the British stage!

SPLITTER 4:   (Irish). If that's what you're up to, the Irish Nationalists who have given you noble support so far will support you no more! Going to Westminster indeed!

SPLITTER 5:   The Socialist Labour Party will have none of your proto-capitalist Bernstinian compromise! We in the Socialist Labour Party — though we may not be strong in numbers — have Karl Marx on our side —

SPLITTER 6:   Marx on your side! You've turned Karl Marx on his head! We in the British Socialist Party are the true heirs of Marx and Engels, and will lead the workers of Scotland to victory over capital, the British bourgeois state, and the SLP!

SPLITTER 3:   Now the SLPs merged with the ILP, the Socialist Labour Party and the BSP can go and fight each other and the SDF and the SL as well, if one of them isn't the same three people as the other, for we in the ILP are about to merge with the SWPRC, and the SWPRC are going to merge with the LRC to produce nothing other than the Labour Party of Great Britain!

ALL OTHERS: Well they're wrong! You're all wrong! (Etc.)

MAY: One last time through: all together now! Arise ye starvelings from your slumbers, etc.

She and the audience sing the verse/chorus of 'The Internationale' as the SPLITTERS are fighting amongst themselves, climbing on to the platform to get at each other.

As the hymn ends, a lone bugler sounds a Reveille: they all turn in horror.

Gunfire, etc. They are handed military caps, and capes, etc, then three of the four platforms are towed off to war, with the men on them, to the sound of the bugle.

One man stays on the last platform: JOHN MACLEAN. On the other TAMMY, watching —

MACLEAN: 'Thou shalt not steal! Thou shalt not kill!' So says the Bible. But as a consequence of the robbery that goes on in all civilised countries today, Britain, Germany, France, the United States — all have had to keep armies, and inevitably our armies clash together. On that and on other grounds I consider Capitalism the most infamous, bloody and evil system that mankind has ever witnessed.

It is our business as members of the working class to see that this war ceases today, not only to save the lives of the young men of the present, but also to stave off the next great war! I am out for an absolute reconstruction of society, on a co-operative basis, throughout all the world. When we stop the need for armies, we stop the need for wars! My appeal is to the working class. They and they only can bring about the time when the whole world will be on one brotherhood, on a sound economic foundation. That and that alone, can be the means of bringing about a reorganisation of society. That can only be obtained when the people of the world get the world, and retain the world!

TAMMY: Try as he would, John MacLean could not stop the Scots going to war for the British Empire against the Germans: and so our working class killed off their working class, and theirs massacred ours, for a war that brought benefits to neither of them: and by the end of it, Scotland was divided as never before — There were the middle and upper classes who had become passionately jingoist, passionately for everything England stood for, because they owed everything they had to the markets and raw materials that Empire had brought. And a working class, inspired by the Soviet, the German, the Hungarian workers' uprisings, with revolutionary stirrings towards overthrowing a United Kingdom that had given them little but the wage-slavery of the factories, the nightmare of the trenches, and after the war, the prospect of mass unemployment.

On Friday 31 January 1919, a huge crowd gathered in George Square, Glasgow, to support the demand for a 30-hour working week. Munro, the Scottish Secretary, panicked, and persuaded the government in London to send 12,000 troops, 100 lorries and six tanks to Glasgow. The police charged the crowd, and turned a demonstration into a riot.

123

SOUND: of mounting riot, screams, — no shots — horses hooves etc.

MACLEAN: I am certain that London will never lead the Clyde or Scotland, so we must lead ourselves! I hold that the British Empire is the greatest menace to the human race: the best interests of humanity can therefore be served by the break-up of the British Empire. The Irish, the Indians and others are playing their part. Why ought not the Scots? A Scottish breakaway at this juncture would bring the Empire crashing to the ground, and free the waiting workers of the world!

ForsometimepastthefeelinghasbeengrowingthatScotland should strike out for national independence. Many of us are convinced that ever since 1707 the Edinburgh politicians have been in the regular pay of London to keep Scotland as the base tool of the English government. Now the reaction is beginning.

I stand for a Scottish Workers Republic, with control in the hands of the workers, male and female alike, each workshop and industry sending delegates to district councils and to the National Council — which is to be established in Glasgow! But the Scottish workers must be joined in one big industrial union with their English and Welsh comrades against industrial capitalism! And we must refuse to murder our fellows on this planet at the autocratic bidding of John Bull!

TAMMY: For his pains, Maclean was arrested and imprisoned, went on hunger strike, and was force-fed, grew weaker and weaker, and died in 1923 at the age of 44.

MUSIC — solo fiddle.

VOICES come crowding in as MACLEAN'S float is dragged off:

KELVINSIDE WOMAN: He was a wicked man, John MacLean . . . one of the worst of these rabble-rousers . . . scum of the earth —

MAN: (pseudo-academic). Of course this 'Red Clyde' nonsense is all a bit of a myth — my research shows clearly that most decent Glasgow people were much more moderate in their demands — there was no revolution going on along the Clyde, I can assure you . . .

KELVINSIDE WOMAN:	We in Glasgow are particularly fond of our working classes — Good Heavens, they're the sweetest wee people you could find, except for those few throwbacks with their staring eyes and frothing lips going on about Workers of the World Unite — the workers of Glasgow *are* united, and they're quite happy with their lot, thank you very much —

TAMMY: The upper classes, the financiers, the industrialists, coalowners, shipyard owners, landowners; the middle classes whose livelihood depended on them — the merchants, the managers, the small producers and the banks; and the professional classes, who owed their income to both lots — the lawyers, accountants, doctors, dentists, academics and establishment artists; all three combined in Scotland against the threat of an aroused and militant working class. They relied heavily on the power of the British state to keep them safe and powerful: they needed England — to protect them from their own workers; and they repaid this service with an almost hysterical devotion.

GLASGOW BUSINESSMAN: Of course we in Scotland are just not self-sufficient — we're bloody subsidised by the English — we should be bloody grateful to them — and we bloody are!

TAMMY: Aye there were many in the Scottish ruling classes who had reason to be grateful to England — and still have today: from Lord James Douglas Hamilton to Lord Polwarth to the Duke of Buccleuch — owner of over 800,000 acres of Scotland, and heir to the noble Duke of Queensberry —

But the people of Scotland were angry, and rebellious — and their anger and rebellion were channelled into the British Labour Party, and in 1922, they sent a huge delegation of Labour MPs to Westminster committed to the socialist reorganisation of society, and Home Rule for Scotland.

On the night they were catching the train to London, a huge meeting was held in St Andrews Halls —

(Singing of 23rd Psalm begins.)

The place was packed to the rafters. Neil Maclean announced the end of the old parliamentary order! John Wheatley and Jimmy Maxton were there — Jimmy Maxton got up to speak:

MAXTON: Comrades and friends, we who are going off to

125

Westminster do not go as so many individuals to
win glory for ourselves. We go as a team — a team
selected by the working people of Scotland to take
on any and all opposition, a team with one great
goal — the establishment of a socialist society in
Scotland!

Scene Five — The Big Match

(WHISTLE)
A whistle, as of a train, but coming from the referee who has run on
to the pitch; the FIVE SPEAKERS strip off their costumes, hats, etc to
reveal full Scottish team tracksuits.

MUSIC FOOTBALL
On the English stage, the FIVE ENGLISH PLAYERS appear in tracksuits
and make rude gestures at the Scots. The goalposts come on, the referee
clears the pitch, the benches are now laid out along the touchlines, a
medley of sporting theme-tunes is playing, and hot pies are wheeled
in at the back of the crowd — on tape: crowd noises, songs.

The COMMENTATOR is on the Bandstand, visible, and he, as well as
giving something like the following lines, also directs the crowd to clear
the pitch, tells them where there are empty seats, etc.

COMMENTATOR: Hello and good afternoon and welcome to Wembley
Stadium, where Scotland are all set to clash head-
on with England in what is undoubtedly going
to be the Match of the Century. (AD LIBS re
crowd/seats/pitch, etc)

Clear the pitch please and the ground staff will
bring on the stands, the terraces, the paddock and
the visiting team's cages, etc, etc.

There is an extraordinary atmosphere of expectation
all around the ground — Scotland of course has
been the loser for over two centuries, both at home
and abroad, but now she has her new team of bright
new players, brilliant tacticians all, and the Scots
crowd are right behind them.

The English team, well, not used to being beaten by
anybody, their victories over Russia in the Crimea,
over practically every country in Africa and Asia
in the Empire Cup, and recently over the Boers
in Natal and their somewhat costly victories over
Germany at the Somme Stadium and the Turks at
Gallipoli.

126

> A sparkling team, confident, strong and ready for a
> hard game with these plucky little Scots — they're
> due on the pitch at any second — for the formal
> presentation to His Majesty the King of course, who
> is I suppose King of both countries, oddly enough,
> but is clearly seen by the English support as *their*
> king — I'm not sure how the Scots see him, or if
> they see him at all . . .

Football lights go on and the TWO TEAMS, jog out, kicking balls to
each other, bouncing them etc, in full track suits.

A whistle and they line up facing the bandstand: a regal figure lights
up, waves, bows, as 'God Save The King' is played, in a short version.

Another whistle, and they strip off their tracksuits, the CROWD NOISES
get more excited, and the referee calls the CAPTAINS, tosses, and
England elects to play towards the Scottish end. The teams line up.

Behind the Scots goal, on the stage, a group of SCOTS FANS, cheering
and waving bottles, wearing the insignia of the Tartan Army, especially
the long Lyon flags flowing back from their shoulders. They also have
saltires to hold up and other banners ready.

During this:

COMMENTATOR: Well there it is, the holy moment when the two teams
stand united and silent as it were entranced by the
royal personage: the King of course is descended
directly from the captain of Hanover City, top of
the Hanseatic or German League, who was bought
by England for a record sum in 1714.

His son, the Duke of Cumberland, played himself
for England against the Scots, hammering them
mercilessly for several seasons, and since then the
Scots have tended to play a defensive game, with
four in the back row, a couple of sweepers, four in
midfield and not many left to attack, but there's
a new aggressive edge to this team, that includes
Maxton, Wheatley, Kirkwood, Shinwell and Ramsay
MacDonald the crafty captain.

The English team seem a little heavyweight in
comparison, maybe a little complacent with their
recent run of success, but I don't think they are
going to miss any tricks in this all- important Match
of the Century.

(Noises from SCOTS FANS.)

There's a lot of high-spirited support from the rather

127

colourful Scottish fans — let's hope there will be
no trouble to mar this sporting contest . . . Play up,
play up, and Play the Game! That is, we hope, what
they are telling their team —

CROWD: Kill the Bastards! Boot the English bastards in the
balls! Rub their stuck-up noses in the shite, lads!
Go for the groin, Jimmy!

COMMENTATOR: Yes, the usual cheery banter from the Scots, I couldn't
quite decipher . . . but good-humoured and witty
no doubt —

The REF blows his whistle to start the game. There is no physical ball,
the players mime it, but otherwise they move around looking for
position, covering, tackling, making runs, etc as in a real game.

Immediately the SCOTS, who have the kick-off, move forward
aggressively toward the English goal.

COMMENTATOR: And my goodness this is a different Scotland moving
already into top gear — Maxton the dashing centre-
forward over to Wheatley Number Eleven over on
the left wing, he kicks with his left foot I believe,
Wheatley back to Kirkwood, Kirkwood to Shinwell,
Shinwell a crafty run towards his own goal, a short
ball to Ramsay MacDonald, MacDonald — well,
well, MacDonald dispossessed there because when
he got the ball at his feet and the English goal wide
open in front of him, he seemed to stop and bow
to the Royal Box, the fans not happy with that.

Beatrice Webb, the English sweeper has snapped
up the ball, out to Baldwin, who fumbles, and
it's skied back to Maxton's head, nods it down to
Archie Kirkwood, this could be a goal — No, no
— Beatrice Webb the English Fabian has the Scots
attack in trouble, she seems to be teaching them
how to drink tea, yes, how to suck lemons, how to
behave in London society. Young Winston Churchill
meanwhile has moved up to Scotland, and rams the
ball into the Scots crossbar, and once again these
plucky Scots seize the ball and with great shouts of
Home Rule for Scotland! they punt it up the pitch.

THREE SCOTS
DEFENDERS: Home rule for Scotland!

COMMENTATOR: Again, it's Maxton, again he's moving inside the
English penalty area — oh! and he's brought down

128

very heavily by the English Health Minister, who stands laughing at him, Maxton gets up . . .

MAXTON: I call you a murderer, and all of you are murderers, who allow children to die for the sake of saving a few pennies!

REFEREE blows whistle, shows Red Card, and orders MAXTON off, WHEATLEY runs over.

WHEATLEY: And I say they are murderers too, every Tory who voted for this parsimonious legislation!

REF sends him off too, amid protests.

COMMENTATOR: Well, there are those who would have called that a clear-cut penalty for Scotland, but it's ended with Maxton and Wheatley taking an early bath for unparliamentary behaviour. The Scottish fans are turning quite nasty now, but the game has re-started with a long punt into the Scots goal-mouth, and it takes all the wiles of Shinwell to get it away from danger.

Up to Ramsay Mac — some very tricky footwork from him — out to Kirkwood, who's moving out to the right wing more, he squares it, the goal's wide open. Ramsay's there, the English defence are in a terrible muddle, it must be a goal —

RAMSAY: Although Home Rule is indeed on our programme, and is partly why we were elected to power, I will not be the last Labour Prime Minister to do some simple arithmetic and see that if Home Rule comes about, that will reduce the number of Labour MPs I can count on in Westminster, and I will lose the next election: I shall therefore pass this ball to a Private Member's Bill, which I shall appear to support but ensure it does not get through the House — so

He boots the ball into his own half. The SCOTS DEFENDER boots it into touch. The ENGLISH TEAM become very active.

COMMENTATOR: Well here's a turn-up, the Labour Party have been thrown out without achieving Home Rule or Devolution, and the Tories are back in Westminster with a vengeance, and the Unionists in Scotland are of course on their side so it's looking like a very unequal contest here —
Now what's going on? Good gracious, it's my colleague Chris Grieve the Sports Reporter who's

run on to the pitch with big Lewis Gibbon, and
he's playing as Hugh McDiarmid, at Number 9!
— and yes, he plays the ball quite well down the
line, and he's run off again, into the Press Box,
and Chris Grieve is phoning in a glowing account
of the brilliant play of Hugh McDiarmid! Now he's
back on the pitch again claiming there's a Literary
Renaissance —
Now the ball's with Gallacher the Communist — and
McDiarmid tackles him, takes the ball and sets off
impatiently for the English goal but Gallacher brings
him down from behind and kicks him into touch!

I must say the English team are not seeing much
of the ball — here comes another attack, another
Labour Home Rule Bill, but there are four hundred
Tories in the English goal-mouth and no chance
of success . . . . A lot of tussling there, the Scots
crowd not quite sure what's going on . . . No (all
the Scots sit down) Ah — a General Strike — the
Tory Government in England take the opportunity
to score a few easy goals — One, Two, Three, Four
— that's Five Nil Scotland trailing, but they're back
on their feet, fighting fiercely, storming up to the
English goal — and oh! McDiarmid brought down
heavily there with a very hostile critical reception
in England, the Lallans kicked from under him in a
most aggressive piece of play, and as he limps off to
write his own review of his work, it's a penalty to
Scotland, and after another General Election, Labour
are back in, Home Rule still in their Manifesto and
with twenty-nine years of the 20th century gone,
Ramsay MacDonald is still Captain — and he elects
to take the penalty himself . . .

(Whistle. RAMSAY takes a run at the ball, then circles round past it
and boots it the other way — the SCOTS KEEPER dives frantically but
it goes in the net —)

And it's a goal for England! 6-0 to England —
the Scottish team don't like that, Maxton has run
back to protest, the Scots are giving their captain
a hard time — and Ramsay MacDonald is taking
off his shirt, turning it inside out, and he's playing
for the other side . . . Well, that's it for Scotland
I'm afraid.

No — maybe help is at hand —

(Two kilted figures, the SNP RIGHTWINGERS; one parades up and

130

down the touchline playing the pipes — briefly — 'Scotland the Brave', the other does a Victorian dance.)

> Now those are the Scots substitutes for Ramsay
> Mac warming up there — thirty-four years gone
> and the Scottish National Party is ready to take the
> field: on they come, what a bonny sight —

(The ref looks at their boots and under their kilts. They jog on acknowledging applause; whistle — ball comes to them. They carefully pass it to each other, moving slowly back then forward, immaculate footwork but getting nowhere. The OTHER SCOTS yell for them to pass the ball, but they don't.)

> Well this is very clever stuff, out on the Scottish right
> wing, the Nationalists passing the ball to each other,
> playing a tight possession game, a very respectable
> game, but not appearing to get anywhere!

(A war time siren sounds: they all run and put on tin hats and gas masks, and come back on. MUSIC — Nazi war music.)

> Thirty-nine years gone, and the century is in a
> mess: a mob of German lager-louts have invaded
> the pitch in Czechoslovakia, and again in Poland
> — they have been banned from European football
> indefinitely, but they show no sign of stopping these
> invasions —
>
> This game is looking very strange now, as the
> two teams line up side by side, salute their royal
> personage, and set off side by side to do battle with
> the Bosch.
> But no — the Scottish left-winger Tom Johnson
> nips back while they are all looking the other way,
> moves the Scottish Office to Scotland, has the
> Scottish Grand Committee meeting in Scotland and
> founds the Hydro Board! Three quick goals there
> for Scotland, and as the whistle goes for half-time,
> it's 6–3 to England, with Scotland looking very
> dangerous!
>
> Down now for a word with Tom Johnson, the scorer
> of that sneaky hat-trick!

(Mike to TOM JOHNSON, with INTERVIEW from COMMENTATOR.)

> Tom I gather you've been pressing hard for some
> time for some action —

TOM JOHNSON: Aye, I have, I wrote Our Noble Families some

time ago to try to get rid of a few really rotten players from our team, and had another go with the paper I edited, called, appropriately enough, 'Forward'! and when the opportunity of this war with Germany arose, well, if they needed us all to unite together, I could see we might just extract a few token concessions from them — not very much, but every little helps —

COMMENTATOR: Well we hope you'll have a good second half, Tom —

TOM JOHNSON: Me? Go back on there? In 1945? No way — I'm away to run the Hydro Board, and leave the country to Clem Attlee and the Labour Party.

TOM JOHNSON goes off. The teams come back on, kicking imaginary balls, etc; they still play the same way.

COMMENTATOR: England's new Captain is in fact a Colonel, Clement Attlee, and Labour once again hold the reins of power. Some of the Scots are afraid that their programme of 'nationalisation' of industry will in fact mean de-nationalisation as far as Scotland is concerned, and Colonel Attlee and his full-backs Morrison and Bevin are not inclined to concede anything at all to the Scottish attack.

(Whistle. ENGLAND attack, the SCOTS move slowly.)

Oh dear, the Scots are very lethargic, very slow to start, and the English are putting on a lot of pressure . . . But what's this? The SNP players have left the pitch and are collecting signatures for a petition of some sort — perhaps our man on the sidelines can tell us more — over to you Tony:

TONY: Well David I've got hold of one of these Maverick players, he's with me now — Mr McCormick, what exactly is this?

SNP PLAYER: It is a National Covenant, sir, to insist we regain our sovereignty —

TONY: I see — will anyone sign it?

SNP: It will be signed by over two million Scots.

TONY: Thank you, Mr McCormick — there you have it, David —

COMMENTATOR: Yes indeed, an appeal direct to the crowd to boycott the game and to give them the victory without even scoring a goal. I don't think the ref will recognise this tactic, nor the authorities — No, the ref (Whistle.) has waved play on without the two Covenanters, who still go on gathering signatures — and of course England now have a great chance to improve their 6–0 lead: Tom Johnson's three goals being disallowed by the ref as being after the whistle —

The game begins, the SCOTS more vigorous. The SNP come on and catch the ball. One announces:

SNP: We have, with due solemnity, to assert the dignity of this nation, stolen the Scottish Stone of Destiny, upon which all our monarchs have been crowned, away from Westminster Abbey where Edward of England and his successors have kept it in contempt of the Scottish nation, and returned it to Scotland, its rightful home!

To a great cheer, they make a rugby-style run down the pitch and make a touch down. The REF blows his whistle all through this, then shows them both the red card, sending them off. An English player with policeman's hat on reports:

ENGLISH PC: The ceremonial object or stone was, after information was received, recovered in a bothy or barn near Brechin, and arrested, and returned to its proper resting-place, behind bars in London.

He takes the free kick, from which he scores direct.

COMMENTATOR: Another try for Scotland, who keep on playing the wrong game for some reason, but it did them no good, and England make it eight or is it nine nil. Some pretty desultory play at the moment, the 50s not proving — ah, here's a little excitement, in the 62nd year: it looks as though, yes, another Scots player is being made Captain of England — it's Alec Douglas-Home.

(DOUGLAS-HOME comes on in cricket flannels, pads, cap, etc.)

He's a descendant of the Border rievers, but he'll be no great threat to England, as long as he thinks he's playing cricket —

(Having faced the bowling, DOUGLAS-HOME is out.)

Poor Alec, did not last very long — another goal for

133

England by the way, making it twelve or sixteen
nil. A word from our expert.

EXPERT: 68 or 69 years gone from this game, and Scotland *not*
showing a lot of the aggression we saw at the start
of the game — of course they've been weakened by
emigration — a lot of their finest players are now
playing for Canada, Australia, New Zealand — and
they've had this curious problem not many teams
face of some of their players actually changing sides,
actually scoring goals against them, in fact of the
twenty-three goals now — twenty-four goals now
scored against them, seventeen or eighteen were
Own Goals —

(Crackle of gunfire, sirens, saracens, etc, crump of bombs.)

Ah, now I think there's something going on just
over the sea in Ulster that *might* liven them up,
might give the Scots some lead in their pencil . . . .
The Irish Republicans are on the offensive again,
trying to break the Six Counties of the north away
from England:

(More genuine, etc. The SCOTS and the ENGLISH move away from
it, together.)

No — no, the Scots don't want to know, the Irish
have frightened them off this kind of thing, they
seem to be settling into a really peaceful acceptance
of England's domination of the game, and the
inevitable run-down of Scotland's resources, with
eventual relegation to the lowest division, down to
the bottom of that and out of the League of Nations
altogether.

There's another goal for England, by the way. The
Scots crowd are getting restless, listen to them now —

CROWD: Scotland! Scotland! etc, etc.
(A chorus of 'O Flower of Scotland'!)

COMMENTATOR: The Scots are about to kick off for the twenty-
seventh time, and it's looking good for England —
but what's going on now? Tony —

TONY: Well David the Scots seem to have struck oil on
their half of the pitch, and they're claiming the
revenues for their own use — but from where I
am I can see that the English are arguing that they
own the pitch, and therefore the revenues belong

134

to them, and the ref is suggesting as a compromise
that both receive a proportion of the revenue —
Some of the Scots are getting very excited now,
refusing all compromise, and I suppose if they
owned oil-wells, this would put them in the front
rank of nations, high in the Premier Division, and
England is declining very steadily, without these
revenues could become the poor man of Europe
— a very interesting argument, one that could go
on for some time . . .

COMMENTATOR: Thank you, Tony — well the fans are joining in,
singing away there — and suddenly it's the Scottish
women players who re-start the game — Winnie
Ewing makes a most extraordinary manoeuvre, the
ball lands at her feet — and it's a goal to Scotland!
Yes, at the Hamilton by-election, Scotland finally
scores — and right away they're on the attack again,
and this time they go weaving skillfully from left
to right, from right to left, and the ball comes high
across the goal-mouth and this time it's Margo
Macdonald who nods it in, at Govan of all places
— who would ever have thought that?

78 years gone, and the English team are looking
tired — Bully-Boy Jim Callaghan keeps bumbling
about all over the pitch, he's meant to be captain
now Sneaky Wilson's taken early retirement, but
he's not very sure. He's got the ball, but I think he
may want to bury it in the ground — no, it's his
own head he's burying, and he's thrown the ball
to anybody who wants it.

The Scots team are watching in amazement as
the English ask them would they like the ball
they're offering them the chance for Devolution,
to play their own game with their own rules —
but England still own the pitch. The Scots are
bamboozled by this, can't make their minds up,
aren't sure what the question means — but they
come forward tentatively, Yes, place the ball on
the penalty spot, as six Geordie MPs fill the goal-
mouth — who's going to take the kick — ? Ah yes,
it's Tam Dalyell of the Binns, trained in England,
of course, surely he won't take advantage of Jim
Callaghan's confusion — No, Tam runs at the ball,
scoops it up, runs for the Scottish goal, places it
two yards from the line — and it's another goal
for England, very like Ramsay MacDonald's great

goal in the 20s. Well the Scottish crowd are not too
pleased — will the ref allow it? Yes —

The REF allows the goal, points to the centre spot. The CROWD now
leap onto the pitch, rush to the English end, where they smash up the
goal-posts and dig up the Astro turf, beat up the REF, rush around with
their Lyon flags flying, terrorise the English team, who run off — the
SCOTTISH team stand worried in the centre as the Tartan Army goes
through another drunken chorus of 'Flower of Scotland' — then:

A HUGE FANFARE of monstrous nature.

The Knoxmobile re-enters with THATCHER on it, driving the SCOTS
supporters away from England — She stands in mock-heroic pose,
with a great booming, echoing voice:

Section Six — Armageddon

The Knoxmobile re-enters with THATCHER on it, driving the SCOTS
supporters and team back towards Scotland. As the Fanfare ends.

THATCHER: Law and Order! I will have Law and Order if I have
to break every law in the land to get it!! As long as
I am Prime Minister we will never, repeat never,
allow the Break up of the Union of Great Britain
and Northern Ireland! Never! I will remind you
that I am an English Nationalist!

I will take your Scottish schools and they will teach
what I want your children to learn! I will take
your ancient universities and I will close them, or
fill them with fee-paying Americans and English
yuppies!

I will starve your splendid hospitals of funds, and close
the best of them down! I will take your industries
and scrap the lot of them, until one-eighth of your
people are unemployed!

I will take your ways of looking after the old, the
disabled, the sick and the homeless, and I will
destroy them!

And then I will go to your Church Assembly and
preach Christian charity and humility. I will tell
your men of God that greed for wealth is the true
message of Christ, and Compete with thy neighbour
is what Moses should have read on the tablets!

And I will impose taxes that take money from
the poor to give to the rich, and I will make you
powerless to oppose my will!

136

And when I have done all these things, I will give
you a Garden Festival so you will think of me as
the Great Earth Mother, bearer of harvest, fruits
and blessings!

I will talk to you of my caring ways, my fairness,
my devolution of power to one and all, and above
all, I will convince you that I bring Prosperity.

And my Public Relations team will start to cast a
spell over you, so that every good thing you do
yourself, will seem to come from me, and every
bad thing I do, will be your own misfortune —

And slowly but surely, bit by bit, I shall destroy
your power to resist, silence any voice that speaks
against me, and take away your individuality,
your culture and your nationhood — slowly but
surely, I will achieve the goal of every English ruler:
you will become mine, indistinguishable from my
followers, slowly but surely Scotland will become
part of England — and you, all of you, will become,
at last, English!

TIMPS from the Scottish stage, individual voices reply, recalling struggles
in the history:

SINGER: (speaks). Ye see yon birkie ca'd a Lord,
                    Wha struts, and stares, and a' that
                    Though hundreds worship at his word,
                    He's but a coof for a' that.
                    For a' that, and a' that,
                    His ribband, star and a' that,
                    The man of independent mind,
                    He looks and laughs and a' that.

BRUCE: We would never defeat the English in open Battle,
                    nor would we resist them in great Castles. Our
                    strength was that we were in our own country.
                    And we were experiencing a new emotion, that
                    was more than self interest, more than the greed of
                    a clutch of Ruling families, more than the simple
                    reaction of the peasant to terror.
                    We were feeling desire for the freedom of our
                    nation:

ISABEL OF FIFE: Ah! Freedom is a noble thing!
                    Great happiness does freedom bring.
                    All solace to a man it gives;
                    He lives at ease that freely lives.

137

ARBROATH: For, as long as but a hundred of us remain alive, never will we on any conditions be brought under English rule. It is in truth not for glory, nor riches, nor honours, that we are fighting, but for freedom — for that alone, which no honest man gives up but with life itself.

JENNY GEDDES: I say unto you that before the poor people of Scotland will bend the knee to you, we will raise a riot in this country like the roaring of the Gales and you and your breed of tyrants will be swept away and hurled over mountain-tops!

MACLEAN: I stand for a Scottish Workers Republic, but the Scottish workers must be joined in one big industrial union with their English and Welsh comrades against industrial capitalism! And we must refuse to murder our fellows on this planet at the autocratic bidding of John Bull!

FLETCHER: My Lord, all nations are dependent, the one on the many this we know. But if the greater must always swallow the lesser and so become greater yet, such a logic is unleashed on the world as will end in — I know not what. We are Scotsmen. Let us set our country in order, and flourish, and add our own, independent, weight to the world.

END

The Cheviot,
The Stag and
The Black,
Black Oil

The Cheviot, the Stag and the Black, Black Oil was given its first public airing at the 'What Kind of Scotland?' conference in Edinburgh on 31 March 1973, and first performed in Aberdeen at the Arts Centre, then throughout the seven crofting counties and many places in the south of Scotland. The composition of the 7:84 Theatre Company who performed it was as follows:

JOHN BETT	Sellar/Duke/Minister/Whitehall, etc.
JOHN McGRATH	Writer/Director, etc.
DAVID MACLENNAN	Stage Management/Indian/Crofter, etc.
DOLINA MACLENNAN	Gaelic Singer/Janet/Mary MacPherson/Gaelic tuition, etc.
ELIZABETH MACLENNAN	Old Woman/Lady Phosphate/H B Stowe/Accordion, etc.
CHRIS MARTIN	Stage Management/Admin./Queen Victoria, etc.
ALEX NORTON	Singer/Donald Macleod/Selkirk/Polwarth/Roustabout/Guitar/Banjo, etc.
BILL PATERSON	MC/Loch/Sturdy Highlander/McChuckemup/Texas Jim/Vocals, etc.
ALLAN ROSS	Fiddle/Indian/Crofter/Bass Guitar/Musicman.

This company worked together on the research, text, presentation and music of the play. They were also the cast of thousands, the Force Ten Gaels Dance Band, and the Nortones Rock Group.

Additional credits:

John Byrne — Pop-up Book
Eileen Hay — Costumes
Ferelith Lean — Administration

The evening begins with the FIDDLER *playing Scottish and Irish fiddle tunes among the audience, in the bar, foyer, etc, as the audience are coming in. The Company are preparing their props, costumes, etc at the side of the platform, talking to friends in the audience, playing drum, whistle, etc to accompany the fiddle; the audience stamp their feet, clap, etc to the music, if they want to.*

The stage is a platform on the floor of the hall, with four chairs on either side of it, on the floor, the same chairs that the audience are sitting on. There is a microphone centre front, and speakers on either side. Every member of the cast has his or her chair, and all their props, costumes, musical instruments, etc are arranged by them, in full view of the audience, around their chair, or hanging on nails in walls, etc behind them.

In the centre of the stage a huge book stands, upright, closed, with the title of the play on the cover.

When the audience is almost all in, and the Company nearly ready and all sitting on stage, the fiddle plays a reel that everybody can stamp their feet to. As it finishes, the MC comes on stage, and, after applause for the fiddler, welcomes the audience, comments on weather, conditions in the hall, etc.

Then he proposes to start the evening with a song the audience can all join in, and by special request, it will be: 'These Are My Mountains'.

A brief intro on the fiddle, and the MC leads the audience in the singing. After a few lines, he says we can do better than that, or terrible, or very good, but let's get some help — and says: 'We've brought some mountains with us — can we have the mountains, please, lads? Go the bens.' He plays a roll on the drum as the rest of the Company lift the book, lay it flat on the actual stage of the hall or some arrangement to lift it higher than the acting platform, behind it. They open the first page, and, as in children's pop-up books, a row of mountains pops up from in between the pages. The MC then calls on the words — and two members of the Company hold up a sheet with the words of the song printed on it. He calls up the accordion, and says we're all set, now we can really sing.

He and the whole Company, with fiddle and accordion, lead a chorus, verse and final rousing chorus of 'These Are My Mountains'.

> 'These Are My Mountains'
> (words and music: James Copeland)
>
> For these are my mountains
> And this is my glen
> The braes of my childhood
> Will see me again
> No land's ever claimed me
> Though far I did roam
> For these are my mountains
> And I'm coming home.
>
> For fame and for fortune

I've wandered the earth
But now I've come back to
The land of my birth
I've gathered life's treasures
But only to find
They're less than the pleasures
I first left behind.

(Repeat verse).

MC: Later on we're going to have a few songs like that one — if you know the words, join in — and then we're going to have a dance, and in between we'll be telling a story. It's a story that has a beginning, a middle, but, as yet, no end —

GAELIC SINGER: *(begins to sing a quiet Jacobite song in Gaelic.)*
Och! a'Thearlaich òig Stiubhairt,
Is e do chùis rinn mo leir eadh,
Thug thu bhuam gach ni bh'agam,
Ann an cogadh na t-aobhar:
Cha chrodh, a's cha chaoirich —

MC: It begins, I suppose, with 1746 — Culloden and all that. The Highlands were in a bit of a mess. Speaking — or singing — the Gaelic language was forbidden. (*Singing stops.*) Wearing the plaid was forbidden. (SINGER *takes off her plaid, sits.*) Things were all set for a change. So Scene One — Strathnaver 1813.

Drum Roll. Page of book turned, a cottage pops up from in between the next two pages.

Enter two Strathnaver girls, singing.

GIRLS: Hé mandu's truagh nach tigeadh
Hé mandu siod 'gam iarraidh
Hé mandu gille's litir
He ri oro each is diollaid
Heman dubh hi ri oro
Hó ró hù ó

As they sing, a YOUNG HIGHLANDER *comes on, watches them, talks to audience.*

YH: The women were great at making it all seem fine. But it was no easy time to be alive in. Sir John Sinclair of Caithness had invented the Great Sheep; that is to say, he had introduced the Cheviot to the North. Already in Assynt the Sutherland family had cleared the people off their land — and the people were not too pleased about it.

FIRST WOMAN: Ach blethers —

SECOND
WOMAN: Cha chuir iad dragh oirnne co diubh. (They won't
                 bother us here.)

FIRST WOMAN: The Countess has always been very kind to us.

YH: Aye, and she's away in England.

FIRST WOMAN: Why wouldn't she be?

YH: With her fancy palaces and feasts for Kings and fine
                 French wines — and it's our rent she's spending.

FIRST WOMAN: Rent! You never pay any rent —

YH: Where would I get the money to pay rent? (*To
                 audience*.) If it's not bad weather flattening the
                 barley, it's mildew in the potatoes, and last year
                 it was both together . . . And now they're talking
                 about bringing in soldiers to clear us off the land
                 completely . . .

SECOND
WOMAN: Saighdearan? De mu dheidhinn saighdearan?
                 (Soldiers — what do you mean, soldiers?)

YH: There were one hundred and fifty of them arrived
                 in a boat off Lochinver.

FIRST WOMAN: Would you get on with some work?

SECOND
WOMAN: Seo-lion an cogan. (Here fill up the bucket.)

*They sing on, as YH goes to a corner of the cottage to pee in the bucket. They
watch him and laugh. Suddenly he panics, does up his trousers and rushes over.*

YH: Here — there's a couple of gentlemen coming up
                 the strath.

FIRST WOMAN: Gentlemen?

YH: (*to audience*). The two gentlemen were James Loch
                 and Patrick Sellar, factor and under-factor to the
                 Sutherland estates.

FIRST WOMAN: Oh, look at the style of me . . .

YH: (*handing them the bucket*). You might find a good
                 use for this. (*Goes.*)

SECOND
WOMAN: I hope they have not come to improve us.

143

FIRST WOMAN: Bi samhach. (Behave yourself.) (*Giggles.*)

Enter PATRICK SELLAR *and* JAMES LOCH, *looking very grand.* SELLAR *sniffs the bucket, ignores the women, who are huddled under their shawls.*

SELLAR: (*with a Lowland Scots accent*). Macdonald has told me, Mr Loch, there are three hundred illegal stills in Strathnaver at this very moment. They claim they have no money for rent — clearly they have enough to purchase the barley. The whole thing smacks of a terrible degeneracy in the character of these aboriginals . . .

LOCH: The Marquis is not unaware of the responsibility his wealth places upon him, Mr Sellar. The future and lasting interest and honour of his family, as well as their immediate income, must be kept in view.

They freeze. A phrase on the fiddle. Two SPEAKERS *intervene between them, speak quickly to the audience.*

SPEAKER 1:   Their immediate income was over £120,000 per annum. In those days that was quite a lot of money.

SPEAKER 2:   George Granville, Second Marquis of Stafford, inherited a huge estate in Yorkshire; he inherited another at Trentham in the Potteries; and he inherited a third at Lilleshall in Shropshire, that had coal-mines on it.

SPEAKER 1:   He also inherited the Bridgewater Canal. And, on Loch's advice, he bought a large slice of the Liverpool–Manchester Railway.

SPEAKER 2:   From his wife, Elizabeth Gordon, Countess of Sutherland, he acquired three-quarters of a million acres of Sutherland — in which he wanted to invest some capital.

Another phrase on the fiddle: they slip away. SELLAR *and* LOCH *re-animate.*

SELLAR: The common people of Sutherland are a parcel of beggars with no stock, but cunning and lazy.

LOCH: They are living in a form of slavery to their own indolence. Nothing could be more at variance with the general interests of society and the individual happiness of the people themselves, than the present state of Highland manners and customs. To be happy, the people must be productive.

SELLAR: They require to be thoroughly brought to the coast,

144

where industry will pay, and to be convinced that they must worship industry or starve. The present enchantment which keeps them down must be broken.

LOCH: The coast of Sutherland abounds with many different kinds of fish. (LOCH *takes off his hat, and speaks directly to the audience*.) Believe it or not, Loch and Sellar actually used these words. (*Puts hat on again*.) Not only white fish, but herring too. With this in mind, His Lordship is considering several sites for new villages on the East Coast — Culgower, Helmsdale, Golspie, Brora, Skelbo and Knockglass — Helmsdale in particular is a perfect natural harbour for a fishing station. And there is said to be coal at Brora.

SELLAR: You will really not find this estate pleasant or profitable until by draining to your coast-line or by emigration you have got your mildewed districts cleared. They are just in that state of society for a savage country, such as the woods of Upper Canada — His Lordship should consider seriously the possibility of subsidising their departures. They might even be inclined to carry a swarm of dependants with them.

LOCH: I gather you yourself Mr Sellar, have a scheme for a sheep-walk in this area.

SELLAR: The highlands of Scotland may sell £200,000 worth of lean cattle this year. The same ground, under the Cheviot, may produce as much as £900,000 worth of fine wool. The effects of such arrangements in advancing this estate in wealth, civilisation, comfort, industry, virtue and happiness are palpable.

Fiddle in — *Tune*, 'Bonnie Dundee', *quietly behind*.

LOCH: Your offer for this area, Mr Sellar, falls a little short of what I had hoped.

SELLAR: The present rents, when they can be collected, amount to no more than £142 per annum.

LOCH: Nevertheless, Mr Sellar, His Lordship will have to remove these people at considerable expense.

SELLAR: To restock the land with sheep will cost considerably more.

LOCH: A reasonable rent would be £400 per annum.

SELLAR: There is the danger of disturbances to be taken into account. £300.

LOCH: You can depend on the Reverend David Mackenzie to deal with that. £375.

SELLAR.   Mackenzie is a Highlander. £325.

LOCH: He has just been rewarded with the parish of Farr — £365.

SELLAR: I shall have to pay decent wages to my plain, honest, industrious South-country shepherds. £350.

LOCH: You're a hard man, Mr Sellar.

SELLAR: Cash.

LOCH: Done.

They shake hands, then prepare to sing — 'High Industry' *to the tune of* 'Bonnie Dundee'.

LOCH & SELLAR: As the rain on the hillside comes in from the sea
All the blessings of life fall in showers from me
So if you'd abandon your old misery —
I will teach you the secrets of high industry:

Your barbarous customs, though they may be old
To civilised people hold horrors untold —
What value a culture that cannot be sold?
The price of a culture is counted in gold.

Chorus:
As the rain, etc.

LOCH: There's many a fine shoal of fish in the sea
All waiting for catching and frying for tea —
And I'll buy the surplus, then sell them you see
At double the price that you sold them to me.

Chorus:
As the rain, etc.

SELLAR: I've money to double the rent that you pay
The factor is willing to give me my way
So off you go quietly — like sheep as they say —
I'll arrange for the boats to collect you today.

Chorus:
As the rain, etc.

LOCH & SELLAR: Don't think we are greedy for person gain
What profit we capture we plough back again
We don't want big houses or anything grand

We just want more money to buy up more land.

Chorus:
As the rain, etc.

At the end of the song they go off. The GAELIC SINGER *stands and says:*

SINGER: 'Mo Dhachaidh' (My home)

She sings the song, in Gaelic. The Company and audience join in the chorus.

SINGER: Seinn he-ro-vo, hu-ro-vo hugaibh o he,
               So agaibh an obair, bheir togail do m' chridhe,
               Bhith stiuireadh mo chasan do m' dhachaidh
               bheag fhein
               Air criochnachadh saothair an là dhomh.

               Seall thall air an aiseag am fasgadh nan craobh
               Am botham beag geal ud 'se gealaicht le aol
               Sud agaibh mo dhachaidh 'se dhachaidh mo ghaoil
               Gun chaisteal 's an t-saoghal as fhearr leam.

               Chorus:
               Seinn he-ro-vo etc.

               'S an ait ud tha nadur a ghnath cur ri ceol,
               Mur e smeorach 's an duilleach 'se'n uiseag neoil
               No caochan an fhuarain ag gluasad troimh lon
               No Morag ri cronan do'n phaisde.

               Final chorus.

At the end of the song, the First Strathnaver GIRL *takes the stage.*

FIRST GIRL: 'A Poem by Donnachadh Buidhe, the Chisholm bard'

               Destruction to the sheep from all corners of Europe.
               Scab, wasting, pining, tumours on the stomach and
               on the hide.

               Foxes and eagles for the lambs. Nothing more to
               be seen of them but fleshless hides and the grey
               shepherds leaving the country without laces on
               their shoes.

               I have overlooked someone. The Factor. May he
               be bound by tight thongs, wearing nothing but his
               trousers, and beaten with rods from head to foot.
               May he be placed on a bed of brambles, and covered
               with thistles.

Enter PATRICK SELLAR. *He pats the baby the* FIRST GIRL *is carrying on
her head, then walks up to audience.*

SELLAR: I am not the cruel man they say I am. I am a business man.

He winks and goes, leaving the Two Strathnaver GIRLS *on stage. Whistles of warning come from around them. They are alarmed, but not afraid. They call other women's names, shouting to them in Gaelic: Hurry up, get down here, there come the men with the papers.* OLD MAN *comes on, anxious.*

OLD MAN: Dé tha sibh a' deanamh? (What are you up to?)

FIRST GIRL: A bheil thu bodhar? (Are you deaf?)

SECOND GIRL: Nach eil thu 'gan cluinntinn? (Can't you hear them?)

OLD MAN: De? (What?)

SECOND GIRL: Tha iad a' tighinn le'n cuid pairpearan, air son 'ur sgapadh. (They're coming with their papers to have us thrown out.) Nach eil thu dol a chur stad orra?

OLD MAN: Oh cha chuir iad dragh oirnne co-dhiùbh.

SECOND GIRL: Cha chuir? Gabh dhaibh le do chromag — (Give it them with your stick.)

OLD MAN: Na bi gorach — (Och, away.)

SECOND GIRL: Mur a gabh thusa gabhaidh mise — (If you won't, I will.)

OLD MAN: The Countess of Sutherland will not leave us without —

FIRST GIRL: Tell that to the people of Eddrachilles.

She thrusts the baby into his arms. Both women call to the other women to come and fight.

SECOND GIRL: Mhairi! Greasaibh oirbh! (Hurry up.)

FIRST GIRL: Kirsti! The men are all gone and the ones that are here are useless!

SECOND GIRL: (*to* OLD MAN). No naire mhor ort. (Shame on you.)

The GIRLS *go out.* OLD MAN *shouts after them.*

OLD MAN: We will form a second line of defence.

He turns to the audience as himself.

When they came with the eviction orders, it was

148

always the women who fought back . . . Glen Calvie, Ross-shire.

He introduces READERS *from the Company, who stand in their places and read from books:*

READER 1: 'The women met the constables beyond the boundaries over the river, and seized the hand of the one who held the notices. While some held it out by the wrist, others held a live coal to the papers and set fire to them.'

OLD MAN: Strathoykel, Sutherland.

READER 2: 'When the Sheriff and his men arrived, the women were on the road and the men behind the walls. The women shouted "Better to die here than America or the Cape of Good Hope". The first blow was struck by a woman with a stick. The gentry leant out of their saddles and beat at the women's heads with their crops.'

READER 3: In Sollas, North Uist, lands held by MacDonald of the Isles. 'In one case it was necessary to remove two women out of the house by force; one of the women threw herself upon the ground and fell into hysterics, barking and yelling like a dog, but the other woman, the eldest of the family, made an attack with a stick upon an officer, and two stout policemen had great difficulty in carrying her outside the door.'

OLD MAN: And again in North Uist.

READER 4: 'McBain put his men into two divisions, and they attacked the women on two sides. They drove them along the shore, the women screaming to their men — "be manly," and "stand up!" Police and women fought on the sand until McBain recalled his officers and the women crawled away to bathe their bloody heads.'

OLD MAN: Greenyards, Easter Ross.

READER 5: 'Sheriff Taylor accompanied by several officers and a police force of about thirty or more arrived at Greenyards, near Bonar Bridge, and found about 300 people, two-thirds of whom were women. The women stood in front, armed with stones, while the men occupied the background. The women as they bore the brunt of the battle were the principal

149

sufferers, a large number of them being seriously hurt, the wounds on their skulls and bodies showing plainly the severe manner in which they had been dealt with by the police when they were retreating.'

READER 6: 'The police struck with all their force, not only when knocking down but after, when they were on the ground, they beat and kicked them while lying weltering in their blood. Anne Ross, 40, struck on the breast, kicked in the head. Margaret Ross, 18, head split, alienation of mental faculties very perceptible. Elizabeth Ross, 25, knocked down, kicked on the breasts, the batons tore away part of her scalp, shattered frontal and parietal bones. Her long hair, clotted with blood, could be seen in quantities over the ploughed land. Margaret Ross, mother of seven, fractured skull from baton wounds, died later. Catherine Ross, who came to help the wounded, struck down until she fell in the river. Grace Ross, felled with a blow on the forehead. Helen Ross, brought home on a litter, and for the space of eight days could not move her hands or feet.'

OLD MAN: But for every township that fought back, there were many more that didn't. The landlords had an ally in the heart of the community.

Fiddle plays: 'The Lord is my Shepherd'. *The Company hum quietly as one of the actors is dressed as The* MINISTER *and the* OLD MAN *places his pulpit in position.*

MINISTER: Dearly beloved Brethren, we are gathered here today in the sight of the Lord and in the house of the Lord, to worship the Lord and sing His praises, for He is indeed, the Lord and Shepherd of our souls. Oh you are sheep, sheep who have gone astray, who have wandered from the paths of righteousness and into the tents of iniquity. Oh guilty sinners, turn from your evil ways. How many times and on how many Sabbaths have I warned you from this very pulpit of your wickedness and of the wrath of the Almighty. For I will repay, saith the Lord. The troubles that are visiting you are a judgement from God, and a warning of the final judgement that is to come. Some of you here today are so far from the fold, have so far neglected the dignity of your womanhood, that you have risen up to curse your masters, and violate the

laws of the land. I refer of course to the burning
of the writs. And everybody here gathered knows
to which persons I am referring. There will be no
more of this foolishness. Be warned. Unless you
repent, you are in great danger of the fire, where
there will be much wailing and gnashing of teeth.
On that fearful day when God divides the sheep
from the goats, every one of us, and particularly
those whom I have spoken of today, will have to
answer for their flagrant transgression of authority.

He goes off.

OLD MAN: And it worked . . .

SECOND GIRL: Everywhere, except in Knockan, Elphin and
Coigeach.

FIRST GIRL *comes on stage and says, to mounting cheers from the others:*

FIRST GIRL: Here the people made a stout resistance, the
women disarming about twenty policemen and
sheriff-officers, burning the summonses in a heap,
and ducking the representatives of the law in a
neighbouring pool. (*Big cheer.*) The men formed a
second line of defence — (*Groan.*) — in case the
women should receive any ill-treatment. (*More
groans.*) They, however, never put a finger on the
officers of the law — all of whom returned home
without serving a single summons or evicting a
single crofter!

*A big hooch from the Company, the fiddle strikes up and they leap onto the
stage to dance to celebrate this victory, the women leading off.*

At the end, all go off except the actor playing the OLD MAN, *who comes to
mike and talks to the audience as himself.*

OLD MAN: What was really going on? There is no doubt that a
change had to come to the Highlands: the population
was growing too fast for the old, inefficient methods
of agriculture to keep everyone fed. Even before
the Clearances, emigration had been the only way
out for some. But this coincided with something
else: English — and Scottish — capital was growing
powerful and needed to expand. Huge profits were
being made already as a result of the Industrial
Revolution, and improved methods of agriculture.
This accumulated wealth had to be used, to make
profit — because this is the law of capitalism. It

expanded all over the globe. And just as it saw in Africa, the West Indies, Canada, the Middle East and China, ways of increasing itself, so in the Highlands of Scotland it saw the same opportunity. The technological innovation was there: the Cheviot, a breed of sheep that would survive the Highland winter and produce fine wool. The money was there. Unfortunately, the people were there too. But the law of capitalism had to be obeyed. And this was how it was done:

Bell ringing. Enter SHERIFF'S MAN, *reading eviction order.*

Enter PATRICK SELLAR, *interrupting him.*

SELLAR: Get on with it, man, you're costing me a fortune with your verbiage: I've got a flock of sheep waiting in Culmailly.

SHERIFF'S MAN: Sheriff Macleod said to be sure and read this, Sir —

SELLAR: Macleod's well known to be a poacher — how would he not be sympathetic to other thieves and tinkers? Who's in there, then?

SHERIFF'S MAN: William Chisholm, sir —

SELLAR: Another tinker.

SHERIFF'S MAN: His family have lived here for some time, Mr Sellar —

SELLAR: Well, he'll no' be here for much longer — he's a sheep-stealer, a squatter who pays no rent, and the Minister informs me he's a bigamist. Get him out —

SHERIFF'S MAN: (*calls at door*). Chisholm! (*From within an* OLD WOMAN's *voice cries out in terror* — 'Sin Sellar, Sin Sellar!')

SHERIFF'S MAN: (*to* SELLAR). There's an old woman in there, sir —

SELLAR: Well, get her out, man!

A WOMAN *comes out in great distress. A man,* MACLEOD, *has come on. He watches.*

WOMAN: Mo mhàithair, mo mhàithair. (My mother, my mother.)

SELLAR: (*annoyed at the Gaelic*). What's she saying?

SHERIFF'S MAN: She says it's her mother, sir —

The WOMAN *goes over to* MACLEOD.

WOMAN: O mhaigstir MhicLeoid, tha mo mhàthair ceithir fichead bliadhna 'sa coig deug — 's ma theid a carachadh theid a mort. (Oh, Mr Macleod, my mother is 94 years old and if she's moved she'll die.)

MACLEOD: She says her mother is 94 years old, Mr Sellar, and if she's moved she'll die.

SELLAR: (*to* SHERIFF'S MAN). Get her out. (SHERIFF'S MAN *hesitates.*) Do your job, man —

SHERIFF'S MAN: I'd rather lose my job, sir —

SELLAR: (*quietly*). Get the torch.

SHERIFF'S MAN *goes out.*

MACLEOD: You have a great hatred for the people of these parts, Mr Sellar.

SELLAR: I am compelled to do everything at the point of the sword. These people here are absolutely a century behind and lack common honesty. I have brought them wonderfully forward, and calculate that within two years I shall have all the Estate arranged.

MACLEOD: Aye, to your own advantage. Have you no shame at what you are doing to these people?

SELLAR: Such a set of savages is not to be found in the wilds of America. If Lord and Lady Stafford had not put it into my power to quell this banditti, we may have bid adieu to all improvement.

MACLEOD: Will you not even give her time to die?

SELLAR: Damn her the old witch, she's lived long enough —

(*Enter* SHERIFF'S MAN *with a torch; he throws it onto the cottage.*)

— let her burn.

Sound of fire, fire-effect on cottage, screams, etc. Blackout. Silence. Single spot on WOMAN, OLD WOMAN, *and* MACLEOD.

MACLEOD: Five days later, the old woman died.

Lights up.

SELLAR: (*to audience*). I am perfectly satisfied that no person has suffered hardship or injury as a result of these improvements.

The Company go back to their seats, and read short sections of accounts of the Clearances from many different areas of the North. Note: *readings to be selected from the following, according to where the show is being done.*

READER: Donald Sage, Kildonan, Sutherland. 'The whole inhabitants of Kildonan parish, nearly 2,000 souls, were utterly rooted and burned out. Many, especially the young and robust, left the country, but the aged, the females and children, were obliged to stay and accept the wretched allotments allowed them on the seashore and endeavour to learn fishing.'

READER: Ardnamurchan, Argyll. 'A half-witted woman who flatly refused to flit was locked up in her cottage, the door being barricaded on the outside by mason-work. She was visited every morning to see if she had arrived at a tractable state of mind, but for days she held out. It was not until her slender store of food was exhausted that she ceased to argue with the inevitable and decided to capitulate.'

READER: Ross-shire. 'From the estate of Robertson of Kindace in the year 1843 the whole inhabitants of Glencalvie were evicted, and so unprovided and unprepared were they for removal at such an inclement season of the year, that they had to shelter themselves in a church and a burying ground. For months there were nineteen families within this gloomy and solitary resting abode of the dead.'

READER: Ravigill, Sutherland. 'The factor, Mr Sellar, watched while the burners tore down the house of John Mackay. His wife, although pregnant, climbed on to the roof and fell through in a desperate attempt to protect her home. Her screams of labour were mingled with the cries of protest of her husband who said: "the law of the country must surely have changed for such things to be done with the approval of the Sheriff's Officer and the Factor".'

READER: Strathnaver, Sutherland. 'Grace MacDonald took shelter up the brae and remained there for a day and a night watching the burnings. When a terrified cat jumped from a burning cottage it was thrown back in again and again until it died.'

READER: Suisinish, Skye. 'Flora Matheson, aged 96, who could not walk, was evicted while all the able-bodied men and boys were away south to earn money to pay the rent. Her three grand-children —

the oldest aged 10 — helped her to crawl along on her hands and knees until she reached a sheep-cot. They remained there until the following December. Meanwhile her son came home from the harvest in the south and was amazed at the treatment his aged mother and children had received. He was then in good health. Within a few weeks, with the cold and damp, he was seized with violent cramp and cough, his limbs and body swelled, and he died. His corpse lay across the floor, the wind waving his long black hair to and fro until he was placed in his coffin. The sick grand-children were removed from the cot by the Inspector for the Poor. The old woman was reduced to a skeleton and had no food but a few wet potatoes and two or three shellfish.'

READER: 'The Island of Rhum was cleared of its inhabitants, some 400 souls, to make way for one sheep farmer and 8,000 sheep.'

READER: Knoydart, Inverness-shire. 'John McKinnon, a cottar aged 44, with a wife and six children, had his house pulled down. The ruins of an old chapel were near at hand and parts of the walls were still standing. There MacKinnon proceeded with his family. The manager of Knoydart then appeared with his minions and invaded this helpless family even within the walls of the sanctuary. They pulled down the sticks and sails they set up within the ruins, threw his tables, stools, chair and other belongings over the walls, burnt up the hay on which they slept, and then left the district. Four times they came and did the same thing.'

READER: 'In 1811 Rogart in Sutherland had a population of 2,148. By 1911 it was 892.'

READER: 'During the time of the Clearances, the population of the parishes of Killarow and Kilmenny — in Islay — was reduced from 7,100 to 2,700. The population of the entire island was halved.'

READER: Ceal na Coille, Strathnaver. 'The people were pushed further and further down to the coast. They suffered very much for the want of houses and threw up earthen walls with blankets over the top, and four or five families lived like this throughout the winter while the last of their cattle died. They were removed as many as four or five times until they could go no further, unless by taking a ship for the colonies.'

155

From the middle of the Suisinish reading, the GAELIC SINGER *has been
quietly humming the tune of* 'Soraidh Leis an ait'. *She now stands and sings:*

SINGER: Soraidh leis an àit',
                 Ad d'fhuair mi m'arach òg,
                 Eilean nan beann àrda,
                 Far an tàmh an ceo.

MC *steps forward.*

MC: Of all the many evictors, Mr Patrick Sellar was the
                 only one who did not escape the full majesty of the
                 law. He was charged with the murder of three people
                 and numerous crimes at Inverness High Court.

The Company become a murmuring JURY.

Enter the JUDGE. *They stand, then sit silently.*

Enter PATRICK SELLAR.

SELLAR: Re the charge of culpable homicide, my Lord —
                 can you believe, my good sir, that I, a person not
                 yet cognosed or escaped from a madhouse, should
                 deliberately, in open day, by means of an officer who
                 has a wife and family, burn a house with a woman
                 in it? Or that the officer should do so, instead of
                 ejecting the tenant? The said tenant and woman
                 being persons of whom we have no felonious intent,
                 no malice, no ill-will.

JUDGE: Therefore, I would ask you (the jury) to ignore
                 all the charges except two. One of these concerns
                 the destruction of barns. In this case, Mr Sellar has
                 ignored a custom of the country, although he has
                 not infringed the laws of Scotland. And the second
                 case concerns the burning of the house of Chisholm.
                 And here we are reminded of the contradictory
                 nature of the testimony. Now if the jury are at
                 all at a loss on this part of the case, I would ask
                 them to take into consideration the character of
                 the accused, for this is always of value in balancing
                 contradictory testimony. For here there is, in the
                 first place, real evidence as regards Mr Sellar's
                 conduct towards the sick — which in all cases has
                 been proved to be most humane. And secondly,
                 there are the letters of Sir George Abercrombie,
                 Mr Fenton and Mr Brodie — which, although not
                 evidence, must have some weight with the jury.
                 And there are the testimonies of Mr Gilzean, and

Sir Archibald Dunbar — (*Sees him in the audience, waves.*) — hello, Archie. All of them testifying to Mr Sellar's humanity of disposition. How say you?

JURY: Oh, not guilty, no, no, no, etc.

JUDGE: My opinion completely concurs with that of the jury.

JURY *applaud* PATRICK SELLAR.

SELLAR: Every reformer of mankind has been abused by the established errors, frauds and quackery. But where the reformers have been right at bottom, they have, by patience, and by their unabating zeal and enthusiasm, got forward, in spite of every opposition. And so, I trust, will Lord and Lady Stafford, in their generous exertions to better the people in this country.

More applause. Distant humming of 'Land of Hope and Glory'.

SELLAR: (*pointing to the mountains, from behind which a giant statue slowly emerges — eventually dwarfing the entire hall*). In lasting memorial of George Granville, Duke of Sutherland, Marquess of Stafford, K.G., an upright and patriotic nobleman, a judicious, kind and liberal landlord; who identified the improvement of his vast estates with the prosperity of all who cultivated them; a public yet unostentatious benefactor, who, while he provided useful employment for the active labourer, opened wide his hands to the distresses of the widow, the sick and the traveller: a mourning and grateful tenantry, uniting with the inhabitants of the neighbourhood, erected *this pillar . . .*

Music turns sour. Statue disintegrates or flies away.

Enter a Victorian GENT.

GENT: And now a poem, by Lord Francis Egerton, in honour of the first Duke of Sutherland:

He coughs politely then performs the poem in a Victorian posturing manner, with vivid gestures — some perhaps a little unlikely.

> He found our soil by labour un-subdued,
> E'en as our fathers left it, stern and rude;
> And land disjoined from land, and man from men,
> By stubborn rock, fierce tide, and quaking fen,
> His liberal hand, his head's sagacious toil,
> Abashed the ruder genius of the soil.

> The fen forbore to quake, the ascent was plain,
> Huge mounds restrained and arches spanned
>   the main.
> He tamed the torrent, fertilized the sand,
> And joined a province to its parent land.
> Recurrent famine from her holds he chased,
> And left a garden what he found a waste.
> A stranger from a distant land he came,
> But brought a birthright where he chose a name;
> And native accents shall his loss bewail,
> Who came a Saxon and remained a Gael.
>
> Thank you.

At the end of the poem, the Company applaud politely.

Enter the GAELIC SINGER.

SINGER: A translation of a Gaelic poem in honour of the Duke of Sutherland:

> Nothing shall be placed over you
> But the dung of cattle.
> There will be no weeping of children
> Or the crying of women.
> And when a spade of the turf is thrown upon you,
> Our country will be clean again.

She goes off. Enter HARRIET BEECHER STOWE *in a large pink bonnet.*

HARRIET B S: Good evening. My name is Harriet Beecher Stowe, and I am a lady novelist from Cincinatti, Ohio. You may have heard of my *Uncle Tom's Cabin. (Confidentially.)* Well, that was about the negro slaves, and my *new* book — *Sunny Memories of a Stay in Scotland* — is about your *dreamy* Highlanders. And my dear friend and namesake, Harriet, Duchess of Sutherland — I've been visiting with her you know, at her delightful home in London, Stafford House, and her country home in the Midlands, Trentham House, and her ancestral home Dunrobin Castle, Scotland . . . where was I? Oh yes — well she is a very enlightened, charming lady, and she is known for her undying support of the oppressed people of the world — the negroes, the slaves, Mr Garibaldi's Italians — she thinks they all ought to be treated much nicer. And as to those ridiculous stories about *her,* one has only to be here, moving in society to see how excessively absurd they are. I was associating from day to day with people of every

158

religious denomination and every rank of life, and
had there been the least shadow of a foundation
for any such accusations, I certainly should have
heard it. To my view, it is an almost sublime instance
of the benevolent employment of superior wealth
and power in shortening the struggles of advancing
civilisation.

COMPANY: Baa. Baa. Baa, etc.

*They come after her on all fours, bleating. She backs away in some confusion.
The* SHEEP *sing* 'These Are My Mountains'.

*Sound of Indian drums, war-whoops, jungle birds, coyotes, hens, dogs barking.
Book turns to an Indian setting. Enter* RED INDIANS. *They dance and
then freeze.*

Enter LORD SELKIRK *in top hat. He passes between the* INDIANS *to the
microphone.*

LORD SELKIRK: I am Lord Selkirk and I have a plan. The people of
the glens have become a redundant population. I
favour their going where they have a better prospect
of happiness and prosperity so long as they are not
lost to Britain. The present stream of emigration must
be diverted so as to strengthen Britain overseas. My
partners and I have recently acquired stock worth
just over £12,000 in the Hudson's Bay Company of
Canada and Fenchurch Street. It is not a controlling
interest, but it is a large interest. Our rivals, the
Northwest Company, a collection of Frenchmen,
have so far ingratiated themselves with the natives
— (*Indicates them.*) — as to become a serious threat
to our trading operations throughout the colony.
They are ruthless and unprincipled. The only hope
for the Hudson's Bay Company is to combine the
needs of the Highlanders for land with our own
most urgent interest, and settle the place. I had at
first thought of settling it with Irishmen, but the
Colonial Officer pointed out that a colony made up
of people so intractable — not to say wild — was
foredoomed and unsuitable for our purposes. So I
have acquired a tract of land five times the size of
Scotland (*Indicates the number.*) and several boat loads
of sturdy Highlanders. There is no point in placing
them on land that is already tamed. They must go
to the Red River Valley and curtail the activities of
the Northwest Company and their Indian friends.

He strikes a post at the side of the stage and waits. Exeunt INDIANS *beating
their drums.*

Enter STURDY HIGHLANDER *punting up a river. He does elaborate pantomime double take at* RED INDIAN *painted on the set, and punts down to the microphone.*

SH: (*to audience*). Has anybody here seen Selkirk?

LORD SELKIRK: (*from his corner*). I was at that time in my house in London anxiously awaiting news.

SH: Ah well, since himself is not here we'll have to get on with the tilling of the land. As you can see by my costume, I'm a Sturdy Highlander and I've been sent here to till the land for future generations and for Lord Selkirk. While I'm getting on with the planting of the brussel sprouts and the runner beans, I am particularly vulnerable to attack from the rear. So if any of you should see any of those big Red Indians I've heard about will you let me know? Will you do that now? I tell you what, you'd better shout something, let me see, let me see — I know. *Walla Walla Wooskie*. Will you shout that? Let's have a practice — after three now, one, two, three — Walla Walla Wooskie!

(*He goes through several attempts to get the audience to join in until they do, with gusto — then:*)

                 Very good. Smashing. Now I can get on with it.

Enter GRANNY *with shawl carrying baby.*

GRANNY: De? What? What?

SH: What?

GRANNY: I can't hear, I can't hear!

SH: Oh I forgot to tell you — that's Granny. She can't hear a thing. She's never been the same since the police hit her over the head at Strathnaver. So as well as the shouting of the Walla Walla Wooskie will you all wave your hands. (*He does.*) Then Granny can see, and I can hear, and a quick bash with the cromach and we'll be all right. All right? Let's have a practice.

(*They all do until he's satisfied.*)

                 Great, great.

(GRANNY *beams, gives the thumbs up and goes off to sit down.*)

                 On with the planting of the radishes!

160

He starts to dig the ground, singing to himself, head down. Re-enter INDIANS *beating drum, tomahawks raised. The audience shouts 'Walla Walla Wooskie'. The* INDIANS *run off before the* STURDY HIGHLANDER *sees them. He accuses the audience of having him on. Repeat this twice. The third time they creep on and after some dodging about, stand towering over him tomahawks raised.*

FIRST INDIAN: Ug!

SECOND
INDIAN: Ug!

SH: (*into microphone*). Gulp!

Enter outrageous FRENCH NORTHWEST TRADER. *He signals the* INDIANS *to leave. They do, tugging forelocks. He taps* SH. SH *collapses thinking it's the tomahawks.*

His WIFE *and* GRANNY *run on and watch with suspicion.*

NWT: I am Nor-west Tra-der! Oo are you?

SH: I'm fine, hoo's yersel'?

NWT: No no, *what* are you?

SH: I am a Sturdy Highlander and this is my Granny.
                   And this is wee Calum.

He indicates the baby she is carrying still.

NWT: (*patting the baby's head*). Thank heaven for little
                   Gaels! I have a très bonne idée!

SH: What?

NWT: A very good idea — why don't *you* go back home!

SH: Because we have no home to go back to, this is our
                   home now.

WIFE *and* GRANNY *nod.*

NWT: That is where you are very wrong my friend, we
                   have ways of making you leave! Où sont mes peaux
                   rouges — (*To audience.*) Anyone who says walla
                   walla wooskie or the waving of the palms will (*He
                   makes throat-cutting gesture.*) Tonto!

RED INDIAN 1:   (*leaps on*). Pronto!

NWT: Hawkeye!

RED INDIAN 2:   (*leaps on*). Och aye!

The INDIANS *come on and stand menacing the group one on each side.*

NWT: These are my little friends. They give me furs, beaver skins, Davy Crockett hats and all the little necessities of life, I give them beads, baubles, VD, diphtheria, influenza, cholera, fire water and all the benefits of civilisation. These — are my mountains, and you're going home.

SH: (*clinging to his womenfolk*). I'll have to speak to Lord Selkirk about that.

Exit NWT *with hollow laugh.*

The INDIANS *remain where they are.*

The group huddle and freeze.

LORD SELKIRK: Things are not going well in the Red River Valley.

SH: (*turning his head*). You can say that again!

LORD SELKIRK: Things are not going well in the Red River Valley. The Governor of the Province seems to have no control over the hooligans of the Northwest Company and their half-breed servants. I have complained to the Colonial Secretary. Unfortunately the Northwest Company denies our allegations and the Governor will not provide troops to protect the settlers. However — the highlanders are a sturdy breed and accustomed to the hazards of life in the wild so I am sending out another three boatloads.

He exits pleased. The lights change to fire on the encampment. The INDIANS *dance round the family, with scalping gestures while they sink down with wails to the ground.*

WIFE *and* GRANNY *remain and hum the song,* 'Take me Back to the Red River Valley', *while* SH *rises, crosses to the microphone and narrates:*

SH: (*out of character*). But we came, more and more of us, from all over Europe, in the intersts of a trade war between two lots of shareholders, and in time, the Red Indians were reduced to the same state as our fathers after Culloden — defeated, hunted, treated like the scum of the earth, their culture polluted and torn out with slow deliberation and their land no longer their own.

(*The humming dies away and the mouth-organ takes over quietly.*)

But still we came. From all over Europe. The highland

exploitation chain-reacted around the world; in Australia the aborigines were hunted like animals: in Tasmania not one aborigine was left alive; all over Africa, black men were massacred and brought to heel. In America the plains were emptied of men and buffalo, and the seeds of the next century's imperialist power were firmly planted. And at home, the word went round that over there, things were getting better.

GAELIC SINGER *stands and reads a poem in Gaelic.*

SINGER: Gur muladach mise 'smi seo gun duine idir
             a thogas, no thuigeas, no sheineas leam dàn
             le durachd mo chridhe soraidh slan leis na gillean
             a sheòl thar na linne gu manitoba.

             Tha luchd fearainn shaor anns an am so ro ghaolach
             air storas an t-saoghail a shlaodadh bho chach.
             's bidh innleachdan baoghalt 's a gaidhealtachd daonan
             gu forgradh nan daoine 's chuir chaorach nan ait.

             Cha labhar mi tuileadh mu euchd nam fear curant
             do Bhreatuinn fuar urram 'gach cumasg is spairn
             'se daoiread an fhearainn a dh 'fhag sinn cho tana
             's gun chuimhne air sebastapol 's manitoba.

Enter two comic-stereotype HIGHLANDERS.

HIGHLANDER 1:   Scene 5, Isle of Skye, 1882!

Roll on drums.

HIGHLANDER 2:   Now at that time, Lord Macdonald was driving the people down to the shores . . .

HIGHLANDER 1:   What shores?

HIGHLANDER 2:   Oh, I'll have a wee dram!

(Roll on drum.)

             No, but seriously though, he was having a bit of an altercation about the grazing rights on a little moor . . .

HIGHLANDER 1:   A little moor?

HIGHLANDER 2:   Oh well, that's very civil of you!

HIGHLANDER 1:   Oh, Sandy, you're a great one for the drink.

HIGHLANDER 2:   Oh Angus I am that, I am.

HIGHLANDER 1:   I tell you what, when I'm dead will you pour a bottle of the Talisker over my dead body?

HIGHLANDER 2:   Certainly, certainly, you won't mind if I pass it through the kidneys first.

HIGHLANDER 1 *drives him off. Drum roll.*

HIGHLANDER 1:   Scene 5, 1882, Isle of Skye, Glendale.

Enter two Glendale WOMEN *in shawls. They cross to read a notice.*

WOMAN 1:   De thann. (What's this?)

WOMAN 2:   (*reads*). 'We the tenants on the estate of Glendale do hereby warn each other to meet on or about 1 p.m. on 7th Feb. 1882 at Glendale Church, for the purpose of stating our respective grievances publicly' — So they're doing something about it at last — 'in order to communicate the same to our superiors'.

WOMAN 1:   De th'ann superiors?

WOMAN 2:   Na daoine mhora! (The great ones.)

WOMAN 1:   Huh.

WOMAN 2:   As if they'd listen.

The rest of the Company, as the MEN *of Glendale, enter discussing the meeting.*

OLD MAN: The whole of the bruachs are being emptied to make way for the sheep, as if they hadn't done enough already.

YOUNGER MAN: Aye, all the crofts in Glendale are being split up to make room for those they've thrown off, and the land's being worked to death till it will grow no more.

OLD MAN: No wonder, when half our own seaweed is taken from us and we have to row all the way round the point to Dunvegan to buy it at 31 shillings and sixpence a ton, and sometimes he's not even in . . .

YOUNGER MAN: Aye, and the rents are going up forbye.

WOMAN 2:   Did you hear, the factor's closed all the shops — he's to open his own meal store and we can only buy from him.

OLD MAN: And it's a helluva long row all the way to Dunvegan . . .

WOMAN 1: And they've stuck up a notice to stop us gathering the driftwood from our own shores.

OLD MAN: And that loch can be very choppy . . .

MAN 3: And do you know the factor has ordered me to shoot my own dog in case he worried the sheep —

OLD MAN: Och what are the sheep worried about, they don't have to row all the way round the point —

YOUNGER MAN: Bith eamh sabhach. (Behave yourself.)

MAN 3: Order! Order!

YOUNGER MAN: (*addresses them all*). Contrary to the opinion of our noble proprietors set forth in the newspapers, notably *The Scotsman*, known hereabouts as The United Liar, they have shown themselves to have no interest in these parts except for the extraction of greater and greater rents, the removal of the people to all corners of the earth and the subjection of those who remain to the will of their factor. Over the last sixty years, we in Skye have put up with just about every indignity a human being can suffer. They have succeeded because we are divided amongst ourselves. It has been proposed that the people of Glendale should unite to take action altogether as one body. We are all in the same situation. Every man and every township has a grievance.

OLD MAN: Och that's right enough.

YOUNGER MAN: If we go one by one to make separate claims, we know what will happen. It should not fall on any one person to be singled out for the wrath of the factor. We must go altogether, and any punishment will have to be inflicted on all of us.

General agreement.

OLD MAN: Ach well I just don't know about that . . .

YOUNGER MAN: To guard against anyone falling out of the ranks, it has been proposed that we one and all subscribe our names in a book, and pledge ourselves as a matter of honour to stand by any demand we may make.

(*Cheers.*)

And until our grievances are met, it has been proposed that we hold back our rent.

WOMAN 2:   No trouble at all!

Cheers.

YOUNGER MAN: That way the situation might strike the factor with
                greater urgency!

OLD MAN: I might strike him with urgency myself . . .

WOMAN 2:   Where's the book — I'll be the first to sign . . .

YOUNGER MAN *produces a book, gives it to* WOMAN 2. *All sign.*

YOUNGER MAN *comes forward, speaks to audience out of character.*

YOUNGER MAN: The idea of united action spread. The tenants of a
                certain Dr Martin of Borreraig were obliged to sell
                their fish and their cattle to the laird at his own
                price, and to give him eight days' free labour each
                year, or 2/6d a day in lieu. They have now struck
                against this labour, and propose to walk in the same
                paths as the men of Glendale. And in the Braes area
                of Skye a mighty confrontation was about to take
                place. Lord Macdonald, in order to settle his vast
                debts, had already driven out the people from most
                of his estate. His tenants in the Braes area resolved,
                like the people of Glendale, to withhold their rent
                until certain of their grievances were met.

                Lord Macdonald made up his mind to put the law in
                force against them and not on any account to yield
                to their demands. The unfortunate Sheriff Officer,
                his assistant who also happened to be the factor's
                clerk and his Lordship's ground officer set out from
                Portree to serve writs of removal on all the people
                of the townships of Peinichorrain, Balmeanach,
                and Gedintaillear.

A SINGER *steps forward and sings, the Company joining in the chorus.*

                'The Battle of the Braes'
                (To the tune of 'The Battle of Harlaw')

                A Sheriff from the factor came
                And he came down our way
                By Lord Macdonald he was sent
                To clear us out frae Skye

                Chorus:
                Oh the battle was long but the people were strong
                You should have been there that day

His depute Martin came along
He could not speak nor stand
They'd filled him up with usique beath
To throw us off our land

Chorus:
Oh the battle, etc.

Oh he had come with fifty men
He could not pass that day
For all the women from the Braes
Went out to bar his way

Chorus:
Oh the battle, etc.

The Laird was angered he was wild
Macdonald must not fail
He sent the sheriff back again
To throw us into jail

Chorus:
Oh the battle, etc.

And next came fifty policemen
From Glasgow they were sent
The Inverness police knew fine
That what we said we meant

Chorus:
Oh the battle, etc.

A wet and dismal morning dawned
As from Portree they rode
The men of the Braes were up in time
And met them on the road

Chorus:
Oh the battle, etc.

All day the cruel battle raged
We showed them we could fight
But five brave men were taken off
To Inverness that night.

Chorus:
Oh the battle, etc.

The judge he found them guilty men
And fined them two pounds ten
In half a minute he was paid

And off they went again

Chorus:
Oh the battle, etc.

Once more Macdonald's anger broke
'Invade the Isle of Skye
Two thousand soldiers, boats and guns
The people must comply!'

Chorus:
Oh the battle, etc.

'Oh if we send one million men'
In London they declared
'We'd never clear the Isle of Skye
The Braes men are not feared.'

Chorus:
Oh the battle, etc.

The police up in Inverness
Demanded extra men
No other town in all the land
Would help them out again.

Chorus:
Oh the battle, etc.

So back the Sheriff came to Braes
All Scotland watched him go
Will you clear off Macdonald's land?
The people answered NO.

Chorus:
Oh the battle was long but the people were strong
You should have been there that day.

At the end of the song, a big 'Heugh!' And all go off leaving the MC *on stage.*

MC: Lord Macdonald was forced, in the interests of his own class, to come to a settlement in the Braes. A victory had been won.

        The men of Glendale did not fare so well. A gunboat was sent in, and three men were imprisoned for two months. But the resistance continued. Two gunboats, a transport ship and a hundred marines were sent in against them. Her Imperial Majesty's Government would move in its own time.

Enter QUEEN VICTORIA. *She waves, and sings:*

168

'These Are Our Mountains'.

QUEEN
VICTORIA:
These are our mountains
And this is our glen
The braes of your childhood
Are English again

Though wide is our Empire
Balmoral is best
Yes these are our mountains
And we are impressed.

Enter shooting party with large armoury. GHILLIE, LORD CRASK, *and*
LADY PHOSPHATE OF RUNCORN.

LADY PH: Her Royal Majesty the Queen is so right about the
charm of this divine part of the world, what? Your
estates, Lord Crask, abound in brown trout and
grouse — what? —

LORD CRASK: Has your Ladyship sampled the salmon?

LADY PH: The rugged beauty hereabouts puts one in mind of
the poetic fancies of dear Lord Tennyson — what?

LORD CRASK: Lady Phosphate of Runcorn you are too kind.

LADY PH: Oh listen for the vale profound is overflowing with
the sound.

Blast of gunfire.

GHILLIE: (*tries to stop them*). No no no no — the beaters are
just having their tea.

LADY PH: As one does. What?

LORD CRASK: What?

Goes to fire; GHILLIE *restrains him.*

GHILLIE: (*to audience*). That's nothing, you should see him
when he's fishing.

LADY PH: How far do your domains extend over this beauteous
countryside, Lord Crask?

LORD CRASK: I have about 120,000 acres down that way, but
most of it's over that way.

LADY PH: Oh Archie . . . Capital, capital, capital . . .

LORD CRASK: Oh yes I've got bags of that too — 200,000 shares in

169

	Argentine Beef, half a million tied up in shipping, and a mile or two of docks in Wapping.
LADY PH:	Topping —
LORD CRASK:	No Wapping —
LADY PH:	What?

LORD CRASK *goes to shoot* — GHILLIE *restrains him.*

GHILLIE:	No no no no no.
LADY PH:	Your highland air is very bracing — I quite fancy a small port . . .
LORD CRASK:	Oh — how would you like Lochinver?
LADY PH:	No no no, I mean I'd like to wet my whistle —
LORD CRASK:	(*waving hand*). We've left a bush over there for that sort of thing . . .

GHILLIE *whistles up the beaters.*

GHILLIE:	Any moment now sir . . .
LORD CRASK:	Here come the grouse, Lady Phosphate —
LADY PH:	What?
LORD CRASK:	The grouse —
LADY PH:	Oh, how lovely. (*She gets out a sten gun.*) I find it so moving that all over the north of North Britain, healthy, vigorous people are deriving so much innocent pleasure at so little cost to their fellow human beings.

Barrage. GHILLIE *aims* LORD CRASK'S *gun up higher, struggles with him.* LADY PHOSPHATE *fires her sten from the hip. Bombs, shells, etc. Barrage ends.*

GHILLIE:	Oh no — Thon was a nice wee boy.

Music — guitar and mandolin begins. LORD CRASK *and* LADY PHOSPHATE *sing a duet.*

BOTH:	Oh it's awfully, frightfully, ni-i-ce, Shooting stags, my dear and grice — And there's nothing quite so righ-it-it As a fortnight catching trite:
	And if the locals should complain,

	Well we can clear them off again.
LADY PH:	We'll clear the straths
LORD CRASK:	We'll clear the paths
LADY PH:	We'll clear the bens
LORD CRASK:	We'll clear the glens
BOTH:	We'll show them we're the ruling class.

Repeat from: 'We'll clear the straths'. *Instrumental half verse.*

LORD CRASK: (*speaking over the music*). Oh they all come here, you know — Lady Phosphate of Runcorn — her husband's big in chemicals — she has a great interest in Highland culture.

LADY PH: How I wish that I could paint —
For the people are so quaint
I said so at our ceilidh
To dear Benjamin Disraeli.
Mr Landseer showed the way —
He gets commissions every day —
The Silvery Tay.

LORD CRASK: The Stag at Bay

LADY PH: The misty Moor —

LORD CRASK: Sir George McClure

BOTH: We are the Monarchs of the Glen —

LADY PH: The Shepherd Boy

LORD CRASK: Old Man of Hoy

LADY PH: And Fingal's Cave

LORD CRASK: The Chieftain Brave

BOTH: We are the Monarchs of the Glen

LORD CRASK: We love to dress as Highland lads
In our tartans, kilts and plaids —

LADY PH: And to dance the shean trew-oo-oos
In our bonnie, ghillie, shoes —

BOTH: And the skirling of the pi-broch
As it echoes o'er the wee-loch

LORD CRASK: We love the games

LADY PH: Their funny names

LORD CRASK: The sporran's swing

LADY PH: The Highland fling

BOTH: We are more Scottish than Scotch

LADY PH: The Camera-ha

LORD CRASK: The Slainte-Vah

LADY PH: Is that the lot?

BOTH: Sir Walter Scott —
We are more Scottish than the Scotch.

They become more serious. They turn their guns on the audience.

LORD CRASK: But although we think you're quaint,
Don't forget to pay your rent,
And if you should want your land,
We'll cut off your grasping hand.

LADY PH: You had better learn your place,
You're a low and servile race —
We've cleared the straths

LORD CRASK: We've cleared the paths

LADY PH: We've cleared the bens

LORD CRASK: We've cleared the glens

BOTH: And we can do it once again —

LADY PH: We've got the brass

LORD CRASK: We've got the class.

LADY PH: We've got the law

LORD CRASK: We need no more —

BOTH (climax):   We'll show you. We're the ruling class!

Song ends.

GHILLIE: You're in fine voice today Lord Crask and Lady Phosphate.

LORD CRASK: Thank you, MacAlister —

GHILLIE: Er — MacPherson, sir —

LORD CRASK: Yes, that's right MacDougall. Do you know, Lady Phosphate, there's a whole lot of trouble-makers, do-gooders, woolly thinkers in the South trying to say these people aren't satisfied in some way or another.

LADY PH: Oh — ghastly . . .

LORD CRASK: Absolute poppycock — look at MacDonald here, he's a bit of a peasant —

LADY PH: Yes, you're a peasant, aren't you?

GHILLIE: MacPherson, sir.

LORD CRASK: Nothing wrong with you is there, Macdonald? No complaints?

GHILLIE: No sir, no sir, not at all.

LORD CRASK: Everything's all right with you, MacAlister —

GHILLIE: Just fine, sir, just fine, everything's just fine.

LORD CRASK: Been with me twenty years. Just like one of the family, aren't you? Mac — er. What's your name again?

GHILLIE: MacPherson, sir.

LORD CRASK: That's right, Mackenzie — none of your people complaining, eh? How's your father?

GHILLIE: Dead, sir —

LORD CRASK: Marvellous, no complaints, marvellous — None of your people had to leave the district, what?

GHILLIE: Oh no sir, my own niece from Skye, Mary, she's away working in the hospital in Glasgow — Mary MacPherson's her name.

LORD CRASK: Oh Mary — bright little girl — always singing happily around the house, never understood a word she said.

Exeunt LORD CRASK *and* LADY PHOSPHATE.

GHILLIE: Aye, Mary MacPherson, happy as a linnie, sir.

The GAELIC SINGER *comes on as* MARY MACPHERSON, *sings a very sad song.*

> Ged tha mo cheann air liathadh
> Le diachainnean is bron
> Is Grian mo leth chiad bliadhna
> A 'dol sios fo na neòil,
> Tha m' aigne air a liònadh
> Le iarrtas ro mhòr
> Gum faicinn Eilean sgiathach
> Nan siantannan 's a' cheò
>
> Ach cò aig a bheuil cluasan
> No cridhe gluasad beó
> Nach seinneadh leam an duan so
> M'an truaighe thainig òirnn?
> Na miltean air a' fuadach,
> Thar chuan gun chuid gun chòir,
> An smaointean thar nan cuantan
> Gun Eilean uain' a' cheò.

At the end of the song, the MC *comes to the microphone.*

MC: During the time of the Clearances, many of the men did not resist because they were away in the Army, defending the British way of life. By the 1850s, it slowly dawned on people that they were being used.

A ridiculous procession, led by bagpipes and drums comes on, followed by the 3RD DUKE OF SUTHERLAND. *He addresses the audience.*

DUKE: Good morning. I have come all this way to Golspie to speak to you, my tenants, because our country is in need.

TENANT: (*from audience*). Baa-aah.

DUKE: The Russians under their cruel despotic Tsar seem to think they are the masters of Europe. Well, they're not. We are. And we're going to show him we are. The Queen, God bless her, upon whose Empire the sun never sets, will not be dictated to by some pesky, Rusky, potentate. Particularly when it comes to the great trading arrangements she has made all over the globe, to the everlasting benefit of all of us, of you — er — and particularly of me. Now she has called upon us, her sturdy Highlanders, to come to her aid in far-off Crimea. In 1800, the 93rd Highlanders was raised, 1,000 strong; 800 of them were from Sutherland — tenants of this estate. They have a long and noble history. They are even now under orders for Scutari; now we have been asked

174

to raise the proud banner of the Second Battalion of the 93rd Highlanders. The Queen needs men, and as always, she looks to the North. My Commissioner, Mr Loch, informs me that the response so far has been disappointing.

Enter LOCH, *now an old man.*

LOCH: Disappointing? A disgrace. In the whole county of Sutherland, not one man has volunteered.

DUKE: I know you to be loyal subjects of the Queen. I am prepared to reward your loyalty. Every man who enlists today will be given a bounty of six golden sovereigns from my own private purse. Now if you will all step up in an orderly manner, Mr Loch will take your names and give you the money.

The DUKE *sits. Silence. Nobody moves. The* DUKE *stands angrily.*

DUKE: Damn it, do you want the Mongol hordes to come sweeping across Europe, burning your houses, driving you into the sea? (LOCH *fidgets.*) What are you fidgeting for Loch? Have you no pride in this great democracy that we English — er — British have brought to you? Do you want the cruel Tsar of Russia installed in Dunrobin Castle? Step forward.

Silence. Nobody moves.

DUKE: For this disgraceful, cowardly conduct, I demand an explanation.

Short silence. OLD MAN *stands up in audience.*

OLD MAN: I am sorry for the response your Grace's proposals are meeting here, but there is a cause for it. It is the opinion of this country that should the Tsar of Russia take possession of Dunrobin Castle, we could not expect worse treatment at his hands than we have experienced at the hands of your family for the last fifty years. We have no country to fight for. You robbed us of our country and gave it to the sheep. Therefore, since you have preferred sheep to men, let sheep now defend you.

ALL: Baa-aa.

The DUKE *and* LOCH *leave.* SOLDIER *beats retreat.*

MC: One man only was enlisted at this meeting. No

sooner was he away at Fort George than his house
was pulled down, his wife and family turned out,
and put in a hut from which an old female pauper
was carried a few days before to the churchyard.

Out of thirty-three battalions sent to the Crimea,
only three were Highland.

But this was only a small set-back for the recruiters.
These parts were still raided for men; almost as
fast as they cleared them off the land, they later
recruited them into the Army. The old tradition
of loyal soldiering was fostered and exploited with
careful calculation.

In the words of General Wolfe, hero of Quebec —
'Some Highland Divisions might be of some use
— they are hardy, used to difficult country and no
great mischief if they fall.'

They were used to expand the Empire and to
subdue other countries, whose natural resources
were needed to feed the industrial machine of Great
Britain.

(*Lights go down. Book turns to a war memorial.*)

Every village has its memorial. Every memorial has
its list of men. They died to defend something. Those
who came back found very little worth defending.

FIDDLER *plays a lament. At the end the lights go up.*

*On stage, the book changes back to mountains. The Company stand in a group,
out of which an* ACADEMIC *emerges, wringing his hands plaintively.*

ACADEMIC: If only the Highlands had some resources, things
would be — much better.

MC1: The figures of de-population increase and increase.

MC2: In 1755, the population of the seven crofting counties
was more than 20 per cent of the population of
Scotland.

MC3: In 1801 it was 18 per cent.

MC4: In 1851 it was 13 per cent.

MC2: In 1901 it was 7 per cent.

MC3: In 1951 it was 5 per cent.

176

MC4: And yesterday it was 3 per cent.

ACADEMIC: If only the Highlands had some resources, things would be — much better.

MC2: In 1861, one hundred and sixty of the islands of the Hebrides were inhabited. In 1941, there were seventy-three.

ACADEMIC *goes to the microphone, holding a book.*

ACADEMIC: All this created a mighty wilderness. In the words of the Highlands and Islands Development Board Brochure — Explore the Highlands and Islands: 'A great open lung, guaranteed to breathe new life into the most jaded . . . Overcrowding? Not in Sutherland . . . a land of solitary splendour . . . mountains, lochs and glens of unrivalled beauty add a sharper poignancy to the scattered stones of the ruined crofting townships.' Yes, the tragedy of the Highlands has become a saleable commodity.

Enter ANDY McCHUCKEMUP, *a Glasgow Property-operator's man. He looks round, takes the mike.*

ANDY: The motel — as I see it — is the thing of the future. That's how we see it, myself and the Board of Directors, and one or two of your local Councillors — come on now, these are the best men money can buy. So — picture it, if yous will, right there at the top of the glen, beautiful vista — The Crammem Inn, High Rise Motorcroft — all finished in natural, washable, plastic granitette. Right next door, the 'Frying Scotsman'. All Night Chipperama — with a wee ethnic bit, Fingal's Caff — serving seaweed-suppers-in-the-basket, and draught Drambuie. And to cater for the younger set, yous've got your Grouse-a-go-go. I mean, people very soon won't want your bed and breakfasts, they want everything laid on, they'll be wanting their entertainment and that, and wes've got the know-how to do it and wes have got the money to do it. So — picture it, if yous will — a drive-in clachan on every hill-top where formerly there was hee-haw but scenery.

Enter LORD VAT OF GLENLIVET, *a mad young laird.*

LORD VAT: Get off my land — these are my mountains.

ANDY: Who are you, Jimmy?

LORD VAT: Lord Vat of Glenlivet. I come from an ancient

	Scotch family and I represent the true spirit of the Highlands.
ANDY:	Andy McChuckemup of Crammem Inn Investments Ltd., Govan, pleased for to make your acquaintance Your Worship. Excuse me, is this your fields?
LORD VAT:	You're invading my privacy.
ANDY:	Excuse me, me and wor company's got plans for to develop this backward area into a paradise for all the family — improve it, you know, fair enough, eh?
LORD VAT:	Look here, I've spent an awful lot of money to keep this place private and peaceful. I don't want hordes of common people trampling all over the heather, disturbing the birds.
ANDY:	Oh no, we weren't planning to do it for nothing, an' that — there'll be plenty in it for you . . .
LORD VAT:	No amount of money could compensate for the disruption of the couthie way of life that has gone on here uninterrupted for yonks. Your Bantu — I mean your Highlander — is a dignified sort of chap, conservative to the core. From time immemorial, they have proved excellent servants — the gels in the kitchen, your sherpa — I mean your stalker — marvellously sure-footed on the hills, your ghillie-wallah, tugging the forelock, doing up your flies — you won't find people like that anywhere else in the world. I wouldn't part with all this even if you were to offer me half a million pounds.
ANDY:	A-ha. How does six hundred thousand suit you?
LORD VAT:	My family have lived here for over a century: 800,000.
ANDY:	You're getting a slice of the action, Your Honour — 650,000.
LORD VAT:	I have my tenants to think of. Where will they go? 750,000.
ANDY:	We'll be needing a few lasses for staff and that . . . 700,000 including the stately home.
LORD VAT:	You're a hard man, Mr Chuckemup.
ANDY:	Cash.
LORD VAT:	Done (*Shake.*)

ANDY: You'll not regret it, sir. Our wee company anticipate about approximately about 5,000 people per week coming up here for the peace and quiet and solitude — not to forget the safari park.

LORD VAT: On safari; hippos in the loch, tigers on the bens, iguana up the burns, rhinos in the rhododendrons.

They go off.

The GAELIC SINGER *comes on, singing:*

SINGER: Haidh-o haidh rum
Chunna mis' a raoir thu

(*Repeat twice.*)

Direadh na staoir' 's a royal

Haidh-o hu-o
Cha ghabh mis' an t-uigeach

(*Repeat twice.*)

Cha dean e cail ach rudhadh na monach.

Haidh-o hair-am
Cha ghabh mis' a siarach

(*Repeat twice.*)

Cha dean e cail ach biathadh nan oisgean.

MC: It's no good singing in Gaelic any more — there's an awful lot of people here won't understand a word of it.

SINGER: And why not?

Drum: 2 chords on guitar. Company members come on stage to answer this question.

MC1: In the 18th century speaking the Gaelic language was forbidden by law.

(*Chords.*)

MC2: In the 19th century children caught speaking Gaelic in the playground were flogged.

(*Chords.*)

MC1: In the 20th century the children were taught to deride their own language.

179

(*Chords.*)

Because English is the language of the ruling class. Because English is the language of the people who own the highlands and control the highlands and invest in the highlands —

MC2: Because English is the language of the Development Board, the Hydro Board, the Tourist Board, the Forestry Commission, the County Council and, I suppose, the Chicago Bridge Construction Company.

(*Chords.*)

MC3: The people who spoke Gaelic no longer owned their land.

MC1: The people had to learn the language of their new masters —

MC1: A whole culture was systematically destroyed — by economic power.

(*2 Chords.*)

MC1: The same people, no matter what they speak, still don't own their land, or control what goes on in it, or what gets taken out of it.

(*2 Chords. They sit.*)

MC: It's no good walking away lamenting it in either language — what have the people ever done about it?

Drum beat begins.

MC4: Easter 1882. Angus Sutherland formed the Highland Land League. In 1884 John Murdoch set up the Scottish Land Restoration League. In 1885 five crofters' MPs elected to Parliament.

MC5: In 1886, Crofter's Commission set up by Act of Parliament.

MC4: Rents reduced by 30 per cent, arrears by 60 per cent; security of tenure guaranteed, hereditary rights established —

MC5: The landlords retaliated. Trouble flared up on the Duke of Argyll's estate on Tiree. The turret ship Ajax, with 250 marines, was sent to quell a population of 2,000.

MC4:   October 1886. Skye: writs served at bayonet point. Six crofters arrested. A medal was awarded for every crofter captured.

MC5:   1887, Lewis. One thousand crofters raided the Park Deer Forest which had been enclosed, and killed 200 deer. A venison feast was held, with a white-haired patriarch saying grace before the roasting stags.

MC4:   1887, Assynt, Sutherland. Hugh Kerr, the crofters' leader, took to the hills pursued by the authorities. The women of Clashmore raided the police station at midnight.

MC5:   1904, overcrowded crofters from Eriskay made a land raid on Vatersay and broke in new crofts.

MC4:   1912, the Pentland Act gave the government power to force landlords to sell their land to the state.

MC5:   This power was never used. 1921–22, impatient with the new government's inactivity, young men from overcrowded areas made more land raids on Raasay, Skye, the Uists, Stratherick and Lewis.

MC4:   1919, Portskerra, Sutherland. Fourteen ex-servicemen drove their cattle on to Kirkton farm, led by the piper who had played them ashore at Boulogne. Their own crofts were small, none bigger than three acres.

MC5:   The land had been promised to them by the Duke of Sutherland. When they came back from the war he had sold it to a wealthy farmer named McAndrew.

MC4:   Legal injunctions were served on them. They resolved to stay put and not to be daunted by threats.

SINGER *moves forward, sings unaccompanied. At final verses, the Company join in, humming and stamping feet.*

SINGER: I will go
I will go
Now the battle is over
To the land
Of my birth
That I left to be a soldier
I will go
I will go

When we went

> To that war
> Oh the living was not easy
> But the laird
> Promised land
> If we joined the British army —
> So we went
> So we went —
>
> Now we're home
> Now we're home
> The laird has changed his fancy
> And he's sold
> All our land
> To a farmer who's got plenty
> Now we're home
> Now we're home
>
> With the pipes
> At our head
> That had lead us into battle
> We set off
> For the land
> That we fought for in the Army
> We set off
> We set off
>
> Oh you Land-
> Leaguer men
> Of Raasay, Skye and Lewis
> Had you seen
> Us that day
> You'd have cheered us on to glory
> Had you seen
> Us that day
>
> Oh the Laird
> Had the law
> And the police were his servants
> But we'll fight
> Once again
> For this country is the people's
> Yes we'll fight, once again

(*Spoken.*) And with these buggers, we'll have to —

MC: And what is happening now?

MC2:   A whole new culture is waiting to be destroyed.

MC1:   By economic power. Until economic power is in the hands of the people, then their culture, Gaelic or English, will be destroyed. The educational system, the newspapers, the radio and television and the decision-makers, local and national, whether they know it or not, are the servants of the men who own and control the land.

MC3: Who owns the land?

MC: The same families — the Macleods, the Lovats, the Argylls, the MacDonalds, the Sinclairs, the Crichton-Stewarts, and the Sutherlands.

MC4: Plus the property dealers.

MC5: The shipowners.

MC3: The construction men.

MC: The distillers. The brewers. The textile men.

MC5: The sauce-makers.

MC4: The mustard kings.

MC5: And the merchant bankers.

MC3: The new ruling class!

Music. Two of the Company sing.

DUO: We are the men
Who own your glen
Though you won't see us there —
In Edinburgh clubs
And Guildford pubs
We insist how much we care:
Your interests
Are ours, my friends,
From Golspie to the Minch —
But if you want your land
We'll take a stand
We will not budge one inch . . .

(*Spoken.*) The Sporting Estate proprietor:

SINGER 1: If you should wish
To catch the fish
That in your lochs are stacked,
Then take your creel
Book, rod and reel
And get your picnic packed.

Now cast away
The livelong day
But don't think it's all free
You own your rods
The rain is God's
But the rest belongs to me!

(*Spoken.*) Doctor Green of Surrey . . .

SINGER 2:   Doctor Green of Surrey
Is in no hurry
For a ferry to cross the Sound
You want a pier?
Oh no, not here —
I need that patch of ground:
This island she
Belongs to me
As all you peasants know —
And I'm quite merry
For I need no ferry
As I never intend to go

(*Spoken.*) The Ministry of Defence . . .

SINGER 1:   The Minister of Defence
He is not dense
He knows just what he's found
The place to test
Torpedoes best,
Is right up Raasay Sound
A few bombs too
In a year or two
You can hear the people groan —
This water's ours
So NATO powers
Go test them up your own.

(*Spoken.*) Continental Tour Operators . . .

SINGER 2:   Herr Heinrich Harr
Says it is wunderbar
To shoot animals is it not?
For a reasonable sum
You can pepper their bum
With bullets and buckshot:
You may call us krauts
Cos we're after your trouts
But listen you Scottish schwein —
This is part of a plan
That first began

184

In nineteen thirty-nine.

DUO: We are the men
Who own your glen
Though you won't see us there.
In Edinburgh clubs
And Guildford pubs
We insist how much we care —
Your interests
Are ours, my friends
From Golspie to the Minch —
But if you want your land
We'll take a stand
We will not budge one inch.

Song ends.

MC: One thing's for certain, these men are not just figures of fun. They are determined, powerful and have the rest of the ruling class on their side. Their network is international.

MC4:   Question: What does a meat-packer in the Argentine, a merchant seaman on the high seas, a docker in London, a container-lorry driver on the motorways, have in common with a crofter in Lochinver?

MC: Nothing at all.

MC4:   Wrong. They are all wholly-owned subsidiaries of the Vestey Brothers.

MC: Ah! The Vesteys — owners of over 100,000 acres in Sutherland and Wester Ross! — and directors of approximately 127 companies, including:

MC4:   Red Bank Meatworks
Monarch Bacon
Blue Star Line
Booth's Steamship Company
Shipping and Associated Industries
Premier Stevedoring
Aberdeen Cold Storage
International Fish
Norwest Whaling
Commercial Properties
Albion Insurance
Assynt Minerals
Assynt Trading
Lochinver Ice and Scottish-Canadian Oil and
Transportation.

185

Music: 'Grannie's Hielan' Hame' *on accordion.*

Enter TEXAS JIM, *in 10-gallon hat. He greets the audience fulsomely, shakes hands with the front row, etc.*

TEXAS JIM: (*to the backing of the accordion*). In those far-off days of yore, my great-great grand-pappy Angus left these calm untroubled shores to seek his fortune in that great continent across the Atlantic Ocean. Well, he went North, and he struck cold and ice, and he went West, and he struck bad times on the great rolling plains, so he went South, and he struck oil; and here am I, a free-booting oil-man from Texas, name of Elmer Y. MacAlpine the Fourth, and I'm proud to say my trade has brought me back to these shores once more, and the tears well in my eyes as I see the Scottish Sun Sink Slowly in the West behind . . . (*Sings.*)

        'My Grannie's Hielan' Hame'

Blue grass guitar in, country style. He changes from nostalgia to a more aggressive approach.

> For these are my mountains
> And this is my glen
> Yes, these are my mountains
> I'll tell you again —
> No land's ever claimed me
> Though far I did roam
> Yes these are my mountains
> And I — have come home.

Guitar continues: he fires pistol as oil rigs appear on the mountains.

Fiddle in for hoe-down. Company line up and begin to dance hoe-down.

JIM *shakes hands with audience, then back to mike and begins square dance calls:*

TEXAS JIM: Take your oil rigs by the score,
Drill a little well just a little off-shore,
Pipe that oil in from the sea,
Pipe those profits — home to me.

I'll bring work that's hard and good —
A little oil costs a lot of blood.

Your union men just cut no ice
You work for me — I name the price.

So leave your fishing, and leave your soil,

186

Come work for me, I want your oil.

Screw your landscape, screw your bays
I'll screw you in a hundred ways —

Take your partner by the hand
Tiptoe through the oily sand

Honour your partner, bow real low
You'll be honouring me in a year or so

I'm going to grab a pile of dough
When that there oil begins to flow

I got millions, I want more
I don't give a damn for your fancy shore

1 2 3 4 5 6 7
All good oil men go to heaven

8 9 10 11 12
Billions of dollars all to myself

13 14 15 16
All your government needs is fixing

17 18 19 20
You'll get nothing. I'll get plenty

21 22 23 24
Billion billion dollars more

25 26 27 28
Watch my cash accumulate

As he gets more and more frenzied, the dancers stop and look at him.

27 28 29 30
You play dumb and I'll play dirty

All you folks are off your head
I'm getting rich from your sea bed

I'll go home when I see fit
All I'll leave is a heap of shit

You poor dumb fools I'm rooking you
You'll find out in a year or two.

He stops, freaked out. The dancers back away from him. He gets himself under control and speaks to the audience.

Our story starts way way back in 1962. Your

> wonderful government went looking for gas in the North Sea, and they struck oil.

Guitar.

> Well, they didn't know what to do about it, and they didn't believe in all these pesky godless government controls like they do in Norway and Algeria and Libya, oh, my God — no, you have a democracy here like we do — so your government gave a little chance to honest God-fearing, anti-socialist businessmen like myself —

Guitar. Two Company members stand in their places to speak.

MC1: Shell-Esso of America, Transworld of America, Sedco of America, Occidental of America — and of Lord Thompson.

MC2: Conoco, Amoco, Mobil, Signal.

TEXAS JIM: All of America.

MC1: And British Petroleum —

TEXAS JIM: A hell of a lot of American money, honey.

Guitar. Enter WHITEHALL, *a worried senior Civil Servant.*

WHITEHALL: You see we just didn't have the money to squander on this sort of thing.

TEXAS JIM: That's my boy —

WHITEHALL: And we don't believe in fettering private enterprise: after all this is a free country.

TEXAS JIM: Never known a freer one.

WHITEHALL: These chaps have the know how, and we don't.

TEXAS JIM: Yes sir, and we certainly move fast.

MC1: By 1963 the North Sea was divided into blocks.

MC2: By 1964 100,000 square miles of sea-bed had been handed out for exploration.

WHITEHALL: We didn't charge these chaps a lot of money, we didn't want to put them off.

TEXAS JIM: Good thinking, good thinking. Your wonderful labourite government was real nice: thank God they weren't socialists.

188

MC1: The Norwegian Government took over 50 per cent of the shares in exploration of their sector.

MC2: The Algerian Government control 80 per cent of the oil industry in Algeria.

MC1: The Libyan Government are fighting to control 100 per cent of the oil industry in Libya.

Guitar.

WHITEHALL: Our allies in NATO were pressing us to get the oil flowing. There were Reds under the Med. Revolutions in the middle-east.

TEXAS JIM: Yeah, Britain is a stable country and we can make sure you stay that way. (*Fingers pistol.*)

WHITEHALL: There is a certain amount of disagreement about exactly how much oil there actually is out there. Some say 100 million tons a year, others as much as 600 million. I find myself awfully confused.

TEXAS JIM: Good thinking. Good thinking.

WHITEHALL: Besides if we produce our own oil, it'll be cheaper, and we won't have to import it — will we?

MC1: As in all Third World countries exploited by American business, the raw material will be processed under the control of American capital — and sold back to us at three or four times the price —

MC2: To the detriment of our balance of payments, our cost of living and our way of life.

TEXAS JIM: And to the greater glory of the economy of the US of A.

Intro. to song. Tune: souped-up version of 'Bonnie Dundee'. TEXAS JIM *and* WHITEHALL *sing as an echo of* LOCH *and* SELLAR.

TEXAS JIM & WHITEHALL: As the rain on the hillside comes in from the sea
All the blessings of life fall in showers from me
So if you'd abandon your old misery
Then you'll open your doors to the oil industry —

GIRLS: (*as backing group*). Conoco, Amoco, Shell-Esso, Texaco, British Petroleum, yum, yum, yum. (*Twice.*)

TEXAS JIM: There's many a barrel of oil in the sea
All waiting for drilling and piping to me

189

> I'll refine it in Texas, you'll get it, you'll see
> At four times the price that you sold it to me.

TEXAS JIM &
WHITEHALL: As the rain on the hillside, etc. (*Chorus.*)

GIRLS: Conoco, Amoco, etc. (*Four times.*)

WHITEHALL: There's jobs and there's prospects so please have
no fears,
There's building of oil rigs and houses and piers,
There's a boom-time-a-coming, let's celebrate —
cheers —

TEXAS JIM *pours drinks of oil.*

TEXAS JIM: For the Highlands will be my lands in three or
four years.

No oil in can. Enter ABERDONIAN RIGGER.

AR: When it comes to the jobs all the big boys are
Americans. All the technicians are American. Only
about half the riggers are local. The American
companies'll no take Union men, and some of the
fellows recruiting for the Union have been beaten
up. The fellows who get taken on as roustabouts are
on a contract; 84 hours a week in 12 hour shifts,
two weeks on and one week off. They have to do
overtime when they're tell't. No accommodation, no
leave, no sick-pay, and the company can sack them
whenever they want to. And all that for £27.00 a
week basic before tax. It's not what I'd cry a steady
job for a family man. Of course, there's building
jobs going but in a few years that'll be over, and by
then we'll not be able to afford to live here. Some
English property company has just sold 80 acres
of Aberdeenshire for one million pounds. Even a
stairhead tenement with a shared lavatory will cost
you four thousand pounds in Aberdeen. At the first
sniff of oil, there was a crowd of sharp operators
jumping all over the place buying the land cheap.
Now they're selling it at a hell of a profit.

Drum. Company step on stage again, speak to the auidence.

MC1:   In the House of Commons, Willie Hamilton, MP,
said he was not laying charges at the door of any
particular individual who had *quote*: moved in sharply
to cash-in on the prospect of making a quick buck.
There is a great danger of the local people being

outwitted and out-manoeuvred by the Mafia from
Edinburgh and Texas . . . end quote.

MC2: The people must own the land.

MC3: The people must control the land.

MC1: They must control what goes on on it, and what
gets taken out of it.

MC3: Farmers in Easter Ross have had their land bought
by Cromarty Firth Development Company.

MC2: Crofters in Shetland have had their land bought by
Nordport.

MC1: Farmers in Aberdeenshire have had their land
bought by Peterhead and Fraserburgh Estates.

MC3: All three companies are owned by Onshore
Investments 'of Edinburgh'.

MC2: Onshore Investments, however, was owned by
Mount St Bernard Trust of London and Preston,
Lancashire.

MC3: A man named John Foulerton manages this empire.
But whose money is he handling? Who now owns
this land in Easter Ross, Shetland and Aberdeenshire?
Whose money is waiting to buy *you* out?

Drum roll.

MC1: Marathon Oil?

MC2: Trafalgar House Investments?

MC3: Dearbourne Storm of Chicago?

MC4: Apco of Oklahoma?

MC5: Chicago Bridge and Iron of Chicago?

MC2: P&O Shipping?

MC3: Taylor-Woodrow?

MC1: Mowlems?

MC2: Costains?

MC5: Cementation?

MC4: Bovis?

MC3: Cleveland Bridge and Engineering?

MC2: These people have been buying up the North of Scotland.

TEXAS JIM: A-a, a-a. With the help of your very own Scottish companies: Ivory & Sime of Edinburgh; Edward Bates & Son of Edinburgh; Noble Grossart of Edinburgh; and the Bank of Scotland, of — er — Scotland.

MC4: And the Sheik of Abu Dhabi's cousin who owns a large slice of the Cromarty Firth . . .

MC2: Mrs Cowan of the Strathy Inn was offered a lot of money by a small group of Japanese.

TEXAS JIM: What can you little Scottish People do about it?

Silence. Exit TEXAS JIM.

MC2: Mr Gordon Campbell, in whose hands the future of Scotland rested at this crucial period, said:

WHITEHALL *gets up, does nothing, sits down.*

Scottish capitalists are showing themselves to be, in the best tradition of Loch and Sellar — ruthless exploiters.

Enter SNP EMPLOYER.

SNP EMPLOYER: Not at all, no no, quit the Bolshevik haverings. Many of us captains of Scottish industry are joining the Nationalist Party. We have the best interest of the Scottish people at heart. And with interest running at 16 per cent, who can blame us?

MC2: Nationalism is not enough. The enemy of the Scottish people is Scottish capital, as much as the foreign exploiter.

Drum roll.

Actor who played SELLAR, *and* WHITEHALL *comes on.*

ACTOR: (*as* SELLAR). I'm not the cruel man you say I am. (*As* WHITEHALL.) I am a Government spokesman and not responsible for my actions . . .

TEXAS JIM: I am perfectly satisfied that no persons will suffer hardship or injury as a result of these improvements.

Drum roll.

Short burst on fiddle. JIM *and* WHITEHALL *go to shake hands. Enter between them, in black coat and bowler hat,* POLWARTH — *not unlike* SELKIRK'S *entrance.*

POLWARTH: I am Lord Polwarth, and I have a plan. The present government seems to have no control over the hooligans of the American oil companies and their overpaid government servants, so the government has appointed me to be a knot-cutter, a trouble-shooter, a clearer of blockages, and a broad forum to cover the whole spectrum. However, I am not a supremo. In this way, the people of Scotland — or at least the Bank of Scotland — will benefit from the destruction of their country.

MC2:   Before becoming Minister of State, Lord Polwarth was Governor of the Bank of Scotland, Chairman of the Save and Prosper Unit Trust, a Director of ICI and was heavily involved in British Assets Trust, Second British Assets Trust and Atlantic Assets Trust, which at that time owned 50 per cent of our old friend, Mount St Bernard Trust.

Musical intro. Tune: 'Lord of the Dance'.

TEXAS JIM *and* WHITEHALL *turn* LORD POLWARTH *into a puppet by taking out and holding up strings attached to his wrists and back. They sing:*

ALL: Oil, oil, underneath the sea,
I am the Lord of the Oil said he,
And my friends in the Banks and the trusts all agree,
I am the Lord of the Oil   Tee Hee.

POLWARTH: I came up from London with amazing speed
To save the Scottish Tories in their hour of need:
The people up in Scotland were making such a noise,
That Teddy sent for me, 'cos I'm a Teddy-boy . . .

ALL: Oil, oil, etc.

POLWARTH: Now all you Scotties need have no fear,
Your oil's quite safe now the trouble-shooter's here,
So I'll trust you, if you'll trust me,
'Cos I'm the ex-director of a trust company.

ALL: Oil, oil, etc.

POLWARTH: Now I am a man of high integrity,
Renowned for my complete impartiality,
But if you think I'm doing this for you,
You'd better think again 'cos I'm a businessman too —

ALL: Oil, oil, etc.

At the end of the song, LORD POLWARTH *freezes.* TEXAS JIM *and* WHITEHALL *let go of his strings, and he collapses.* MC2 *catches him on her shoulder and carries him off.* JIM *and* WHITEHALL *congratulate each other, then turn to the audience.*

TEXAS JIM: And the West is next in line.

WHITEHALL: And the West is next in line.

GAELIC SINGER: And the West is next in line. Even now exploration is going on between the Butt of Lewis and the coast of Sutherland.

WHITEHALL: Don't worry it will take at least five years.

GAELIC SINGER: They've started buying land already.

WHITEHALL: We can't interfere with the free play of the market.

TEXAS JIM: Leave it to me, I'll take it out as quick as I can and leave you just as I found you.

GAELIC SINGER: Worse, by all accounts.

WHITEHALL: Now look here, we don't want you people interfering and disturbing the peace — What do you know about it?

GAELIC SINGER: We'd like to know a hell of a lot more . . . (*Exit.*)

WHITEHALL: As our own Mr Fanshaw of the HIDB said: 'These oil rigs are quite spectacular. I hear they actually attract the tourists — '

Enter CROFTER *and his* WIFE.

               You can give them bed and breakfast.

Doorbell rings.

WIFE: Get your shoes on, that'll be the tourists from Rotherham, Yorks, and put some peats on top of that coal — they'll think we're no better than theirselves.

CROFTER: Aye, aye, aye — go you and let them in . . .

WIFE: Put off that television and hunt for Jimmy Shand on the wireless.

(CROFTER *mimes this action.*)

Oh God, there's the Marvel milk out on the table, and I told them we had our own cows —

Bell rings again.

CROFTER: Aye, aye, aye, they'll be looking like snowmen stuck out there in this blizzard —

WIFE: Och, it's terrible weather for July —

CROFTER: It's not been the same since they struck oil in Loch Duich.

WIFE: Now is everything right?

She wraps a shawl round her head; he rolls up his trouser leg, and throws a blanket round himself to look like a kilt, and puts on a tammy.

WIFE: Get out your chanter and play them a quick failte.

CROFTER: How many would you like?

WIFE: Just the one —

He plays a blast of 'Amazing Grace'. *She takes a deep breath, and opens the door. The visitors are mimed.*

WIFE: Dear heart step forward, come in, come in. (*Clicks fingers to* CROFTER).

CROFTER: (*brightly*). Och aye!

WIFE: You'll have come to see the oil rigs — oh, they're a grand sight right enough. You'll no see them now for the stour, but on a clear day you'll get a grand view if you stand just here —

CROFTER: Aye, you'll get a much better view now the excavators digging for the minerals have cleared away two and a half of the Five Sisters of Kintail.

WIFE: You'll see them standing fine and dandy, just to the west of the wee labour camp there —

CROFTER: And you'll see all the bonnie big tankers come steaming up the loch without moving from your chair —

WIFE: You'll take a dram? Get a wee drammie for the visitors —

CROFTER: A what?

WIFE: *A drink*. I doubt you'll have anything like this down

	in Rotherham, Yorks. All the people from England are flocking up to see the oil rigs. It'll be a change for them.
CROFTER:	Here, drink that now, it'll make the hairs on your chest stick out like rhubarb stalks.
WIFE:	When the weather clears up, you'll be wanting down to the shore to see the pollution — it's a grand sight, right enough.
CROFTER:	Aye, it's a big draw for the tourists: they're clicking away at it with their wee cameras all day long.
WIFE:	Or you can get Donnie MacKinnon to take you in his boat out to the point there, to watch the rockets whooshing off down the range — but he'll no go too far, for fear of the torpedoes. Himself here would take you but he gave up the fishing a while back.
CROFTER:	It's no safe any more with the aerial bombs they're testing in the Sound. Anyway all the fish is buggered off to Iceland.
WIFE:	What does he do now? Oh, well, he had to get a job on the oil rigs.
CROFTER:	Oh, aye, it was a good job, plenty money . . .
WIFE:	He fell down and shattered his spine from carelessness. (*Clicks her fingers at him.*)
CROFTER:	(*brightly*). Och aye!
WIFE:	And now he can't move out of his chair. But he has a grand view of the oil rig to give him something to look at, and helping me with the visitors to occupy him.
CROFTER:	No, no, no compensation —
WIFE:	But we'll have plenty of money when we sell the croft to that nice gentleman from Edinburgh.
CROFTER:	Aye, he made us an offer we can't refuse.
WIFE:	And we can't afford to live here any more with the price of things the way they are, and all the people from the village gone, and their houses taken up . . .
CROFTER:	We were wondering now about the price of houses in Rotherham.

WIFE: Or maybe a flat. I've always wanted to live in a flat. You'll get a grand view from high up.

CROFTER: (*taking off funny hat*). One thing's certain, we can't live here.

WIFE: (*very sadly*) Aye, one thing's certain. We can't live here.

The GAELIC SINGER *comes forward: they stay sitting. She sings the verse of* 'Mo Gachaidh'. *The rest of the Company comes on to join the chorus.*

At the end of the song, all stay on stage and speak to the audience in turn.

The people do not own the land.

The people do not control the land.

Any more than they did before the arrival of the Great Sheep.

In 1800 it was obvious that a change was coming to the Highlands.

It is obvious now that another change is coming to the Highlands.

Then as now, the economy was lagging behind the development of the rest of the country.

Then as now, there was capital elsewhere looking for something to develop.

In those days the capital belonged to southern industrialists.

Now it belongs to multi-national corporations with even less feeling for the people than Patrick Sellar.

In other parts of the world — Bolivia, Panama, Guatemala, Venezuela, Brazil, Angola, Mozambique, Nigeria, Biafra, Muscat and Oman and many other countries — the same corporations have torn out the mineral wealth from the land. The same people always suffer.

Then it was the Great Sheep.

Now it is the black black oil.

Then it was done by outside capital, with the

connivance of the local ruling class and central
government —

And the people had no control over what was
happening to them.

Now it is being done by outside capital, with the
connivance of the local ruling class and central
government.

Have we learnt anything from the Clearances?

When the Cheviot came, only the landlords benefited.

When the Stag came, only the upper-class sportsmen
benefited.

Now the Black Black Oil is coming. And must come. It
could benefit everybody. But if it is developed in the
capitalist way, only the multi-national corporations
and local speculators will benefit.

At the time of the Clearances, the resistance failed
because it was not organised. The victories came
as a result of militant organisation — in Coigeach,
The Braes, and the places that formed Land leagues.
We too must organise, and fight — not with stones,
but politically, with the help of the working class
in the towns, for a government that will control
the oil development for the benefit of everybody.

Have we learnt anything from the Clearances? In
the 1890s Mary MacPherson, whose family was
cleared from Skye, wrote this song:

GAELIC SINGER: (sings). Cuimhnichibh gur sluagh sibh
Is cumaibh suas 'ur coir
Tha beairteas bho na cruachan
Far an d'fhuair sibh arach og
Tha iarrann agus gual ann
Tha luaidhe ghlas is or
Tha meinnean gu 'ur buannachd
An Eilean Uaine a 'Cheo.

MC: The song says:
'Remember that you are a people and fight for your
     rights —
There are riches under the hills where you grew up.
There is iron and coal there grey lead and gold,
There is richness in the land under your feet.
Remember your hardships and keep up your
     struggle

The wheel will turn for you
By the strength of your hands and the hardness of
   your fists.
Your cattle will be on the plains
Everyone in the land will have a place
And the exploiter will be driven out.'

COMPANY: Cuimhnichibh ur cruadal
Is cumaibh suas ur sroill,
Gun teid an roth mun cuairt duibh
Le neart is cruas nan dorn;
Gum bi ur crodh air bhuailtean
'S gach tuathanach air doigh,
'S na Sas'naich air fuadach
A Eilean Uain a' Cheo.

END

Blood
Red Roses

Original programme note

Fashion is a double-edged sword. On the one hand the rippling flow of clothing-styles, ideas, excitements and prejudices gives colour and richness to life. More, it can give the feeling of humanity trying out an endless variety of postures in its restless search for progress towards a better life — a feeling of positive explorations . . . trouser-suits, Cohn-Bendit, structuralism, the Anti-Nazi League.

On the other hand, fashion can perform a valuable role for the capitalist state. For it can effectively safeguard the status quo by seeing every form of opposition to the status quo as a flash in the pan — the seven-days-wonder of the burning bra, the trendiness of Leftyism, the passing of the Winter of our Discontent — now made glorious summer by this hero of Bovis: and even Sir Keith, and monetarism, and Milton Friedman, they too will pass on as fashions come and go . . .

But beneath the glittering surface of punk and ska and Carrington and Abba, the status quo goes marching on, to coin a phrase. The struggles of the working-class to protect the advances made in their standards of life, go on. But they have suffered, are suffering serious setbacks. And militancy in those struggles — particularly industrial militancy — is now distinctly out of fashion . . . Once the media got the message, a series of vicious campaigns against 'The Wreckers' — (remember Red Robbo, who ate babies) — has undermined the already shaky morale of the shop-floor organiser. Managements all over Britain are getting away with murder — sometimes quite literally. And people are now beginning to suffer for it.

In this situation, it seemed important — if a little unfashionable — to take a longer look at one of these militants, and at the whole question of what 'fighting' means in the age of the multiple war-head. And to try to see where exactly the battlefields are, and who is on whose side . . . At the same time, the play tells a story, an adventure story in its way . . . about some people — real in many particulars, not based on the life of any one individual, but on the experiences of many.

John McGrath
August 1980

Blood Red Roses by John McGrath, musical arrangements by Mark Brown. First presented by 7:84 Theatre Company (Scotland) at the Church Hill Theatre, Edinburgh, 18 August 1980 with the following company:

JOANNA KEDDIE	Ella/Janey/Mrs Dundonald/Midwife
PHYLLIS LOGAN	Catriona/Alison/Isobel
ELIZABETH MACLENNAN	Bessie McGuigan (née Gordon)/Accordion
BILLY RIDDOCH	Sandy Gordon/Pablo/Mr Eagleton/Harry Sim
LAURANCE RUDIC	Alex McGuigan/Policeman/Rev Murdo
ALLAN WOLFE	Announcer/Production Manager
and	
ALASTAIR BROTCHIE	Set Painter
MARK BROWN	Musical Arrangements
CHRISTIE HAMILTON	Administrator
DAVID MEEK	Deputy Stage Manager
SUE RUMBALL	Stage Manager
ALASTAIR McARTHUR	Lighting
JOHN McGRATH	Writer/Director/Lyrics
JANETTE MACKIE	Secretary
PAUL PENDER	Production Associate
ANNIE RUBIENSKA	Publicity/PR
JO THOMPSON	Design Assistant
JENNY TIRAMANI	Design
DEREK WATSON	Repetiteur

The play was toured over Scotland, and presented at the Theatre Royal, Stratford, London E15.

ACT ONE

A stage-picture, bold and colourful. Modified for each scene as it happens. The scene-changes, which should be very economically managed, are made during the songs. There can be one singer, or several. They 'tell the story' very directly to the audience — involve them in it.

I

A story, a story
Of Anger and War
A story of Death and Adventure
A story that starts in the high heelan hills
And ends in the far distant future —

A father A father
Comes hame frae the war —
But where is his wife and his daughter
His wife she has gone to the ends of the earth
And his lassie's at hame by the fireside —

So watch now and question
The tale that unfolds —
Is it true or a lie or a fiction?
Is it right or mistaken the story we tell —
Is it fit tae be tellt tae your children?
(Tune: 'Charlie oh Charlie . . .')

Scene One

(A formal announcement, very dead pan. Opposite of the songs.)

ANNOUNCER.   *(announces)* Scene One: The Soldier From the Wars Returning . . . The Year — 1951 . . . The Government: Tory . . . The Place *(Indicates set.)* — a Council House somewhere in the Highlands. Sound: Curlew calling —

(Bessie, a 12-year-old highland girl, sits by the fireside.)

SANDY: *(calling off)*. Janey! Janey! Mrs Gordon!

(A figure looms up — Sandy Gordon, now 31, a sergeant in the Seaforths, in uniform, but looking pale and ill, with a stick, and a stiff leg.)

SANDY: Bessie?

BESSIE: Dad? Is it you Dad?

SANDY: It is I — present and correct — well *(Taps leg.)* almost correct — *(Pause.)* Where's your mother?

BESSIE: *(turns and looks at him)*. I feel as if I'm seeing a ghost.

205

SANDY: Do you? Ha. Well many's the time I damn near was a ghost, Bessie — that's a soldier's luck, good luck, bad luck, both together, I couldn't say — almost a ghost, many's the time and many a matey gone and come back to haunt me too, but not now, no more, it's over, all over all that nonsense — I've come home, girl: oh it was not my choice, no no: it was a Chinese weapon of war took the legs from beneath me but it was time — I missed you, my little girl, soldier that I may be.

BESSIE: I missed you too . . . Have you really come home?

SANDY: It is I in the flesh — apart from the tin bits — eh? The day after you were — how can I say this? Made, er — started —

BESSIE: Conceived —

SANDY: Exactly, conceived, the day after you — yes — in March 1939 I was 19, I went off to Glasgow, I made my way to the Army Recruiting office in Bath Street, and I volunteered for the Seaforth Highlanders. I thought they would take me there and then, but no — they took my signature, my pulse-beat and my temperature and sent me home to await my papers. Six weeks later, on the platform at the railway station, Janey told me the news: of you. Two days later, I was a soldier. The day I finished my basic training, war broke out: and I was everywhere — Norway, Singapore, Italy, Normandy — I never saw you until 1946 . . .

BESSIE: I remember the day —

SANDY: I'm glad I stayed in though — Palestine, Malaya: interesting. Got made up — three stripes: Sergeant Gordon . . . Then the Chinese bazooka got me (*pause*) Home now, though. (*Pause.*) As I walked along from the train, I knew it was the right thing. (*pause*) I didn't expect a hero's welcome — getting your leg blown off is just plain bloody stupid, incorrect military procedure, fit only for National Service Second-lieutenants and nig-nog privates from Paddy-land. But I did think she'd at least be *in* after twelve years.

BESSIE: She said to tell you she's gone.

SANDY: Oh. When is she returning to base?

206

BESSIE: (*cautious*). She's gone away. For ever. With a man.

SANDY: (*pause. He takes this in*). That's not very good.

BESSIE: She tried to take me with her. But I wouldn't go. I wanted someone to be here when you — (*she stops, near to tears*). She tried to drag me, but I bit her till the blood came. And he tried to hit me, but I threw the teapot over him. I wanted to be here. I wanted to run to meet you, but I was too — shaking — to do that: but I am here.

SANDY: Yes. Yes. Thank you, Bessie. I'm proud of you.

BESSIE: What shall we do now?

SANDY: Go to Glasgow. My sister stays in Glasgow now. We'll go there.

BESSIE: Shall we go tonight?

SANDY: No. I'm tired now, and I'm under orders not to walk more than ten paces, yet: but I was determined to walk home from the train — determined to — to show her I was still able.

BESSIE: Tomorrow then, Dad?

SANDY: Yes. Tomorrow.

BESSIE: Would you like a cup of tea?

SANDY: Yes. Thank you. A cup of tea would be very acceptable.

(*Music*)

II

SINGER: Oh pack your bags my bonnie lass
And lie without sleeping till the morning
In pain and fear your father lies
Tho' he'll no' shed a tear come what may —
Then off they set for Glasgow town
Never feart, the lassie leads the way
And not a care will cast them down —
They've lost but they will fight another day . . .

Scene Two

ANNOUNCER: Scene Two: Blessed Are The Meek for They Shall Escape the Attention of the Authorities. The Time — still 1951. The Government

> — still Tory. The Place: a street in the
> centre of Glasgow . . . It is approaching
> midnight.

(*Enter Sandy and Bessie carrying two suitcases and various bags round her neck. Sandy is now in civvies: wearing an old mac and a cap.*)

(*Sound: The last tram —*)

SANDY: (*pointing to building*). There it is, Bessie — just think — in 1939 I signed my legs away in that very building — the Bath Street recruiting office.

(*Bessie puts the cases down and looks at it, wearily.*)

SANDY: Well? Are you tired, girl? Here, let me take the suitcases —

BESSIE: No, Dad, I can manage, just a wee rest —

SANDY: That's right — a wee rest — now we've seen it.

(*Two women stalk past — sniff at Sandy's state*)

WOMAN 1: (*indicating Bessie*). Startin' early —

WOMAN 2: (*laughs*). Aye — it's amazin' what some men'll do for money.

WOMAN 1: It's amazin' whit some women'll do for money. (*They laugh and go.*)

SANDY: (*nervous*). I don't understand why my sister was not there to meet us — I wrote to her — she will have received the letter this morning.

BESSIE: The train was very late, Dad.

SANDY: So it was, so it was — but that's a poor excuse.

BESSIE: Perhaps she's moved to another address.

SANDY: No, no. East Kilbride she lives, East Kilbride *near* Glasgow — if it's *near*, she could have come to meet us . . . But never mind, we shall find our way there —

BESSIE: In a wee whiley . . . You shouldn't be walking so far with your new leg. Is it sore?

SANDY: Painful, very painful: I strongly disapprove of drink, Bessie, and I hope you will never let a drop cross your lips. But at a time like this, a wee drop of whisky to kill the pain. Do you object? (*Produces miniature.*)

BESSIE: No Dad.

(*Sandy swigs the whisky. As he does so, a PC enters, young, clever and corrupt. He sees Sandy drinking. Bessie on the street.*)

PC: Hey You —

SANDY: Are you addressing me, constable?

PC: Aye, you — what's the game?

SANDY: Perhaps, young man, you would be so civil as to direct me to Poplar Drive —

PC: Aye, very good — never heard of it —

SANDY: Poplar Drive in the East Kilbride area of Glasgow.

PC: Don't you take the mickey out of me, you — now move along or I'll clap the baith o' ye in the Marine!

SANDY: (*bristling*). Oh you will, will you, constable — well I'll just remind you that I am still a Sergeant in His Majesty's Army, and when you address me you will address me as Sergeant. You will put your heels together, and you will stand to attention, or you will be put on a report to your superior officers first thing in the morning.

PC: Aye, very good. Now shift or I'll run you in for drunk in charge and her for soliciting — a wee bit young for that game, do you no' think Sergeant?

SANDY: You foul-mouthed young pup — you'll regret that —

PC: You're drunk sergeant, you reek of it — ye can hardly stand up — look (*Pushes him — he rocks, slips.*)

BESSIE: Leave him alone!

PC: Look at ye. (*Pushes again, Sandy falls.*) Ye cannae stand on your feet —

BESSIE: I'll kill you for that.

PC: You will — will you? (*Backing away.*)

BESSIE: Aye, I will —

(*She throws both suitcases at him one after the other, and as he dodges she*

209

swings a bag from her shoulder round and round till she hits him, knocking him to the ground, then she jumps on him — but he's banged his head and is out cold.)

SANDY: What have you done to him?

BESSIE: That'll teach him — come on Dad.

(She helps him up, and gathers their bags together.)

We'll go back to Buchanan Street and queue up for a taxi.

SANDY: Bessie Gordon — if you were anyone else I'd put you on a charge.

BESSIE: Come on Dad!

SANDY: It was just here that the Bolsheviks used to stand to try to stop our lads volunteering for the first war, you see — traitors, they were —

BESSIE: *(sorting bags)*. Maybe, but I wish one of them had stopped you, whoever they were — we wouldn't be in this mess, would we?

SANDY: Sh! Don't say such things —

(A groan from the PC.)

BESSIE: Come quick, Dad. I wonder how near this Kilbride place is, by the way, what's a Marine?

(They go.)

III

SINGER: So hold your head up bonnie lass
And never let your pride be easy broken
You're strong in heart, you'll no go wrong,
You'll see him safe and guard him come what may
Then off they set and journeyed on
Till they came to a door that took them in
But blood runs thick till cash runs dry,
And soon they'll be off travelling once again . . .

Scene Three

ANNOUNCER: Scene Three: Domestic Arrangements. Time: two weeks later, Government: unchanged, the place: a new duplex in East Kilbride, the residence of Sandy Gordon's sister, Ella.

(Enter Ella, in her early thirties, a hard woman making her way to respectability. She is still in her dressing gown, and carrying a long letter which she is looking at in suppressed fury. She calls up the stairs.)

ELLA: Sandy! Sandy, come down!

SANDY: *(off).* Come down? Come down? I've already peeled six pounds of tatties, woman, and I'm plucking and trussing this fowl I killed last night — d'you think I lie in bed all day like a high-born lady?

ELLA: There's a letter for you.

SANDY: *(coming on, hands red with chicken blood.)* Oh is that so, Ella — well well — Are you going to let me read it?

ELLA: You have given this address —

SANDY: Well I didn't exactly give it. I lent it to them for the purpose of sending me this letter, which from the shape of it could be my Disability Pension Book, you see —

ELLA: I'm sorry Sandy but this address is not yours to give or to lend — this letter does not even say 'care of Mrs Wilson' to imply that it is only temporary, this letter says Mr Gordon, 24 Poplars Drive as if it were *your* house, *your* address — well I'm telling you Sandy, turning up unannounced with that poor little daughter at three in the morning, that's one thing. I could hardly have turned you away — you were made welcome, both of you. But using this house as if it was your own, peeling great mounds of potatoes all day long and frightening Catriona with your tin leg — well — and now this — this is quite another thing: it's not your address to give — if the Development Corporation got to hear of it, they could throw us out, back to the misery of Bridgeton that we've now risen above.

SANDY: I *am* your brother, Ella.

ELLA: So you keep informing me but where have you been since 1939 — don't tell me, don't tell me. Where are those girls? Would you look at the time? *(Shouts upstairs.)* Catriona! Bessie! Come down this minute — *(To Sandy.)* Did you make some tea?

SANDY: Oh no, no — I never thought of tea.

ELLA: *(going off).* Never thought of tea —

211

SANDY:	(*alone*). Three months ago, I killed twenty-three men in one afternoon. Couldn't miss, mind you, they were running up the hill straight at me. Chinese of course. Twenty-three. They had to be kept in check, you see. The North Koreans were infringing the border of the South Koreans, well the Yanks couldn't allow such things of course, so there we all were, United Nations peace-keeping patrol — me, up a hill, in a concrete redoubt — the Chinese running up at me, in twos and threes, all afternoon. I personally couldn't see much to choose between the North Koreans and the South Koreans, they were all Gooks: but it appears that those Gooks north of the 48th Parallel were all Communists and dear to the heart of Joe Stalin: and those books to the south of it were not, so they were all dear to the heart of President Truman, so that was all there was to it. Ours not to reason why. I am a professional soldier. I was. (*Opens envelope.*) Yes, my Disability Pension (*Reads, sad.*) Twenty-five shillings per week. I suppose I shall manage —

(*Bessie comes in.*)

BESSIE:	Dad — I'm going to school with Catriona —
SANDY:	But you've no uniform. We don't live here.
BESSIE:	I can explain to the headmistress. And you're to go to the Allocations Office at the Development Corporation and tell them you've been shot, and they'll give us a special house, pretty well right away.
SANDY:	It'll be one of those wi' bars on the windows, eh?
BESSIE:	Now don't forget, you're to go this morning. Aunt Ella's getting fed up with us, and I'm getting fed up with her — so go and show *them* your tin leg, and see if *they* scream. Poor Catriona — she's my friend, so leave her in peace. I'll see you this afternoon. (*goes*) Wait for me Catriona — Dad says that's just fine!
SANDY:	Three months ago grown men jumped at the sound of my voice. Sergeant Gordon, the black bastard of the Seaforths — I put a man on a charge for going into battle without braces —

(*Ella comes in.*)

ELLA:	Cup of tea, then, Sandy?
SANDY:	Coming, coming —

ELLA: I hear you're going to the office this morning, to
see about a house . . .

(*They go off.*)

IV

SINGER: A soldier's a man till
He's shot or he's shelled:
And then he's a soldier no longer —
He's thrown by the wall
To grow old and to grieve,
And to think of his life and to wonder . . .

A woman's a lass till
She fights for her pride
And then she's a lassie no longer
Then she walks in the world
With her head held up high
And *no* man shall dare be her master . . .
(Tune: 'Charlie, oh Charlie . . .')

Scene Four

ANNOUNCER: Scene Four: Bessie Makes Her Mark. The time —
Autumn 1955. The Government — yes Tory. The
place — a classroom in a High School not a million
miles from East Kilbride.

(*Catriona and Bessie, both 15, sit at desks. The Rev Murdo Smith is about to
address the class*.)

REV MURDO: Now you'll be wondering why I have asked your
teacher to take the lads off to another room: well
I'm not going to say anything it would do them
any harm to hear — no, it's just so we can be more
relaxed together: for you are all fifteen, coming
up sixteen, many of you leaving us next summer
for the big wide world, and all of you, I should
imagine, young women. And what I want us to
discuss today is marriage. Now boys are inclined
to scoff and crack jokes about marriage, perhaps
because they *think* marriage is not so important in a
man's life. A man will, usually, have so many more
things with which to occupy himself. But to you
girls, well — marriage is what life is all about: so
let's discuss it without the boys making silly jokes
about it, shall we?

CATRIONA: Sir, what should you do if you think you're pregnant?

213

REV MURDO:	That is a *large* question, Catriona, which can only be answered in the context of even larger questions still. But they are not the ones we are discussing today.
CATRIONA:	It's legal —
REV MURDO:	Marriage, my dear, is something that rises above the merely legal — it is a sacrament, a sacred bond, a pledge to God and to your partner — only those who are weak or incapable of carrying their burden have to slither down into the gutter of divorce.
BESSIE:	Now wait a wee minute —
REV MURDO:	You will all, I am sure, have your vision of your Dream Man — perhaps tall, perhaps dark, perhaps handsome —
CATRIONA:	Perhaps rich, perhaps sexy, perhaps wi' a car — and stamina . . .
REV MURDO:	Quite, Catriona — but are these the qualities you should look for when a man presents himself to you as your partner for life? Now tradition has it, of course, that the man takes the initiative in these matters, he 'pops the question' so to speak —
BESSIE:	He makes me sick. (*Murdo looks at her.*) You make me sick . . .
REV MURDO:	(*recovers, then* —). But we all know you have your little feminine wiles, your flutterings and enticements, to draw the man of your choice into your snare, as it were —
BESSIE:	I'm gonnae stick one on him —
REV MURDO:	So you must know exactly what you are looking for in a man — the qualities that will make for a lasting marriage — one that will not end in the tragedy, the shame of the Divorce Courts, as so many do —
BESSIE:	(*seething*). Hold me down, Catriona, would you?
REV MURDO:	For he is, after all, the man whose children you will bear and rear and devote your life to, whom you will have to send off happy to his work in the morning and welcome home with good food and good cheer in the evening —
BESSIE:	(*loud*). Shite.

REV MURDO:	I beg your pardon Bessie —
BESSIE:	(*stands*). You're speaking a load of shite — Sir —
REV MURDO:	Am I? Sit down, Bessie, thank you for your contribution. (*To class.*) You see, being a Christian means turning the other cheek on such mindless provocations — though I shall of course be speaking to your headmistress. I said sit down, Bessie . . .
BESSIE:	I'll get you. One day. Mr Smith. (*Sits.*)
REV MURDO:	So — what are the qualities we must look for in a man? Kindness, I suppose, patience, a good, hard worker, diligent and uncomplaining, at the factory and at home, a steady, sober, reliable person, above all — one who will listen to your complaints and understand your little problems, who will guide you on the path of life to acceptance and contentment: a lot to ask of a man? Yes — but then: you'll be giving him a lot: your life . . .

(*Through the end of the last speech, Bessie has been bearing down on him carrying her desk. At the end she raises it, and brings it down on his head.*)

(*Blackout*)

Scene Five

(*Sandy comes on alone, talks confidentially to the audience.*)

SANDY:	Her mother of course was a fighter — my God, she was! — from a long line of fighting women, I'm told: now they all had to take the names of their men, so they were of a different name in each generation: but I sometimes think it would have been better had they kept their own name through the centuries — if only as a fair warning to all who came in contact with them: the daughters of Boadicea.
	The headmistress sent for me on several occasions: I did my best to explain to Bessie that the direct physical onslaught on her elders and betters was unwise, even self-defeating. But it was of no use. If anything, she was becoming even more of a fighter.
	And then, in my studies of military history, I came across a Roman military man called Marcellinus and to my delight I discovered this: I'll read it to you:
	'A whole troop of foreigners would not be able to

215

withstand a single Gaul if he called his wife to his assistance. She is usually very strong, with blue eyes. Especially when, swelling her neck, grinding her teeth, and brandishing her sallow arms of enormous size, she begins to strike blows mingled with kicks, as if they were so many missiles sent from the string of a catapult.'

Suddenly, not only did I begin to feel the greatest sympathy for the Reverend Murdo Smith, and Bessie's English master, and the PT mistress and the school janitor, all of whom had to endure her missiles — but also I began to take a pride in the antiquity and dignity of her profession: for she was a Celtic fighting woman, of a very long line of Celtic fighting women, and I admired her for it.

And many's the night, as she grew, I saw her mother flashing out of her. And I wept for what I had lost. Not my leg: no. Her. Jane Fraser. You see, I had run away from her fight, the battle she offered me. I'd chosen to fight Adolf Hitler, Rommel, Mussolini — then Palestine, the Stern Gang, the Chinese in Korea, anybody, rather than do battle with her. And now it was too late.

I made a home for us, in the new town: like Bessie said, they gave me a wee house with all I needed. It was hard while Bessie was at school, and there was no work for a cripple like me: I just kept the house clean, and read my books: war books, history sort of thing: and soon, aye too soon, she was out of school and hunting for a job. I told her: you take it easy: you go battering people you're for the boot — or maybe worse — She said she'd try.

Scene Six

ANNOUNCER: Scene Six: One for All, and All for One. The time — 1956. The Government — still Tory. The place — the Scottish Accounting Machines factory in East Kilbride — boring repetitive slog department . . .

(*Sound: the rhythmical clatter of a factory floor.*)

(*Catriona and Bessie work side by side on coil-winding or soldering points — on a bench. Catriona is feeling sick. It is morning.*)

CATRIONA: I feel sick. What time is it?

BESSIE: Half past nine —

CATRIONA: That's it — every morning this week at half past
                   nine — it's got to be the morning sickness.

BESSIE: The phantom pregnancy strikes again . . . Tell me
                   something — do you ever do anything to justify
                   these sensations?

CATRIONA: Oh, here — aye — listen (*Overcome with nausea.*)
                   oh no — don't listen — I'm gonna puke . . .

BESSIE: Well turn that bloody machine off!

CATRIONA: (*holding her mouth*). I cannae dae *that*, she'd stop
                   my wages — she'd give me the heave.

BESSIE: (*stops her own machine, goes over and stops Catriona's*).
                   Come on, let's go to the toilet — you're not well.

CATRIONA: (*moans with nausea, giddy, but resisting*). No, don't
                   — it's OK — it's just the morning sickness.

BESSIE: You need some fresh air —

CATRIONA: No — start the machine — here, she's coming.

BESSIE: (*angrily*). Would you stop being so bloody servile!

CATRIONA: Oh Bessie, I'm done for anyway — see if I'm
                   pregnant, what'll I dae?

BESSIE: Stop worrying, you're gonnae get some air — (*she
                   practically lifts her to her feet and carries her out. As
                   they go, Mrs Dundonald, the Supervisor, appears on one
                   side, and, unobtrusive, Alex Mcguigan on the other. He
                   just stands and watches, and listens.*)

MRS D: And just what do you two young ladies think
                   you're playing at?

BESSIE: Catriona's not well, Mrs Dundonald —

MRS D: And why are your machines turned off? You know
                   that is against regulations . . .

CATRIONA: I'm sick, miss — I was gonnae puke —

MRS D: Sick? You came to work, you expect to be paid.

BESSIE: (*restraining herself*). She began to feel sick a few
                   minutes ago, Mrs Dundonald sir, and now she needs
                   to go to the lavvy to vomit — you know what that

                   217

	is — it comes from your belly and out doon your nose, like this —
MRS D:	And why are *two* machines turned off?
BESSIE:	Because I'm going with her —
MRS D:	Are you? And who are you? What's your name?
BESSIE:	Bessie Gordon, Miss —
MRS D:	And are you suddenly incapacitated as well, Bessie Gordon: Is there an epidemic?
BESSIE:	No, I'm not ill: I'm helping her out because she can hardly stand up . . . and if you want to know why, it's because this place is hot and airless and it stinks of chemicals and human beings shouldnae be working in it, and if Scottish Accounting Machines are making money out of this place, they can put a ventilator in and some windaes — there's a wee clump of trees just the other side of that wall, I'd love to see them, and to have a windae to close when it rains — OK?
MRS D:	Bessie Gordon, if you wish to continue your employment here, you will go back to the bench, start your machine and get on with your work.
BESSIE:	No. I'm taking her to the cludgie — it's only right. I'm her cousin.
MRS D:	It is not allowed: now — one malingering miss is quite enough without another to hold her hand — And if you have any complaints about the ventilation, kindly make them through the proper channels —
BESSIE:	And what are the proper channels?
ALEX:	Me.
MRS D:	(*notices him, sniffs*). Mr McGuigan is a Shop Steward. The proper channels is the Suggestions Box. Now, back to your machine, you — no more excuses for lazy behaviour — work!
BESSIE:	I've told you: I'm taking her out —
MRS D:	You are stealing time from the company, and time after all is money —
BESSIE:	Are you accusing me of stealing money?

MRS D:	I am your supervisor — you are a lazy, deceitful girl, disobedient and, yes — a thief —
BESSIE:	Right you —
MRS D:	Don't offer violence to me or you will suffer for it.
BESSIE:	You cow — what is this bloody company? What have they done to you?
MRS D:	And *don't* question my loyalty to the Company!

(*Catriona finally retches, running off with her hanky over her mouth. Bessie goes after her, but Mrs Dundonald hangs on to her arm.*)

MRS D:	You will not leave your post?
BESSIE:	Let me go or I'll kill you —
MRS D:	You little tyke!

(*Bessie batters her. Alex comes over and, after admiring the sight for a while, holds Bessie off.*)

ALEX:	Aye very good, darlin': but that's your lot.
BESSIE:	And you let go of me or I'll gie you one too —

(*Mrs Dundonald picks herself up, weeping, hysterical.*)

MRS D:	I shall call the police! I shall have her carted off to prison!
ALEX:	Fine, fine — OK.
MRS D:	She'll get six months for this. Assault and battery!
ALEX:	Aye, good, good, excellent —
MRS D:	(*going*). You won't work in this town ever again, Miss Bessie Gordon.
ALEX:	Ah, now wait a wee minute . . . you're talking about unfair dismissal there, and you've threatened to jeopardise her employment potential in future years: you know that's a serious offence, Mrs Dundonald, and could well cost you a lot of money in damages —
MRS D:	Damages? What about the damages she's done to me? You're talking nonsense —
ALEX:	Well what's a few wee bruises to a woman like

	yourself! Nae mair nor your man gies you of a Friday night, from the look of him —
MRS D:	How dare you?
ALEX:	Besides, it was you laid hands on her first: I was watching. She no more than shook herself free, like a spaniel scratching a flea — a natural reaction.
MRS D:	You lying, insulting criminal.
ALEX:	Do you think? But I'm your only witness — Come on now, Bessie — let's see what she's done to you — my God — do you see that, Mrs Dundonald? You scratched her face there, I think when you attacked her . . . I think you'd best get along to the hospital with that, lassie, it could turn nasty . . . Tut, tut, Mrs Dundonald.

(*Mrs Dundonald shakes her first at him, speechless with anger.*)

	And now offering violence to *me*, a mere bystander — for any's sake, woman, no jury would send her down for six months without putting you away for eighteen — and you with a record, too —
MRS D:	Alex McGuigan, you're an evil, bigotted man, I'll tell you what *you* are — and don't bother to deny it: you're a member of the Communist Party.
ALEX:	Is that an offence now, is it? Oh Christ, I'd better resign quick — everybody else has since the Russians invaded Hungary — how no' me? Aye, you're right — it's time I got out —
MRS D:	Don't get too smart, Alex — you can still get the sack —
ALEX:	Not without reasonable cause —

(*Catriona comes back, relieved.*)

	Ach, here's the source of all the worries, wee Catriona — are you feeling better for your outing?
CATRIONA:	Aye — that fresh air did me the power of good — see, first thing in the morning it's not so bad in here, but after about an hour it really gets through to you —
ALEX:	Well there again, Mrs Dundonald, SAM really have got to take steps. I mean, Bessie here is quite correct

— it's contrary to the provisions of the Factories
Act of 1843, let alone the Mines and Quarries Act
of 1954. Now the poisoning of this young girl's
system will I'm afraid, have to be laid at the door
of the supervisor of this bay — namely yourself . . .
Why don't you go and have a wash and a wee
rest, put your feet up for five minutes and you'll
be as right as rain, and we'll forget all about your
threats, slanders and offers of violence. And we'll
handle the poisoning of the atmosphere through
the normal channels, eh? Come on girls — I need
to talk to you.

MRS D: My God — if that's what your union is supposed
to be for — perjuring yourself for the likes of her
— then all I can say is if anything's poisoning the
atmosphere, it's *you*. You'll be hearing more of this,
all of you.

(*She goes. Alex watches her go, then.*)

ALEX: Aye well. I don't think we will — Now listen to me,
Miss Welterweight Champion of Scotland 1956 —
you do that one more time and you'll end up in
jail — you're damn lucky you're not on your way
there at the moment: are you listening to what I'm
telling you?

BESSIE: Aye. Now lay off me, or I'll start on you next.

ALEX: Oh will you now?

BESSIE: Just who are you exactly?

ALEX: I'm sorry — Alex McGuigan, I'm your Shop Steward,
and I should have been to visit you before now:
could I see your cards please?

CATRIONA: Cards? What cards? We gave them in at the office —

ALEX: I mean your union cards — if you work here, you
have to belong to the AEU: I'm afraid it's a closed
shop: no join, no job —

CATRIONA: That's a bit —

BESSIE: Why?

ALEX: Well, put it this way: if you want to fight her, and
her superiors, you're wasting your time with the
fisticuffs: they can deal with that sort of stuff any

day of the week. The only way to fight, and win, is to join the union. That doesn't mean just one or two of us, or those of us who feel like it — but all of us — so we have a rule: no join, no job.

BESSIE: That's no' right. What if I don't like unions?

ALEX: (*serious*). Listen you, I just saved you from six months in Peterhead breaking rocks — with your teeth — stop provoking me: you know fine why you've got to — we're fighting a war on this shop floor, and the enemy are the meanest bastards in creation: and we're fighting for our lungs, and our eye-sight, and our food and our clothing, and our right to have the job in the first place. Give those bastards half an inch, and they'll take away your job, dilute your food till it's tasteless, lifeless muck, take away your house and put it on the market to the highest bidder, and make those who do work powerless to improve the conditions they work in. That's what they want, and I for one am not going to give them half a chance. You call yourself a fighter, eh? Well, so am I — and I cannae afford to lose. You join the union, now, or I'll stop the whole plant until you've gone. OK?

CATRIONA: Aye, OK.

BESSIE: I'll need to think about it. Are you married?

ALEX: What? No . . .

BESSIE: Then you can come for a wee blether up to the house — do you drink?

ALEX: Not a lot —

BESSIE: I'll get something in for you. Now I've got work to do. Will you come tonight?

ALEX: Er — no, I can't tonight —

BESSIE: Tomorrow then — I'll meet you at the gate at five — what's your name?

ALEX: Alex.

BESSIE: No, the other one —

ALEX: McGuigan —

BESSIE: (*sniffs*). Aye well — and you're a Communist?

222

ALEX: Yes. I am.

BESSIE: My father's legs got blown off by one of yous —
                 he'll be pleased to meet you. Come on Catriona,
                 start the motors up: nobody calls me lazy and gets
                 away with it.

*(Motors begin again. Alex goes, a bit dazed. They get back to work. Bessie
winks at Catriona. They laugh.)*

Scene Seven

(Sandy resumes his chat to the audience.)

SANDY: Yes, my daughter brought home a Bolshevik. Of
                 course, I'd come across them before — during
                 the war it was quite usual to find one of them by
                 your side, even sharing a dug-out, or a bivouac.
                 So I was not altogether disturbed by this aspect of
                 the man, no. But McGuigan — oh dear — could
                 be anything, I suppose — not a football supporter
                 either — so it was hard to tell. But I was happy
                 for Bessie, if she was happy, and with not a word
                 from her mother — and me having precious little
                 interest in marrying again — well, it was natural
                 for her to want a home, as soon as possible . . . And
                 that is what she arranged. At the wedding it turned
                 out I was right about McGuigan — but they were
                 nice enough people, and the ceremony took place
                 in the registry office. I wore my medals.

                 Bessie and her man got a new house in East
                 Kilbride, and invited me to move in with them —
                 very kind. I offer no opinions, I make myself useful
                 about the house, and I continue my readings in
                 military history. One week, out of interest, I began
                 to explore some military activities nearer to home.
                 And I got quite a shock — Do you know how many
                 times the British Army has been used against the
                 Scottish people, in Scottish streets? No? Well neither
                 do I — because it is impossible to add them up —
                 Culloden — oh aye we all know about that. But the
                 Food Riots that were put down, what they called
                 the King's Birthday Riots in 1792, the Friends of
                 the People agitation, the militia riots at Tranent,
                 the Clearing of the Highland straths, the Weavers
                 Uprising in 1820 — right through to the marines
                 landing on Skye and Tiree in the Crofters War in

223

1882, and the tanks in the streets of Glasgow in 1919 — my goodness — the British Army never seemed to stop turning out for action against the population of Scotland. I found this area of great interest, and began to try to organise my findings into book form, but the wee man at the local library assured me that no publisher would find such a thing of interest.

Then something else came along to command my attention. I must say, life continued to be extremely interesting . . . (*He goes.*)

Scene Eight

ANNOUNCER: Scene Eight: A Turn-up for the Books. The year: 1959. The Government: Tory — BUT: there has been a General Election, and the results are coming in thick and fast — Will the Tories be given their marching orders? We shall see. The year: 1959. The place: A Maternity Hospital in the West of Scotland: outside the Delivery Room . . .

(*Sound: distant babies crying — and distant TV election broadcast.*)

(*On an uncomfortable bench sits Catriona, terribly nervous, clutching a suitcase. Pacing up and down, Alex.*)

CATRIONA: Will it be very painful, Alex? Do you think? I mean — the size of a baby's head! And the tearing, you know . . . I'm terribly worried about it —

ALEX: It's just as well it's no' you having it then.

CATRIONA: Aye. Och she's awfy brave — and strong, eh?

ALEX: Aye.

CATRIONA: Alex will you stop prowling up and down — you're like a leopard in the zoo.

ALEX: Well I cannae change my spots, eh?

CATRIONA: What are you so anxious about? She'll be OK.

ALEX: Her? Aye, she'll be OK. But will the Tories get in again? Can you no' hear the bloody London BBC crowing away there? They can hardly contain their delight when another reactionary lackey of imperialism succeeds in bamboozling another constituency — sh! Listen, listen —

224

CATRIONA: Why don't you go down and watch it on the telly?
              I mean, Bessie won't mind, she'll just be in there
              gettin' split asunder —

ALEX: Do you think? Listen, I'll be back in five minutes
              — right? If anything happens, come and get me:
              I'll be in the TV room down the stair — Will that
              be alright by the nurse, do you think?

CATRIONA: Oh aye — she's not having the baby either — away
              you go.

(*Alex goes off. Catriona looks down her jumper.*)

CATRIONA: (*to audience*). I'm getting a lump on my breast — but
              I'm too scared to tell anyone (*pause*) This hospital,
              it's really new — so how do they manage to make
              it smell really old? (*pause*) At least I'm not pregnant
              this week . . . After all those false alarms I had —
              she gets married and six weeks later — DING DONG
              she rings the bell — This young man I'm goin' out
              with, from the Income Tax office: he cannae even
              swing the hammer.

(*The Midwife appears.*)

MIDWIFE: Mr McGuigan?

CATRIONA: Oh, I'll get him — is she? Has she? What's happened?

MIDWIFE: Has he gone away?

CATRIONA: Just to watch television — is she OK? I'm her cousin.

MIDWIFE: She's fine — She's had a little girl . . .

CATRIONA: Can I see?

MIDWIFE: Husbands only I'm afraid — for the moment —

CATRIONA: I'll get him — can I tell him?

MIDWIFE: If you like —

(*Catriona goes off to find Alex. Midwife wheels on Bessie in bed, holding her
baby, but zonked out.*)

MIDWIFE: Nine pounds two ounces, Mrs McGuigan: quite a
              big girl —

BESSIE: Aye — you can say that again —

MIDWIFE: Have you got a name for her?

BESSIE: My mother's name was Jane.

MIDWIFE: Jane? I think Jane's a lovely name —

BESSIE: (*looking at baby*). Janey McGuigan. Born 8th October 1959: in East Kilbride. I wonder where your granny is — she'd be proud of you. I miss her. So will you, Janey. Just wait till you see your Dad — he's awfy serious. But he'll be proud of you too. (*To Midwife.*) Can he come in now?

MIDWIFE: Any minute, he'll be here — that's him now I think.

(*Catriona comes on pointing Alex to the door.*)

CATRIONA: In there — just go in!

ALEX: Will I knock?

CATRIONA: Just go IN!

(*Alex comes in — sees Bessie.*)

ALEX: It's Harold Macmillan — for another five years!

BESSIE: It's Janey McGuigan — for life.

ALEX: Is that her?

MIDWIFE: Would you like to hold her?

ALEX: Aye — I would. (*Midwife passes him the baby.*) Would you look at that? Are y'another bonnie fechter? We're gonnae need you to get rid of these Tories, eh? (*To Bessie, ignoring the baby.*) Christ Bessie what are we gonnae do? *Another* five years of the Tories . . . how can folk no' see what they're up to? What they *did*? After eight years that's included Hola camp and Cyprus and invading the Suez Canal and manufacturing H-bombs — I'm ashamed of the working-class of this country. I'm ashamed and disgusted that we are so stupid, self-centred and ignorant.

BESSIE: Give me the baby, Alex —

ALEX: I'm sorry pet — but —

BESSIE: I know, I know. But I'm too tired, and she's too wee for that sortae thing.

ALEX: (*looking at the baby*). Aye. If you're anything like your mother — God help the Tories —

BESSIE: When she grows up, there'll be no more Tories in Scotland —

ALEX: Do you think?

BESSIE: That's what we're fighting for, isn't it?

ALEX: Aye — but the buggers canne take a hint.

BESSIE: Give her back to me.

ALEX: She's lovely. Aren't you? (*Hands baby back.*) Here.

BESSIE: Did I do well?

ALEX: Aye. You did.

BESSIE: Well, tell me then — never mind her (*Midwife.*) — she's heard it all before —

ALEX: Bessie — you're great.

BESSIE: (*pleased*). You didnae do so bad yourself. Now I'm going to rest — Tell my Dad will you? I'll see him at visiting time, tell him. And tell him she looks just like my mother, OK?

ALEX: Right.

BESSIE: And tell Catriona there's nothing to it —

ALEX: Right. Cheerio. See you tomorrow —

(*Alex goes out. Catriona is waiting.*)

ALEX: (*to Catriona*). Any more results in?

CATRIONA: How was she? Who does she look like?

ALEX: What did she ever look like?

CATRIONA: No' Bessie — your daughter.

ALEX: Oh her — aye —

CATRIONA: (*as they go*). Has she got any hair?

ALEX: Aye — Bessie said there was nothing to it —

CATRIONA: I bet . . .

(*They go off. Bessie looks at Midwife. She is very upset.*)

BESSIE: He didnae kiss me —

227

(*Midwife comes and holds her hand.*)

MIDWIFE: She's a beautiful baby. And you did very well.

BESSIE: Thanks . . . I mean, what's politics for — if he couldnae say that — ?

V

SINGER: See oh see her dark eyes opening,
See her fingers jimp and sma' —
Hear her skirling, brave wee wifie,
Long the journey brings her here —
Here's a world that's full of sorrow
Here's a hard world were she'll grow —
Cling a moment to your mother
Rest awhile before ye go . . .

(Tune: 'Loch Duich')

Scene Nine

ANNOUNCER: Scene Nine: Normal Service Will Be Resumed as Soon as Possible. The Time: 1961 — the Government, still Tory. The place: the McGuigan family residence — a wee bit shieling in East Kilbride . . .

Auntie Ella has come, not to interfere you'll understand, just to pay a visit —

(*Ella sits with a cup of tea harassing Sandy, who is now doing the ironing.*)

ELLA: But how can she do it? You're not *fit* to look after a two-year-old and besides she needs her mother — what if she took ill? What if *you* took ill? It's heartless, heartless — the poor baby . . . what kind of a woman is she?

SANDY: Ella — you're speaking about my daughter.

ELLA: And what kind of a woman will that little girl grow up to be — deprived of a mother's love?

SANDY: And now you're speaking about my grand-daughter —

ELLA: It's wicked. It's altogether shameless —

SANDY: But I quite enjoy looking after the wee girl — and we need the money —

ELLA: There are some things money can't buy . . .

SANDY: Aye. Self respect. See me, Ella: I can't work. I've

228

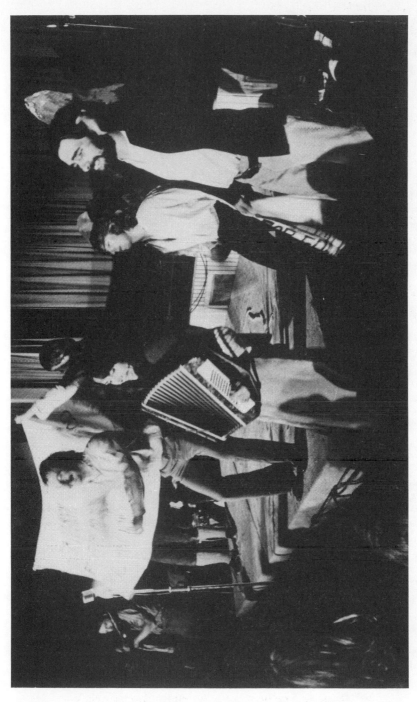

The Cheviot, the Stag and the Black Black Oil, from left to right: Allan Ross, Bill Paterson, Dolina MacLennan, Elizabeth MacLennan, John Bett and David MacLennan.

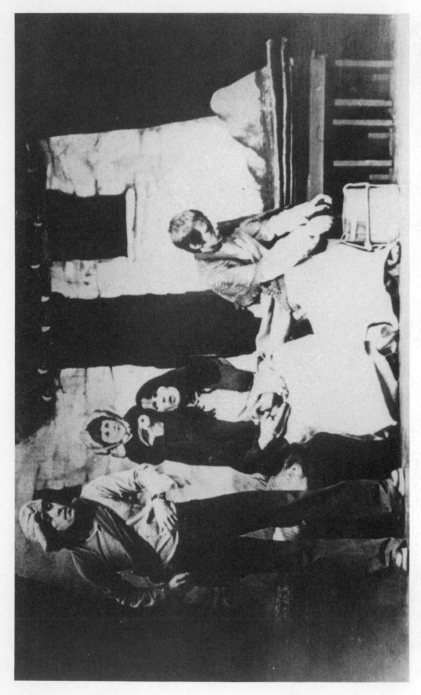

'Na daoine mhor . . .' scene from *The Cheviot,* left to right: Alex Norton, Elizabeth MacLennan and Dolina MacLennan.

Blood Red Roses, Laurance Rudic as Alex and Elizabeth MacLennan as
Bessie, 1981.

Joe's Drum, Sandy Neilson as Thomas Muir.

Out of Our Heads, left to right: Allan Ross, Terry Neason, Billie Riddoch at back, Elizabeth MacLennan, Dave Anderson and Neil Gammack.

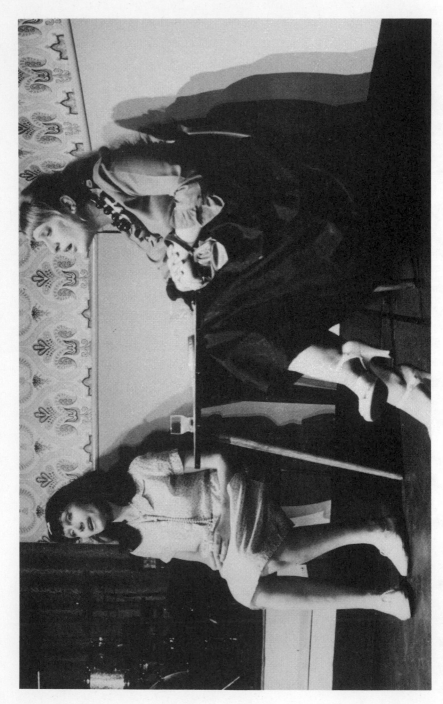

Out of Our Heads. Elizabeth MacLennan as June and Terry Neason as Janice.

played my part in the world, I know, but I still feel . . . ach, useless — a burden on Bessie and her husband — on the world. I'm not old, but there's days I feel — geriatric . . . I can see how she'll want to go out to work.

ELLA: She's a mother.

SANDY: Aye, and I'm a father and you're a sister, and I'm a brother and you're a daughter and Winston Churchill was almost certainly an uncle.

(*Pause. Hostility.*)

ELLA: You defeat my powers of understanding sometimes, Sandy Gordon. Thank you for the tea. I'll be off.

SANDY: Are you not going to wait to see your grand-niece? Bessie picks her up from the nursery at four — she'll be in any minute . . .

ELLA: Well — I don't know if I can be trusted to keep my mouth shut, Sandy: I think it's a crime —

SANDY: Aye, so we gathered — well go then, I'll tell her you called —

(*Noise off — Bessie and Alex come in.*)

Too late — you're trapped —

(*Bessie and Alex come into the room.*)

BESSIE: Dad — did you not — ? Hello Aunt Ella — Where's Jane?

SANDY: You were to pick her up on your way home.

BESSIE: Oh no! Did you not get my note?

SANDY: Note?

BESSIE: I'll go and get her — she had to be uplifted by three thirty today, the woman said, the woman had to go — I promised her you'd — ach, never mind . . .

ALEX: I'll go, I'll go — you've got visitors —

BESSIE: No, no —

SANDY: I didn't see any note —

BESSIE: (*waving piece of paper*). What's that then? Dear Dad,

229

	please go and get Jane by 3.30 as Miss Coates is leaving early —
SANDY:	I never saw *that* — let me have a look.
ALEX:	Stay there Bessie, I'll go on the bike.
BESSIE:	I've told you Alex, I'll go — I *want* to go —
SANDY:	Dear Dad Please go and get Jane by 3.30 as Miss Coates is leaving early . . .
ALEX:	(*overlap*). You stay here Bessie, Ella's come to see you —
BESSIE:	No no NO NO NO!
ELLA:	Oh don't worry about me — it's that poor little child you should be concerned about —
SANDY:	Where did you leave this?
ALEX:	I'll go on the bike — now where is this nursery exactly?
SANDY:	I'll tell you what — I'll go — I know where it is.
BESSIE:	(*shouts*). STOP IT!

(*Silence. Broken by Ella tut tutting.*)

	(*to Ella*). And you shut up.
ELLA:	(*getting up*). Well, I'm not going to stay here to witness scenes like that one and then be told to shut up!
BESSIE:	Away you go then.
ELLA:	You're as hard and heartless as that mother of yours. And if you go off and desert your daughter, as your mother deserted you, that little girl will grow up as bad as both of you . . .
BESSIE:	(*looks at her*). I'm no' deserting my daughter —
ELLA:	Then where are you all day?
ALEX:	(*reasonably*). Ella, listen, you've no right —
BESSIE:	Keep out of this, Alex. (*To Ella.*) I'll tell you where I am all day — I'm at my work. I'm staying up till late with the grown-ups, OK? And when my daughter

grows up she'll love me and respect me for it, just as I love and respect my mother for doing what she had to do.

ELLA: Well —

BESSIE: And if you say one more word, I'll do something I'm likely to regret, so don't. I'm away for Jane . . . she's *my* daughter. My responsibility. And she's going to be alright.

(*Bessie goes. Ella gets up with attempted dignity.*)

ELLA: Well — I suppose I'm just old-fashioned . . . but if I had been that lassie's father, I'd have put her across my knee. And if I'd behaved like that in front of my husband, I'd have had a few bruises before the morning — and no worse for it either —

ALEX: Is that a fact?

ELLA: Yes — there's still time to mend her ways. Cheerio.

(*Ella goes out, the men wave her off vaguely.*)

SANDY: I've got some moussaka in the oven — Greek.

ALEX: Sandy — I admire your daughter —

SANDY: I should hope so, you married her.

ALEX: Aye — but . . . she scares the hell out of me . . .

SANDY: Good.

ALEX: I'm no' sure I'm gonnae stick the pace —

SANDY: No, maybe you won't. Her mother had the same effect on me. I was fortunate of course: World War Two.

ALEX: Aye. What do you advise?

SANDY: St Bruno.

ALEX: What, pray to him?

SANDY: No, smoke him: a pipe-smoking man has more chance of survival, in my experience — a slower, more deliberate manner — a great deal of parapheranalia to hide behind, in times of stress, and the delusion of a philosophical attitude to life . . .

ALEX: Thanks.

231

SANDY: You won't feel any better, but you'll look as if you feel better — it's a sly sort of revenge.

ALEX: Aha.

SANDY: Pity it's over, really, World War Two —

ALEX: Well, there's always the class war, *that* continues — the trouble wi' that, of course — it's hard tae get an overseas posting. I am gettin' to Italy this summer though.

SANDY: Italy? Aye, I was there in '43 — Salerno, second wave — fourteenth landing-craft from the left . . . They were very bad at hiding their emotions, the Italians — what takes you there?

ALEX: The Italian Communist Party: a big Festival in Bologna —

SANDY: Well, I trust for your sake they make better communists than they did fascists — pathetic — old Benito — they hanged him, you know. By the knackers.

ALEX: Good God —

SANDY: The Allies were none too pleased.

ALEX: A sly sort of revenge — eh?

SANDY: The secret of health and happiness is to keep on winning: but even if your side is winning, you personally could be dead. Or maimed for life. For a soldier, a military victory is an abstract thing, like pure mathematics — of interest to all, of benefit to none. Are you planning for a victory, in your class war?

ALEX: Victory? Don't frighten me. My father was a red, my mother knew John Maclean, my grandfather was put in prison in 1916 and again in 1923; and I've been fighting the class war since the day I was born: it's my element, like the birds need the air and the fish need the sea . . . Christ knows what I'd do if we actually *won*. I'd be useless, out of date, without the necessary skills . . . I think I'd suffer that, though — I've given up a lot of my life for the day capitalism crumbles . . . everything I believe in follows from that . . .

SANDY: What do you think will happen on that day?

232

ALEX: Chaos. Confusion for years and years. But *eventually* . . . well, put it this way — with capitalism, we've no chance to go anywhere except backwards — back to the 1850s. With socialism, we *might* stagnate for a year or two — but at least we have the conditions for moving forward —

SANDY: Where's forward?

ALEX: Well — first things first: to a longer life and a healthier life and a more comfortable life: for everybody. After that — well — onwards to different ways of being better, eh? Wee Janey — she'll see all that. No' me.

SANDY: And that's what you're fighting for?

ALEX: Aye. And her — Bessie. What about you? Still fighting?

SANDY: No. 1956 finished me off. I always believed that you fought for only one thing: to win. And in the British Army — for as long as anyone can remember — we won. Then we invaded the Suez Canal — my God, a few thousand wogs and a strip of sand: did you ever see the Egyptian Army? What a shower — (*demonstrates their military bearing*) — And then? We lost. They, *them*, they beat us. I've no interest in that sort of fighting any more — soldiering's done for: these nuclear weapons make soldiering into like a game for grownups: a hobby. I'm happier to look after wee Janie — she's got something to say. I'm interested. If you talk to wee children — I mean, really get down below their eye-line, so they can see you — you learn a great deal. But soldiering? No . . .

(*Music, as he goes off. Fade to Blackout.*)

Scene Ten

ANNOUNCER: Scene Ten: The Veil is Rent Asunder. The Time: 1964. The Government: still Tory — but with Sir Alec now leading them towards certain disaster. The place: back in the Scottish Accounting Machines, under-capitalised, non-electronic factory in East Kilbride, also heading towards certain disaster.

(*Bessie and Catriona at work on the bench.*)

233

BESSIE:	There's word of a take-over.
CATRIONA:	Aha.
BESSIE:	Aye — a big firm from England —
CATRIONA:	That'll be right —
BESSIE:	But which one?
CATRIONA:	Don't ask me — I only work here. You're my Shop Steward.
BESSIE:	I suppose it's better than closing the place down. But then what they usually do is take a place over to stop it closing, for which they get a big government grant, then two months later they close it anyway. Are you alright?
CATRIONA:	Aye.
BESSIE:	Aye nothin'. What's wrong?
CATRIONA:	I'm OK.
BESSIE:	Listen, I'm getting fed up with you being OK — you're about as OK as a leper colony — what is it?
CATRIONA:	Nothin'.

(*Bessie goes and closes down both machines.*)

BESSIE:	Tea-break. Now come and tell Aunt Bessie.

(*Catriona breaks down into tears.*)

CATRIONA:	I'm too scared to say.
BESSIE:	Oh come on, Catriona, you don't look after yourself — what's the story?
CATRIONA:	Start the machine eh? Mrs Dundonald —
BESSIE:	Forget Mrs Dundonald: now what is it?
CATRIONA:	I've got lumps. They started in my breast — now they're all over the place . . . I was too scared to tell anyone. But —
BESSIE:	Where else are they?
CATRIONA:	Well — here (*Top of chest.*) — and here — (*In lower stomach. Bessie feels them.*)
BESSIE:	You daft wee bezom. Come here. (*Gives her a hug.*) You must have been going out of your mind.

234

CATRIONA: Aye. I have —

BESSIE: Have you no' even told your mother?

CATRIONA: Her? No, she'd kill me — say I was making it up.
She hates anything emotional.

BESSIE: My God, the state of Scotland — listen you, you're
going to the doctor, *now*. And I'm coming with you.

CATRIONA: No.

BESSIE: Yes. And thanks to my hero husband, 'in the event
of an employee being taken sick in working hours,
one other employee is permitted to accompany him
or her to receive medical attention without penalty
to either' — Good, eh? Get your coat, we'll catch
young Doctor McCorquodale before he goes on his
rounds.

CATRIONA: I don't want to.

BESSIE: You're going to — so shift.

CATRIONA: I havenae had a bath.

BESSIE: He's going to inspect you, no' eat you — shift . . .
It'll be OK. Get your coat.

CATRIONA: I cannae go to the doctor's. I'll be sick. Listen —
forget I said anything, eh. I've got it — right? Cancer.
I've got it. I'm what they call — riddled with it. So
that's that.

BESSIE: So that's what? You've got to fight it —

CATRIONA: Why? I'm no' a fighter . . .

BESSIE: Well — you must.

CATRIONA: I cannae see why. I mean — if I'm gonnae die, I'm
gonnae die, and I was gonnae die anyway so what's
the difference? I'm no' gonnae change just cos I'm
gonnae die —

BESSIE: It's human nature to want to stay alive.

CATRIONA: No' mine. What goods' it do? I thought once or
twice maybe I'd do something crazy, like going in
an aeroplane to America, or getting drunk — but I
couldnae see why — I'm no' that sort of person. I
was thinking of coming to work late this morning,

just lying in my bed: but I couldnae — I'm the sort of person that gets tae work on time. Why should I change my personality just because of a few lumps? That seems to me to be very vain . . .

BESSIE: You must fight for your life.

CATRIONA: Well — I lost that fight. About ten years ago. I mean . . . The only thing I wish I'd had was a baby.

BESSIE: Now listen — you're going to stop talking like that: have you got a pain?

CATRIONA: Aye.

BESSIE: Well, the very best you can do is to get some aspirins — come on . . . get your coat. That's an order.

(*Catriona goes reluctantly to get her coat. Bessie picks up her stuff*).

(*Alex comes in, grinning.*)

ALEX: Hey — I got the job —

BESSIE: Did you?

ALEX: Thirty-two pounds fifteen and six a week.

BESSIE: That's less than you're getting here.

ALEX: Only a pound or two — it's worth it, eh?

BESSIE: Aye — so long as you don't go the way of all trade union officials —

ALEX: Things are gonnae move in this country this year — we'll have a Labour Government, with Harold Wilson in Number Ten, and a new self-confidence in the working class and a fighting TUC at long last — if I have my way, that is —

BESSIE: Are you sure you're no' doin' a better job where you are?

ALEX: No, I'm no' sure. But its pathetic going on and on about how useless the trade union bureaucracy is if you're no' prepared to take the responsibility yourself when it's offered to you. There's folks moved heaven and earth to get me this job: I'm gonnae do it. It's all down to you to keep the good work going in here — eh?

BESSIE: Me?

236

ALEX: Aye — you; we're wanting you as Senior Shop Steward for the women.

BESSIE: Nae chance —

ALEX: What are you saying? It's your duty.

BESSIE: Aha.

ALEX: Educate Agitate Organise — all they fools in Hampstead can educate and agitate: it's up to you and me to organise: I mean it.

BESSIE: Alex — my life's too short already just wi' trying to work and be a mother — how can I go to all those meetings, negotiating committees, combine committees — they're trying to close this place: you know what that means for the Senior Shop Stewards — work, work, work. You're not on.

ALEX: Think, Bessie. Think what it's all for.

BESSIE: Aye, a better life — for some other people, at some other time, in the future. Well, I'm here now. I want my life.

(*Catriona comes back in, overhears last remark.*)

CATRIONA: Aye. Me too. Come on.

BESSIE: (*looks at her*). Are we going then? (*Catriona nods.*) Good. (*To Alex.*) OK. I'll try. For a bit (*Goes over to him.*) By the way — you're alright.

(*She goes out with Catriona. Alex is amazed.*)

ALEX: She must be going to have another baby . . .

(*Cross-fade to spot, down stage. Bessie comes back, talks to audience.*)

BESSIE: And I was. But Catriona dying took all the joy out of it. She was very what they call 'brave'. That means she screamed inside instead of out loud . . . at night, not during the day. All the time the baby was growing in me, those lumps were growing in her — it was gruesome. If only she'd said when she first felt the bloody thing, she'd have had a chance . . . if only she hadn't been afraid — of losing her breast, of her mother, of me. She died a week before Alison was born — aye, another girl. She was quiet from the word go, a douce wee miss, and my father gave her everything she wanted — she

237

had him twisted around her little finger . . . And I went back to work. And Aunt Ella wouldnae speak to me. And by 1966 they voted me Senior Shop Steward for all the women in SAM. It was then we discovered who owned us . . .

(*Romanian music.*)

Scene Eleven

ANNOUNCER: Scene Eleven: All is revealed. The time is 1966. The Government — Labour. The place — a concrete hotel on the Black Sea, Romanian Section, full of members of the British Communist Party on a Progressive Tour, and various assorted reds and lefties from all over Europe.

(*Pablo and Alex sit under a coloured umbrella, sipping Bulgarian wine.*)

PABLO: Madrid — she is full of Maoist. They blow up the palm trees in front of big hotel.

ALEX: Blow up? Wi' explosives? What have they got against palm trees?

PABLO: Now they in prison, many, many. The children of the rich become Maoist, blow up palm tree, go in prison: under the street they keep them like in graveyard — you walk round Madrid, see El Prado, buy postcard — under your feet, rich Maoist in prison. Franco love his little joke.

ALEX: What about the poor people?

PABLO: They in prison too — in the head — they afraid of police, of the soldiers, of the priest, of God — they very quiet — but not all . . .

ALEX: How?

PABLO: We organise. We wait.

(*Bessie comes in smothered in calamine lotion.*)

BESSIE: Would you look at the state of me — I'm burnt purple — (*To Pablo.*) Hello . . .

ALEX: This is Pablo — frae Spain — he's a comrade —

BESSIE: Oh aye? From Spain?

PABLO: Barcelona. It is like your Glasgow, no?

BESSIE:	So I've heard —
ALEX:	Bessie works in business machines too — (*To Bessie.*) Pablo here works for MME Barcelona.
BESSIE:	Good luck to you — I work for SAM.
PABLO:	Ha! So we are brother and sister —
BESSIE:	How d'you mean?
PABLO:	Because we both work for IRM no?
BESSIE:	IRM? No, SAMs been taken over by Inter-Trust, London Limited —
PABLO:	That too is IRM. My factory is owned by Corunna Holding Company — that too is IRM. Our organisation has a list — your SAM is on this list. When you have a strike in Glasgow, we work extra in Barcelona — International Registration Machines play with us.
BESSIE:	What do you make?
PABLO:	Parts of the A27s, R33s —
BESSIE:	Aye, but which parts?
PABLO:	Buzz-bars, frames — just like you, no?
BESSIE:	How come I never knew this? That explains a lot. Every time we go on strike, they're laughing at us — they're getting the same parts from you lot — cheaper —
PABLO:	Well — maybe it could be arranged —

(*Bessie is thinking hard.*)

ALEX:	IRM eh? If you're up against the multi-nationals, you've got to do better than that, love. They've got plants all over Europe —
BESSIE:	(*spoiling for a fight*). Right, you bastards — you want a fight, you're gonna get one.
ALEX:	(*to audience*). At last, Bessie McGuigan had found some worthy opposition. Would she win? See Act Two.

(*Music.*)

END ACT ONE

ACT TWO

Scene One

ANNOUNCER: Are you all back? Right — Act Two. Scene One: Boadicea v. The Roman Empire — The time: January 1968. The Government — well, Labour. The place: Scottish Accounting Machines plant in East Kilbride, the new young Personnel Manager's office.

(*Bessie and young Mr Eagleton, a keen young English personnel manager, confront each other across his desk.*)

MR EAGLETON: Please sit down Mrs McGuigan —

BESSIE: You explain to me just exactly what you're up to, Mr Eagleton . . .

MR EAGLETON: I'm not up to —

BESSIE: You know fine no senior Shop Steward is allowed to discuss business with you or your infinite superiors without at least one other shop steward present. You asked me in here privately son, to discuss my personal position: now you're trying to tell me you're gonnae sack fifty of my women.

MR EAGLETON: Mrs McGuigan, I mentioned the possibility of rationalisation purely out of courtesy —

BESSIE: Aye, and the next week you'll be saying you discussed it with me — which means I agreed to it. Don't try those tricks on wi' me, son — if you reckoned you were only dealing wi' a handful of women so you could trample over them, don't go down in the woods today, cos you're sure of a big surprise — and it'll no' be a picnic.

MR EAGLETON: There are too many women —

BESSIE: Listen son: you're representing the interests of International Registration Machines of Delaware Inc. and their mighty managers and their eighty thousand, mostly American, shareholders and their global policy of economic imperialism and exploitation: me, I've got five hundred and fifty women frae East Kilbride who need the money. I think you'll find that although that situation gives you more power, it gives me more motivation, which means that in the end, I'm gonnae win. Right?

MR EAGLETON: Is this notification of your intention to take strike action, Mrs McGuigan?

241

BESSIE: This is courtesy, son.

MR EAGLETON: Then I must warn you of the consequences —

BESSIE: Say no more, I'm not continuing this conversation without a witness. Stop right there. I'll be back . . . wi' a pal.

(*She goes. Eagleton quickly dials a number.*)

MR EAGLETON: (*on phone*). Mr Grundyen please — it's urgent . . . Hello Mr Grundyen, Eagleton here — this rationalisation plan we discussed in London on Monday — there's going to be a lot of local opposition — I've just had the female senior shop steward in here . . . Yes, bloody Bessie McGuigan. She's gone off sounding all militant, threatening to bring production to a stop . . . But would we get an import licence to bring the parts in from Holland, it's a Labour government? . . . Ah, I see — well, how accommodating of them . . . so — we go ahead — . . . do you mean we could last out indefinitely — . . . I see, so we actually save money? Fine, say no more, I'll be the Rock of Gibraltar . . . yes — have a pleasant meeting in Paris, Eric — bye.

(*Bessie comes back in with Janice, a girl off the line, who doesn't know what's going on.*)

BESSIE: Right Janice, stand there. And listen. (*To Eagleton.*) OK — say that again. In front of her.

MR EAGLETON: Very well. Certain technological advances in coiling procedures have enabled us to install a plant in Cumbria which will produce more and better components in one day than the two shifts on Area D produce in a week. We intend therefore to transfer production of all European magnetic-B coiling to Barrow, and consequently to cease production in Area D. The two shifts will be given adequate notice and redundancy payments will be made. Area D will be used for storage. (*Shrugs.*) I don't *have* to explain this to you, Mrs McGuigan, but I'm quite happy to keep you in the picture. And your witness.

BESSIE: OK Janice, you come with me to see the Convenor.

MR EAGLETON: I ought to warn you that we are not in breach of any agreement —

BESSIE: Oh yes you are: this government paid you a bloody fortune to expand production in this town — to provide employment for these people. You took it. Now you're taking away jobs and giving them to a machine in Cumbria. That's a serious breach of agreement. Secondly, there are agreed methods of consultation with unions and shop stewards in the event of even thinking about sacking folk — this bloody multi-national has never consulted anyone. That's another breach. Yon Grundyen in London thinks he's God Almighty — well he's no' — nor are you God Almighty's wee boy . . . though you're gonnae need to turn some water into wine before this strike's over —

MR EAGLETON: And you, Mrs McGuigan, are going to need more than five loaves and two little fishes . . .

BESSIE: Aha. Right. We'll see. Come on Janice. (*They go.*)

MR EAGLETON: (*on intercom*). Esther — get me the manager's office.

VII

SINGER: *There* they go out the door
Hard and angrily
Soon they'll come beat on it
Wild and hungrily
No man dare speak tae them
Sae insultingly
*Wi'*oot he kens
The women are up again —

Come and dae battle then, chairmen and managers
Come and dae battle directors and shareholders
We'll stand all day till we close down your factory
Bugger the lot of ye big multi-nationals —

We'll —
Turn away artics
and send them back hame again
Turn away scabs and
we'll a' be ashamed of them —
Picket by night and day
Mair than just six of us
Show ye the women are
no' just a walk-over —

Come and dae battle then, chairmen and managers
Come and dae battle directors and shareholders
We'll stand all day till we close down your factory

Bugger the lot of ye big multi-nationals —

Here we stand side by side
No they will *no'* get in —
Polis are terrified
Yes we are gonnae win —
Yankees go home again —
Out wi' the racketeers
Hame wi' a bloody nose —
Out wi' the profiteers —

Come and dae battle then, chairmen and managers
Come and dae battle directors and shareholders
We'll stand all day till we close down your factory
Bugger the lot of ye big multi-nationals
(Tune: 'Donald McGillivray')

Scene Two

ANNOUNCER: Scene Two: Divide and Rule. Time — April 1968.
Government — still, well — Labour. The place: a
picket line outside SAM, East Kilbride, too early
one morning.

(*Isobel and Janice stand or sit, with umbrellas and a placard saying 'Picket Line'
looking very unofficial. It is cold and wet and six-forty-five in the morning.*)

JANICE: What time's it?

ISOBEL: Quartae seven.

JANICE: Hurry up, Bessie, my man'll be late for work —

ISOBEL: Can he no' get himself up in the morning?

JANICE: Him? Cannae brew a cup o'tea — cannae pour out
a plate of Cornflakes wi'out some remark aboot
burning brassieres and the demise of a man's
self-respect.

ISOBEL: Aha.

JANICE: They're a' the same —

ISOBEL: Well — Billy's no' so bad. He'll bring me a cup
of tea on a Sunday morning, take the kids out
on a Saturday, do a bit of paintwork, you know.
Who's this?

(*Enter Alex in a suit.*)

244

ALEX:	Morning ladies — no sign of Tommy?
JANICE:	Tommy who?
ALEX:	Tommy Dolan your district official —
ISOBEL:	Never heard of him let alone seen him — we're unofficial.
ALEX:	Aye. I know — well he's coming down this morning — I'm to meet him — how's it going?
ISOBEL:	Fine, fine — cold wet, and pointless, but we're havin' a wonderful holiday, eh Janice?
JANICE:	Aye. Who are you then?
ALEX:	Oh I'm from the union head office in Glasgow . . . Glad to see you're keeping the struggle going still —
JANICE:	Well it's no thanks to you lot, is it? I mean — it was three weeks out then they sacked the Convenor, then two more weeks out and they took him on again so we all went back to work and three days later they sacked him again so Bessie got us all out again and it's been five weeks this time — that's three days' pay in ten weeks and no' a penny strike pay frae the union — what do we pay our dues for, I wonder — to keep you lot in smart silk suits is it?
ALEX:	I know, I know — we tried to have it declared official, but they wouldnae hear of it in London — if you're wanting a change of policy, you'll need to change the Executive —
ISOBEL:	It's because we're women: they'll no support women on strike, will they?
JANICE:	But there's men out here as well, Isobel —
ISOBEL:	Aye — but where are they? He's the first man I've seen on this line before eleven in the morning.
ALEX:	Aye. Well . . .
JANICE:	Well what?
ALEX:	There's trouble from the men — they're supporting families, rent to pay, kids . . . they've got on to Tommy Dolan, and he's got on to me. They want to go back to work.
ISOBEL:	The bastards. Here, you'd better speak to Bessie about that —

ALEX: I have. I'm married to her.

JANICE: Oh — I see . . .

(*Bessie comes in; sees Alex, stops.*)

BESSIE: (*to Isobel and Janice*). Well — has he told you the great news?

ISOBEL: Aye. Apparently the men have got responsibilities — and we're just doin' it for fun —

ALEX: Now, now, I never said anything of the kind.

BESSIE: I'm surprised you can show your face at all — Tommy Dolan didnae summon up the courage — he wants to meet you in his office.

JANICE: I'm away now Bessie, OK? I'll be back about nine wi' some coffee.

BESSIE: OK Janice. You stay here, Isobel, I'm needing a witness —

ISOBEL: I'm no' running after my husband's breakfast — he can cook it himself . . .

JANICE: Aye well I'm wanting some bottoms left in my pans, so I'll away — cheery bye . . .

(*Janice goes. Bessie turns to Alex.*)

BESSIE: Well?

ALEX: There's no chance of winning, Bessie. They're getting all the parts they need from Eindhoven, with an import licence from the Labour government — you're no' going to get your fifty women's jobs back, and your ex-Convenor is a man — and he agrees with the men — get back to work. Think again.

BESSIE: So it's no' just the multi-nationals we're fighting. It's our own union — and the men we work with as well —

ALEX: Aye. It is.

(*Silence.*)

BESSIE: Right well. And guess who's gonnae be our next Convenor? You'll no' get away with that wi' me — None of you. OK, Isobel — back to work, ten weeks out for nothing — sorry about that, it was my fault.

I underestimated the divisions within the working class: and above all the treachery of the male of the species: but I won't do that again — oh no. Alex — get back to your office in Glasgow and telephone London and tell them I'm wanting to make direct contact with the International Department of the TUC right away — and I'll be doing that whether they say yes or no. I'm going away to Barrow-in-Furness tomorrow — I'm wanting to talk to the folk there — and then I'll be convening an IRM shop stewards' combine meeting in Liverpool as soon as maybe — and I'll be contacting shop floor organisers in every IRM plant in Europe — personally. OK?

ALEX: (*wearily*). Aye — OK, Bessie —

BESSIE: Ever since you got that job you've been trying to lead a quiet life: well there's nae chance, understand — nae chance, Alex. Come on Isobel — I've got five hundred women to apologise to, on behalf of one hundred and twenty men. (*To Alex.*) I'll see you at home.

(*They go.*)

ALEX: (*to audience*). Two weeks later, in May, there were ten million workers on strike in France. Everything seemed possible in 1968. Everything.

VII

A battle's a battle
And hard she must fight —
A faint heart will soon be defeated:
As they twist and they turn
She must cling to their heels
Let them go and she'll find she's been cheated . . .
So follow their footsteps
And hold to their trail
Through all of the lands that they master —
They're rich and they're fly
And they don't give a damn
If they're fast then she just must be faster . . .
(Tune: 'Charlie, oh Charlie')

Scene Three

ANNOUNCER: Scene Three: The Price of a Phone-call. The Time: 1971. The Government: Tory again — Edward Heath variety. The place: The McGuigan family residence, now bulging at the seams with growing little girls — Janey is now twelve, and Alison is nearly seven . . . Sandy is holding the fort.

SANDY: You'll have to speak more slowly — MORE SLOWLY — SENHOR — Si, Si, No, NO — My daughter is in the toilet . . . The cludgie — lavabo, Si — Don't get so excited you foreigners are all the same, now just calm down and she'll be with you — OK — Hang on eh? Si, si, wait a wee minute!

(*He goes out yelling*). Bessie!

(*Alison, now seven, comes in and picks up the phone.*)

ALISON: Hello who's that? I want a bike for Christmas not Janey's old one but a new one all for myself . . . Yes, I can ride a bike — what's that funny noise? You should put some more money in —

(*Janey, now twelve, comes in.*)

ALISON: It's a man! I'm having a conversation with a man!

JANEY: Don't talk rubbish —

(*Janey tries to take the phone, but Alison won't let go and it develops into a fight. Alex comes in, sorts it out. The phone is left lying there. He goes and picks it up and hangs it up. Bessie comes in just as he does so, followed by Sandy.*)

BESSIE: Don't! Oh Christ that poor man — he's tried to get me five times from a call-box in Lisbon because the secret police are tapping his phone and every time he goes out he gets followed by a man in a mac and just because I'm in the lavvy for two minutes . . .

ALEX: Was there somebody on that phone?

ALISON: Aye, he was going to buy me a bike . . .

SANDY: Was it Portuguese he was? That explains how I could not understand one word he was saying —

(*The phone rings. They all look at it. Janey picks it up.*)

JANEY: Hello — oh hi Phillipa — yes, I know, he said he never wanted to speak to me again, I think he's *horrible* . . . mm, yes Phillipa, I know . . .

BESSIE: I am sorry to interrupt this vital conversation but is that the same Phillipa who left this house ten minutes ago, who lives in Donald Drive and whom

you will see again in approximately twelve hou
on your way to school?

JANEY: Oh mum — Just a minute, Phillipa —

BESSIE: Hang up. Put the bloody phone down. Raccrochez
s'il vous plait, there's a man in a street in Portugal
risking his life to get in contact with me, and all
you can do is blether!

(*She takes the phone and puts it down.*)

JANEY: Bye Phillipa! (*Pause.*) What do you mean — risking
his life?

BESSIE: There are some countries in Europe where you
arenae allowed to go on strike, or picket your
own factory, where anyone who is suspected of
even *trying* to organise anything or of being in the
Communist Party gets taken away in the night and
never seen again. There are some people who'd love
to see that set-up here, and that's why we have to
be political and boring and go on demonstrations
against this government we've got now, to make
sure they know they won't get away with what
they get away with in Portugal and Spain, and now
Greece. Mr Varga is a very brave man.

(*The phone rings again. Alex picks it up.*)

ALEX: Hello — Mrs Gorgon? — aye . . . (*To Bessie.*) Medusa,
it's for you.

BESSIE: Hello — oh yes, hello Mr Varga — I'm sorry about
the confusion . . . Thank you for phoning . . . OK
I'll be quick — we go on strike — aye, yes, si —
on strike.

(*Alison and Janey have punch-up.*)

Alex, would you sort those two — aye, en grève —
next Wednesday — Mercredi — aye, mercolleddy
— Do not increase production of M33 frames or
parts, OK? . . . You've got it, correct, no overtime,
no increase, good, good, you're wonderful . . .
magnifico . . . give my love to Amalia — right —
don't forget — no more frames for M33s. We'll do
the same for you one day — see you in Toulouse . . .
look after yourself, comrade —

(*She hangs up. Sniffs.*)

Right, that just leaves the Italian lot, they should be no bother at all — if a Signor Umberto Collini rings, don't hang up — he'll no' be risking his life, but he's very impatient and he'll no ring back — now, where was I?

ALEX: In the lavvy —

BESSIE: So I was, no wonder I'm constipated . . . (*To Janey and Alison.*) Now you two, off to your beds — it's ten to nine — and I've got half a dozen phone-calls still to make and the washing's up to the ceiling —

JANEY: Why should I have to go to bed?

BESSIE: Just look at the state of Alison, off you go —

JANEY: She's six!

ALISON: I'm nearly seven —

BESSIE: You're both to go to your beds. (*To Janey.*) Have you found that tie yet?

ALISON: I'm hungry.

BESSIE: You had it yesterday morning going to school, where is it now?

ALISON: I'm needing something to eat, mammy — I'll no' be able to sleep for hunger —

JANEY: I want you to tell me some more about that man —

ALISON: *I* spoke to him — he was *my* friend —

BESSIE: Tomorrow, tomorrow — Alex, will you put that paper down and exercise some control over your off-spring? I've got to get Trevor Edwards before nine or he'll be away to the pub or the Eisteddfod or wherever he goes — BED!

(*Bessie starts dialling a row of numbers.*)

ALEX: Aye — right. Alison, come on, I'll take you up to bed — (*To Bessie.*) Is she to have a bath?

SANDY: No, no, she's had her bath — haven't you my darling?

ALEX: OK — up we go then —

ALISON: I'm not going if she's not going — it's not fair, just

250

	because I'm the younger . . . Mammy says we're all equal in this house —
ALEX:	Well you've got to go to bed —
ALISON:	Well I'm no'. I'm hungry. I'm gonnae make a sangwich . . .
BESSIE:	(*on phone*). Can I speak to Trevor please?
ALISON:	Mum will you make me a sangwich?
BESSIE:	Sh: I'm on the phone — Go up and I'll be up to say goodnight —
ALEX:	Janey, will you no' get tae bed?
JANEY:	I've got homework —
ALEX:	Oh no —
JANEY:	Mrs Law will kill me if I've no' done my homework *again*.
BESSIE:	(*on phone*). It's Mrs McGuigan from East Kilbride —
JANEY:	Mum never gave me a note last time.
ALEX:	You've had all night — what've you been doing?
JANEY:	Mum said we could go to guides.
BESSIE:	Mum never!
ALEX:	Guides? Christ — Alison come here, you're no' to go cutting bread at your age . . .
BESSIE:	(*on phone*). Oh no! See if you can catch him . . .
ALEX:	Janey, your mother says you're to go to bed, so go!
JANEY:	I've got *homework* — Mum, I've got *homework*.
BESSIE:	Well do it in bed.
ALEX:	Come on pet — you'll get both of us in terrible trouble.
BESSIE:	(*hand over phone*). Alex will you stop trying to be so bloody *nice* and get those two into their *beds*! (*Back to phone*.) Sorry, Trevor — aye, next Wednesday.
SANDY:	Alison! Janey! If you're no' in your beds by the time I get to your room, you will not hear the next exciting episode in the story of the massacre

of the Macdonalds of Glencoe — the treachery of the Clan Campbell and the perfidy of the English King — how the red-coats crept up in the night, through the pure white snow, and just as dawn was breaking — . . . Are you not in your beds yet? Hurry up, hurry up —

BESSIE: (*hand over phone*). Night night — (*Calls.*) do your teeth! (*They go.*) No, no, not you Trevor! . . . OK, I'll see you on the 15th at Stafford — What a dump, eh, never mind, next time the Riviera . . . (*Hangs up, looks up next number.*) (*to Alex*) I hear you're having it away wi' some bit of stuff from your office (*starts to dial*)

ALEX: Aye — we've given Jane Fonda a start in the Education Department — what are you saying?

BESSIE: If y'are — don't. Stop it. Now. (*Listens.*) Curses — engaged. (*Hangs up, looks for next number.*) Harlow 371432 — Where's the code book?

ALEX: Were you serious just then?

BESSIE: That's what I was told . . .

ALEX: Jesus Christ — who's your friendly informant?

BESSIE: Never you mind.

ALEX: Do you believe them?

BESSIE: No. Or I'd batter you. But there's something going on. Mind you, I'm no' surprised, I mean I'm away a lot, eh, and no' exactly doin' the female thing.

ALEX: Bessie — hold on a wee minute — what are you saying?

BESSIE: (*anger*). It's OK — I'm just taking on a multi- national corporation, pretty near single-handed — certainly wi' no help from you and your union. So are you surprised I'm no' all coy and sexy when hubby comes hame frae the boozer?

ALEX: Bessie, you're talking a load of crap, will you stop it?

BESSIE: Oh aye, crap is it? Christ, you couldnae even get the girls tae bed —

ALEX: What's that got to do with it?

BESSIE: Trying to be bloody *nice*. You're too concerned about your own image —

252

ALEX:	Bessie are you trying to provoke me?
BESSIE:	(*exasperated*). Why should I, stand here, apologising to you, for no' coming on all feminine, when I do everything in this house, *and* a job of work, *and* fight a war against a multi-national in my spare time, and you sit there reading the paper and worrying about your image. If they need sleep, they must go to bed, whether it makes you feel unkind or whether it doesnae. Now where's the code book — shift your bum.
ALEX:	It's no under my bum.
BESSIE:	Well look for it — or is that no' union policy?

(*Janey comes in.*)

JANEY:	Mum, Grandpa's going to give Alison bad dreams with that story at this time of night — it's horrible.
BESSIE:	Perhaps she likes horrible stories —
JANEY:	Well it's me she'll wake up in the night.
BESSIE:	Send her through to me — and you too, if you get bad dreams, you're not too big to come through are you Janey McGuigan?
JANEY:	Will you get him to stop?
BESSIE:	Aye, I will . . . But once he starts —
ALEX:	Will I go up?
BESSIE:	No, it'll need to be me — could you find the code book?

(*The phone rings. All groan. Alex picks it up.*)

ALEX:	Funny noises . . . Hello — ah yes, Signor Collini, from Novara — one moment please —
BESSIE:	Tell the snooty bugger to hang on . . . Talk to the man.
ALEX:	He's ringing from Italy.
BESSIE:	And she's gonnae have nightmares — get your priorities in order. (*To Janey.*) Come on you, let's go and sort out your Grandpa — Massacre of Glencoe, indeed — he reads too many war books, does he no'?

253

ALEX: (*holding phone but to audience as Bessie and Janey go*). Priorities. That's what's worrying me — (*laughs*) (*into phone*) Eh, Umberto — si, si, she'll no' be long —

(*Blackout.*)

IX

SINGER: (The) workers are marching now
All over Italy
Demos and rioting all over Germany
Wars in Chicago and
Fighting in Washington
What are we waiting for
Let's get stuck intae them —
Come and dae battle then, chairmen and managers
Come for a scrap for you're no' tae big for us
We'll find our comrades in all of your factories
Bugger the lot of yous
Big multi-nationals . . .

(Tune: 'Donald MacGillivray')

Scene Four

ANNOUNCER: Scene Four: Victory. The time: two years later: 1973. The Government, aye, Tory — the place: the McGuigan residence, late one Thursday night.

(*Sandy is in, alone.*)

(*Sandy resumes his chat to the audience as he DIYs a book- case.*)

SANDY: This shelf is for Janey's books — this for Alison's. Same size, of course. This is for Alex's murky tomes, mostly Karl Marx's mumbo-jumbo — and this is for my classics of the art of warfare — Clausewitz, Julius Caesar, British Army manuals, Mao Tse Tung, various Greeks and the wit and wisdom of Attila the Hun. The library service is quite good, of course, and the odd television or radio programme will illuminate some unexplored facet of military history. I have a strict routine of reading and note-taking, and a rudimentary form of filing system in my bedroom — the facts at my fingertips.

None of this can compensate for my lack of involvement in a good scrap. For the last twelve weeks, I've seen Bessie go out of that door at six on the morning and come home at midnight exhausted, and up again

254

at 5.30, ready for more. Why? She's a good fight on her hands . . . This phone here — my goodness, for two years — I've been speaking with Spaniards, Greeks, Dutchmen, Algerians, even members of Parliament. Oh yes, we were all roped in for what they call 'the struggle'. And this last effort — after twelve weeks — she's won . . . I could have advised the gentlemen in New York not to bother — if you cross our Bessie it's just a matter of time before you get a bloody nose. But the difference in her . . . and me, well I'm baby-sitting wee Alison while they're away celebrating — and I suppose I'm quite happy. To my way of thinking, there's two purposes in living, there's enjoyment like reading or playing with the grandchildren or growing scarlet runners, that's one, but there's no flavour to that, no value in it, without the other: and that's fighting — the struggle. Either one, without the other, is foolish: but together, they are the reasons for carrying on. (*Hears the others*) And victory? Ah, victory is sweet — but never complete . . .

(*Enter Alex, Janey and Isobel from the celebration, singing — or trying to sing 'Imagine'.*)

Hello Isobel — what's this Janey McGuigan, the bugler has blown Lights Out some two hours ago, and here you are out on the tiles with the other roisterers —

JANEY: It was great Grandpa — there was a band — and singing — and everybody gave Mum a huge cheer and stood up and clapped and stamped their feet —

SANDY: Is that right?

(*Enter Bessie, a bit tiddly, in a new trouser suit.*)

JANEY: I was really proud of her —

ISOBEL: Aye, she's right, we were all proud of her —

ALEX: And with good cause. Bessie, you did a good job — you fought and you won . . .

BESSIE: Och, away the lot of you. Isobel here fought, and the other women fought, and even some of the bloody men fought when it looked as if we were gonnae win: I just used the telephone —

ISOBEL: Maybe — but I mind when that guy frae Carlisle

255

> decided to drive his truck through the picket line
> to collect something, eh? (*She and Bessie laugh.*)

ALEX: What did she do?

ISOBEL: She pulled him out of his wee windae by the scruff of the neck, set him down against the fence and gave him a brief lecture on trades unionism including illustrations of the penalties for breaking the rules.

ALEX: I hope the press was no' around at the time —

ISOBEL: No, it was OK — he got back in his truck and went home to Carlisle, bleating like a wee sheep.

BESSIE: (*laughing*). Oh, he was no' such a bad wee mannie — Janey! Do you know what time it is?

JANEY: Oh mum!

BESSIE: Oh Mum nothin'.

ALEX: I'm just makin' a cup of tea — can she no' have just a cup of tea?

BESSIE: Alex, you're terrible — she's got school in the morning —

ISOBEL: It'll be a night to remember, eh, Janey?

JANEY: Aye . . . Mum, you said Grandpa would sing us a song —

SANDY: Oh no no. I couldnae do that.

ALEX: (*producing bottle*). Not wi'oot a wee dram, eh?

SANDY: No, no — well, just to clear my throat, if you insist —

ISOBEL: (*as drinks are poured*). Why you should never forget tonight, Janey, is because tonight we're celebrating the first time a big multi-national corporation has had all its workers in all its plants in the whole of Europe organised to support each other over a dispute. And we won. And they lost. They couldnae win, because we were better organised even than they were. It's a day of history, Janey, and you're lucky to witness it.

ALEX: I'll drink to that. Bessie, you and the women at SAM have succeeded where the mighty trades union organisations of Europe have failed. I feel proud, and a bit ashamed. Here's to Victory . . .

ALL: To Victory!

(*They drink. A silence.*)

JANEY: Is Grandpa going to sing now?

SANDY: (*laughter*). Aye — Bessie, to celebrate your victory
                   — I'll give you a song. Get your box out, Bessie —
                   I'll need a chord.

BESSIE: Och, I've no' played for years —

SANDY: No no, it's there in the corner and I heard you play
                   only a week ago — 'Dark Lochnagar'.

ALEX: (*as Bessie puts on her accordion*). Sandy, do you think
                   that's a suitable song for a victory over international
                   capital and the American imperial machine?

SANDY: It's what I fancy singing at this point in time — and
                   it's not entirely inappropriate — have you found
                   your fingers Bessie?

BESSIE: No but you'll have to put up with it — (*She plays a
                   big chord.*)

(*Sandy sings 'Dark Lochnagar'*)

SANDY: (*With feeling*). Away ye gay landscapes
                   Ye gardens of roses
                   In you let the minions of luxury roam
                   Restore me the rocks where the snowflake reposes
                   If still they are sacred
                   To Freedom and Love
                   And yet Caledonia
                   Though dear are thy mountains
                   Around their white summits though elements war,
                   Though cataracts foam
                   'stead of smooth flowing fountains
                   I sigh for the valley of Dark Lochnagar.

(*Bessie and the others encourage him to sing another verse, which he does with
the help of another dram.*)

                   Oh the years have rolled on
                   Lochnagar since I left you
                   And years will elapse till I see you again —
                   Though nature of verdure and flowers has bereft you
                   Yet still thou art dearer than Albion's plain —
                   England thy beauties
                   Are tame and domestic

>To one who has roved on the mountains afar
>I sigh for the crags
>That are wild and majestic
>The steep crowning glories of Dark Lochnagar
>(*Based on words by Byron*)

(*Sandy finishes with a fine flourish, and all applaud, and demand more. As they swing in to 'Maxwelton Braes Are Bonnie', fade to black. A discord on the accordion. A single spot comes up downstage.*)

Scene Five

(*Alex comes forward, speaks to the audience.*)

ALEX: I *was* ashamed, too. Embarrassed by my own job, embarrassed by the realities of the world we live in. For four or five years Bessie had worked up to that moment when the people who slave away at SAM East Kilbride could withdraw their labour — in the hope of improving their pay or conditions — and not be made to feel stupid. I didn't push too hard for my union to take over the organisation. And I'll tell you why. It wasnae laziness. Since the late 50s a string of International Trades Union Confederations had been springing up for one trade then another, and the unions in this country had been joining in with true internationalist fervour — only to discover as the years wore on, and these confederations achieved nothing, that they had been founded, funded and subsequently foundered by the Central Intelligence Agency of the USA. And what's more, if any official union set up any such confederation without their money, it was no problem at all for them to infiltrate it, and then either take it over or failing that, bugger it up. It's a pretty obvious thing for the CIA to do, if you come to think of it. And as we know, the CIA and the multi-nationals dine at the same trough. The year is 1973, the year ITT and the CIA together assassinated Allende, and conspired at the butchery of hundreds of thousands of Chileans. In Glasgow we organised marches and protests and God knows what. Oh aye! But when it came to fighting the multi-nationals, what Bessie was doing was the only way . . . a massive combine, at shop-floor level — based on personal contacts. The CP had some role to play in this — most of the continentals were comrades or known to our comrades . . . you cannae

258

have working-class action against multi-nationals
without an international political organisation . . .
and the Communist movement is precisely that. I
feel — well, I hesitate to mention it because some of
you will already have started thinking — conspiracy.
Well — you'd be right. But what else are ITT or IBM
or Unilever or Esso or General Motors or United
Fruit if they're not conspiracies: no, the CP had a
role to play, and I'm no' going to stand here and
apologise for it. But when it came to organising,
and co-ordinating the action, against IRM, then
Bessie had to do it all herself. The Party couldnae
help — my God, what a field day that would have
been for the *Sunday Post* . . . Jings, crivens, so help
ma bob . . . 'It makes you think.' And the unions
couldnae help — no, too easy to infiltrate — and
anyway we were swinging away to the right, slowly
but surely, one way or some other way — No there
was no-one to help but Isobel and a few of the
women, and their men wanted their tea on the
table at half past five, or there'd be trouble. And I
must confess — I didnae find it easy either when
she went waltzing off to Marseilles for the weekend
wi' a bunch of handsome young Spaniards — and
me left doing the washing and the heavy father
act . . . I know, I know — too bad, eh? Aye — but —
I quite *liked* her, you know — I would have loved
to have a chat with her one day . . . Aye, you'll
have seen through that, too eh? . . . OK then: I
fought against my instincts, but I failed to overcome
them. I was fed up. If it hadnae been for Sandy,
those two girls would have grown up into Hell's
Angels or something . . . But was that a reason for
me getting fed up? For thinking about leaving? No,
surely not . . . me leaving would only have made
it worse. I didnae leave her — but I was thinking
about it . . . I suppose, if I was going to leave, I
should have left then, in 1973, when she was at the
peak of her achievements — but who's to know a
peak's a peak until you start slithering down the
other side? I try to be honest. I try to change myself,
and to see politics reaching into all areas of my life.
But I can't help it: politics has got to be a fight to
overthrow the capitalist state — first and foremost
— it's no good relating beautifully to each other if
you're still being robbed and exploited: it doesnae
make sense. And unfortunately, along with that
attitude, there seems to go an old-fashioned need

for the wife to look after the weans. Till after the
revolution. I'm trying to be honest, and I think
that's how it is. Anyway, I didn't leave her. Not
then. No . . . Just thinking about it, I feel such a —
aye well . . . but I'm not happy with the set-up . . .

(*He goes.*)

X

SINGER: He walks to the door
Then he walks back again
He'll cause her no trouble
He'll cause her no pain
There's a feeling of sadness he'll never explain
So he closes the door
And he walks back again.

But she knows he is restless
She knows he must go
She casts down her eyes
But her bitterness shows
They gaze out at angles till neither one knows
The stranger beside them
The cold wind that blows

(Tune: 'Bonnie Moorhen')

Scene Six

ANNOUNCER: Scene Six: The Slippery Slope. The Year: 1976. The
Government — 'Well Labour' again. The place: the
SAM plant East Kilbride, now making components
for International Registration Machines Computers,
employing some eight hundred women and two
hundred men. We are, as they say, in the disused
lavvy known generously as the Convenor's office.
Bessie and the three Senior Shop Stewards are
digesting a piece of information . . .

(*Bessie and Isobel and Harry, the Men's Senior Shop Steward, and Janice are
all reading a piece of paper. They move away, one after the other. Harry is
left holding it.*)

HARRY: I knew that was tae come — I tellt ye, but ye
widnae listen.

ISOBEL: Harry can ye no' shut up?

HARRY: Aye well — here it is, eh — now it's upon us.

'With effect from 7th of July — ' That's what? Two
months — 'Total closure', 'transfer of *all* production
elsewhere', 'sale of the site' — 'Redundancy of *all*
personnel' . . . What a time for this tae happen eh?

JANICE: How come ye've no' resigned yet, Harry?

HARRY: What are ye sayin'?

JANICE: You usually resign when things look a bit tricky.

HARRY: A bit tricky? Christ, this is disaster — complete
shut-down — you cannae call that 'a bit tricky' —
I should have resigned four years ago, when she
started all her International Hands Across the Sea
Communist business — I never wanted to be Senior
Shop Steward anyway, it was just somebody had
tae be . . . will we get support frae the unions, do
you think? Official, I mean?

BESSIE: Oh aye — now it's too late.

JANICE: I've never heard you say anything like that before
Bessie. Are you for giving up the struggle?

BESSIE: No. We'll struggle. But we'll lose —

HARRY: Christ, now I've heard it all. Listen Bessie McGuigan
— we were always going to lose: you know that,
and you always knew that — and you played about
wi' the livelihoods of all the folk employed here —
well now you've got what was coming to you —
and we're gonnae suffer for it. You're worse than
a criminal, do you know that? You're a mindless
militant, that's what they call your sort, and you
are a burden on the working class of Scotland. You
can stuff your heroic struggle against the multi-
nationals — they're laughing at us: they've had us
for breakfast, and now they're spitting out the pips.
Aye, I resign. For ever. From everything.

(*He goes. Janice is tending to agree with him.*)

ISOBEL: Pay no attention to him, Bessie. He's aye been a
sneaky bugger, that Harry Sim —

JANICE: Aye, but maybe he's no' so far wrong. I mean —
this is the end, eh? And we've been led here —
oh aye, grand fighting words, Bessie — but when
they up sticks and away, where are we left? Any
of us? I'm no' blaming you, Bessie — you did what

you thought was best — but, well — you took the three cheers when we were winning . . . I'll stick by you though. I'll no' behave like that yin. We'll stick by her, won't we Isobel?

ISOBEL: Well I hope you'll no' behave like that wee snotter. Aye. Don't worry, Bessie. We're with you.

BESSIE: Are you? Well pass the gelignite — I'm off to see the nice new manager —

JANICE: Will it do any good, do you think?

BESSIE: No. But it'll do me good — I'll be back —

(*She goes out. They sit a moment.*)

JANICE: She's gone for a wee greet . . .

ISOBEL: Aye.

JANICE: How could she no' have had a wee greet wi' us?

ISOBEL: It wouldnae be right — in here. This is official.

JANICE: Oh Christ, are even the tears unofficial round here?

ISOBEL: Aye — the union cannae afford to cry . . .

(*Fade . . . Fade up on Bessie.*)

Scene Seven

(*Bessie speaks to the audience.*)

BESSIE: The next six months were very bad. We did the lot, short of occupying the factory. We had meetings with the management, meetings with the unions, meetings with the government, the Scottish Office, the District Council, the Regional Council, with the local MPs and the Provost and the Church of Scotland and every Trades Council in the area. And we had mass meetings, aye — but as the months went by and we were just keeping the gates open by pure will-power, the meetings got smaller, and quieter, and sadder.

Because it was only a routine: the ritual struggle against closure, as seen in factories throughout the land. We gained a certain amount of time, but we knew we couldnae win. And *that* is terrible tae bear.

262

To fight, knowing you are gonnae lose, well — it takes away the dignity of the combat — it turns fighting words into speechifying, and worst of all — it induces cynicism — and if I hate anything, I hate cynicism. No, those six months were bad. And harder to bear without Alex: he, of course, had left me — he went off to live in Glasgow with a nice, quiet wee woman that worked for the corporation, and I'm sure they were very happy. He sent money for the girls — just as well, with the price of things, and Janey away tae University and Alison having to be turned out just so or she'd go to her room and cry — aye — it was just as well we got some money from him. Especially when it all came tae its inevitable conclusion, and the gates of SAM East Kilbride closed for the last time. Because we'd fought so hard, most of the folk got other work — but not all. And certainly no' me. I was out. Infamous Bessie McGuigan — her that closed down SAM — her the communist that lost all they folk their jobs — her the unemployable . . . Well, I was due a spell in the house, and I had plenty to occupy my mind, and my old accordion to squeeze a tune out of, and my father to clean up round. And the girls. Oh aye, the girls — my darling daughters —

And — I acquired a young man . . .

Scene Eight

(*Alex comes on, to make the announcement, self- conscious.*)

ALEX: Er — Scene Eight: Young Lochinvar Rides Again. The time: 1978. The Government — well — Labour. The place — my bloody house . . . (*He goes off, a bit put out.*)

(*Sandy and Alison are playing cards, noisily. Janey is trying to write an essay. Bessie is sternly reading the newspaper.*)

BESSIE: By Christ, this Labour government's gonnae get such a kick up the bum from the working people of this country one day and boy will they deserve it!

(*No reaction. The game gets noisier.*)

JANEY: How can I write my dissertation with you two sounding like World War Three?

SANDY: No, no Janey — World War Three will be completely

263

	silent. Except for the groans of the dying. It will be chemical, not nuclear, I fancy, and silent.
JANEY:	What I'm trying to say is: shut up.
ALISON:	Shut up yourself' — what's a dissertation anyway? Grandpa you're looking —
SANDY:	I deny your imputations, young lady — I was not looking, you were revealing —
BESSIE:	For God's sake! After all that UCS occupation and glorious triumph, they're closing down John Browns.
ALISON:	(*to Janey*). What is it?
JANEY:	It's a sort of long essay you do at University on some topic you're really interested in . . .
ALISON:	What's yours about? Men?
JANEY:	No.
ALISON:	What then?
BESSIE:	Would you look at that?
JANEY:	'Attribution: the Cultural expression of structural pressures towards the creation of a whipping boy caste —'
ALISON:	Whit?
JANEY:	'With special reference to gypsies in Finland 1950–1975, and coal miners in Scotland 1700–1750'. Well — you asked me.
ALISON:	And you're really interested in that?
JANEY:	Aye. It's vital.
SANDY:	Are you playing this game, Alison? Or shall we pack it in?
ALISON:	No, I want to play — I'm winning — but did you hear that rubbish Janey's writing about? She must be cuckoo — I'm no' going tae the University, they're all snobs —
JANEY:	(*angrily*). It's about why people like you need to think it's clever to be stupid — OK? So you can be ruled from on high without a murmur.

ALISON:	Oh — it's politics —
BESSIE:	(*still reading the paper*). What's all this about gypsies in Finland? How about unemployed mothers in East Kilbride? I'm getting stupefied —
JANEY:	Aye, well. It must be twenty-one years in the CP. How come you never resigned when they invaded Czechoslovakia?
BESSIE:	You probably won't remember but we protested about that — but you ultra-lefts have gae convenient memories.
SANDY:	(*to Alison*). There we are now — remember: Sevens are wild.
ALISON:	I think they're gonnae argue about politics again. (*Defiant.*) Well I'm no interested in politics, I never have been and I never will be — it's boring and pointless, and it makes people look all prim round the mouth when they discuss it, and it kills people. And it puts people out of work. And it drives away your dad . . .
BESSIE:	That wasnae politics.
ALISON:	No. It was you. And what are you but one long party political broadcast —

(*Silence.*)

I want a nice house of my own — and a nice man — with enough money to keep me at home all day playing cards with Grandpa — no arguments about politics . . . That's what I want, and I'm gonnae make sure I get it. (*Looks at cards.*) What's this? You've been going through this pack.

SANDY:	I certainly have not — A gentleman never cheats at cards —
ALISON:	This is a load of rubbish —
JANEY:	Would you keep it quiet, Alison. Even if you *are* content to be stupid, ignorant, prejudiced and unprincipled — at least try to be them quietly.
ALISON:	Away to your Anti-Nazi League Perverts Against Racism Punks Against Polytechnics Rock In — If you want to write, go to the bedroom — we want to make a noise, and we've got every right to.

BESSIE: What do you mean — you've got every right to? That's a political demand. If you don't hold with politics, how are you going to fight for your rights? How are you even gonnae say what they are?

ALISON: It's alright for your generation, you were interested in that sort of thing . . . you thought you could change things. Well we know we can't —

JANEY: Oh do we?

ALISON: You're as bad as her — wi' your Socialist Worker and going off to Lewisham to batter a policeman.

SANDY: Lewisham? Did you go to that rammy at Lewisham? (*Bessie looks at him.*) My goodness —

JANEY: Alison will you shut your face you wee clipe —

ALISON: (*to Sandy*). I'm gonnae change the lot —

SANDY: Yes. Seven it shall be . . . (*Counts them out thoughtfully.*)

(*They play on. Janey writes. Bessie stops reading, and looks at her watch. Around at the others nervously, then at her watch again. She clears her throat, but can't say anything.*)

JANEY: Anyway, Bessie went to Govan Town Hall the night the Nazis came, and she got put in jail —

BESSIE: No no — only in the van. They took us tae Pollockshaws and turned us out — so we all stood around the John Maclean memorial and sang a wee hymn, then got the bus back to Govan. (*Laughs.*) One of the boys got arrested *again*, and taken wi' about twenty others to some cop-shop, and this old constable came by in the middle of the night and said he'd never been so ashamed of the Glasgow police, and wouldn't they all like to relieve themselves in the cludgie — so they did: and here — the windae was wide open, and they all flew away — what time is it?

SANDY: Bessie — are you no' getting a bitty old for that kind of escapade?

BESSIE: No. I'm still fighting and I'm gonna carry on fighting till they count me out — the trouble wi' this bloody Labour government is it's so bland, and the alternative is so terrifying, none of us know where tae land the first punch —

JANEY:	Some of us manage to fight —
BESSIE:	Aye, yous ultra-lefts have to fight your way out of the fog of your own verbiage — I'm talking about politics, lassie, no' teenage psycho-drama.
JANEY:	Politics? D'you call holding hands wi' Tony Benn politics? When you Stalinists talk about politics in that tone of voice you either mean you're going to sell out the working class, or you're going in for some more brutality —
SANDY:	(*getting up*). You'll excuse me, Alison, I'm away to oil my leg — (*Goes.*)
BESSIE:	When has the Communist party ever sold out the working class?
JANEY:	Greece 1945, Berlin 1953, Hungary 1956, Czechoslovakia 1968, Paris 1968, Chile 1973 —
BESSIE:	You've been reading too many Trot comics —
JANEY:	You've been wasting your time in the CP —
BESSIE:	Do you think?
JANEY:	They're just as repressive and manipulative as Healy and Callighan.
BESSIE:	Janey — I've spent my life fighting for a better life for myself and the women I work with, I gave my best to that struggle, I lost my job and, aye, Alison's right, I wrecked my marriage for it. But I would not regard that as wasting my life, and I'm certainly not finished yet — not by a long way. OK?
JANEY:	Good. Well I'm fighting too, *and* I know where to land the first punch — I'm going to London to stand in front of a bus at Grunwicks, and nobody's going to stop me, right?
BESSIE:	Are you? Good. (*Pause. Bessie looks at her watch again.*) Terry's going down there next week . . .
JANEY:	Who's Terry?
BESSIE:	Oh — he's a friend of mine . . .
ALISON:	Mum — what have you been up to? You've got a guilty look on your face —
BESSIE:	I havenae —

JANEY: You have too — explain yourself —

BESSIE: Well — he's a man, that's all —

JANEY: And — ?

BESSIE: Well — I quite like him —

ALISON: You dirty beast — Can we meet him?

BESSIE: Aye —

(*Ring on door bell.*)

SANDY: (*off*). I'll get it —

BESSIE: That'll be him now —

ALISON & JANEY: Oh no!

(*They start tidying themselves up.*)

BESSIE: Would you stop? It is me he's come to see —

ALISON: Is he divorced?

BESSIE: No! He's twenty-two! (*They all shriek.*)

(*Sandy leads in Terry, a young man — previously seen as the announcer. He is very nervous as well he might be.*)

SANDY: Bessie — it's, er — this young man — has come calling on you —

(*She goes and stands beside him — links his arm.*)

BESSIE: Well now everybody: this is Terry —

(*Slow fade.*)

XI

SINGER: 'The Tamosher'
                 There were twa bonnie lassies
                 And they were dressed in blue
                 And they went out
                 Some rushes for to pu'
                 And yin o' them caught a wee thing
                 Before she did return
                 And she dandled and put it in her apron —

                 Well the first man that she met
                 Was her faither on the stair
                 'Oh daughter, dear daughter

What have you got there?
Who gave to you the Tamosher
To wear the starched gown
And you dandled it
And put it in your apron?'

'Oh was it to the baker
Or was it to the clown
Or was it to the bonnie boy
That sails the world around —
Who gave to you the Tamosher
To wear the starched gown
And you dandled it
And put it in your apron?

'It wasnae to the baker
It wasnae to the clown
It was to the bonnie boy
That sails the world around
He gave to me the Tamosher
To wear the starched gown
And I dandled it
And put it in my apron'

(Repeat verse one)

(Words and Tune: Trad)

Scene Nine

BESSIE: (*to the audience*). Things are looking up. I mean,
young Terry, well, he wasnae gonnae last forever,
but it was quite nice, while it did last. And — I got
a job, aye. I decided to fox the employers' Secret
Police — them that keep files on the militants —
and to strike a blow for women's dignity at the same
time — by reverting to my maiden name. Bessie
Gordon. I started visiting the Job Centres in Glasgow
under my rightful name, and within three weeks —
I was working. McArdles's Electronics down by the
Silvery Clyde: it's the technological version of the
sweat-shop. Four hundred women doing footery
bits of soldering all day for thirty-eight quid a week
— in 1979 — anyway, it was work.

And then: they discovered who I *really* was. Frae
the PAYE I suppose: I don't really know. I just got
summoned to the Personnel Office, and this man I'd
never seen in my life before accused me of deceiving

269

the company and making false declarations on my
application form. I said I thought I was taken on
for my skills not for my surname — that was it . . .
Exactly, he said — Exactly the tone of voice that
has brought Britain to her knees and consigned
Glasgow to the Third World. I got half an hour of
pure class hatred, then he told me he was a miner's
son frae Fife, the wee shite. But I kept my mouth
shut. Well — as much as I was able — then he
said: We are reviewing your situation. Oh no, I
said — you'll no' sack me so quick as that. He said
they would if they wanted to — in the first three
months they can suit themselves. So I went as an
ordinary member to my Union Branch Office. And
they said there was nothing they could do. Then
I got my jotters — no reason given, just: Out. So
I went to my Union Head Office: and guess who
I get to protect me? Aye — Alex. Right, says Alex
— we'll have a mass meeting of the members
at McArdle's, and we'll resolve that if they give
you the heave, we'll all come out — no problem.
And that's what's going on right now — the shop
stewards' committee requested that I was not to
be present . . . but there cannae be any problem —
though it has been going on for quite a long time
now. I'm fairly confident. But I'm getting a wee bit
nervous. I wish I could speak to them myself . . .

(*Alex comes in, looking shaken. She knows it's bad news.*)

ALEX: I cannae believe that out there . . .

BESSIE: They wouldnae support me would they?

ALEX: No by about one hundred and fifty votes to fifty.
              Two hundred abstained.

BESSIE: Abstained? Two hundred? Abstained — that's a
              good word for it. One hundred and fifty against.
              Right — are they still out there? Let me have a wee
              word with them —

ALEX: Don't Bessie — They've dispersed.

BESSIE: Aye dispersed. Abstained. These bloody words
              you're using Alex — they've spat on me, rejected
              me, and now they're away hame tae their tellies
              — the Bastards —

ALEX: Aye. You're right. But there's no good calling folk names: find the reasons for it all — fight *them*. And that's a long, boring fight, Bessie —

BESSIE: I know about long boring fights — I fought one — it cost me you.

ALEX: No. I lost you. Bessie — you must never underestimate yourself. You're a bonnie fechter, none better. I'm not — I'm a coward, at heart — but I'm trying to make it work for me . . . Know what I mean?

BESSIE: Aye. You just keep going on and on. And one day it'll turn out the union's no so right-wing as we thought . . . I know your game fine. But they — that lot — that just slunk away wi'out a murmur . . . they're still bastards —

ALEX: No. They're people who've been manipulated by the capitalist state: which is enemy number one . . .

BESSIE: Aye — but how are you going to get rid of it, without them? Don't tell me 'they'll be back' —

ALEX: Sooner than you think.

BESSIE: You're a terrible naive optimist under all that shrewd cynical pessimism, Alex McGuigan: Maybe that's what I saw in you, all those years ago . . . Poor Catriona. I think of her a lot these days, wi' her phantom pregnancies —

ALEX: Do you?

BESSIE: Well — she should have had a better life and lived longer.

ALEX: Come on. The divorce is through — I can buy you a drink.

BESSIE: Oh — your woman'll kill you . . .

ALEX: Just the one —

BESSIE: (*laughs*). Aye — that's right, just the one.

(*They go.*)

Scene Ten

SANDY: The Romans had their legions, built their baths and villas, their roads and their walls — a fine civilisation. They failed to subdue the population of Scotland —

271

nevertheless a fine civilisation. To protect it, they had their cohorts, their legions of fighting men. The Mongol emperors had their Mongol hordes — not a group of people to be taken lightly, I should say — and with their help, the Mongol emperors held sway over vast portions of the globe.

Our own empire — how was that kept in check? The Blood Red Roses — the red-coats, the English — or should I saw the British soldier, has kept order throughout the world for centuries . . . Feared, and respected by untold millions, of all colours and creeds. Enforcers of England's will.

But who now rules the world? Of whose empire are we the colonial people? Look around — we see no soldiers, no military parade with drums and fifes, bugles or bagpipes. No gun-boats, no show of strength . . . And yet there is fear — I can smell it . . . long black hulks glide underwater out of the Holy Loch, full of terrible destruction, quiet as the grave. In East Kilbride a factory closes, and a whole town discovers it is dependant on the will of the imperial power. Here, there is only fear, and silence. There is no more soldiering, no more spit and polish, no more display — the British army still sits in Germany, unable to move out — they go there to recover from pursuing phantoms in Belfast, shooting down school boys, to no purpose: not wanting to be there, dying because they cannot go away. War — it's best left to computers, they are the weapons of the new empire: a man does not need to be a man any more — the fight is inside our heads: all we need is will-power, and clear thinking, and the determination to refuse to comply. If I was a soldier now — and we are all soldiers now — those would be my weapons. I would not need legs.

(*He goes off.*)

Scene Eleven

ANNOUNCER: Scene Eleven: Where you Went Wrong was . . . The Year: 1979. The Government: Well — Labour, but a New Dawn is about to break over the charred industrial battlefield that is Britain: the corpses of our empty factories and yards will be brought back to life; the wounded — the unemployed and the

youth — will be tended with healing care; and a new
pride and confidence will burn in our breasts — for
there is about to be an election: now is the Winter
of our Discontent to be made glorious summer by
Sir Keith Joseph . . .

(*Sound: cheering on telly.*)

(*In the McGuigan sitting room, about one in the morning, Alison and Bessie
are watching the results come in.*)

BESSIE:	Turn it off, I've seen it all.
ALISON:	It's interesting.
BESSIE:	No quick, here comes that self-satisfied bastard wi' his swingometer — aye, we know, a twelve and a half per cent swing to the Tories — that should be enough to win Stevenage and bring back the cat o' nine tails — OFF! (*Silence.*) Oh Christ. What have the people of Britain let happen to them?
ALISON:	It's quite understandable. I mean, look at the mess everything's in. Strikes all the time. Inflation. The country going bankrupt.
BESSIE:	Oh aye — where do you get all that story from?
ALISON:	It's obvious — it's the Trades Unions taking control of the country. Not even the unions — it's these militants, they're wrecking industry —
BESSIE:	What?
ALISON:	Aye — see that Any Questions we had after school last week with the Headmaster and the Provost and a man from the *Glasgow Herald* and a Trades Union official — It was quite obvious who was right and who was wrong — to my mind anyway.
BESSIE:	And they said it was the militants who'd wrecked industry and that the Trades Unions were running the country?
ALISON:	Well no' exactly, but — well — you could see.
BESSIE:	Listen — I *am* what you call a militant —
ALISON:	I know: they mentioned you — how you'd given the whole place a bad name and driven away the investors —
BESSIE:	Did they say how I'd been victimised, how I've

273

no been able to get a job for two years. And what happened when I did get one?

ALISON: No. I don't think that's fair. Well — from their point of view it is, but from yours it's terrible — from mine too.

BESSIE: Never mind! Now we've got the Tories, there'll be no more jobs anyway —

(*Janey comes in from the street. Utterly despondent.*)

JANEY: I cannae believe that out there. Have you seen?

BESSIE: Aye. It's pretty definite. What did your boy get?

JANEY: Don't. (*Laughs.*) One hundred and two votes. He had more people campaigning for him than voting for him . . .

BESSIE: Oor Wullie got 403 — including two wee punks who thought it was a concert . . . The New Wave hits the CP.

JANEY: Aye well . . . It'll have washed over it —

BESSIE: We're all in it now — up to our necks. I just hope we can all work together for a change. This woman's off her heid. The John Knox of monetarism — And that Keith bloody Joseph, he shouldnae be let out . . . But if it's any consolation — it's no' the first time the working class have been taken in by Tory promises —

JANEY: It's a disaster.

ALISON: It's the English, that's what it looks like to me . . .

BESSIE: No. It's the erosion of class consciousness, if you want to know. Working people in England and quite a few in Scotland see their own, individual interest — less income tax for some, buy your own council house for quite a few, and the price of a loaf of bread for millions — but they don't see themselves as part of a class, that must stick together . . . they've been driven into their own private cosy selfish fantasy-world, and now they're gonnae suffer for it. Because the others know they're a class, and they'll stick together until the day we drive them out.

JANEY: Shall we turn on the telly, see what's happened?

BESSIE: No. Sell it. That's what's done it as much as anything

— the private fantasy-machine. Robert MacKenzie and his swingometer, Robin Day and his fearless questions —

JANEY: Well they do tell you the results.

BESSIE: No. We *know* the results. (*laughs*) But I'll tell you a wee secret. I've had some results too. The most positive ones this year — I'm pregnant . . .

JANEY: Mum!

ALISON: Oh that's lovely . . .

BESSIE: Good eh? I thought we'd better have something to cheer us up.

JANEY: But — is it Terry?

BESSIE: Aye — nice wee Terry —

JANEY: (*worried*). But —

BESSIE: I know, I know. He's working at Sullom Voe, and as far as I know he'll no' be coming back — that's OK. We can manage — do you no' think?

ALISON: Aye — I think it's great.

JANEY: What about Dad?

ALISON: He's OK — he's probably having a baby too —

BESSIE: Alex will understand . . . He knows me quite well. I'd like him back, but he'll no' come back now . . .

JANEY: Well — it's your life —

BESSIE: No — it's his: or hers — Fight on, eh?

(*Crossfade to singer.*)

XII

SINGER: Now that is our story
A tale that goes on
Is it true or a lie or a fiction?
Is it right or mistaken the story we tell:
Is it fit to be tellt tae your children?

(*Fade.*)

END

Joe's Drum

Original programme note

JOE'S DRUM was written in April and May 1979 as a direct response to two major events: in March, a majority of those voting in Scotland voted for a Scottish Assembly, but due to 'arrangements' made in Westminster, they did not get a Scottish Assembly. In May, at the General Election, a tiny *majority* in SCotland voted for the Conservatives, and, due to events south of the Border, they *did* get a Tory government. At the same election, the vote for an ever-more-Right-leaning Scottish National Party was dramatically reduced, and the SNP seemed destined to a massive decline.

These events came at a time of confusion and apathy in Scottish politics, and yawning tedium in Scottish cultural life. The younger generation of students seemed just not interested in politics, and the young marrieds of all classes seemed content to scrape together their own pile of consumer goods and cosiness, to the exclusion of any involvement in public life. Within the working class organisations, many of the unions had recently elected right-wing leaders, and the TUC in London seemed content to follow a line that must have satisfied the CIA. The political groups of the far left got less support in the election than the National Front, and the Labour Party under Callaghan was distinguishable from the Conservatives only by being marginally less rhetorical in its pursuit of a smoother-running capitalist economy. And the inflation that had changed all our lives seemed to be caused by factors way beyond our control.

The overall effect of these events and feelings was to give the individual person, at work and at home, the impression that she or he was powerless to affect any decisions or even to be involved in any decisions. There was a dangerous bored fatalism in the air, an uncharacteristic passivity, that amounted almost to acceptance of defeat.

In these circumstances JOE'S DRUM was both an expression of anger and frustration, and a tocsin to alert the audiences to the full monstrosity of what was going on. In performance, it clearly aroused many echoes, and seemed to say what a lot of Scots wanted to hear in 1979. It is to be hoped that the drum will go on beating into the '80s, to waken us from our curious hibernation.

John McGrath

Note: Several of the songs used in the play were written by Nick Keir and John Wilson of Finn MacCuill, and Embro Embro by Lewis Spence with music by Ed Miller. To them, and to the company who contributed so much to the show, my deepest thanks.

Joe's Drum by John McGrath, Music by Finn Maccuill. First performed in Aberdeen Arts Centre 21 May 1979 with the following company:

NADIA ARTHUR	Costume Design, Wardrobe
JIMMY CHISHOLM	Duke of Hamilton, Robert Dundas, Robert Hamilton
TONY IRELAND	Guitar, Vocals
JIM IRVING	Lighting
BILLY JOHNSTONE	Tour Manager
JOANNA KEDDIE	Jeannie
NICK KEIR	Whistles, Mandoline, Vocals, Guitar
JOHN McGRATH	Writer, Director
PEIGI MACKENZIE	Stage Manager
DOLINA MACLENNAN	Publicity
CAMPBELL MORRISON	Director
SANDY NEILSON	Fletcher of Saltoun, Thomas Muir
ANNIE RUBIENSKA	Administrator
BILLY RIDDOCH	General Joe Smith
IAN SOMERVILLE	Lighting Design
JOHN WILSON	Bass, Vocals

Thanks to:
Archie Fisher, Ed Miller, Kenneth Logue, Hamish Henderson, Bob Tait, Bob Marshall, Liz Maclennan.

ACT ONE

Opening: set of reels from the band. At the end of set, the house lights are down and the audience in. One of the band introduces the show.

SINGER: Hello, and welcome to the show. It's called Joe's Drum, and it's about a man called Joe Smith who really lived — in the 1700s, and who really did get up to some of the amazing things that you'll hear about. He lived in Edinburgh. And contrary to what they think in Glasgow, Edinburgh is a working-class city. And the working-class of Edinburgh has a history as proud as any, and it goes back a long way.

SONG: 'Embro, Embro'

If a' the blood shed at thy Tron
Embro Embro
Were shed intae a river
T'would ca' the mills o' Bonnington
Embro Embro
T'would ca' the mills o' Bonnington
For ever and ever

If a' the psalms sung in thy kirks
Embro Embro
Were gaithered in a wind
T'would shake the taps o' Rosslyn birks
Embro Embro
T'would shake the taps o' Rosslyn birks
Till time was oot o' mind

If a' the broken herts o' thee
Embro Embro
Were heapit in a howe
There would be neither land nor sea
Embro Embro
There would be neither land nor sea
But yon red brae and thou

If a' the tears that thou has shed
Embro Embro
Were shed intae the sea
Whaur wud ye find an Ararat
Embro Embro
Whaur wud ye find an Ararat
Frae that fell flood tae flee

(music Ed Miller, lyric 'Capernaum' by Lewis Spence)

(*At end of SONG, a drum beat outside the door, JEANNIE comes rushing onto the stage.*)

281

JEANNIE: Is that a drum? Oh no! It's my man — Would you
             listen to that?

(*She runs through audience to the door, opens it.* JOE SMITH *comes in, beating
his drum. She follows him, five paces behind, down the hall, onto the stage,
and round the stage until he stops and speaks to the audience.*)

JOE: My name is Joe Smith (*drum*)
             General Joe Smith I'm cried in Embro (*drum*)
             I'm a puir cobbler to trade,
             and I stay in the Cowgate — (*drum*)
             And I'm angry. (*Silence*)
             And by — when I'm angry — I beat my drum (*big
             drum beat*)

             I've been deid and cauld in the earth two hundred
             year, and I've slept in my grave through mony's
             the disaster — aye — through Napoleon's wars
             and the Kaiser's wars and Hitler's wars too. But
             the thunderous apathy of the devolution vote has
             finally roused me from the sleep of the just — Ye
             had yer chance to beat yer ain drum — And what
             did you dae? Oh, I'll tell you what you did — Oh
             I've been watchin ye — 'What me?' ye'll be saying,
             'Ah've done naethin', Wisnae me.' Aye right, that'll
             be correct. *Naethin'* ye've done *naethin'*.

             And what's happened to Scotland while ye were
             dain' naethin'? It's crumbled awa' — Wi' ancient
             slum-dwellin's worse nor the worst in Europe,
             worse nor Naples, worse nor Barcelona — aye, and
             brand new council houses that are worse nor the
             slums — Aye, I've seen ye — dain' naethin'.
             So where is Scotland noo?

             What have yae let happen tae it?

(*Goes and peers at the audience.*)

             From the look of ye — well maist of ye — ye're the
             common cry — ye're what the ancient Greeks used
             to call the Hoi Poloi — or what the politicians call
             the Great Unwashed — ye're what I'd call the Mob.

             And if you are entitled, if you are *qualified*, to belong
             to a guid auld Scottish Mob — then you have a
             responsibility: and in my day, every man, woman
             and child took their responsibility seriously.

(*Beats drum.*)

             A puir wife and her bairns livin' snug in the Pleasance,

while her man was away: along came the landlord
and flung them out in the street for no' payin' the
rent and he roupit her furniture, every stick of it:
what does the puir man dae when he comes hame
to find his woman and his pretty ones oot in the
weather? He gangs tae a stable wi' a rope and he
hangs himsel'! What does that say to you? or to
you? I'll tell you what it says tae *me* . . .

I've a responsibility. I wheeks on my drum, and I
beat it up the Cowgate and I beat it down the West
Bow and I beat it along the Grassmarket, and wha
hears it? Your great-great- grandfather hears it, aye
— and my drum says to him: you've a responsibility
— so he shifts himsel'.

Three four thoosan' of us noo, following the drum tae
Thomson's Park, and up I gets on tae the shoulders
o' six o' my lieutenant generals an' I tells them:
'It's no right. Yon landlord's as good as killed the
puir man, and turned oot his wife and bairns to
perish in the cauld — what'll ye dae? Will ye see
some justice? Will ye take it wi' yer ain hands, or
will ye let it go by?'

(*To audience, individuals.*) What would you have
done? What would you do? Eh? What do you think,
eh, my friends? You couldnae go tae the Police —
the Town Guard were mair corrupt and useless than
your police are today. And don't think you could
take him tae court — because the judges, and the
landlords, just like they are today . . . (*links fingers*).
What did we dae? We took some responsibility!

(*Beats drum.*)

We took every article he had in his house. We built
a pyre in the street with his ill-gotten goods. And
if he hadnae slipped awa' like an eel into the tide,
we'd hae pit himsel' on top o' it.

(*Tune in.*)

And wi' this hand I set a light tae it, and up it went.
And for half an hour we danced around it, singing
and laughin', and up starts the music and on we
go, three four thoosan' of us, dancin' and singin'
and laughin' for joy. (*Tune on and then ends.*)

Aye, in my day, if you were a human bein' at a',

283

you took your responsibility to your fellow-man
upon your shoulders, you walked down the street
wi' it, and if a man was to be hangit or whippit or
pilloried, you went alang wi' your responsibility
tae see it done. But noo?

It's a' hidden awa' If a man's done an evil thing,
ye put him behind a high wall and ye forget aboot
him. Let some other chiel attend to him. (*Beats
drum.*) Ye think ye can buy people tae punish yer
evil-doers, buy people tae police yer streets, buy
people tae tak responsibility fer yer bairns, people
tae govern ye, tae think fer ye: so's ye can sit and
watch telly wi'oot another thocht in yer heids. Well
I'm angry. And I'm angry wi' *you* lot. Who am *I* to
be angry? I'm General Joe Smith frae the Cowgate,
and I'm a man that speaks my mind.

(*Whistles. JEANNIE comes up beside him.*)

That's the wife, Jeannie.

(*To her.*) Tell them Jeannie — tell them who I am —

(*To audience.*) I'll be back.

(*He goes off, not beating his drum.*)

JEANNIE: Oh aye, he's a man that speaks his mind. As for
me — I'm a woman, and a woman's a second-rate,
unco' stupit class o' creature, accordin' tae him —
so I'm the one that has tae walk alang five steps
behind him catchin' his farts — aye — an' when
he wants to speak his mind in my direction, ye'll
hear him whistle me up like a cowerin' collie dug,
to hear his wards o' wisdom. And when he's had
his say, I'm to drap back again, in case awbody sees
me walkin' up alangsides o' him. 'General Joe'?

He's a *cobbler* — no' even a shoe-maker —

(*Re-enter JOE.*)

JOE: The Riots, wumman, the Riots! Set the scene for
my moment of glory!

JEANNIE: Aye, I will — away ye go. (*JOE goes.*)

Aye, well it all began, as usual wi' the English. An' jist like
aethin' since, at the root of it was the Union wi' England
in Seventeen hundred an' seven, the year I was born.

(*JOE re-appears.*)

JOE: 1707! Wull ye' no' go sae faur back wumman, ye'll never get tae the Riots afore the pubs shut!

JEANNIE: I will, I will — but they're gae fond o' the Act of Union (*To audience.*) Are ye no'?

(*Back to him.*) And they *love* to hear aboot it — don't ye? Whaur wid ye be withoot it?
(*To JOE.*) Away you, and put on yer breeks while I speak to the folk here aboot the union wi' England —

He's a guid man, that, a' the same. He's never the once gi'en me a dunt in the face — a kick in the ribs, maybe, but not where it shows, ken. That's what I call a thoughtful husband. Where was I? Och aye — the English — We werenae very fond o' the English at that time, no. They'd no' exactly come oot and gi'en us a dunt in the face, but I'm tellin' ye, they'd gi'en us a few kicks in the wame afore they bought us into their Union . . . Here's a wee song aboot one o' their tricks, will ye hear it? It's a sad yin —

SONG: 'Darien'

Now Scotland was a pedlar-man
He tramped from door to door
He cried his wares at the market fairs
Till he could cry no more:
Oh, will ye buy? But they passed him by
For his goods were old and thin:
And the English mocked his misery
Not a door would let him in.

Now the King of Spain has an Empire ta'en
In far-off Mexico
There's silver, gold, aye there's wealth untold
If o'er the seas ye'll go —
So the pedlar man he arranged his plan
For to sail across the sea —
And the English mocked his desperate bid
Ye'll no' find your Liberty.

On the morning tide sailed old Scotland's pride
Six hundred bold young men
As their mothers sighed, cross the ocean wide
They sailed to Darien
But the fevers raged, would not be assuaged
And we wished we'd never been born
To Jamaica we had to send away

285

For medicine and corn —

Now Jamaica was a colony
Of England's cruel brood
And the English laughed and gave to them
Nor medicine nor food:
So back they sailed to certain death
Back sailed those brave young men —
And soon we heard that one and all
Had died in Darien.

JOE: Dae ye ken what we did in Embro when we heard that news? We had a riot. Oh aye, it was our responsibility, d'ye see. I was nae there mysel', no' bein' born at the time, but my faither and my grandfaither were livin' in Niddry's Close, so they were oot on the street when the word came back frae Darien. My faither was apprehended by the Town Guard for beatin' his drum, thereby causing a riot. Noo they put him in the pillory and he was to be whippit alangsides of a handful of other riotous worthies frae the Mob, the following Friday. Well — that day, alang comes the hangman, wi' his whip in his fist and what does he see? There, in the pillory, the prisoners, garlanded wi' floors, and each man wi' a present of a bottle o' wine. And standin' all around, six thoosand of the common cry, waitin' tae see wad he harm them. Silent as the grave. And there, lookin' at him, the magistrates of the town, come to see the punishment writ in letters of blood on the bare backs of my faither and the floral prisoners.

Up comes the whip — and down like a feather from the breist o' a doo. Not a mark on the flesh of a single hero. The mob is smilin' but the magistrates is glowerin', and they send in a rage for the Haddington executioner, tae flagellate the flagellator, to scourge the unwilling hangman — But when he came the next day, we were there afore him: to supervise: and he took a glance at the six thousand, and a glance at the magistrates, and skippit off up a close and away' hame tae Haddington.

(*To audience*.) Were we right, do you think? Or are *you* on the side of Law and Order? What would *you* have done my friends? (*Music in.*) We had a night o' it, tae celebrate —

(*Music.*) 'Fisherrow'

286

As I came in by Fisherrow
Musselburgh was near me:
I threw off my musslepock
And courted wi' my dearie.
Upstairs, downstairs, timberstairs fears me,
I thought it lang to lie my lane, when I'm sae near
    my dearie.

Oh had my apron bidden down,
The kirk wad ne'er hae kent it,
But since the word's gane thro' the toun,
I fear I canna mend it.
Upstairs, downstairs, timberstairs fears me,
I thought it lang to lie my lane, when I'm say near
    my dearie.

But I maun mount the cutty-stool
And he maun mount the pillar,
And that's the way that poor folks do,
Because they hae nae siller.
Upstairs, downstairs, timberstairs fears me.
I thought it lang to lie my lane, when I'm sae near
    my dearie.

(*Then musical change into: 'Union Song'*)

JOE: The one thing we couldnae prevent: The Union wi'
England. Oh don't think we didnae take up our
responsibilities — oh aye we did. We turned over
Lord Seafield's carriage for him, we set about the
corrupt Lords of Scotland, the bought-up Dukes
of Argyll and Queensberry, the purchased Earls o'
Marchmont, Eglinton, Glencairn, Cromarty and
Sutherland — Aye, and the cheaper-to-come-by
common or garden Lords of the realm, like the guid
Lord Banff, whose vote cost the English treasury
the mighty sum of eleven pounds two shillings . . .
Aye we knew our responsibilities. We 'set about' the
buggers, but we had nae gowd nor siller tae change
their minds wi'. (*Music ends.*) And just the one man
we had tae lead us was a puir glakit creature who
was feart o' his mammy — aye — wi' a leader like
him, we'd nae necessity for enemies: here he is noo
— the noble Duke o' Hamilton — I'll let him talk
to you, but only so ye can see for yersel's how the
Union wi' England cam by, and how for that true
reason the people of Scotland were betrayed then,
and for that very same reason are betrayed today
— Tak tent noo, for he's a canny wee Dukie.

DUKE OF	
HAMILTON:	Well I'm a patriot.

My heart beats firmly in my breast for Scotland.
Argyll, Queensberry, Seafield, they're all traitors
— of course I can't say that too loudly, because
we've all got lodgings in the same building — Palace
of Holyrood House, actually, we're all stuck in it
together, the Campbell's bed-chamber looks straight
into my dining-room, and I've got Breadalbane
above me and Queensberry below — it's a dashed
difficult situation when you're trying to have them
all hanged, but then that's politics, I suppose. To
tell you the truth, I find the Campbells absolutely
terrifying. I believe you will be familiar with an
organisation in Sicily called the Mafia. I'm told their
methods are remarkably similar to those of the
Campbells, except that the Campbells are strictly
legal. Of course the English spend their time bum-
licking the Campbells, and the Campbells will do
anything the English want. At a price.

But they will not succeed. Not while my quicksilver
brain is darting hither and yon through their every
trick and turn. I've a trick or two of my own,
I can tell you. This Act of Union with England;
the Duke of Argyll's come back from the wars
in Flanders to bully the Scots Parliament into
submitting to it. Not before they'd made him a
Major-General, and promised to make him Duke
of Dover, and slipped him a cool five thousand
pounds as a personal bribe — *and* discovered a
soft job for his brother Archie. Never mind about
that. He's not going to get his Union with England;
I have other plans in mind. Look at it this way.
The monarch of Scotland — at the moment —
is also the monarch of England — good Queen
Anne. But she's failed to produce an heir — I
can't say she hasn't tried, sixteen brats and not
one of them survived, but that's neither here nor
there. When she dies, the English want some wee
German lairdie from Hanover to be their King. All
well and good. But do we? No — we don't. The
Scottish people want a Scottish King — like myself.
So when she dies, Scotland won't have a King. As
for the Stuarts — well, they've been kicked out
twice already for being hard-line Papists. No. A
Presbyterian people need a Presbyterian King —
like myself.

So I think I'm in with a very good chance. Sh! I'm playing a very crafty game.

The Highlanders and the Cameronian fanatics from Galloway and the mob from Glasgow and the mob from Edinburgh were all set to sink their differences, march into Edinburgh and overturn the parliament. Well, I let them get on with their little scheme until the very last minute, then I thought: Well who stands to gain? Certainly not me. Not one of them was singing a song saying that *I* was their rightful king. And then I thought What if they fail . . . I mean, the English had thousands of troops massing at Berwick and at Carlisle, and thousands more in Belfast and Flanders, all ready to embark for Scotland — Who'd be for the long walk up the ladder and the short drop down? Yours truly. Nothing to gain, everything to lose. I sent them all a message, calling the whole thing off.

I had an idea. I thought all those against the Union should just walk out of the parliament, that would cause them no end of delay and worry. It was all organised. But when the day came to do it, I woke up with a terrible toothache. It was this one (*tongue in cheek*) one of my wisdom teeth, you know what I mean. So they didn't walk out — just because I wasn't there — what a pack of weaklings, I ask you.

Now I'm not too sure of the next step. The mob give me such cheers when I drive through the streets. I think they put an awful lot of trust in me, and I *do* want to do the right thing. I'll do anything to be King of Scotland . . . and I should be. I really should. But the big question is, what to do? Oh dear. All those people trusting me . . . I find it quite oppressive. I'm sure I'll think of something — I mean, that is politics.

(*Exit HAMILTON.*)

JOE: Aye — that was our noble chieftain, that —

JEANNIE: (*interrupting*). He couldnae help the way he was brought up.

JOE: But ye see, politicians is a' the same: they are a' oot for theirsel's, if they're no' bought wi' money, they're aye bought wi' dreams o' place and power —

JEANNIE: No. Not all o' them —

289

JOE: Wad ye remember we're in public, woman, and stop interrupting me —

JEANNIE: Well — ye were speakin' stupit: there's aye one or two that mean what they say —

JOE: (*looks around*). Whereabouts? I've never seen a politician that means what he says. (*To audience.*) Have you ever seen a politician that means what he says?

JEANNIE: (*angry*). Well ye're going to see one noo — This is the man, Fletcher, Laird o' Saltoun — he's a man o' the people —

(*Enter FLETCHER.*)

FLETCHER: No, I'm no' a man o' the people, ye'll understand, but I appear to be the people's man. Or at least I was, in this matter of the Union, in the late Parliament of Scotland. I'm telling you now, I stood firm against it. And so did they — and I spoke for them. And I've came here tae tell ye, that if ye're thinking they were just a galraviching mob o' Ganders wi' no' a thought in their heids nor an ounce of reason in their drunken riots — you're wrong. I had good strong reasons of statecraft, and the future prosperity and happiness of Scotland in my mind when I spoke against this Union: and so had they.

They *knew* they were bein' cheated. One small nation was forced under threat of armed invasion tae join with another larger nation lying next to it. They knew from common observation that sik a thing could only be for the benefit of the larger nation. So don't go away thinkin' they were just stupid — or Calvinists — or Jacobites. They were speakin wi' reason.

(*Turns to go, JOE and JEANNIE have been watching.*)

JEANNIE: Tell them what ye said.

FLETCHER: What I said?

JEANNIE: In the Parliament.

FLETCHER: Would they listen, do you think?

JEANNIE: (*to audience*). He spoke for us, this yin — will ye hear what he said?

Well, tae set the scene: the auld Scots Parliament
was debatin' whether tae dismiss theirsels for ever;
half of them were bribed wi' money frae the English
Parliament, put aroon on the sly by the Duke o'
Queensberry: he's the Duke of Buccleuch and
Queensberry noo, and he owns mair acres than any
man in the land: oh aye, they did well they folk.
There they were, all waitin' tae vote Scotland doon
the dunnie. And then up jumps himself, Fletcher
of Saltoun, and he spoke for us all:

FLETCHER: My Lord Chancellor, I beg your indulgence for my
late arrival. I have met with an accident on my
journey here. But it is as nothing to the calamity I
find on my arrival. I have a poor memory, my Lord,
yet even I can recall that but two years ago there
were not ten men to be found in this house, no —
in the whole of Scotland — to support a complete
incorporating union with England. Today I hear loud,
indeed overwhelming murmurs of sanctimonious
approval for a hypocritical speech for just such a
union. Have I come into a tailor's shop, where so
many coats are turned in so short a time?

What has intervened? Nothing — save that the
English Ministers, that have ruled us by indirect
means since the Union of the Crowns, have now
concluded they must now rule us completely and
directly — in fact, they have concluded Scotland
must be removed from the geography of the world,
and North Britain be the designation of a nation,
a people, a tradition once free, self-governing and
in control of its own destiny.

They have decided that, and — let it come as no
surprise — suddenly that is what our Queen most
earnestly desires us to accept. And her Scottish
Ministers who sit here before us on thrones and
carved chairs beseech us to obey. More, they oblige
us to obey, if we will improve our personal fortunes.

I do not speak, my Lord, as one who desires to
replace one Monarch now living in London with
another now living in France. There are some who
are so absurd as to believe this country must be
made a field of blood in order to advance a Papist
to the throne of Great Britain. No. If we may live
free, I little value who is King. It is indifferent to
me, provided this parliament is free, to name or not

291

name Hanover, Stuart, or whom you will. Therefore I argue no lost causes, my Lord. I argue the freedom of the Scots parliament — not the Ministers, who frequently mistake bad former practice for good precedent.

Our parliament is not perfect. We must improve it, set our constitution to rights, and restore our trade by reaching some understanding with England to our mutual benefit.

It was for that purpose, and that alone, that we despatched our Commissioners to London. Could we then — not ten months ago — have believed what they have achieved? Are we not here, by right of our just demands on the Monarch that we should make the laws of Scotland, we, the people of Scotland? If we propose to abandon this duty to others, do we not cease to be Representatives of Scotland? Those commissioners who went to England to make a trading settlement, and who came back with a plan to end our Parliament and our Nation — are they not guilty of High Treason? Are we not all, merely to consider it, guilty of High Treason?

JEANNIE:

Oh and they yelled and shouted at him — they telt him tae apologise or they'd throw him oot —

FLETCHER:

I must not lose my vote, therefore I must apologise, which I do, most humbly, for having caused concern in the breasts of so many in this noble parliament, which I respect above all other institutions.

I have much to say about the effects on our trade of abandoning our border and our safeguards against the merchants of England, but it is well known that my view is this: that we have long been held back by our dependence on England in this matter, and that were we, in our wisdom, to pursue a more, not less, independent policy, we should grow in the health of our industries, the improvement of our agriculture, and the strength of our export to the rest of the world.

If we are to be protected by forty-five Scottish members in an House of Commons full of Englishmen, we shall improve but slowly, and always follow behind the greater power of England.

If this treaty be approved by us, I shall leave all

my concern with politics, for I shall know that government is but a puppet show, to please the onlookers — and I for one am not for playing the marionette.

But that must not be. My Lord, all nations are dependent, the one on the many, this we know. But if the greater must always swallow the lesser, and so become greater yet, such a logic is unleashed on the world as will end in . . . I know not what.

We are Scotsmen. Let us set our country in order, and flourish, and add our own, independent, weight to the world.

(*He goes off, JEANNIE comes forward quietly.*)

JEANNIE: And they lost the vote.

And he walked oot the door, and hame tae Saltoun, and he worked his land and never spoke in public again. And the world was the worse for it.

Aye, oor Parliament took their vote, and twenty thousand pound of English gold, and the fear of the English Army, and the greed of the merchants for to have England and its Empire to sell their goods in, all went crashing down on the one side of the scale:

JOE: CRACK! And the puir wee Duke of Hamilton went skitin' up in the air off the other side — and with him went Scotland. Aye, it was no jist the stinkin' Parliament of lords and merchants that went away that day. It was the power to fight for oorsels, to think for oorsels, to be oorsels, that went away that day.

JEANNIE: Och, we chased the buggers doon the High Street, and smashed a few windaes that night I'm tellin' you — but the deed was done —

JOE: Put not your trust in Princes.

JEANNIE: Aye — well, nae mair we will —

JOE: Neither in Scottish Dukies —

JEANNIE: Nor in German Lairdies —

JOE: Nor the Bonnie Prince Charlies.

JEANNIE: Ever since that day, we've had tae mak oor ain way —

JOE: The best we can.

SONG: 'Farewell to a' oor Scottish fame'

Fareweel to a' our Scottish fame
Fareweel our ancient glory
Fareweel even to the Scottish name
Sae fam'd in martial story!

Now Sark rins o'er the Solway sands
And Tweed rins to the ocean,
To mark where England's province stands,
Such a parcel of rogues in a nation.

O would, or I had seen the day
That treason thus could sell us
My auld grey head had lien in clay
Wi' BRUCE and loyal WALLACE!
But pith and power, till my last hour,
I'll mak this declaration;
We're bought and sold for English gold
Such a parcel of rogues in a nation!

(*Music continues*.)

JOE: So I grew up to be a man when the rulers of Scotland sat in a foreign land, mair nor seven days journey to the South, and the King of us all could speak neither Scots nor English, and he never even came to Scotland in the whole of his life. But he wanted oor siller to build himself a palace, and the English Parliament wanted oor siller as well — so they tried to tax us. Oh aye — they tried.

But they tell me these days, when they want your money, they tak it away before ye even get it in your pouch. Ye say nothin', ye dae naethin', ye jist pay up. But it wadnae dae for me, no, we had a strange feeling o' 'responsibility' when it cam to paying taxes tae a foreign government.

(*Music in*.)

CHORUS: There never were such taxes,
I'll tell ye it's a fact
They're laying on us burthens that
would break your back
Unless we join together, and see what we can do
They'll tax us for the very air we're breathing

The King and Lords of England had a party

it was grand
There were mealie pudding suppers and
　a six piece band
Ah but who will pay the reckoning
　for the brandy and the wine
Ye'll find out when ye go to pay your taxes

There's taxes laid on beer and ale
　and worst of all on bried
On corn and malt and, very soon,
　on potted heid.
But if the poor folk can't buy food,
They're gaun tae end up deid;
And then who's gaun tae pay
　their English taxes?

If the English King wants soldiers
　or a trumpet and a drum
Or just a velvet cushion on which to rest his bum
Or if he wants a Scottish laird to turn
　and stab his chum
Ye'll find the bribe is paid by Scottish taxes

JOE:　　　　　Aye — we couldnae be fashed wi' taxes, and that
was that.

So the English tried to gather in oor siller wi' the
Excise duty, on wine and brandy and a' that frae
o'er the sea — but they were no' gatherin' oor siller
quite quick enough, for the smugglin' is a trade
that flourishes when the Excise duty goes up, and
declines when the duty goes down. Frae this, any
intelligent person could see that the only way tae
put an end tae smugglers is tae abolish Excise duty
a' thegither. But the English were nae sufficiently
intelligent. They aye suffered frae a lack o' that
kind o' intelligence. Whit did they dae? They sent
for mair Excise-men, English Excise-men, wi' cold
piercin' eyes, and drippin' red noses, and an unco
sma' sense o' humour. And one fine night they
apprehended a couple o' bonnie lads in Fife —
Andrew Wilson and Geordie Robertson — and the
Edinburgh magistrates said they must be hangit in
the Grassmarket. Noo these two smugglers had a
plan. They asked tae go tae the Kirk, for tae pray —
and when they were there, Andra starts tae struggle
wi' the guard, and Geordie's guard runs tae help,
leavin' Geordie unattended — an Geordie skippit
awa' and never was seen again. Noo the feeling

295

in the toon was that a man who would create a
diversion so his friend could escape the gallows,
but stay tae face it himself was a hero — a selfless,
noble person — and was in no way fit to be hanged.

(*To audience.*) Would ye agree wi' that? Ye would
— no? I mean tae say, he was only a *smuggler*: it
was only the English, wantin' their Excise Duty,
that he'd done any harm to — Ye'd surely no' stand
and watch them hurdle him through the streets
tae the gibbet?

Ye would hae come wi' us tae set him free? Ah?

Ye would — aye — well more 'n likely ye would
have been shot. Deid. Because Black Jock Porteous
wis the captain o' the Town Guard, taking Andrew
Wilson tae the gibbet: when we intervened in the
name o' natural justice, he ordered his men to fire
right intae the mob; tae fire tae kill. And they did.
Six people they killed.

So if you'd come, that could have been you. And
they hang'd the noble Wilson.

And puir Jockie Porteous? The magistrates put him
in jail, and said, they'd hang Black Jock as well,
for murder. But we heard they were planning tae
kinda let him slip awa' ye see, and that was no
right. (*Drum.*) If Black Jock Porteous was tae hang
oor hero fur the crime o' no payin' Excise duties;
then we wad hang Black Jock fur murderin' six
innocent people o' Edinburgh — (*Drum*).

And we broke intae a rope-makers in the West
Bow, and we took a stout length of rope — leaving
one guinea in full and just payment (*Drum*).

And we took Jock Porteous tae the Grassmarket
and hang'd him oorsels — very quiet and orderly
— (*Drum*).

(*To audience.*) Would you hae done that?

JEANNIE: They've stopped a' this hangin' folk an' whippin'
an' sickerlike cruelty, and quite right too —

JOE: No — Yon wee mannikie cried Nicholas Fairburn
wants tae bring it a' back again: a right fanatical
sectarian that yin — what I'm sayin' is — wad he
dae it wi' his ain hands, like we did? Would *they*?

JEANNIE: Ach, times have changed since oor day — they're no' savages, like we were —

JOE: Maybe no'. But they'll vote for savages.

JEANNIE: Aye — some o' them will. Maist o' them will nae. They've got their different way o' doin' things.

JOE: Aye, so they have. Democracy, they cry it; where 33 per cent of the Scottish people vote for an Assembly and don't get it, and 35 per cent vote for a Tory government and they do get it.

     Their Parliament was no' very pleased wi' us for hangin' Jockie Porteous. There was a Commission of Enquiry. But when their Commission enquired: naebody saw naethin'. But we had tae let them understand . . . the common cry o' Scotland have a voice. (*Drum.*)

JEANNIE: And a will. (*Drum.*)

JOE: And will act. (*Drum.*)
     And naebody makes monkeys oot o' us —

     (*To audience.*) Is aebody making monkeys oot o' you? (*Looks at audience, beats his drum and goes off beating it. JEANNIE follows.*)

The next sequence is in the form of a kitchen opera, with minimal demonstrated action, and formal song presentation. Enter three singers downstage: they sing, unaccompanied.

SINGER 1:   Did ye hear aboot the price o' meal?

SINGER 2:   Did ye hear aboot the price o' meal?

SINGER 3:   Did ye hear aboot the price o' meal?

ALL: What are we goin' tae dae?

MERCHANT (1):   (*sings*). My granary is full of meal
And corn and barley too
And if you'll pay my price, my friends,
There's lots for all of you.

     But if you can't afford to buy
I'll have to bar my door
And ship it off to Newcastle
For they're offering sixpence more . . .

JEANNIE: A shillin' a peck, och it's terrible dear

297

> And they're wantin' some more very soon so I
> hear —
> The bairns'll be hungry the rest o' the year —
> What are we gaun tae dae?

(*Enter JOE, sings.*)

> His granary is full of meal
> And corn and barley too
> And if we pay what we can pay
> There's lots for all of you
> But if he won't accept our price
> Then why should we pay more,
> We'll take an axe and with this hand
> I'll burst that merchant's door —

SINGERS &
JEANNIE:

> Well, we knocked at the door of the oatmeal shop
> We sent in and asked for the prices to drop
> The merchant refused so we gave him the chop
> An' did what we had tae dae —
> Yes we knocked at the door of the oatmeal shop
> (*etc, repeat*)

MERCHANT (2):

> The laws of trade in heav'n are made
> But they don't understand
> If I can sell for eighteen pence
> In some part of this land
> And if I charge them generously
> One shilling as I planned
> Oh can't they see I give them all
> Six pennies in their hand

(*Music continues quietly under.*)

JEANNIE: (*sings to merchant*). Oatmeal, eight pence per peck, same as it was in March. Serve!

MERCHANT (1): What'll ye dae if I refuse?

JEANNIE: Dinnae provoke me, I've got a vivid imagination.

MERCHANT (1): Obadiah, bring me the measure!

(*Enter Obadiah, sneaky with a fixed measure.*)

OBADIAH: Is this the yin ye're wanting? Sook, sook, Tee, hee.

MERCHANT (1): Serve!

JEANNIE: Eight pence per peck! Oatmeal! —

MERCHANT (1): (*sings*). If brutes use force to rob my till

And make their threats so vile
Then all that's left for me to use
Is cunning, stealth and guile —

(*OBADIAH turns grinning and sings to audience.*)

OBADIAH: They think they're robbing him, tee hee,
But see his strategem
The measure's fixed, it gives short weight
And so he's robbing them —

(*Music repeats as OBADIAH grins at MERCHANT, points to measure, laughs, gets carried away, grins at SINGER — points to measure. MERCHANT sends OBADIAH off.*)

SINGER 1:   Did ye hear aboot the measure was light?

SINGER 2:   Did ye hear aboot the measure was light?

SINGER 3:   Did ye hear aboot the measure was light?

ALL: What are we gaun tae dae?

(*JEANNIE passes the news to JOE, who beats his drum.*)

JOE: (*sings*). We'll go back tae the merchant and make him repay
Two pennies to all he had robbed yesterday
Then we'll give him a beatin' and so on our way

ALL: We'll dae what we have tae dae . . .

We went to the merchant and made him repay
Two pennies to all he had robbed yesterday
We gave him a beatin' and went on our way
We did what we had tae dae.

(*At end they all go off leaving JEANNIE.*)

JEANNIE: I don't suppose ye'd get away wi' that doon your local Asda, Eh?

Ach, ye'll hae tae excuse us if you're thinkin' we were a bit wild — but they were wild times in Scotland. Bonnie Prince Charlie and his Heelan' army cam marchin' intae Edinburgh — and oot again, a' the way back tae Culloden Moor. That was when the English showed what they could dae to the Scots if they had a mind tae it.

And puir Scotland fell into the hands of the English in London, and we were ruled at home by the

Clan Campbell, and the hard-eyed fraternity o'
Edinburgh lawyers.

But when it came tae oor ain affairs, well, we had
a voice.

The magistrates o' Edinburgh used to meet every
Wednesday in the forenoon tae consider the affairs
and improvement of the city: but they knew fine they
could arrange naethin' — wi'oot oor permission.

(*JOE comes back on in a hurry.*)

JOE: Well of course not, woman — there'd hae been a Riot!

JEANNIE: That's just what I was tellin' them — och you should
                hae seen him when they sent fur him tae gie his
                guid advice tae the magistrates — show how you
                stood, Joe —

                (*JOE declines modestly.*) Go on, dae as you're tell't —

(*JOE assumes an air of great importance and condescension, and a peculiar pose.*)

JOE: (*without moving his lips*). I stood like this so they
                wad see I wasnae inferior —

JEANNIE: What do you think, Mr Smith — they'd say — what
                do you think? And he'd speak up for everybody.

JOE: And they knew better nor tae argue.

(*Enter MAGISTRATE.*)

MAGISTRATE: Mr Smith — to business. A great many of the worthies
                of Edinburgh are considering the construction of
                a New Town, on the other side of the Nor' Loch,
                with wide streets and gracious homes all laid out
                in a systematic plan. Would your friends have any
                objection to such a scheme?

JOE: Well — on the one hand — no. Because we'd be
                getting rid o' you frae the best apartments in the
                Cowgate. On the other hand — aye! For if ye're
                awa' the other side o' the Nor' Loch, how will we
                keep an eye on what ye're a' daein'?

MAGISTRATE: (*pouring drink*). Is this objection insurmountable?

JOE: (*with dry throat*). Aye. Insurmountable.

MAGISTRATE: (*calls*). Alistair!

(*JOE thinks he's going to get a glass. Enter ALISTAIR with flagon.*)

ALISTAIR: Would ye fancy a firkin?

MAGISTRATE: Thank you, Alistair. (*Exit ALISTAIR.*) It will provide
                 employment . . .

JOE: (*sniffs flagon, is satisfied*). Aye — so it will —

MAGISTRATE: I'm sure, Mr Smith, you will find a way —

JOE: (*takes bottle as well*). Aye — I'm sure I will.

(*Exit MAGISTRATE. JOE passes bottle to JEANNIE, who passes it to BAND.
JOE turns to audience.*)

JOE: You see, the magistrates o' Edinburgh were all
                 merchants. Now there was a famous book written at
                 this time called 'The Wealth of Nations' — currently
                 I believe much admired by Sir Keith Joseph — and
                 that book says: 'When the merchants make the laws,
                 we maun gie them most suspicious attention. For
                 the merchants are an order of men 'whose interest
                 is never exactly the same wi' that o' the public, who
                 have generally an interest to deceive and even to
                 oppress the public, and who accordingly have, upon
                 many occasions, both deceived and oppressed it.'
                 I think Sir Keith must hae ripped that page oot o'
                 his copy, Eh? That was how Mr *Adam* Smith put it.
                 Noo he was one o' the Smiths frae Kirkcaldy: no
                 relation ye'll understand — as Mr Joseph Smith
                 frae the Cowgate puts it: I'd trust the Edinburgh
                 Corporation as far as I could throw one o' their
                 buses. No, my friends, we didnae hae votes, nor
                 referendums — but we let them know what we
                 wanted, and if we didnae get it: there was trouble.
                 (*Drum.*)
                 If they put up the prices, we took them doon again.

JEANNIE: This we did, and money's the time. (*Drum.*)

JOE: If they tried tae send their meal awa' tae Newcastle,
                 when oor bairns were hungry — we turned their
                 carts aroon' —

JEANNIE: This we did, and money's the time — (*Drum.*)

JOE: If they did load their boats at the dockside we
                 chopped down the mast, so they couldnae sail off —

JEANNIE: This we did, och aye we did. (*Drum.*)

JOE: And, at the time o' the year, when the sun shone bright, we'd a' gang doon tae Leith races and get drunk. (*Drum, exit.*)

JEANNIE: This he did, and mony's the time. (*Drum into Song.*)

SONG: 'Leith races' (part one)

       In July month, ae bonny morn,
       When Nature's rokelay green
       Was spread o'er ilka rigg o' corn,
       To charm our roving een;

       'Whan on Leith-Sands the racers rare,
       'Wi' Jocky louns are met,
       'Their orrow pennies there to ware,
       'And drown themsel's in debt
       'Fu' deep that day.'

              (Lyric: Robert Ferguson)

(*At the end of the song, enter ADAM FERGUSON, Professor of Moral Philosophy, at Edinburgh University, brought up a Gaelic speaker from Perthshire.*)

FERGUSON: As Professor of Moral Philosophy at the university of Edinburgh, I do not get invited to a great many parties. I was not invited along here tonight but I trust you will forgive a gate-crasher from beyond the grave. My name is Adam Ferguson. I am very taken with the arguments of your friend Mr Smith. I find it ironical to recall that, at the very same time that Mr Smith and his mob were rioting in the Cowgate, not two hundred paces away, in the University, the most profound and advanced thinkers in Europe were giving voice to enlightened thoughts about the future. Unfortunately this philosophy resulted in Mr Smith having even *less* to do with the governance of the realm than he ever had.

       For we saw the growth of the factories, and we saw that men and women employed in these factories were to become but animated parts of a machine. We saw them becoming so reduced from their wholeness as human beings as to be incapable of any decision at all.

       In the new commercial state, we saw man to be a detached and solitary being: we saw profit to be the object which sets him in competition with his fellow-creatures, and we saw man dealing with his fellow-man as he does with his cattle and his soil, for the sake of the profits they bring. The mighty engine which we suppose to have formed society only sets its members at variance, and breaks the bonds of affection.

We may, with good reason, congratulate our species on trying to escape from a state of barbarous disorder and violence into a state of domestic peace and regular policy. But when they have sheathed the dagger, and the weapons with which they contend are the reasoning of the wise, and the tongue of the eloquent, there arises a fresh danger, perhaps more dangerous than the dagger or the over-ready sword. Civil order, and regular government are advantages of the greatest importance: but we have reason to dread such political refinements when we consider that their main object is repose or inaction.

And so every dispute of a free people, with this object, amounts to disorder, and a breach of the national peace. There are indeed politicians who would model their government not merely to prevent injustice and error, but to prevent agitation and bustle.

Men must take precautions against each other to repress crimes. The vyper must be held at a distance, and the tyger chained. But if a policy is applied to enslave a population, rather than to restrain them from crime, then it has an actual tendency to extinguish the spirit of a nation: If Its severities be applied to terminate the agitations of a free people, if forms be applauded because they tend merely to silence the voice of mankind, then we may expect that many of the boasted improvements of civil society will be mere devices to lay the political spirit at rest, to chain up the active virtues of the people.

The dangers to liberty can never be greater from any cause than from the remissness, indeed the apathy, of a people. This liberty is never less secure than it is in the possession of politicians who consider the public only as voters to advance them on the road to power and fortune.

Thank you.

(*Enter JEANNIE.*)

JEANNIE: Joe Smith is deid —

FERGUSON: Long live Joe Smith.

(*He goes: JEANNIE turns to the audience.*)

JEANNIE: He fell off the back o' the coach comin' hame frae Leith Races — he wis drunk as a lord, and my one consolation is, he never felt a thing.

(*Enter Funeral Procession. JOE's body apparently being carried aloft. JOE, however, follows behind holding his head.*)

JOE: Never felt a thing? That'll be right. And my horse came in fourth — One minute I'm on top o' the coach, fleein'. Next minute I'm aff the top o' the coach, fleein' — Wallop! I woke up in the box, and that was me.

I'm away for a wee refreshment, so I'll let you do the same — but I'll be comin' for you in ten minutes . . .

'Leith races' (part two)

Now, money a scaw'd and bare-ars'd lown
Rise early to their wark,
Enough to fley a muckle town,
Wi' dinsome squeel and bark.
'Here is the true an' faithfu' list
'O' Noblemen and Horses;
'Their eild, their weight, their height, their grist,
'That rin for Plates or Purses
Fu' fleet this day.'

They say, ill ale has been the deid
O' money a beirdly lown;
Then dinna gape like gleds wi' greed
To sweel hail bickers down:
Bedown Leith Walk what burrochs reel
Of ilka trade and station,
That gar their wives an' childer feel
Toom weyms for their libation
O' drink thir days.

END ACT ONE

ACT TWO

At the end of the Interval, JOE storms round wherever the audience may be, beating his drum, followed by JEANNIE.

JOE: Come back, come back, my friends and take your seats for tae hear what I have tae say — it's yer ain true story told in biased argument, highly selective history and emotional folksong. Are ye all back that's comin' back? Right — lock the doors — for I'm wanting tae speak tae ye aboot yer responsibility — Noo — just in case any of ye have to leave, before the end, like, for a bus, or a baby-sitter, or just because ye're no likin' what ye're seein' — I'll tell ye how the story ends. It ends today: wi' democracy. Wi' you gettin' the vote, that's democracy; so's ye can choose atween two sets o' politicians. Ye may not like either o' them, but ye *can* choose. That's democracy. And then once you've voted, and they get into power in London, they dae exactly the opposite of what they said they'd dae, and there's naethin' ye can dae aboot it. That's democracy. Aye — that's the end of the story — the people o' Scotland sittin' at hame, watchin' telly, content wi' the thocht that in five years' time they can repeat the whole procedure all over again — with the same result. That's democracy. And the very politicians that three-quarters o' you voted *against* is sittin' in England rulin' Scotland. So it's a happy endin', eh? Do ye no' think? (*Drum.*) Eh? (*Beats Drum.*) Do ye no' think? (*Produces cobblestone.*) Dae ye see that, my friends? That's a cobblestone frae the Lawnmarket. (*Walks away.*) (*Drum as he marches round the stage, followed by JEANNIE.*)

JEANNIE: Ye see, folk died for tae get you the vote. They died because they thocht it would *mean* somethin'. They died so ye could decide yer future for yersels, all quiet and reasonable: and there would be no kings nor lords nor merchants set above us to rule. 1789, in France, that's where it all began. King Louis and his Marie-Antoinette were thrown intae their ain dungeon. The people of France took over their ain affairs, and the rulers o' England were rattlin' inside their boots.

JOE: Tom Paine, him that had supported the Americans when they broke away, Tom Paine comes out with a book called 'The Rights of Man'. Och, they banned it straight away wi'oot another thocht — if it was aboot the rights o' man, then it had tae be

306

subversive. But the Tree of Liberty was sproutin'
a' over England, and a' over Scotland as well. *The
Rights of Man* was read doon every close; it was even
translatit into the Gaelic for the Highland folk, and
did they no' have need o' it! And Rabbie Burns
wrote a wee song aboot the Tree of Liberty. Sing,
Jeannie.

JEANNIE: Aye, I will.

JOE: There's some folks say Rabbie Burns didnae write
            this, because it's a wee bit strong — but he did:

SONG: 'The Tree of Liberty' (part one)

            Heard ye o' the tree o' France,
            I watna what's the name o't;
            Around it a' the patriots dance,
            Weel Europe kens the fame o't.
            It stands where ance the Bastile stood.
            A prison built by kings, man.
            When Superstition's hellish brood
            Kept France in leading strings, man.

            Upo' this tree there grows sic fruit,
            Its virtues a' can tell, man;
            It raises man aboon the brute,
            It makes him ken himself, man.
            Gif ance the peasant taste a bit,
            He's greater than a lord, man,
            An' wi' the beggar shares a mite
            O' a' he can afford, man.

            Without this tree, alake this life
            Is but a vale o' woe, man;
            A scene o' sorrow mixed wi' strife,
            Nae real joys we know, man.
            We labour soon, we labour late,
            To feed the titled knave, man,
            And a' the comfort we're to get
            Is that ayont the grave, man.

            Wi' plenty o' sic trees, I trow,
            The warld would live in peace, man;
            The sword would help to mak a plough,
            The din o' war wad cease, man.
            Like brethern in a common cause,
            We'd on each other smile, man;
            And equal rights and equal laws
            Wad gladden every isle, man.

JOE: Aye, the Tree of Liberty was bearing fruit in 1792. The King's birthday, June the Fourth. The Lord Provost o' Edinburgh invites a few o' his cronies tae drink the king's health. Up in the Lawnmarket the toast is ringin' out loud: 'Tae George the third an' last!'

And just tae show we didnae care, we chased the soldiers and set their sentry-boxes afire in the High Street. Aye — we had a party a' right. The Home Secretary in London was the very same Henry Dundas who had ruled Scotland on behalf of the English, and his own private fortune, for very nearly forty years. King Harry the Ninth they cried him in Edinburgh. But neither kings nor Henry Dundas were very popular in Scotland in 1792: in May, they burnt his effigy in Fife, and handbills and posters were tae be seen in Edinburgh that were highly uncomplimentary. So he sent four troops of Dragoons, and the 53rd Regiment of Foot to Edinburgh Castle, tae quell the people's fire.

And he sent his wee nephew Robert, the Lord Advocate, to rule the unruly, and in turn tae be ruled by him . . .

(*Enter ROBERT DUNDAS, with a letter he has written.*)

DUNDAS: 'Dear Uncle Henry, Sorry to trouble you with my little problems when you have such big ones of your own, but I thought I ought to let you know that most people in Edinburgh are trying to kill me. And I suspect this to be only because they cannot lay their hands on *you* — you being in London.'

Hm — maybe that's a bit too strong. No, if I'm to be murdered as a poor substitute for him, at least he ought to know about it.

'The evil spirit of the French Revolution seems to have reached us in Scotland. I was in hopes John Bull would have kept it to himself, but no. There is a lawless force of mob roaming the streets of Edinburgh which even the Dragoons which you so kindly provided cannot dispel.

'The present riots began on the King's birthday, with disloyal toasts, and the burning of an effigy of yourself, dear uncle, which I'm told occasioned almost universal happiness.

308

'I was in your mother's house in George Square,
with Colonel Francis Dundas, when the mob
appeared with yet another effigy of your good self,
dear uncle — this time hanging from a scaffold.
They tried to smash the windows of your mother's
house! Colonel Francis bravely set out to repel them,
armed only with Lady Arniston's crutch. But alas
the brave warrior was seized and beaten with his
own weapon. Thankfully the troops arrived and
saved him.

'We thought the mob had gone away to burn down
the Lord Provost's house in St Andrew's Square.
Imagine our chagrin when they returned in even
greater numbers, crowding into George Square as
thick as they could stand. We thought our final hour
had come, when the Dragoons once more came to
our rescue and fired into the crowd. We saw five
or six fall — whether dead or merely wounded I
know not — and the crowd dispersed, but for how
long we dare not say.

'The whole of Europe is in the grip of this dreadful
revolutionary fervour, dear uncle, and you Home
Secretary too. Fortunately the mob here do not know
exactly what they want, except a vague desire for
blood — yours, mine and His Majesty's — which
I hope will not be satisfied, alarming as it may be.

'There is however another element within Edinburgh
society which *does* know precisely what it wants. A
young advocate, one Thomas Muir, expelled from
Glasgow University not five years ago, is the prime
mover of a most articulate and cunning organisation
of disaffection known as the Friends of the People.

'Now: Alone, they have no strength. And the mob,
alone, have no direction: but should they combine
the one with the other, I fear our days are numbered.
I am resolved to insinuate a spy into the heart of
their counsels, and to set about clapping Mr Muir
into the Tolbooth for High Treason, and thence to
the gallows or at worst Van Dieman's Land, the
very moment I can find a scrap of evidence.

'Meanwhile, dear uncle, I shall continue to
administer Scotland in the calm, fair and benign
spirit which you yourself have taught me, and to
carry out your every wish in so far as my frail
person is able.

309

'Your respectful' — no better — 'Your *obedient* nephew, Robert.'

Hm. That should give him a few sleepless nights.

(*As ROBERT DUNDAS starts to go, enter THOMAS MUIR, a young advocate and revolutionist.*)

MUIR: They call me a trouble-maker. But I don't make the trouble. The trouble is there already. I just refuse to walk around it looking the other way.

DUNDAS: (*to audience*). That's him. That's Thomas Muir. Don't believe a word he says . . .

MUIR: There are forty-five Members of Parliament elected in Scotland. Thirty of them from country seats, fifteen from the Burghs. Well, the Burghs are as rotten as any in England, to be bought and sold like haddock in the market. And the thirty country members for the whole area of Scotland are elected by a grand total of 2,662 voters. Now I'd call that trouble. And I didn't make it. All I did was to follow the example of the French, and the precepts of Mr Tom Paine, and the spirit of my own teacher, John Millar of Glasgow — and set up an organisation called the Friends of the People to agitate for reform of this corruption.

My God, ye'd think I'd raped the Queen.

DUNDAS: There were scoundrels like him in England, but at least *they* charged two pounds per annum to join their Friends of the People, and that kept the riff-raff out; but not Mr Muir, oh no — sixpence per annum to join in Scotland. So they *all* joined. Branches of his evil organisation everywhere — fifty-seven of them, I'm told.

MUIR: And I was everywhere too — Aberdeen, Dundee, Edinburgh, Glasgow. We held our first meeting in Edinburgh, one month after the King's Birthday Riots: in Glasgow three months later; soon, all over Scotland; we became famous all over the world, we sent messages to our comrades in Paris, in London, in America. And in Ireland.

DUNDAS: Aha!

MUIR: We called a National Convention in Blackfriars Wynd, Edinburgh: the Friends of the People were going into action.

DUNDAS: Aha!

MUIR: It was a great success. We resolved unanimously to live free or die.

DUNDAS: The latter, if *I* have anything to do with it.

MUIR: And we read an Address from our brothers the United Irishmen, praying we should succeed — 'Not by a calm, contented, secret wish for a reform in Parliament, but by openly, actively and urgently *willing* it, with the unity and energy of an embodied nation.'

DUNDAS: Just what I needed.

MUIR: Aye. It was just what he needed. I was arrested. I had not caused trouble. I had simply refused to avoid it. I was charged with High Treason.

DUNDAS: I've got him by the heels, the renegade.

MUIR: I was released on bail. So I went to London to address the English Friends of the People. There I heard that the French Revolutionists were planning to chop King Louis's head off. I dashed over to Paris to plead with them not to do any such thing; for the reaction to an act of terror like that would set back the cause throughout the world; but I arrived in time to see the guillotine fall on the neck of that unfortunate monarch. Instantly war broke out with England, which made it very difficult for me to get back to Edinburgh for my trial . . .

DUNDAS: Wining and dining with the Jacobin murderers, the toast of Paris, the Scottish Traitor! He has failed to answer his bail — he is guilty as charged.

MUIR: I eventually managed to get a passage to Philadelphia, where I should have enjoyed meeting the American Revolutionists, but the boat stopped unexpectedly at Belfast. I got off, and took the opportunity to visit our United Irish friends in Dublin. They received me very kindly.

DUNDAS: More murderers and traitors! The man's whole life is dedicated to evil men and evil deeds!

MUIR: But after a week I journeyed back north with a heavy heart, I crossed from Larne, and was met at Stranraer by a Government agent, who put me in chains. I was put on trial in Edinburgh before Lord Braxfield. I had no hope of mercy, so I was my own defending counsel.

(*Enter LORD BRAXFIELD.*)

My Lord, if the real cause of my standing here is for actively engaging in the cause of parliamentary reform, I plead guilty. It is a good cause; it shall ultimately prevail — it shall finally triumph.

BRAXFIELD: Gentlemen of the jury, the prisoner is charged with sedition. Is he guilty? Or not guilty? Well, there are two points upon which no proof is needed: one — the British constitution is the best that ever was since the creation of the world, and it is not possible to make it better; And two — there has of late been a spirit of sedition and of revolt against this Constitution.

This cannot be allowed to continue. Was it entirely innocent of the prisoner to talk of 'reform' among ignorant country people, and of preserving their liberty among the lower classes of the towns, who, but for him, would never have known it was in danger. He must know that Parliament will pay no attention to such a rabble.

A Government in every country should be just like a Corporation, and in this country it is made up of the landed interest, which alone has a right to be represented. As for the rabble, who have nothing but personal property, what hold has the nation of them?

Gentlemen of the Jury, it is quite clear to me, at least, that the prisoner is guilty. I urge you to return such a verdict as will do you honour.

MUIR: All fifteen members of the jury were also members of Government-funded loyalist groupings. Of course, they did as they were told.

BRAXFIELD: Thank you, thank you. The Court highly approves of your verdict. Mr Muir, I see little difference between your crime and treason. I feel no punishment for your crime is sufficient now that torture is, er, happily abolished, but fourteen years of transportation to Botany Bay should keep you out of contact with our society while you learn to better your ways.

Should you return to any part of Great Britain, you will hang.

(*Goes, as does ROBERT DUNDAS.*)

MUIR: I never made trouble. The trouble was there for all to see.

(*He goes off. JOE steps forward.*)

JOE: He was 27 years old when he was sentenced. There was some sort of plan tae rescue him frae the Tolbooth, but Dundas's spies were amongst us, and he was shifted quick tae London, to wait in the convict hulk.

Tae defy the Government, The Friends of the People had another Convention: but the Lord Provost of Edinburgh and thirty constables broke it up wi' truncheons, and arrested mair o' the leaders. Ye see, Mr Muir and his friends never quite made contact wi' the mob, and the mob werenae quite sure whether they would want the vote or no', anyway — so the reformers had no power. And once their leaders were arrested, and transported, that was them for twenty years, quiet as the grave.

JEANNIE: And Thomas Muir's health was broken. With great determination he made his way back to France, but things had changed there as well. He died alone and unknown in lodgings in Chantilly, at the age of thirty-three.

JOE: He died for yous tae have the vote. (*Drum.*) He died tae end the rule of kings and aristocracy. (*Drum.*) He died so every man —

JEANNIE: — and woman —

JOE: — would rule their ain lives

JEANNIE: And have a powerful voice in the management of Scotland.

JOE: Did he die for naethin'? (*Drum.*)

SONG: 'The Tree of Liberty' (part two)

For Freedom, standing by the tree,
Her sons did loudly ca', man;
She sang a sang o' liberty,

Which pleased them ane and a', man.
By her inspired, the new-born race
Soon drew the avenging steel, man;
The hirelings ran — her foes gied chase,
And banged the despot weel, man.

Let Britain boast her hardy oak,
Her poplar and her pine, man,
Auld Britain ance could crack her joke,
And o'er her neighbours shine, man.
But seek the forest round and round,
And soon 'twill be agreed, man,
That sic a tree can not be found,
'Twixt London and the Tweed, man.

Wae worth the loon wha wadna eat
Sic halesome dainty cheer, man;
I'd gie my shoon frae aff my feet,
To taste sic fruit, I swear, man.
Syne let us pray, auld England may
Sure plant this far-framed tree, man;
And blythe we'll sing, and hail the day
That gave us liberty, man.

JOE: Och, a' the same, she was a braw city, Embro, in those days. The castle up there, bonnie, eh? Full o' soldiers tae run doon in their boots tae fire bullets at us — oh, aye, a bonnie sicht, the castle. And the Old Town, cascading doon the sides of the ridge o' Castle Hill, like the mane frae the neck of a proud racehorse: where you could breathe an atmosphere of romance: six inches deep in human shite. One third dung, one third smoke and one third disease: gae romantic.

That was why the city worthies built their New Town the other side o' Nor' Loch, wi' their Princes Street, and their George Street and their Hanover Street. Oh aye — but don't enquire too deep aboot hoo the gracious New Town was financed, my friends — it was financed by the Hielan' lairds who paid their rents by emptying the straths of people to get higher rents themsel's frae sheep farmers. It was financed by the lairds in the South, who paid their rents by investing in the slave trade and the coal mines, where the miners were slaves themselves. And it was financed by the merchants who paid their rent by buyin' cheap and sellin' dear — and paying wages ye couldnae live on. Then along came

314

the most monumental robbers o' the whole crew:
the captains o' industry. By, they were the boys.
They took the money frae a' the other criminalsals
and bocht great machines, and set men and women
— and children — tae work them frae mornin' tae
nicht, and they made their fortunes. And they paid
dividends tae a' the other criminals, and they made
their fortunes. And Edinburgh New Town became
the grandest place in Europe: where the grandest
thieves and the grandest rogues used to meet for
the purpose o' plannin' even greater thievery and
roguery and legalising their tricks.

But who really paid for it? The men and women
and children racking their bodies at work, livin' wi'
disease and hunger a' their days. They paid for it.
And the Hielanders driven oot o' their homes and
across the seas — They paid for it. And the honest
folk, like the weavers, that were put oot o' business,
they paid for it.

But no' everybody took it lyin' down. The bold
weavers rose up, tae fight for their work, their
freedom and their lives. But they were crushed by
the military at Bonnymuir.

SONG: 'Bonnymuir'
                 (Tune: 'The Haughs o' Cromdale')

With pikes and guns we did engage
With lion's courage did we rage
For Liberty or Slavery's badge
Caused us to fight that morning

Although our lives we ventured fair
To free our friends frae toil and care
The English troops we din't to dare
And wished them a good morning

But some of us did not stand true
Which caused the troops us tae pursue
And still it leaves us here to rue
That e'er we fought that morning

Oh we are all condemned tae dee
And weel ye know that's no a lee
Or Banished far across the sea
For fighting on that morning.

(*Music continues.*)

315

JOE: The man who wrote the words of that song, Allan Murchie, was transported to Australia, along with sixteen others. But three men, Baird, Hardie and Wilson, were hanged. They died so you could have the vote. In a few years' time, they made a wee Reform — you know the way it goes: last year's radical extremism gets watered down till it becomes this year's Tory policy. And for a few years Edinburgh was as quiet as the grave, or even as Peebles.

SONG: (*Song ends.*)

Oh we are all condemned tae dee
And weel ye know that's no a lee
Or Banished far across the sea
For fighting on that morning.

JOE: Then a new storm shook Great Britain: a People's Charter was written, demanding votes for everybody, and a secret ballot, and the right to change the government once a year. Huge fiery meetings of the common folk were held in every village, town and city. Great orators arose, as if from nowhere, and demanded the repeal of the Corn Laws, the repeal of the Union with Ireland, the nationalisation of the land, and — in 1838 — self-government for Scotland.

JEANNIE: They had great banners, did the Chartists — 'May the People awake to the Recognition of their Rights: have the fortitude to demand them; the Fortune to obtain them, and henceforth sufficient wisdom and vigour to Defend them.'

JOE: Aye — but what happened tae the People? What was goin' on in Embro. All over England, and Wales, and maist o'Scotland, the Radicals could see fine that if they wanted their rights, they'd hae to fight for them — but in Embro some Reverend gentleman led fifty delegates to the top o' Calton Hill one dark night, and there they voted for something I consider to be extremely dangerous: something called 'Moral force'. What does that mean? It means nae riots. How are the mighty fallen. They were doomed to failure.

JEANNIE: And fail they did, for ten years. Till 1848 came, and the French had another Revolution, and all over Europe revolution was what was happening.

JOE: Not tae be outdone, the Edinburgh Chartists go

back up Calton Hill, ten to fifteen thousand of them. And up stands a mild kindae gadge by the name of Robert Hamilton, and he spoke tae the crowd.

(*Enter ROBERT HAMILTON.*)

HAMILTON: Fellow-democrats, friends: for fourteen years I have preached moral force. And I am tired of it. I urge every man here tonight to purchase a musket or a pike. To join one of the excellent arms societies — like the Muir Club, the Baird and Hardie Club, or the Burns Club — in order to learn how to use his musket. And to join a National Guard to defend the People's Convention, and the Charter. This is not the time for speeches — the time has come for action: While a revolution will not be for the benefit of *any* class, still we must show our hard task-masters that we are determined to be slaves no longer. If perish we must, let it be by the sword rather than by hunger. The Government's new Security of the Community Act would put every man who speaks at a public meeting into a dungeon. Well, fellow-democrats, I intend to speak, and I intend to speak sedition. Let every one of you ten thousand make the same stand as I do, and this base, bloody and tyrannical government will soon discover the jails will not be sufficient to hold us all. They can never put down the united force of the working classes.

JEANNIE: The government spies and informers rushed away tae clype in' their hundreds and puir Robert Hamilton was arrested.

JOE: But no before there were a thousand men under arms in Edinburgh, and another thousand in Aberdeen, and 800 in Alva.

HAMILTON: Physical force was defeated. And moral force? In capitalist, imperialist Britain, there was no morality. And if there had been, it would have had no force.

(*ROBERT HAMILTON goes.*)

JOE: Aye — but in that very year, 1848, Karl Marx and his matey Engels wrote the Communist Manifesto — and a slow fuse was lit under the bums of the ruling classes of Europe — and the world: a fuse that's still splutterin' away the day, so they tell me.

JEANNIE: Aye, and the New Town was full o' cobblers.

317

JOE:	Jeannie!
JEANNIE:	Tell them about the worthies.
JOE:	Aye, the worthies and the captains of industry were sitting pretty — confident, ruthless and rich. So a few years later they permitted another reform: a few million more got the vote.
JEANNIE:	But no' the women! They knew better nor tae gie the women the vote: they only gied it tae the men because they were a' sooks, and wad vote for the nice prosperous merchants and lawyers that stood for parliament — there was nae danger, no' from the men!
JOE:	Much as it sorrows me tae agree wi' ye, ye're right. There was no danger. Somehow or other, the mob had lost its voice. And anyway, if ye cried out in Scotland, who was tae hear ye? The parliament was in London, wi' no' even a Scottish Secretary tae yell at. A' the Scots thinkers, and writers, and men o' science and learnin', a' were away tae London as well. The only powerful men who stayed in Scotland were those who stayed tae mak money — and they were very hard o' hearin', when it came tae the voice o' the people.
SONG:	'The Rich They are so Sensitive'

The rich they are so sensitive
To poetry and rhyme
At songs by Brahms and Schubert
They swoon — sublime, sublime —
But when it comes tae starvin' folk
They havenae got the time:
When it comes to us
They're very hard of hearing.

The ladies in their velvet gowns
Appreciate the arts
They palpitate at Tennyson
With tender fluttering hearts
But when it comes to poverty
Their tenderness departs
When it comes to us
They're very hard of hearing

They love the little children
If they're crippled or they're blind

318

For babies born in Africa
Six pence, they'll always find
If workers' kids are starving
Out of sight is out of mind
When it comes to us
They're very hard of hearing

Industrialists' and landlords' wives
And others of that ilk
Insist on careful dieting
To keep their skins like silk
But when it comes to poor folk's kids
They take away their milk
When it comes to us
They're very hard of hearing.

JEANNIE: But there was one man came up out o' the lower
            depths o' Edinburgh, who was goin' tae *make* them
            listen: in Scotland, and all over the world. He was
            born in the Cowgate and his faither worked for the
            Edinburgh Corporation removing night-soil and
            dung frae the streets after dark. And he himself
            started work at the age of ten, washing down the
            inky rollers on the presses of the *Evening News*.
            By the time he was twenty, he was speaking tae
            crowds of thousands in the East Meadows, speaking
            socialism.

JOE: Very good — but will ye no' tell them what his
            name was?

JEANNIE: I will. James Connolly his name was. And he was
            the one for me.

JOE: Aye, aye —

JEANNIE: He made his livin' sweepin' the streets, but at one
            stage he sunk to become a cobbler —

JOE: Him? He was one o' the worst cobblers ever tae
            botch a shoe, he lasted six months then he had to
            shut up shop. He said he was away tae buy a mirror,
            tae watch himself starve tae death —

JEANNIE: But he didnae. He was offered a job organising the
            Dublin Socialists, then he went on tae America, tae
            organise the International Workers of the World,
            then he came back to Ireland tae fight for a socialist
            Ireland. He lead the Easter Rising in Dublin in 1916,
            but he was wounded and captured by the English

319

soldiers. In Mountjoy prison he was so weak they had to strap him to a chair and carry him out, to shoot him.

JOE: Wherever there was a fight for the rights of the people, frae the Cowgate tae Chicago, Connolly was there . . .

JOE: Aye: Connolly was there.
He was a wee man, wi' bowed legs frae a touch o' the rickets, and a squint frae readin' by firelight, and a stammer. But by, when he got goin' he was as good as any man I've ever heard. Aye, they listened to Connolly, and John McLean and Willie Gallacher — but they couldnae take the responsibility: they began the long journey from aff the streets tae inside their ain heads. And the politicians played wi' them: played wi' *you*. For why? Because more and more people were getting the vote. *That's* the way tae dae it, said the politicians, create this mighty machine tae *represent* the working class — and ye'll no' need tae rise up — just vote, once every five years, and the Labour Party will do it all for ye! Spend your vote wisely and well, my friends, and you will get your package of socialism — eh? — alang wi' a year's supply o' Valium, free, and a video-cassette of Denis Healey singing 'A Working Class Hero is Something To Be'.

SONG: 'Who will Buy my Rubbish?'

JOE: Who will buy my rubbish
Promises for sale
Fresh until ye've voted
Then they're quickly stale

CHORUS: Buy braw rubbish
Fresh frae London town
Promises a-plenty
Keep the rabble down

JOE: Here's a manifesto
Fantasy and lies
Fine to wipe your bum on
Good for swattin' flies

CHORUS

Here's a pretty wage-rise
For each nice P.C.

320

Fine protection money
So they'll keep you from me

CHORUS

Here's a map and compass
Bloodhounds one two three
London pocket guide
For finding your M.P.

CHORUS

Here's an honest conscience
Might a saint adorn
Made for politicians
So was never worn

CHORUS

Once you've made your purchase
And the vote's arranged
As you leave the Poll Booth
Mind and check your change

CHORUS (Twice)

BAND: 'Tree of Liberty' (part three)

But vicious folks aye hate to see
The works o' Virtue thrive, man;
The Courtley vermin's banned the tree;
And grat to see it thrive, man;
Awa' they gaed wi' mock parade,
Like beatles hunting game, man,
But soon grew weary o' the trade
And wished they'd been at hame, man.

For freedom, standing by the tree,
Her sons did loudly ca', man;
She sang a sang o' liberty;
Which pleased them ane and a', man.
By her inspired, the new-born race
Soon drew the avenging steel, man;
The hirelings ran — her foes gied chase,
And banged the despot weel, man.

JOE: (*referring to song*). That's wishful thinking, boys —
blind optimism. I like it — but I'll need tae see some
action, as well as some singin'. For the world's gan
round some twisted ways since I fell aff the back
o' the coach from Leith. Like auld Adam Ferguson

321

the professor could see, a' they years ago, what a' this 'democratic' votin' and law and order is for, is *inaction*. For the government to be completely satisfied, the whole people would need tae go to sleep for five years, then wake up just in time tae vote them in again. (*Drum*) Well, that's no' for me. (*Drum*) Is it for you, my friends?

Well, maybe it's no'. But I'm tellin' ye, there's one third o' ye didnae even wake up long enough tae vote when it came tae this Assembly they were offering. Aye — I know it wisnae very guid — but noo where are ye? Ye've got a bunch o' English public schoolboys in London tellin' ye what's what, and George Younger in Edinburgh just a wee bit surprised tae suddenly find himself sellin' council houses instead o' beer.

Scotland voted *against* they buggers. (*Drum*.)

Scotland didnae want them. (*Drum*.)

Did *they* get forty percent of the Scottish vote? (*Drum*.)

Come on, noo. Are you surprised I'm angry wi' ye?

Are ye surprised I'm beatin' my drum? Ye've let them get away wi' *murder*. And like I said: what have ye done? Ye've done naethin'.

(*Produces cobble stone*). See that? That's a cobble stone frae the Lawnmarket, that. (*Looks at it, puts it away agin*.)

Remember Thomas Muir? He took action.

Remember Andrew Fletcher of Saltoun:

(*Enter FLETCHER.*)

FLETCHER: My lord, all nations are dependent, the one on the many. We are Scotsmen. Let us set our country in order, and flourish, and add our own, independent weight to the world.
(*He stays on.*)

JOE: Remember James Connolly —

JEANNIE: If you remove the English army tomorrow and hoist the green flag over Dublin Castle, unless you set about the organisation of the Socialist

322

> Republic, your efforts would be in vain. England would still rule you. She would rule you through her capitalists, through her landlords, through her financiers, through the whole array of commercial and industrial institutions she has planted in this country.

JOE: Remember Robert Hamilton —

(Enter ROBERT HAMILTON.)

HAMILTON: If every one of you makes the same stand as I do, then this base, bloody and tyrannical government will soon discover that the jails are not big enough to hold all of us. They can never put down the united force of the working class.

JEANNIE: And remember him. (*JOE.*)
He was no' perfect. I'll grant ye. There's a lot that you could teach him, aboot this an' that, an' no' least about me. But he took his responsibility seriously.

JOE: I used tae look at it this way: if aethin' happened in the world — it was because I let it happen. If it was wrang, and I couldnae sort it mysel' — that's what I had ma drum for. OK?

(Drumbeat.)

(Blackout.)

END

Out of Our Heads

Out of Our Heads, by John McGrath, music by Mark Brown:
first performed by 7:84 Theatre Company, Scotland.

The Company:

DAVE ANDERSON	Teacher, McCloy, Piano-Player, Vocals
NADIA ARTHUR	Costume Design, Wardrobe
NEIL GAMMACK	Alec, Bass guitar
JAMES GRANT	Davey
FERI LEAN	Admin, Publicity
JOHN McGRATH	Writer, Director
ELIZABETH MACLENNAN	June, Mrs McCloy, Piano
KRIS MISSELBROOK	Barman, Stage Management
TERRY NEASON	Janice, Vocals
MAREK OBTULONICZ	Lighting, Sound
BILL RIDDOCH	Harry, Drums
ALLAN ROSS	Gus, Fiddle, Mandolin

Poster by JOHN BYRNE, Choreography by Pat Lovett.

ACT ONE

The full stage picture will be taken up with a Glasgow Public bar, with a small alcove where there's a piano, and the band and the singers will entertain from.

However, as the show begins, we find JUNE, an 'average' young housewife from Glasgow, standing in a spot at her small kitchen table, counting out her cutlery, worried.

After a while, she speaks to the audience.

JUNE: I'm not normal. No, I'm really not — in fact, I'm completely and utterly abnormal. I'm not even normal for a looney. Well . . . I'm not. Normal loonies kid on they're Napoleon or Jesus Christ or the Queen of Sheba when any fool can see they're no' the Queen of Sheba — I kid on I'm 'normal', so I get away wi' it.

I got this thing about being average, right? I *know* what that means. I've just got the two weans, right? In Britain the average woman has 2.4 weans. I spend a lot of time in my bad spells working out how I could get .4 of a wean, just to be upsides with the average. Very difficult problem that.

Or take wages. His wage is £5.30 below the average for an industrial worker. What he doesnae know is that I take in wee jobs from a toy factory: I earn £5.30 every week, no more nor less — and I know we're average. Now that's no' normal — but the best bit is — it *is*. That's why I radiate self-confidence.

See him drinkin'? A lot of women wouldnae stand for that. He's pissed out of his head five nights out of seven. Well — I don't mind. Because as I see it, that's normal — quite usual anyway for this part of the world. I don't like it when he's drunk. He batters me, quite hard, most nights. But inside of me I get this mad satisfaction: he's just behaving in a normal manner, so it's OK.

I've started getting a bit unreasonable though, these last few months: I'm wanting everything to be *equal*. There's twenty-five houses the other side of the street. There's twenty- six on this side. That's unequal and a wee bit abnormal in a street. I keep thinking I'll burn our house down, just to even things up.

Or take this with the cutlery. Twelve knives, twelve

forks, twelve big spoons — only five teaspoons. I've got to do something about that. First thing in the morning I'll be down to Woollies for my seven teaspoons. Where's it gonnae end up? In my bad spells I get to screamin pitch about bein' normal and I can only stop it by telling myself that it's not normal to scream, in fact it's quite rare, so I don't.

Nobody knows I'm a looney. Not even him.

One day they'll find out. I'll slip up and do something crazy. Then they'll put me away, give me electric convulsions and cut the bad bits of my brain out. Mebbe I won't mind though, d'you think? That's the normal thing to do with a looney. (She flinches as she hears her husband, HARRY, coming in from work, via the pub.)

(HARRY comes in, a little the worse for wear.)

HARRY:	Hey June: come here —
JUNE:	We need another seven spoons.
HARRY:	Come here.
JUNE:	We need another seven spoons. We need another seven spoons.
HARRY:	Come here, I'm gonnae give you somethin' tae remember.
JUNE:	We need another seven spoons.
HARRY:	Come on — this time you're gonnae *enjoy* it.
JUNE:	One two three four five — no more.
HARRY:	For once in your life you're gonnae *enjoy* it you miserable bonefaced cow, ye —
JUNE:	Not enough — we need seven more.
HARRY:	Shut it and do as I tell ye —
JUNE:	Twelve forks — twelve knives —
HARRY:	Come here before I belt ye —
JUNE:	Twelve soup spoons —
HARRY:	Right —
JUNE:	One bread knife.

329

HARRY: You're gonnae enjoy yourself right! Right?

JUNE: One bread knife.

(HARRY moves.)

One bread knife.

(HARRY hits her — she goes flying to the floor — curls up — whimpers.)

But we need another seven spoons.

HARRY: (looks at her). Ach — I cannae dae anything with that.

JUNE: It's not equal.

HARRY: You've put me off, you've got no life in you.

JUNE: It's no' normal.

HARRY: (shouts). You've finished me off, you looney. (Morose.) I was all for makin' you enjoy yoursel' for once in your life — (Laughs, sour.) You're mental.

JUNE: Twelve, twelve, twelve: Five: who took my teaspoons? The children never took my teaspoons —

HARRY: (aggressive). You're mental! You put me right off it! You ruined my night!

JUNE: My mother never took my teaspoons —

HARRY: (shaking her). You're mental!

JUNE: You took my teaspoons —

HARRY: (belts her. She falls). Get up . . . I havenae even started on you. (She cries. He kicks her.) Shut your moanin' face. (Sits at table.) Where's ma tea?

JUNE: Oh Christ aye, your tea — here — it'll be dry as a bone — it's still hot for you though — d'you want a cuppa tea or what?

HARRY: Aye — I'll take some tea.

(As JUNE puts his tea in front of him at the table, and he eats it complacently, the BAND start to play, and the SINGER comes on to the set, watching, and sings, with other SINGERS joining later:)

SINGER: This is the story of a looney and an alchy
Ordinary people
Ordinary people

330

	Ordinary people Like you —
JUNE:	What me? I'm no looney.
BAND:	That wee wifie's out of her head.
SINGER:	This is the story of a looney and an alchy. Ordinary people Ordinary people Ordinary people Like you —
HARRY:	You callin' me an alchy?
BAND:	That bloke's steamboats — out of his head.
JUNE:	I'm bananas — (MUSIC 'Cakewalk').
HARRY:	I'm — a drunk (MUSIC 'Nellie Dean')
BOTH:	We're
JUNE:	Certifiable.
HARRY:	Dipsomaniac.
JUNE:	Maladjusted.
HARRY:	Uncontrollable.
BOTH:	Ordinary people.
HARRY:	Who get drunk.
JUNE:	Or go round the bend.
HARRY:	In a perfectly ordinary way —
SINGER:	Ordinary loonies
HARRY:	Ordinary alchies.
HARRY/JUNE:	Ordinary people — Like you.

(HARRY philosophies to the audience as he finishes his tea.)

| HARRY: | I'm a man that never believes in violence, drunk or sober. It doesnae suit my temperament. That's what the wife says, if ever I should thump her one — it doesnae suit you. Aye, but it's the drink does that — I mean I wouldnae lay a finger on her if I was sober: the drink does the fightin' and the thumpin — but that with her, with the wife — now that's |

331

no what I'd call violence — I've seen too much of
men kickin' other men's heads in, broken ribs, I
saw a murder one night, on my way home — that's
violence, men fightin' other men, or the polis —
I'm a man who doesnae believe in violence. I'm
pretty steady really.

And sex? Well, that's somethin'. The wife's gone
right off it these days, no sense of enjoyment —
I say to her, if she'd have a wee drink maybe —
you know — maybe she'd feel a bit more like it . . .
But no. She doesnae want to enjoy hersel'. I'm no
sayin' I'm a great lover or anythin', no no . . . Well:
it's no the be-all and end-all of life, is it, sex? It's
somethin' we have in common wi' animals, wi' the
Animal Kingdom: that's all. I can do wi'out it, same
as the booze — take it or leave it, doesnae worry
me. I'm a man that can take it or leave it, when it
comes tae sex or booze. Or politics — ach, Christ,
a right bloody mess that's made of the country.

No — I'm no' a boozer — Anytime you fancy comin'
to my house — drop in — we've got nothin' to hide.
I'm just an ordinary bloke that likes his pint. (He
gets up, throws on his jacket, heads for the door,
calls to JUNE.)

HARRY: I'm just away for a minute or two, love. OK?
Anythin' you want?

JUNE: Aye, if you see the weans in the street, tell them
I'm wanting them —

HARRY: Aye — well . . . if I see them —

JUNE: Away you go — (He goes. She speaks to audience.)
Of course this isn't *my* story. No — it's his: I mean
— he's the man — his story's more interestin', sort
of thing. I'll just shift this stuff, so yous can see the
problems of bein' a man — (To BARMAN.) Come
on, gie's a hand — I'm only a woman — I need
help, right?

(As she takes her stuff off, and BARMAN re-sets pub and the BAND
settle back in their places, HARRY comes on downstage, i.e. outside
the pub; before he goes in, he talks to the audience.)

HARRY: See what I mean? Mental.

Right now — just to fill yous in — I've had a few
wee bevvies on my way home, I've had my tea,

and now — I'm gonnae sit wi' my pals and enjoy
a bit of company — what's wrong wi' that? I've
done my day's work, I've attended to my family
responsibilities — and all work and no play makes
Jack a dull boy — so — in we go.

It's a great wee pub this — nothin' done up about
it, none of your whore's parlour plush. It's no'
for sippin' your martinis and discussin' the Stock
Market, this one! It's a pub for gettin' pissed in —
and that's what you do.

You get some rare characters in here, but — (MUSIC
in, and HARRY starts off the song.)

HARRY: There's a bloke wi' a nose like a strawberry
There's a bloke that's always plastered
There's a bloke drinks a pint while you count to three
There's a bloke that's a right wee —

BARMAN: No language please
No fish, no chips, no ices —
No pies, no peas —
Just toasted plastic slices

CHORUS: For: our wee pub's a great wee pub
Of all the pubs the best — you can meet
Aye: our wee pub's a great wee pub —
The finest in the West — of our street

HARRY: There's a guy has a pint every Friday night
He's a regular — never missed it —
But the beer's pretty queer on a Saturday night
For it tastes like the dog has —

BARMAN: No language please
No fish, no chips, no ices
No pies, no peas
Just toasted plastic slices —

CHORUS: For: our wee pub's a great wee pub
Of all the pubs the best — you can meet
Aye: our wee pub's a great wee pub —
The finest in the West — of our street.

HARRY: Now at closing time comes the CID —
And they think they're God Almighty —
But when we're goin' home, they get Drinks
for Free —
Now I think that's pretty —

BARMAN: No language please

No fish, no chips, no ices —
No pies, no peas —
Just toasted plastic slices

CHORUS: For: our wee pub's a great wee pub
Of all the pubs the best — you can meet
Aye: our wee pub's a great wee pub —
The finest in the West — of our street.

HARRY: Now we're all pretty free an' the Round's on me —
But if you're down on your luck son —
On your feet, down the street — What a Liberty
For we couldnae gie a —

BARMAN: No language please
No fish, no chips, no ices —
No pies, no peas —
Just toasted plastic slices

CHORUS: For: our wee pub's a great wee pub
Of all the pubs the best — you can meet
Aye: our wee pub's a great wee pub —
The finest in the West — of our street.

(At end of song HARRY goes to Gents; then DAVEY comes in, and crosses to bar.)

DAVEY: Ten whiskies —

BARMAN: (Looks over bar) Ten whiskies —

DAVEY: On a tray —

(DAVEY looks around bar. Everyone else is looking at him.)

DAVEY: Grand night.

OTHERS: Aye — so 'tis.

(PIANIST plays a few notes, then stops.)

BARMAN: Ten whiskies. Three pounds.

DAVEY: Three pounds.

(DAVEY takes tray and goes and sits alone at a table. The others watch. ANDY moves over to get a better look.)

DAVEY: In case you're wonderin' — I'm celebratin'.

ALEC: Whit?

DAVEY: I've resigned frae the workin'-class: I cannae afford it —

334

ALEC: Oh.

DAVEY: Fourteen years in the Communist Party (Drinks one glass.)
Ten years a shop steward (Drinks another.)
Six years on the Scottish Executive of the Union — (Drinks another.)
Three years on the Trades Council (Drinks another)

Two thousand seven hundred meetings,
Fifty-three marches and demonstrations,
Thirty-one committees,
Twenty-nine wage negotiations,
Ninety-eight mannning disputes,
And one fine of fifty pounds for gettin' hit on the heid by the polis at a rally —
Cheers (Drinks another.)

I never see my wife, or my kids, and when I do they don't recognise me —

And I never get drunk — cheers (Drinks another.)

(Sits, waiting, arms outstretched.)
Aw Christ, it's no workin' . . .

(Enter HARRY — goes to bar. TERRY points out DAVEY, whispers to him. HARRY peers at DAVEY, goes over to him.)

HARRY: Is that you, Davey?

DAVEY: Aye — it's still me.

HARRY: (looks at glasses, then). What'll ye have?

DAVEY: No no — I'm fine — a half-pint of heavy —

HARRY: Ye'll take a pint, and somethin' wi' it, you big lassie, ye —

                 What's wrong wi' ye?

(Goes over to bar, gets two pints and two whiskies.)

DAVEY: What's wrong wi' me? I spend my life doin' battle with the capitalists on behalf of the workers, tryin' to organise for a better life for myself, for my kids and for everybody else: and where is everybody else? In the boozer. They don't even want to know.

The flower of the Scottish working-class: polluted.
The agents of social change; incapacitated, nightly.

335

Put out of action by the guerilla tactics of McEwans, Youngers, Scottish and Newcastle and the Distillers Company Limited. Chemical warfare.

If I've been to one meetin' where half the people that should've been there, werenae there because they were in the boozer — I've been to a thousand.

If there's one man that's prepared to put his energy into even readin' a book, there's a thousand sittin' in the pub talkin' rubbish.

(HARRY comes over with the drinks.)

HARRY:	Christ, Davey, you're a hell of a man.
DAVEY:	Am I?
HARRY:	Ten whiskies, eh? Feelin' like cuttin' loose tonight?
DAVEY:	Aye.
HARRY:	Ach, great — just great — do you a power of good.
DAVEY:	Do you think?
HARRY:	Here — chase 'em down wi' that — I havenae seen you in here for months — the wife been lockin' you in your kennel?
DAVEY:	Meetin's.
HARRY:	Ach, that's bad for ye, all that stuff — Sit back and relax a wee bit, there's a piano player here Thursdays, Fridays and Saturdays, have a wee sing-song.
DAVEY:	Aye — right — that sounds just about great — Here it's beginning to work . . .
HARRY:	What is?
DAVEY:	The whisky.
HARRY:	Good on you.
DAVEY:	Do you know what happens to you, when you take a drink?
HARRY:	Aye, ye get drunk.
DAVEY:	No — but what *happens*?
HARRY:	Well — not exactly.

DAVEY: I do. Exactly. Will I tell you?

HARRY: (doubtful). Aye —

DAVEY: In a single whisky there's nine grammes of pure
            alcohol, right?

HARRY: Is that a fact?

DAVEY: It is. Now — what happens when your nine grammes
            of pure alcohol hits your stomach?

HARRY: Er — whit?

DAVEY: Nothin'. If you're unlucky it burns a wee hole in
            your belly, but nothing much — it gets passed on
            to your liver. That's round about — there — you've
            only got one, and if you damage it, you're dead:
            right? So what happens when the alcohol hits your
            liver? I'll tell ye: Inside your liver there's things
            called enzymes, and they're the things that turn
            food and drink into the proteins and the vitamins
            and the carbohydrates that your body needs to keep
            going. But what happens when your nine grammes
            of pure alcohol hits your enzymes?

HARRY: Christ, Davey — you're getting a wee bit morbid
            there — could you no sing us a song or tell us a
            wee joke?

DAVEY: Your enzymes stop workin'. Your body doesnae
            get its proteins. And your brain doesnae get any
            vitamins — and it needs its vitamin Bs, to keep the
            oxygen circulating, to keep it going — And the same
            with your whole nervous system — No vitamin
            Bs, it slows down — your brain gets stupid. Your
            body gets clumsy. You drink enough and your body
            gets numb and your brain stops altogether — you
            pass out.

HARRY: Are you feelin' a'right, Davey —

DAVEY: Aye, fine. Cheers (Takes another whisky, drains it.)

HARRY: Cheers — Christ, you're a hell of a man, Davey —

DAVEY: You think so? Well I'm tellin' you — I'm half a
            man. I'm half the man that I was when I came in
            that door. I cannae stand up. I cannae talk right. I
            cannae think right. I'm stupid. And I'm tellin you,
            I did that to myself, I mutilated my mind, to get

337

	away from reality. But I'm no succeedin' quite well enough. I'd better get a few more grammes down me to block off the oxygen from my brain-cells completely. Cheers. (Drinks.) That's ten.
HARRY:	What's bitin' you tonight, Davey?
DAVEY:	Apathy. Do you know what that means?
HARRY:	Aye — well, not exactly, but — ach never mind about it —
DAVEY:	Aha. What I want to ask you, Harry is: do you suffer from apathy because you're a boozer, or are you a boozer because you suffer from apathy?
HARRY:	Davey — could you no jus' — take it easy?
DAVEY:	You couldn't care less, about anythin', as long as you've got your pint in your hand — am I right or am I wrong? That's what the union is for, that I spend my time at — isn't it? To keep that pint in your hand — that's what socialism's turned into, isn't it? For you — Harry — and for every man in this bar — look at them —
AL:	You lookin' at me pal?
DAVEY:	Aye well, maybe better not look at them —
AL:	(comes over). I said are you lookin' at me, pal?
HARRY:	No, no, he was tryin' to see the time —
AL:	Right — well tell your pal the clock's over there — keep your eyes off-a me, OK?
HARRY:	Aye, sorry about that —
AL:	(to DAVEY). OK?
DAVEY:	OK, OK —
AL:	Don't you OK, OK me, son or I'll blatter ye. (to BARMAN.) Eh Jimmie — see that guy — he's gonnae cause trouble in here.

(AL goes and sits.)

HARRY:	You shouldnae go lookin' at people, Davey —
DAVEY:	I'm lookin' at you, Harry.
HARRY:	(getting up). Aye — well — take it easy, eh? You're my mate, right? Take it easy — I'll be back. (Goes.)

DAVEY: Aye — take it easy. That's what I'm here for. Stop
                lookin' at people. Stop askin' questions about
                anythin'. Stop my brain workin'. That's what I'm
                here for — I've retired, given up, packed it all in
                — For fourteen years I've been trying to get things
                moving — here in Scotland. In that time, in Vietnam,
                a few people defeated the entire military might of
                the USA — kicked them out: what have we done?
                Ach, forget it — that's what everybody else has
                done — forgotten it — just forget it — close your
                eyes, close your mind, pour your whisky down
                your gullet, and float away —

(The BAND plays a sweetly ironic pop melody, and the SINGER sings
seductively, as DAVEY drinks his last whisky, and the OTHERS in the
bar dream, stare into space.)

SINGER: Float off Float off Float off . . .
                Float off round your private Bahamas
                Float off live on nuts and bananas
                Float off
                On your own psy-cho-dramas —
                Float off . . . Float off . . . where nothing can harm us

                Come on in, the water's lovely and warm
                Spread your wings, and glide
                Come on in, it's like before you were born —
                Trouble's locked — outside —

                Underwater wonder-world awash in the coral
                Sub aquatic rainbows that would dazzle Cousteau
                Other-worldly water maidens slipping and sliding —
                Work on your wet-suit and go — down down down
                    below —

                Float off — to a land of illusion
                Float off — it's the only solution
                Float off — you can live in confusion

                Float off . . . Float off . . . mix desire with delusion —

                Come on in, the water's lovely and warm
                Far below the tide.
                Come on in, it's calmer under the storm
                Dive down deep and hide.

                Up above the thunder-clouds are threatening
                    lightning
                Up above the hurricanes are starting to blow
                Crashing waves and clashing seas are threatening,
                    frightening

> Work on your wet-suit and go — down down down
>   below . . .
>
> And now you're there
> You're past all care
> And no-one dare
> Upset you —
> Wave your arms
> Admire the charms
> Of ocean farms
> And let the world forget you —
> And let the world
> Forget you —

(HARRY comes over to DAVEY with another two pints.)

HARRY: All my life, Davey — I've been a man that does . . .
what he wants to dae. Know what I mean? Ah
wannae dae somethin' — I dae it. Right?

DAVEY: You're a hell of a lucky bloke there, Harry — unusual.

HARRY: Unusual? No. Just take a look around this place.
What do these blokes want to dae? Uh? — Drink!
So they're daein' it . . . Ah'm a man that's lucky.
Lucky in his friends. You, Davey, now take you —
you are ma friend. Am I right or am I wrong? Ah?

DAVEY: You are correct, Harry.

HARRY: So I'm LUCKY! — Er, now — what was it I was
jus' sayin' there, there was a point tae it — Christ
I can never remember a bloody thing.

DAVEY: You do — what you wannae do.

HARRY: Aye — right — Christ, you're a good friend tae me,
Davey. Ah'm a man that does — whit he wants to
dae — right? No disputes?

DAVEY: No — you are meticulously exact in your wording
there, Harry.

HARRY: Aye — aye, so I am. And what ah want to dae, the
noo — is sing a little song. And — a-a-and . . . I'm
gonna dae it — right?

DAVEY: Aha. Away ye go, Harry —

HARRY: (SINGS) Ah- ah- (Speaks.) Ah'll just find my key —

(SINGS, romantically). Ah luv yuh,

As I've never loved before —
Since first I met you on the village green . . . etc.

DAVEY: It must be great to be drunk. See that? When you're
           drunk, you can sing. Harry's no jus' singin', but
           he's showing some romantic soul, sentimentality.
           What do you want to call it? Something we've all
           of us got, but society says: for Christ's sake don't
           show it, unless you're drunk. If you *do* show it, and
           you're sober, he's exactly the same guy — but he
           can only tell you about it when he's pissed out of his
           head: then, of course — nobody gets embarrassed:
           it's just an old Scottish custom, like pickin' your
           nose in the bus.

(HARRY does a wee jig with another customer.)

           Oh aye, and you can dance, too — you can even Touch
           Another Man: Christ, accidentally brush against
           some bloke when you're sober. 'You touchin' me,
           eh, Jim? I'll kick your heid in — fung pouf.' Know
           what I mean? Look at that — they'll be holdin' each
           other up baying at the moon before the night's out.
           (Bays at moon, holding up imaginary mate.) Have
           you seen it once? You've seen it a hundred times
           — but have you ever seen a Scotsman wi' his arm
           round another fella when he's sober?

(Shriek from TERRY at the bar. HARRY has been trying to touch her
up. ALLAN surfaces.)

AL: Hey yuh — you been botherin' that lady? I'll blatter
           ye. (Collapses.)

HARRY: (to BARMAN). He's harmless.

DAVEY: Sex too. When you've had a few bevvies, you're
           free to chance your arm. See a nice pair of tits —
           you gie'em a squeeze — worst can happen is a wee
           squeak and a slap on the wrist. Try it on at ten in
           the morning, you'd get three months in Peterhead,
           you're a sex-maniac.

(HARRY comes over to DAVEY again, grinning.)

HARRY: Right wee sure thing, that yin — did you see the
           look she gie me? Oho —

DAVEY: Harry — do you realise — you broke nearly every
           taboo in Scottish history there?

HARRY: Whit?

DAVEY: I saw you — bein' emotional — in public.

HARRY: Ah well, now, I wasnae being emotional —

DAVEY: I saw you — Touch Another Man —

HARRY: Aw come on —

DAVEY: I saw you Dancin' wi' Him!

HARRY: Aye but —

DAVEY: I saw you squeeze that lady's bosom!

HARRY: Aye — just in fun —

DAVEY: But you're not allowed to do any of those things in Scotland — they're Taboo!

HARRY: Well — I was pissed —

(Music in: TABOO — ALL join in a big choreographed number.)

'Taboo'

Indians on their reservation
Tell you with no hesitation
Scalping Grandma's not so droll,
Like widdling on the totem pole:
It's Taboo — . . .
Among the Sioux . . .
If you're a Sioux,
It applies to you,
It's what you —
Must never do . . .
Otherwise a tomahawk, Otherwise a tomahawk
Splits you right in two —
Oo.

But. In. Scottish Nation.
We've. More. Sophistication
Don't reveal your real emotion
Till you've drunk your magic potion
It's Taboo . . .
You no can do . . .
It's no' quite right
It's a terrible sight
If you're bright:
You'll stay uptight —
Otherwise your attitude, Otherwise your attitude
lands you in a fight — shite!

INDIAN WOMAN: Squaws in wigwams.

SCOTTISH WOMAN:	Cleans like white tornado.
INDIAN MAN:	Braves on war path.
SCOTTISH MAN:	Droppin' doon the boozer for a pint.
ALL:	Indian call — ending with: 'Scotland!'

Indian brave got masculinity
Next best thing to Holy Trinity
Hoovering Wigwam: not so cool —
That's no job for Sitting Bull —
It's Taboo
Among the Sioux . . .
If you're a Sioux
It applies to you
It's what you
Must never do . . .
Otherwise a tomahawk, Otherwise a tomahawk
Splits you right in two —
Oo.

And in Scottish City
Sitting Bull still sitting pretty —
Squaw must wash and squaw must cook,
Brave must never even look —
It's Taboo
You no can do —
Since time began
A manly man
Must always plan
From mind to ban —
ish any thought of woman's work — Any thought
    of woman's work —
Or the shit will hit the fan: Man!

INDIAN MAN: (spoken, drums behind). Me heap big Chief. Me
fill squaw many many papooses. Me drink many
bottle fire-water. Me rule wigwam iron fist. Me fight,
me eat meat, me God Almighty. Me just average
Indian Joe.

(African drums.)

Natives in the darkest jungle
Can't afford to make a bungle:
Don't eat nephews, don't eat nieces,
You'll end up in savory pieces —
It's taboo

343

In Timbuctoo:
In Timbuctoo
It applies to you —
It's not what you
Must not do:
Otherwise an assegai, Otherwise an assegai
Lands you in the stew — Oo.

And in darkest Edinburgh
Retribution's just as thorough:
If a man's not drunk and hairy
It's gae weel kent he's a pouf or a fairy —
And that's taboo
In Edinbroo —
Ooyah Ooyah, Smile at me I'll do yah.

Glasgow's soft and sentimental
They kick your head in awfy gentle:
Celtic's green and Ranger's blue
You'll die if you confuse the two.
It's Taboo
I'm tellin' you:

There's tribes here too
Like Timbuctoo:
Things that you
Must not do:
Otherwise the UDA — Otherwise the IRA —
Splits you right in two — Oo.

Umpyah Umpyah, Look at me I'll thump ya —
SCOTLAND!

(HARRY resumes with DAVEY.)

DAVEY: Ach — taboos. I'll tell you the greatest taboo of the
                   lot, Harry — talking to people. I mean, would I be
                   talking to you, like this, straight, if I was completely
                   sober? No. I couldn't. But once you've got a glass
                   in your hand — away you go — you don't even
                   need to drink the stuff — doesnae matter, you're
                   released — friendliness pours out of you, wit,
                   banter, impersonations of Andy Stewart, your whole
                   personality scintillates — and you feel — well —
                   pretty good — You feel, part of your world, at one
                   with the society you live in, an active contributor
                   to the cut and thrust of the great debate that is
                   Scotland today: a communal man. Wonderful. Ah?

                   Forget it. We're kiddin' ourselves on —

344

	Who does the talking that matters? Sober men with no names and no faces, in Zurich, and the City of London, and Wall Street and Washington: Christ, we need a few pints, to make us feel important. The way things go — we're nothin'.
HARRY:	Davey — you're my mate — right? You and me — school together, lads together, work together — everythin' — you're my good mate — I think you're a good bloke — Davey — you're first-class. But: — you're hell of a political.
DAVEY:	Harry — I apologise. I'm doin' my best. I'm trying to retire from the working-class.
HARRY:	There you go again, see!
DAVEY:	What?
HARRY:	'Working class' — that word is political. It annoys people. Look — why don't you just — get pissed.
DAVEY:	Harry — I cannae do it.
HARRY:	What?
DAVEY:	Get drunk. It's in there — my nut: won't stop workin'.
HARRY:	You're tryin' too hard, maybe.
DAVEY:	You know the kid's joke about the man with the bananas in his ears? This other bloke keeps yellin' at him. Hey, yuh, you've got bananas in your ears — Heh yuh — you've got bananas in your ears! Eventually he turns round and says — What are you saying? I cannae hear you, I've got these bananas in my ears.
HARRY:	Aye. I heard it.
DAVEY:	For fourteen years I've been yellin' at you — Harry, your life's bein' mucked about by capitalism — Any minute now, You'll turn round to me and say I cannae hear you, Davey, my life's being mucked around by capitalism.
HARRY:	Oh. No. It's no' that. It's these bananas in my ears.
DAVEY:	Harry — what made you into what you are? You've no lived in Glasgow all your life, have you?
HARRY:	No — I'm a chuchter —

345

DAVEY: I remember you that first day you came into our class — we were just back from the Christmas holiday — and there you were — standin' in front of us, lookin' terrible innocent.

HARRY: I was only twelve — Aye, I suppose I was a bit backward —

DAVEY: You had to learn what we'd all had to learn years before — the hard way —

(Scene has changed to a classroom, with GUS, ALEX, JANICE sitting in a row, HARRY standing — DAVEY moves his table and chair, as MR THOMSON, History Teacher, enters and whacks a desk.)

MR THOMSON: Good morning — I hope you all had a good holiday . . . I hope you've all come back thirsting for knowledge.

GUS: Thirsting for somethin' —

(Noise. MR THOMSON whacks the table with his tawse.)

MR THOMSON: Shut up! (To DAVEY.) Move yourself into line Matheson — (To HARRY.) Who the blazes are you?

HARRY: Harry McCall, sir —

(Bleats from boys in class.)

MR THOMSON: Shut up!

GUS: Just helpin' the chuchter feel at home, sir —

DAVEY: He's awfu' keen on the sheeps, Mr Thomson —

MR THOMSON: You have a sparkling wit, Matheson, but I'll remind you that civilisation is repression — so be civilised and repress it.

DAVEY: What's he sayin'?

MR THOMSON: What's he sayin'? He's sayin' Shut Your Stupid Face — got it? Right now, McCall, I'm supposed to be teaching these baboons about history — did you learn anything about History in the Heelans?

HARRY: The what sir?

MR THOMSON: The Heelans. Are you tryin' to take the mickey out of me, son?

HARRY: No, sir.

MR THOMSON:	Well don't. Turn to page 146 in your blue books. You can count up to 146, can you, McCall?
HARRY:	Oh yes, sir.
ALEX:	He counts his sheeps at night, sir.
GUS:	One two, oo that's a pretty one.
MR THOMSON:	Shut up! Right — reading — Janice — Oh God, what's the matter with Janice?
JANICE:	I'm still hungover frae Hogmanay, sir.
ALEX, D & G:	Scotland!
JANICE:	When Scotland's free we'll be gettin' free school milk, free school dinners, an' free black coffee and alka-seltzer at play time — so yous shu' up.
MR THOMSON:	McCall were you talking?
HARRY:	Yes sir.
MR THOMSON:	See that? (Tawse.)
HARRY:	Yes sir.
MR THOMSON:	Know what it's for?
HARRY:	Yes sir.
MR THOMSON:	What is it for, McCall?
HARRY:	Beating people up sir — damaging their bodies.
MR THOMSON:	If . . . ?
HARRY:	If you can't damage their minds, sir.
MR THOMSON:	McCall, you and I are not going to get on — understand?
HARRY:	Yes Mr Thomson. I do.
MR THOMSON:	Excellent — in that case you will know exactly what to expect if you step one quarter of an inch out of line.
HARRY:	Yes.
MR THOMSON:	Sir.
HARRY:	Sir — sir.

MR THOMSON: Good. Read: History. Page 146. James the Fourth —

HARRY: (reads from text book.) 'James IV of Scotland was a kindly monarch, a man of culture and civilisation, who encouraged the gentler arts of poetry, the drama, music and painting. Men of wit and wisdom were to be found at his court, and an elegant style of living flourished there. He came to the throne when only fifteen years of age, but his advisers, men of patience, learning and honour, ensured that the young king grew up into one of the flowers in the garland of Scotland's history.' Sir.

MR THOMSON: OK. OK. So you can read. Out with your exercise books, you lot, and copy that paragraph into them — read, learn and inwardly digest — and no talking.

(They do so. MR THOMSON to audience.)

MR THOMSON: What have they learnt from this lesson on a cold January morning?

(They put their hands up one by one and answer.)

DAVEY: We've learnt that a teacher is licensed to stand up or sit down — Walk around or leave the room — sir.

GUS: Tell you to speak —
Tell you to shut up — sir.

ALEX: Tell you to read.
Tell you to write — sir.

HARRY: *Why*? Because he's got something we haven't got — sir.

DAVEY: He's licensed to intimidate, sneer, bully —

ALEX: To be friendly, funny or familiar —

GUS: To shout, threaten, make you feel like nothin' —

DAVEY: By using his superior brain and experience —

HARRY: To smash you with a custom-built leather tawse Which he is licensed to hit you with — *Why*?

ALEX: Because he's got something we haven't got.

JANICE: And we've learnt from his tone of voice that we're never likely to get it, no way, no how, no time —

GUS: We've learnt that our jokes are rubbish.

ALEX: That what we know about life is irrelevant —

HARRY: Because they belong to us.

DAVEY: And real wit and wisdom belong to someone else.

TERRY: We have learnt that we shall never appreciate
Robert Burns.

HARRY: Though we might sing his songs till our hearts burst
open —

JANICE: Because we don't know how to appreciate these
things — in the right way.

DAVEY: We have learnt that it is our role in life
To be laughed at, knocked into a manageable
conformity:
And we have learnt that lesson well.

GUS: Send a stranger amongst us, we will laugh at him,
Knock him into a manageable conformity.

HARRY: And we are all strangers to each other:

ALEX: So we do it to each other all day long.

(MR THOMSON goes out.)

DAVEY: We have learnt that hostility is natural,
Aggressiveness is natural,
Violence is natural,
Repression is natural,
Conformity is natural,
Fear is natural,
Inferiority is natural
Taking orders is natural.

HARRY: And we have learnt that the greatest of these is
Charity —
But we can't find it on the list.

GUS: We have learnt that everything we stand for is
wrong.

ALEX: And everything teacher stands for is right.

JANICE: But we can never have it:

DAVEY: So we are doomed to frustration, repression and
failure.

HARRY: So we are split — inside our skulls.

(MR THOMSON comes back in.)

MR THOMSON: Right — anybody finished that lot?

ALL: Gie's a break — Jesus Christ — My hand's droppin' off, etc.

MR THOMSON: Hm. Janice.

JANICE: Aye?

MR THOMSON: What insights into Scottish history have we acquired today?

JANICE: James the Fourth, sir — we've done him.

MR THOMSON: And did anything characterise his reign?

GUS: Aye, it was wet.

MR THOMSON: Silence. Janice?

JANICE: James IV?

MR THOMSON: Yes. What did he do?

JANICE: Smashed the English sir — giein' them poison sangwiches at Killiecrankie snack bar.

MR THOMSON: Sit down, rest your weary head.

JANICE: Thank you, sir — I will.

(Enter JUNE.)

MR THOMSON: Oh hello June. Nice of you to come. Might I ask where you've been?

JUNE: Sick.

MR THOMSON: Do you have a note?

JUNE: Aha.

MR THOMSON: Sit down. Get out your history exercise book. Now, we'll all write down three headings for next week. Border Warfare.

(JUNE looks at HARRY. Neither write anything down.)

Divide and Rule. Dominate Or Be Dominated.

JANICE: What?

MR THOMSON: Dominate Or Be Dominated . . . OK?

(Bell rings. Turbulence.)

MR THOMSON: Release! Off you go! Into the playground and smash each other's skulls in! Smokers to the lavatories, poker-players to the bicycle sheds, let gang-war commence!

(They rush out.)

MR THOMSON: (to audience). I'm very fond of these kids — really. But — what can you do? There's no hope for them. No hope. 'What characterised the reign of James IV?' 'It was wet, sir' (Laughs.) That'll go down well in the staff-room. Great kids. Full of life. No hope. No. Hope. (Goes.)

(HARRY sits on his own, having a crafty smoke.)

JANICE: Hey — yuh — chuchter —

HARRY: (guilty). Yes?

JANICE: My friend's wantin tae speak to you:

HARRY: Oh.

JANICE: Well be a bit bloody friendly, can't ye? She's shy.

HARRY: Oh. Hello.

JANICE: June — her name's June.

HARRY: Hello June.

JUNE: Are you frae the Highlans?

HARRY: Aye.

JUNE: What's it like?

JANICE: She wrote a poym once about the Highlans — she's never even seen a hill.

JUNE: Shut up. What like's it?

HARRY: Oh — quiet. Hills.

JUNE: That's what I said.

JANICE: Go on. Get on wi' it . . .

JUNE: Shut up.

JANICE: See what it is — Gus got her up a close and stuck

351

> his hand up her skirt, and did things to her, and
> she didnae like it. I tellt her what can y'expect,
> and Gus has got a gang an' that so what can you
> do about it, but she's stupit, and she winnae wear
> make-up nor decent clothes an' look at the state
> of her shoes, she's retarded.

(Pause.)

JUNE: I didnae like it.

JANICE: So are you gonnae gie Gus a doin', or what?

HARRY: Me?

JANICE: Aye, yuh. Christ, do you no get it?

HARRY: No.

JANICE: Gus knows — about her and you. He's comin' to
                 gie y'a doin' anyway. There's the others wi' him.

HARRY: (amazed). Her and me?

JANICE: Aye — see, he knows she's tellt you to gie him
                 a doin'.

(GUS, DAVEY, ALEX, come on bleating. Stand round HARRY.)

HARRY: (quietly). Be quiet . . .

(During next bit, his voice goes from West Highland to thick Glasgow.)

> Stupid people.
> Away to the looney bin
> Get off me
> Gie us a break, will ye?
> Up your flue, ye eejits.
> Shut your face, ye great babboon
> One more poke and I'll kick your teeth in
> Right, you bastard — ye

(HARRY, now totally Glasgow, and in a vicious wild temper, flies at
GUS and, in ritual motions, does him over — as he holds his boot over
GUS's face, the GIRLS scream. He stops, turns to DAVEY.)

HARRY: Right — you can jine ma gang.

(DAVEY, then ALEX, move over behind him.)

DAVEY: Can Gus jine your gang?

HARRY: Aye. (To JUNE.) Come on, you. (Spits on GUS.)

(He goes off with JUNE.)

DAVEY: (to audience). And he took her up a close-mouth, and put his hand up her skirt, and did things to her. And still she didn't like it. But she couldn't do anything about it, because she was his girl. And that was Harry — one of us.

END ACT ONE

ACT TWO

Lights go up in the bar. BARMAN finishes mopping tables, unlocks door, takes towels off the taps.

HARRY, aged 15, comes on stage, outside the bar, leading GUS, ALEX and DAVEY. A bit tentative. They are very unsure of how to behave themselves in a bar. HARRY is now the ring-leader. He examines them, says, without too much confidence:

HARRY: Just dae whit ah dae, right?

(He leads them into the bar, with a certain amount of You go first going on among them. The BARMAN looks at them. HARRY goes over to him.)

HARRY: Four pints of heavy lager —

BARMAN: What age are you, son?

HARRY: Make that four vodkas.

BARMAN: I'll check with the governor.

HARRY: Four vodkas. I'm eighteen, right?

BARMAN: Don't get touchy — four vodkas.

(The others come over and collect their vodkas singly and go and sit at one table.)

HARRY: Get the girls.

(ALEX goes out. When the boys have sat down, JANICE and JUNE come in, JUNE in paroxysms of embarrassment. HARRY motions them to the bar.)

JANICE: Two vodka and orange, wi' some ice and a bit of lemon in 'em, now — and some crisps.

(BARMAN serves them. HARRY goes over and puts money in juke-box. Nothing happens.)

HARRY: (to BARMAN). Hey yuh — what's the matter wi' this thing?

BARMAN: It doesnae work.

HARRY: Oh. (Sits.)

(The GIRLS sit on the other side. A huge void between them. Silence. BARMAN watches. Nothing. A bloke on his way home from work drops in for a pint. Stops. Looks at set-up.)

BLOKE: Christ almighty. (To BARMAN.) The other bar open?

(BARMAN nods.)

BLOKE: Do you serve grown-ups in there?

BARMAN: No — hot pies —

BLOKE: Aye. (Goes.)

(Very tentatively, JUNE starts to sing 'The Black Hills of Dakota'. The OTHERS join in.)

DAVEY: (to audience). From that night on — that bar was ours.

(Through the SONG, the Bar changes back to the present day.)

DAVEY: (After song ends) What's it mean — to be a man? To us, it meant pushin' a woman around, fightin' — and drinkin'. That night, in that bar, we were men.

                      The schoolteachers, and the policemen and the good people they represent told us we were not: in their eyes we were less than human: and they had power, so they knew. But in that bar, that night, we were men. We've been drinkin' ever since to prove it.

(ALL are as they were, back in the bar.)

(JANICE and JUNE remain at their separate table. The MEN go over to the bar. DAVEY has gone off to the gents. JUNE steps forward, speaks, as herself today.)

JUNE: I know it isnae my story, but I'll tell you what happened to me. I was Harry's girl for a month, then he got fed up wi' me, for bein' a spoilsport — Janice gave me a talkin' to —

JANICE: You needed one —

JUNE: See, I tellt Harry to stop takin' me round the back —

JANICE: Aye, but that's what the lads all *want* — that's what you're his girl for —

JUNE: I don't like it —

JANICE: No, I know — but you should *get* tae like it — otherwise they'll think there's something wrong wi' you —

JUNE: I'm not going to get to like it —

JANICE: Well *pretend*. You don't need to let them go too far

— in fact you shouldn't — but don't put them off
— Look at the state of you . . . You're fifteen, you
should be doing somethin' about your appearance
— I'm gettin' worried about you . . .

JUNE: What's wrong wi' me? I like this dress . . .

JANICE: Aye but a man likes to see some make-up, somethin'
done to your hair, decent clothes, a bit of uplift,
and some *shoes* — you cannae get a decent man in
your sannies —

JUNE: But I don't think I want a decent man —

JANICE: You know what they'll be saying about you . . .

JUNE: What?

JANICE: You're not normal —

JUNE: But I'm normal for me.

JANICE: Listen — if you're normal, you want a man. And
what's the normal way to get a man? Do yoursel'
up like a normal woman — see here — I'm gonnae
take you in hand —

JUNE: Do you think?

JANICE: What do you think the chemists and the hairdressing
salons and the clothes shops and the shoe-shops
and all the adverts are for? To tell you how to be
normal —

JUNE: Aye — well, maybe — I don't want to be a freak . . .

JANICE: No — and you're not gonnae be — I'm gonnae see
you right. (Goes.)

JUNE: (to audience). And she did — It took quite a while,
because I had nae money for all they things, but I
got a job in a hotel, makin' the beds an' cleanin',
and Janice made me spend all my money getting
to look normal, and she taught me how to do eye-
shadow and deodorants, and green shoes and bras
that stuck out like tent-poles, and one night she
made me go in the pub again, and Harry didn't
recognise me, and he was awfy nice to me, and that
was how we got married, and had the two weans,
and lead the normal life. But I'll let yous get on —
sorry for holdin' yous up . . . (She goes.)

(Piano starts up again. GUS, unsteady, gets up and threatens HARRY.
DAVEY watches at top of steps.)

357

GUS: Don't come that wi' me, son —

ALEX: No no no — sit down, man —

GUS: I said Don't come that wi' me, son —

ALEX: Sit down, sit down —

GUS: I said —

HARRY: I heard you — now sit down.

(GUS sits. ALEX sits.)

GUS: Just don't come that wi' me.

DAVEY: Harry's life. A roundabout. Round and round —
                non stop, no gettin' off: just keep on payin' your
                sixpence every time the man puts his hand out —

                Brutalised, by his own life. How can he no put an
                end to that happenin'? He cannae — because he's
                brutalised. He's had it walloped intae his skull — at
                school, at work, by the clothes he wears on his back
                down the street — that he is unimportant, stupid.
                How can he no stop that happenin' all over again to
                his kids? He cannae — even if he wanted to, because
                it's there, in his skull, that he's unimportant, and
                stupid.

                And he's been told: everything you stand for is wrong,
                what you know about life is not acceptable, your
                house is not like the houses in the ads on the telly,
                your wife is not like the women in the magazines,
                your face not like the faces on the hoarding selling
                motor-cars, and your class, the working-class, are
                a mob of greedy gangsters intent on destroying the
                country.

                So he's split inside his skull, and how can he no
                do anythin' about the lies he's been sold? Well
                of course he cannae — he's split inside his skull,
                he's confused by the lies, he's unimportant and
                stupid — so he goes for a pint. And he feels better.
                Wi' a few pints and a few whiskies inside you,
                you can live with it all. The great lubricator of the
                merry-go-round — booze.

                So he gets pissed: and how can he no see that
                getting pissed is no' making anything better? Well
                of course he cannae see that — he's pissed.

(HARRY comes over to him with another couple of pints.)

HARRY:	Davey, you're my good friend, right? I'm gonnae tell ye. See me: I'm nothin'. Nothin'.
DAVEY:	You're OK, Harry —
HARRY:	Ach there's millions of blokes like me. Millions.
DAVEY:	What's wrong wi'em all?
HARRY:	Wrong wi' em? Nothing at all — great blokes.
DAVEY:	So what's wrong wi' being like millions of great blokes? That makes *you* a great bloke, Harry — and so y'are.
HARRY:	No. I'm nothin'.
DAVEY:	Remember you at school, Harry — don't kid me on: you were a hero — a great lad for the fightin', and the girls.
HARRY:	I'm done wi' fightin. I could smash every man in this boozer: what's tha' make me? Nothin'. And the women? Christ, even June thinks I'm nothin'. So I am.
DAVEY:	Of course you're no nothin'. You're a great bloke.
HARRY:	Davey — you're my mate — tell me somethin'. What is it I'm tryin' tae say?
DAVEY:	I don't know, Harry. There's something wrong with your life: is that what you're tryin' to say?
HARRY:	Aye — aye — but what? I mean — I've got a job, I've got a hoose, I've got a cooker and a fridge and a pile of furniture, food, clothes, a bed, money. I've got a wife and weans, ma mates — what's wrong wi' that? I mean — I could do wi a wee bit more of this, and a wee bit less of that — but who couldnae: thing is — I just feel I'm nothin'. What am I tryin' to say, Davey?
DAVEY:	You're just saying you're a human being.
HARRY:	Aye, but see — there's somethin' missin'.
DAVEY:	Where do you work, Harry?
HARRY:	McGoverns Chemicals, same as you —
DAVEY:	Did you want to work there?

HARRY: Want to? Last time I was out of work the feller at the Broo says: You interested in Chemistry? I says Aye, what's the money like? Noo I'm shovellin' chemical muck a' day in Shettleston. It's no a bad job, cannae complain.

DAVEY: But you enjoyed workin' in the yard?

HARRY: So I did, after a manner of speakin' . . .

DAVEY: What for did you pack it in?

HARRY: Wasnae ma idea — two thousand of us got laid off.

DAVEY: Whose idea was that?

HARRY: Christ knows — here — what are you sayin'?

DAVEY: Where do you live now?

HARRY: MacIver Tower: Eleven flair up.

DAVEY: What did you want to live there for?

HARRY: I didnae want to live there — that was where I was put.

DAVEY: And June?

HARRY: What about her?

DAVEY: Why did you want to marry June?

HARRY: I had tae. She was in the club. What are you gettin' at?

DAVEY: Can you think of one thing you're doing that you really want to do?

HARRY: Aye — drinkin' . . .

DAVEY: Do you really want to drink?

HARRY: No . . . Aye — what else can I dae?

DAVEY: Plenty.

HARRY: You talkin' about politics?

DAVEY: I'm talkin' about the hole in your heart.

HARRY: That's politics you're talkin' — We've got blokes like that down McGovern's: it's rubbish — class war, smash the bosses, down wi' capitalists — see that guy McCloy, Works Manager — couldnae

360

meet a straighter bloke. Knows everybody's name
in the whole works, and he's a very clever man.
Now how should he no have a decent wage? He's
worked for it. I'm no gonnae rise up and cut his
throat because he doesnae live down our street.
He deserves a decent life, know what I mean?

DAVEY: Aye, maybe. But is he getting one?

HARRY: I should bloody hope so — the money he takes home.

DAVEY: I feel sorry for the man.

HARRY: Away — I thought you hated his guts —

DAVEY: No his guts, no. Just what he does — and what
            it's done to him. He's got a great job for Apex
            Pharmaceuticals International, makin' drugs cheap,
            for them to sell at ten times the price to the Health
            Service, that is, to you and me.

HARRY: Aye, well that's no right, but you cannae blame *him*.

DAVEY: No. We're good pals, me and Andrew McCloy —
            just like that.

HARRY: Aye —

DAVEY: Do you know why I came in here tonight? Because
            I went to see my friend Andrew in his office after
            work tonight. Just a personal chat, you'll understand
            — Will I tell you about it?

(Tables moved to office setting.)

HARRY: You? And McCloy? Having a nice wee chat? On
            your way —

(Lights change. Enter McCLOY, a 35-year-old Glasgow business man,
thoughtful and ambitious. He sits and sips tea, reading reports. A knock
on the door.)

DAVEY: Mr McCloy?

McCLOY: Oh hello, David, come in — nice of you to come
            by — sit down.

DAVEY: Thanks —

McCLOY: I hope I'm not keeping you back from something
            important — It seemed more appropriate to have
            a chat after working hours, as what I have to say

361

	is by way of being more personal than our usual confrontations. Will you take a drink? A whisky perhaps?
DAVEY:	No — no thank you.
McCLOY:	You're quite a sober sort of man, David — I've been very impressed by the way you conduct yourself. Which is why, I suppose, I wanted you to hear my good news —
DAVEY:	Mr McCloy, I must point out that I am not entitled to enter into any negotiations, official or unofficial, without at least one other steward present —
McCLOY:	That's another thing I like about you, David — absolutely straight — no no, you can relax — I'm not trying to swing a deal with you — that's not the way I work either — we're very alike in that. No no. My news is of a much more personal nature. I'm leaving this job.
DAVEY:	Leaving McGoverns?
McCLOY:	Well not exactly. McGoverns will still be a subsidiary of Apex. And I've been offered a seat on the board of Apex Great Britain Limited — with special responsibility for Personnel. It's a big move up for me, as you can appreciate — it'll mean up sticks and away to Reading.
DAVEY:	Congratulations —
McCLOY:	Thanks — I must admit I'm looking forward to it. But I'm going to have one hell of a fight on my hands down there.
DAVEY:	Oh?
McCLOY:	Davey — I'm not satisfied with our industrial policy. Wages — well, there's not much we can do about wages, even our bonus schemes are tied to the government's pay code. But manning — we're in a hell of a mess there — with proper re-training schemes we could give a lot of blokes who are stuck in dead-end jobs a much better chance to get on in the firm, to move from subsidiary to subsidiary, up the ladder, so to speak — a bit of upward mobility, to motivate the bright sparks. I want to get our people moving. Would that not be a good thing?
DAVEY:	It has its problems —

McCLOY: Exactly. I knew you'd say that — And that is why
              I asked you in for a chat, because you are familiar
              with those problems: more so than I am, or any
              member of senior management. You see, the first
              step I'm going to take when I get to Reading, is to
              survey the entire career-structure pattern of Apex
              Pharmaceuticals, from tea-boy to Managing Director,
              and then proceed to re-create it, step by step, so
              that every man or woman has the same chance
              to get on — onwards and upwards. Why should
              Harry McCall rot away in Shettleston, scraping
              out the same vats year after year when he could
              be re-trained, with Government assistance, and be
              producing more and better goods, for more money,
              by pressing the right buttons in our new plant in
              Gravesend? Upward mobility — more opportunity
              for every employee, more interest in life — and a
              happier Apex family.

DAVEY: Are you asking me if I think it would work?

McCLOY: No. I'm asking you to come with me to Reading
              and make it work.

DAVEY: Me?

McCLOY: Industrial Relations Adviser: your own office, five
              thousand a year plus, a house and a car. We can
              work out the details. I can see you're surprised.
              Good. I hoped you would be.

DAVEY: I'm amazed —

McCLOY: If this scheme works, David, a lot more people are
              going to be amazed. It's an opportunity to make life
              better, more interesting, for the working man, to
              give an aim, an incentive, to men with no future.
              I've known you for some years now — one of the
              finest convenors in Scotland, a first-class negotiator,
              a militant for what you believe in, and a member
              of the Communist Party — am I right?

DAVEY: It's no secret —

McCLOY   Some people might think I've taken leave of my
              senses — but you're the man I want for this job.
              Because you have the good of the employees very
              close to your heart, as I do, and you understand
              their problems, which maybe I don't, and you speak
              their language, which I can't. And I don't believe

363

a man like you will pass up this opportunity. Ask yourself: what are my alternatives? The usual man for the job is some sold-out superannuated Trade Union bureaucrat, who will say what we want him to say, and miss the point of the whole operation. What do you and I both want? We want Apex to be a desirable firm to work for. Right — let's make it that way.

DAVEY: I want Apex to be nationalised under workers' control —

McCLOY Good — that's your opinion: it's not mine, but I'm not going to argue with you. The point is: at the moment, it *isn't* nationalised. So let's make it at least civilised.

DAVEY: And how is all this going to affect profits?

McCLOY: With a happy, motivated work-force and a statutory incomes policy, profits will look after themselves. Make no mistake — I admire a lot of what you people stand for: it can, and must, affect our thinking.

DAVEY: But. You are the people who think.

McCLOY: But that's what I'm saying — I'm asking *you* to think with me —

DAVEY: In an office in Reading, with a lot of thousand a year, a house and a car? Let me get this straight — in my head — You're asking me to join you, not to improve the profitability of Apex Great Britain, not to sell your schemes to the workers, not to whizz-kid your way to the top, but for me to have a wee shot at thinking?

McCLOY You've forgotten something. I'm asking you to join me to help me make the working lives of every man and woman in the Apex Group, more interesting, and more fulfilled. You're an intelligent man, David — don't hark back like a record with a stuck needle to the old days of class conflict, evil bosses, noble workers and blacker-than-black villains in the board room. Those days are over. I'm an employee, just like — Harry McCall. I earn my living by doing my job, just as he does. I'm a manager, he's a labourer — what's the difference?

DAVEY: Are you asking me? I'll tell you. You think. You decide. You instruct. He is thought about. What

364

he does is decided for him. He is instructed. You
are active. He is passive. You are the subject of the
sentence. He is the object.

The old class divisions might appear to have gone.
But they've only been made more confusing. It's
quite simple, really. To be in your position, you need
to have taken into yourself the real interests of the
shareholders of Apex Pharmaceuticals International.
You need to have joined the logic of capital: profit,
growth, amalgamation, monopoly, multi-national,
imperialism. Once you've joined, you're on the
ladder to power — and you too can become the
President of the United States of America. Given
time, and money.

But if you don't join, or you don't have the
qualifications, you're out. You're the object of
history, the passive receiver of instructions from the
foreman, the boss, the teacher, the policeman, the
government, the gnomes of Zurich and the Chase
Manhattan Bank.

There's your class-system *now*, Mr McCloy. But
there's two problems for you in it, and they're
the same as they always have been. One, your
system's not working too well, is it? It's looking a
bit patched and tattered. And Number Two, these
people, these things, these objects of your decisions
are human beings: they know there's something
missing from their lives. So they get pissed, to make
them feel complete for a while. But it doesn't last.
Sooner or later they're going to demand the right
to think for themselves, to decide for themselves,
to control their own work and their own lives. And
when they do, your system is not going to be able
to accommodate them: is it?

McCLOY: And will yours accommodate them any better? Do
               they not drink in Russia?

DAVEY: Russia? Is that what you're throwing at me?

McCLOY: It's your Utopia, isn't it?

DAVEY: Ten per cent of the entire income of the USSR
               comes from duty on vodka. The statues of Stalin
               have been pulled down, the streets re-named and
               Stalingrad is suddenly Volgograd: but the spectre of
               Stalin walks the streets, and terrorises the Western
               World. We can do better than that.

McCLOY:	When?
DAVEY:	Sooner or later —
McCLOY:	And meantime — you want people's lives to get worse — so they can see how evil capitalism is?
DAVEY:	No —
McCLOY:	Is that why you're turning me down?
DAVEY:	Of course not —
McCLOY:	What I'm talking about is real, starting next month, with an actual effect next year — it's a way to make people's lives better *now*. Not in eighty years' time; or never —
DAVEY:	I don't think —
McCLOY:	It's your methods, man: you'll never win — you frighten people. They don't want to think, or decide — they want a quiet life with a pint in their hand and their tea on the table, maybe a holiday in Spain every two years — what I'm offering is a *better* quite life:
DAVEY:	With two pints in their hand, caviare for tea, and holidays in Haiti?
McCLOY:	Yes. And I'm going to win, and you — whatever you're dreaming of — are doomed. Why? Because it's asking ordinary people to do *too much*. And they won't do it. Ask Harry McCall: would he rather have another twenty pounds a week from a better job in Apex Plymouth, or a bloody revolution — ask him.
DAVEY:	(pauses). I don't think you can buy people's minds — his or mine. I will not be trapped in the logic of profit, repression and exploitation.
McCLOY:	We all are.

(Enter MRS McCLOY. It is not apparent at first that she is pissed out of her head.)

MRS McCLOY:	Andrew — are you still there?
McCLOY:	Oh — excuse me: I'm here Shona —
MRS McCLOY:	I want to borrow the car — (Sees DAVEY.) Oh.

	Am I disturbing you? He works such terrible hours, sometimes I have to come and drag him home —
McCLOY:	This is David Matheson, dear. (To DAVEY.) My wife.
DAVEY:	Pleased to meet you —
MRS McCLOY:	Oh — union matters: perhaps I shouldn't say this, Mr Matheson, but you people give my husband a pain in the arse.
McCLOY:	Here are the keys for the car, dear — but: do you think you should?
MRS McCLOY:	Should what?
McCLOY:	Drive?
MRS McCLOY:	(to DAVEY). He thinks I'm an alcoholic — (Fiercely.) Of course I should, I need to go somewhere, stop bossing me around, I'm not one of your employees —
McCLOY:	Well — I have almost finished — if, David, you would excuse us, perhaps —
MRS McCLOY:	You're not coming with me —
McCLOY:	Where are you going to?
MRS McCLOY:	Mind your own fucking business —
DAVEY:	Er — if you don't mind, I'll be on my way.
MRS McCLOY:	Perhaps I can give you a lift somewhere?
DAVEY:	No no, there's a perfectly good bus — thank you.
MRS McCLOY:	Hm. No. I'm giving you a lift. You're interesting. (To McCLOY.) Give me the keys.
McCLOY:	I don't think so, Shona.

(She is defeated, crumbles, cries, sits.)

MRS McCLOY:	Why can I never do anything for myself?
McCLOY:	(helping her up and out). Come on, my dear — I'll look after you . . . (Turns to DAVEY.) Perhaps we can talk again.
DAVEY:	Er — of course —
McCLOY:	We're all trapped —

(He goes, distressed, with MRS McCLOY)

DAVEY: Poor bastards . . .

(DAVEY goes back to HARRY, lights change.)

DAVEY: And I went home. And I told the wife. And she said
                I should have taken the job. My own wife.

HARRY: Quite right too — that sounds like a rare opportunity
                — are you going to see the man again?

DAVEY: I resign. I have retired. All those years. I was kidding
                myself on. (Feels sick.) Oh Christ — (Recovers a
                bit.) We're all men — right, we're all men. Fourteen
                years, since I started work — batterin' away: for my
                mates — my class — saying: do we want something
                better? Yes. Do we want dignity? Yes. Do we want
                pride? Yes. Do we want self-respect? Yes. Do we
                know how to start on the long march towards all
                these things? Yes, yes, yes — And are we gonna
                do anythin' about it? Away, we're off for a pint —
                you do something.

                Well, I've resigned. I've retired — (Dizzy again.)
                Oh no, my head — Am I gonnae do somethin'? —
                No. (Collapses. Slowly recovers, sighs deeply.) Yes.

(Piano begins — 'My Way'.)

DAVEY: I've been standin' watchin' this for too long — I'm
                gonnae get you, Harry — I'm gonnae get you. You,
                Harry McCall, at this very moment, are the most
                important man in Western Europe —

HARRY: Davey, you're my pal —

DAVEY: No — I mean it. You could create somethin', here in
                Scotland, that would change the course of history:
                do you know that?

HARRY: Are you tryin' tae take the mickey out of me,
                Davey —

DAVEY: No. I'm tellin' you the simple truth: you are the
                most important man in Western Europe. What are
                you going to do about it?

HARRY: Excuse me —

(HARRY goes over and SINGS, with some passion, the Frank Sinatra
standard — 'My Way'.

DAVEY watches. Song ends with HARRY rising to a fine crescendo on the last line — 'I'll Do It My Way'. HARRY finishes and sits, taking the applause of the OTHERS in the bar.)

DAVEY: Can y'no' hear what I'm saying? Take the banana out of your ear, Harry —

BARMAN: Clear the bar now please, clear the bar —

DAVEY: Shut up!

HARRY: Ach he just wants to watch his telly — don't get carried away —

DAVEY: Aye — I'm gettin' angry, and bunched up — why? Because I think that guy's pushin' me around. Multiply that by ten thousand — orders, demands, frustrations, indignities — and you've got your average working man — you've got me, and you. Our minds are split into pieces, we're told we're wrong, fools, on the rubbish-tip — and we get a drink inside us and out they come — The Wild Things, Things with no Name, Creatures of Dreams, Fantasies, Deep-repressed Desires — to be Loved, to Dominate, Covered-up Despair — The Truth of our Situation that we can't speak, the Visions of Freedom and Wholeness and Peace with the world, that we all need — to feel whole, complete, and in charge of our destiny.

BARMAN: Come along now please —

DAVEY: The rearguard of Calvin and Knox walk Scotland with straps, crushing the feeling and the singing and the emotion out of our lives, and we take a drink to let it out, and we're singing and laughing and crying and holding on to each other with a great gush of sentiment and love for other human beings —

(GUS and ALEX start pushing each other — it grows into a fight.)

And then we take a few too many, and start to thump and kick — at anything we can reach, best mate, anything — because we cannae kick at the market machine that sticks us in jobs we hate, then lays us off when it wants to, then undermines whole cities, whole countries, if it has to — we think we cannae kick that in the balls — don't we? But we can, we can — but we're drunk and all our energy goes on some poor bastard that's just as screwed up as we are — look at it — every bloody night,

369

all the energy we've got left after working for their bloody system, we spend kicking each other.

BARMAN: Outside please. Outside please. (Loud and sharp.)

(ALEX is carried off, out cold.)

DAVEY: Finally — oblivion. They've won. The working class has committed mental suicide. The guerilla tactics of McEwans, Youngers, Scottish and Newcastle and the DCL have paid off. We've been wiped out by chemical warfare. What's wrong wi' all of us — have we all gone mental?

HARRY: Come on now, Davey, the wee mannie's gettin' restless.

DAVEY: Aye, come on — out in the street — scatter to our homes — divided, hopeless, pissed. Come on, Harry.

(They go out, stop in the street.)

HARRY: Davey — what you're saying: See: I think that's just human nature.

DAVEY: Oh no! Once upon a time, it was human nature to own slaves. It was human nature to buy your wife from her father. If you were a Pict, it was human nature to wear woad — If you were a cannibal it was human nature to eat people. No, Harry — it's no' human nature. It's capitalism. Getting something better in its place. And getting it to work — there's a lot needs doin'.

HARRY: Will you come back for a wee drink, maybe? See — I've a quarter bottle somewhere or other.

DAVEY: Aye — well: aye, I will. Is June at home?

HARRY: Aye.

DAVEY: Good: aye, I will — I'm, er — wanting to talk to you . . .

(They go. The SINGER and The BAND, left in the bar, sing — OTHERS join in as the BARMAN counts the takings.)

People have been meeting in the cities
People have been gathering in the towns
Meeting and talking in a whisper
Talking of the life that keeps them down

Counting the takings

Counting the giving
Counting the joy and the sorrow
Counting the days
The small change of living
Counting all the hopes for — hopes for tomorrow . . .

People have been meeting in the cities
Nothing much been ventured, not much won,
Trying to forget —
But having to remember —
All the clouds that are blocking out the sun:

Drowning your sorrow
Is drowning tomorrow,
And crying in your drink won't make things good —
Forget your sorrow
And drink to tomorrow
For things won't change unless we think they could.

You can choose your meeting in the city
You can choose your meeting in this town
You can buy your head-ache from the brewers
Or you can turn this world right upside-down

Drowning your sorrow
Is Drowning tomorrow
And crying in your drink won't make things good
Forget your sorrow
And drink to tomorrow
For things won't change unless we think they could.

END

Random Happenings in the Hebrides

Random Happenings in the Hebrides was first presented by the Lyceum Theatre for the Edinburgh International Festival in August 1969.

It was directed by Richard Eyre, designed by John Gunter, lit by Andy Phillips, with costumes by Lorraine McKee.

JOHN THAW	Jimmy Litherland
JOSEPH GREIG	Aeney McPhee
JOHN CAIRNEY	John James McPhee
ELIZABETH MacLENNAN	Catriona McPhee
ZOE HICKS	Irishwoman
KATE BINCHY	Rachel
BROWN DERBY	Andy
JOHN SHEDDEN	Calum
MAGGIE JORDAN	Mary
MOREEN SCOTT	Pauline
BILL McCABE	Macalaster
BRYDEN MURDOCH	Tom
MICHAEL HARRIGAN	Peter Fraser
JIMMY GAVIGAN	MacDonald
MATT McGINN	Donaldson
IAIN AGNEW	Fishermen
DENIS LAWSON	
IAN (KENNY) IRELAND	
MARTIN HELLER	Doctor
KEVIN COLLINS	Mr MacDonald
SHEILA LATIMER	Mrs MacDonald
MAY HENRY	Andy's wife
SANDRA BUCHAN	Teresa

The action of the play takes place between 1964 and 1970

The poem read in Act 1 Scene 4 is by Sorley Maclean, translated from the Gaelic by Iain Crichton Smith, which translation was first published in Lines 28.

ACT ONE

Scene One

Graveyard overlooking sea. January, 1964.

The first sound heard is that of the sea, loud and insistent: amongst the crashings of the waves should be heard the spatter of rows of drops on the tops of the rocks, and the awful suck of water away from cliffs. No seagulls. Land and water, angrily meeting.

This sound continues through the first scene, making it almost a dumb show. It is, anyway, dreamlike, and operatically lit. The main events should take place against the sky line, and be done with slightly exaggerated gestures. If there is to be music, it must not be louder than the waves.

The curtain goes up in darkness, then, after the lights have come up to reveal an incline running up from the audience's left to right, and the huge bulk of a chapel in the centre, a coffin is carried on and up the hill. It is followed by a small group of mourners, in grey and black tweed suits, who straggle out behind the chief mourners. These are: AENEAS McPHEE, 52, the village schoolmaster, short, voluble, violent, looking slightly incongruous in this role; his daughter CATRIONA, a strong, hidden, rather beautiful girl with clear eyes and unstarved figure, aged twenty-three/four; and his son, JOHN JAMES, a rebellious spirit whose reaction to his father's slightly 'respectable' position — even if he has failed to be respected for it — was to leave school at fourteen and go straight to work with all the roughest lads of the village on the fishing boats. He, too, looks incongruous, is unsure of how much emotion he can show, but is deeply troubled underneath.

The action is as follows:

The coffin is pushed right across the stage, followed by the mourners, who halt at the highest point to watch it being lowered off-stage.

While this is going on, a young man appears, obviously late. He is JIMMY LITHERLAND, twenty-six, attacking, very intelligent, nervous. He was evacuated here from Liverpool during the war, and considers it his home. He is now returning here for good.

He goes straight into the chapel, but re-emerges a moment later having seen that it is empty. He is about to leave when he sees the group up the hill. He goes and stands at the foot of the hill, waiting, his hands clasped together. He has a shapeless, black overcoat on, over grey flannels and a jacket, and no tie. He tries to conceal this fact by clutching his coat lapels together at his throat, nervously, compulsively.

The group slowly break away and stand aside waiting for the family. JOHN JAMES moves away first and he, too, waits for his father and CATRIONA. In a moment they turn, and together lead the way back down the hill. JOHN JAMES follows at a distance. When they get close to JIMMY, McPHEE looks up and is pleased to recognise him.

(*Freezes for four seconds.*)

CATRIONA is not so pleased, but smiles. McPHEE quietly nods, shakes his hand, and JIMMY walks on beside him, in JOHN JAMES' position. This is not lost on JOHN JAMES, who watches this as if it were a calculated insult to him. JIMMY puts a hand on McPHEE's shoulder; (*Freeze action.*) JOHN JAMES stops. The other mourners, in their subtle way, are acutely aware of this. So is CATRIONA, who looks back and reaches out a hand to JOHN JAMES; (*Freeze action.*) he ignores it and walks off alone, full of black thoughts.

As the other mourners shuffle off after them, the lights fade, and the sound of the sea swells up.

Scene Two

Public bar and saloon bar, Morna Hotel. January, 1964.

The chapel revolves, or is transformed, into the Morna Hotel. This is a multiple set which forms the basis of the action.

It consists of: (i) a scruffy public bar of a type common on the west coast of Scotland (and of Ireland) — a bare wooden bar, a couple of wooden tables with chairs around them, a piano, a one armed bandit, a few bottles on the wall behind the bar, and very little else. (ii) This interconnects behind the bar — so one barman can serve both — with the saloon bar, or resident's lounge: armchair, sofas, low tables and even a bowl of flowers. And (iii) above both, a hotel bedroom, with two single beds, clean, neat, sparsely furnished.

The 'Incline' of Scene One has moved over to the right and now has a wooden bench on it, looking out over the audience, or the sea. This is another playing area.

At the moment, the wake is prepared for gloomily in the saloon. Some sandwiches and cakes are laid out on the tables, and some small glasses of whisky. There is an atmosphere of constraint over the whole thing. The women of the funeral party wait in uneasy silence. McPHEE and CATRIONA come in, followed by the MEN. JIMMY goes up to his room, starts looking for a tie.

CATRIONA:	Oh, God, we didn't ask the minister —
McPHEE:	This is not the marriage feast at Cana — we do *not* require any water turning into wine.
CATRIONA:	Oh, Dad!

McPHEE: The year is 1964 AD, not BC.

DONALDSON: Sad day, Mr McPhee.

McPHEE: Aye, lad, it is. Drink up.

ANDY: Aeny — (Mournful pause.) I'm terribly sorry.

McPHEE: Can't be helped.

ANDY: The Lord moves in mysterious ways . . .

McPHEE: Aye (Irritated.) So he does.

ANDY: We can't always follow His pattern . . .

McPHEE: You mean *I* should have gone first?

CATRIONA: Oh, Dad.

McPHEE: What's the man talking about? If cancer of the
                womb is one of the Lord's ways, the Lord's not so
                much mysterious as plain evil — what's got into
                Andy? Is he scared of dying, or what?

Inside the saloon, the mourners have been awkwardly drinking and
mumbling amongst themselves. MacALISTER and MARY serve out
more drinks and sandwiches.

CATRIONA is trying to make the best of things going around talking
to everyone, but McPHEE himself is being very difficult, sitting on the
arm of a chair, picking his teeth with his thumbnail, lost in a trance.

CATRIONA now comes over to him.

CATRIONA: Dad — (She gestures to the guests.)

McPHEE: (pulling himself together). Oh, great Gods, yes, I
                suppose I must. (Looks rather amazed at the petite
                glass of sherry he has in his hand.) What am I doing
                drinking sherry? Will you get me a dram for God's
                sake, and half a pint of heavy.

CATRIONA: Dad, you're not in the public bar on a Saturday
                night . . .

McPHEE: (looks around). I can see that, Catriona.

CATRIONA takes his sherry glass, sinks it down, and goes over to the
bar to get him his drink. A WOMAN MOURNER comes up piously.

TERESA: She was a grand woman was Bessie . . .

McPHEE: Aye, and she died of a grand disease. Did you ever read 'The Black Swan' by Thomas Mann? No, I can see you didn't. Do you know, I recognise that look on your face, Teresa — that boy of yours wears it when I catch him fiddling under the desk . . . Not that I would discourage him, you understand.

CATRIONA: Dad, will you stop insulting people — we all know you're upset, and so are we, too.

McPHEE: Did you get my dram?

MARY brings his whisky.

MARY: Here you are, Mr McPhee. (Turns to CATRIONA.) Have you seen who we've got staying in the hotel, just now?

CATRIONA: Jimmy, is it?

MARY: *You'll* be pleased.

CATRIONA: It's been a long time . . .

McPHEE: (jumps up on chair, clears his throat — silence). Ladies and gentlemen, good neighbours, I won't say many words. We have already been constrained by the customs of our small community to sit through twenty minutes or so from the reverend minister which neither comforted the living nor eulogised the dead.

JOHN JAMES comes in, goes to door of saloon, listens, rejects the idea of going in, goes around to the public bar, and listens from there.

McPHEE: So I'll be brief. Bessie was well beloved. Since her death on Saturday we have had tributes to her not only from all over our islands, but also from all over the globe. To these, I shall, at this moment, add not one word.

You will have noticed, by contrast, how few of you there are present here. This was by design — one might almost say by her request. We were told, some thirty-one years ago, when we first came to these islands as young schoolmaster and beautiful bride, that they were characterised by one main feature: hypocrisy. We have found this to be more or less accurate.

Ladies and Gentlemen, you constitute the few that Bessie has treasured through her lifetime: you are the ones that she would have chosen to be present at this time — the friends we can speak our minds to. And what I have to say is this: I know you will miss her. You know I will miss her. We all loved her. She died too young, cruelly young, and we are bereft.

But life must go on, so no two minutes' silence: eat up and drink up — it's all paid for. And thank you for coming.

McPHEE gets down from the chair. There is an embarrassed silence as JOHN JAMES, who has been listening in the bar next door, claps ironically — meanly and cynically. McPHEE sits down.

Inside the Public Bar, the IRISH WOMAN, also known as ROSITA is sitting by the fire with her back to us, looking like a tied-up bundle of old mackintosh and headscarf. She turns as JOHN JAMES comes in and we see a surprisingly young, weather-beaten face: she could be thirty, forty or even forty-five.

She is considered slightly mad by the locals — she sleeps rough and is always in the bar as soon as it opens, sipping half a pint of stout through three or four hours, never leaving until closing time. Her one accomplishment is to be able to sing, in a wild, high, very loud voice, the popular ballads of ten or fifteen years before.

She nods at JOHN JAMES and turns back to the fire. He acknowledges her with a curt dip of his chin and goes straight to the bar. He waits, leaning, in a posture comfortable through long familiarity.

The IRISH WOMAN, without turning, speaks.

IRISH WOMAN: Bad cess to the day your own mother goes under. (She turns.) She'll be smarting now for the lack of you, somewheres, as bad as you will be for the lack of her.

JOHN JAMES: Aye. (He savagely punches the bell on the counter.) Where the hell's MacAlaster?

IRISH WOMAN: (eyeing him). Waiting on the mourners . . . would you have the price of a nip, would you, to keep a woman warm?

JOHN JAMES turns and looks at her. There is mischief in her eyes. He goes over to strike her in a sudden fury.

JOHN JAMES: You mischievous old bitch.

She stays quite still and stops him with a look.

IRISH WOMAN: I'm sorry she's gone, boy. (Pause.) Buy me a nip and a dram for yourself: do you good. (Nods to the bar.) Here's MacAlaster now.

JOHN JAMES goes over to the bar.

JOHN JAMES: Pint of heavy and a half — (Grudging.) And a nip for herself — (Jerks his head.)

MacALASTER: (shocked). Are you not coming through, John James?

JOHN JAMES: Aye. Mebbe later.

He resumes his stance at the bar. MacALASTER pulls the drinks, puts them on the counter; goes back to the saloon with a look at JOHN JAMES.

Upstairs, JIMMY tears the red tie off and looks around desperately. Inside the suitcase is a sort of strap of black material. He gets out a pair of scissors and cuts it off and ties it round his neck. It works a treat.

In the bar, the IRISH WOMAN comes over to get her nip of whisky from the end of the counter.

She raises it to JOHN JAMES.

IRISH WOMAN: God bless you, son. May you never harm a woman . . . Remember her as she was, not as she is now, and you'll not go far wrong.

She drinks and goes back to the fire, warmed by the whisky.

JOHN JAMES drinks up and goes out.

After JOHN JAMES has gone out, JIMMY comes dashing in wearing a terrible piece of black stuff round his neck, that looks ridiculous. Some of the MOURNERS recognise him, but not all. He stands at the door.

McPHEE: Jimmy — good boy, good boy — (Sees tie.) What in the name of Moloch is that black abortion you've got round your neck?

JIMMY: This? I thought I ought to wear a tie.

McPHEE: A tie? Is that what it is?

CATRIONA: Where did you get it?

JIMMY: I — I didn't have one. It's the strap from inside my suitcase —

McPHEE: Take it off, for God's sake.

381

JIMMY:	Shall I?
CATRIONA:	(nods). Jimmy.

He takes it off, as he goes over to AENEY.

JIMMY:	I'm sorry about the missus, Aeney.
McPHEE:	Ach, the world's a dim brute place, and to hell with it.
JIMMY:	It has its moments.
McPHEE:	You're still an optimist? We're trapped, boy, inside an inanimate vortex — irrational and meaningless — does a rock have logic? Does the sea have meaning? No. And neither do we.
JIMMY:	Come on now, Aeney —
CATRIONA:	How are your parents?
JIMMY:	Happy now they're back in Liverpool among the grit and the effluents; my father's struggling to become the first fully automated electronic man.
McPHEE:	Is he working?
JIMMY:	In a clock factory.

People start to leave, come up to McPHEE to say goodbye, etc . . .

MR MacDONALD:	Well, Aeney, you'll excuse us if we're away —
McPHEE:	I'm ashamed of myself — I've not had one word with you.
MRS MacDONALD:	Not to think about it, Mr McPhee.
MR MacDONALD:	It was a grand speech, Aeney.
McPHEE:	Do you know who this is? Hey? You remember our boy from Liverpool?
MR MacDONALD:	Jimmy Litherland? Who'd have believed it?
JIMMY:	Mr MacDonald, isn't it?
MR MacDONALD:	Meet my wife — I'm married again, you know . . .
McPHEE:	Hey — right through Liverpool University — first class honours in Economics — and two years higher research at Wadham College, Oxford . . .
JIMMY:	And glad to be away from it, I can tell you . . .

McPHEE:	B. Litt.
JIMMY:	Aeney, you must stop showing me off like some prize Aberdeen Angus —
MRS MacDONALD:	You should be proud of it, Mr Litherland. It's education gets you places . . .
JIMMY:	I'm prouder of the time I spent here, Mrs MacDonald, and that's God's honest truth.
McPHEE:	Aye — proud you survived, no doubt.
JIMMY:	(coughs). You haven't changed a bit, Aeney.
McPHEE:	Hm — cynical to the end.
MR MacDONALD:	Goodbye, Jimmy — I hope you'll give Iain a shout if you have time — he'll be looking for you —
JIMMY:	I'll be over tomorrow, whenever he gets in.
MR MacDONALD:	Do that. Goodbye now Aeney. And don't forget — we'll be there. Catriona, be sure and remind him.
CATRIONA:	I will. Goodbye now. Thanks for coming.
McPHEE:	That's got shot of the burgers — now for the peasants and the troglodytes: not forgetting the quack. God, boy, this place — you've got no idea — and this is the pick of them . . . (He goes, leaving JIMMY with CATRIONA.)
JIMMY:	He loves it really.
CATRIONA:	You know him very well all of a sudden, Jimmy Litherland: what makes you so sure?
JIMMY:	There's something about this place, Catriona, you don't find anywhere else. They may be a bit short on logic here, but they can still dream.
CATRIONA:	A-ha. I do live here Jimmy.
JIMMY:	I know. Catriona — you were one of the reasons I had to come back.
CATRIONA:	A-ha.
JIMMY:	Do you not believe me?
CATRIONA:	Mebbe so.
JIMMY:	(getting serious). Listen, Catriona —

CATRIONA: (putting up a hand). We'll talk of it another time, Jimmy.

JIMMY: Of course. I'm sorry. Where's John James?

CATRIONA: He — didn't show up.

JIMMY: Is he teaching now?

CATRIONA: No. He's a skipper on the boats. He went to the fishing three years ago — just to spite father.

JIMMY: You're hard on him.

CATRIONA: Acha. You don't have to scrub out his underclothes stinking of beer and mackerel.

JIMMY: Neither do you.

CATRIONA: No. I don't. Before this term's over, Dad'll be handing in his notice, and we'll both be away.

JIMMY: (laughs). You're not — (Realising she means it.) Leaving the island? (She nods.) Where on earth would you go to?

CATRIONA: Nashville, Tennessee.

JIMMY: I don't believe you.

CATRIONA: Here, look they're all away to their dinners —

JIMMY stands alone frowning and thinking as the people shove off with a certain amount of formality and hand shaking. McPHEE turns round as the last one goes and looks hurriedly at his watch, then drops his arm.

McPHEE: Aye, well — there's no hurry back — MacAlaster, would you ever replenish these glasses, the big ones and the wee ones —

MacALISTER: Mr McPhee — if I may say so, it's a wicked disgrace, your Bessie, I mean — and will you kindly take these on me . . .

McPHEE: Thank you, Neil. We will. Never been known to refuse.

MacALASTER nods to MARY and goes off to get them. She remains to collect the glasses and tidy up. McPHEE and JIMMY settle in chairs, CATRIONA perches and prowls.

McPHEE: I feel as if there's a great pressure lifted, somewhere inside me — now she's down that awful hole.

384

CATRIONA: Oh, dad, how can you say that?

McPHEE: I speak with no disrespect: that pressure moulded my life, squeezed me into shape — that's what I married her for. Without her, it all feels a bit — slack. (Pause.) Still, that's supposed to be the modern panacea, is it not — relaxation, cool, slackness, inertia . . . perhaps I'll give lessons in it . . .

JIMMY: In Tennessee?

McPHEE: Did you tell Jimmy about that? (She nods.) Well, what do you think? Life begins at fifty-four . . .

JIMMY: Aeney, you're a valuable man, and shoving off to America of all places — for Christ's sake!

McPHEE: Maybe Nashville, Tennessee *is* a trifle extreme, Jimmy, but right now, I feel I'm finished with this little island. I need to move on.

Silence. MacALASTER goes. The glasses rattle as MARY puts them on a tray. JIMMY hands one up to her as she hovers round him. There is a look of something between them — MARY blushes; CATRIONA doesn't miss a thing, looks at them, wondering. MARY goes off.

JIMMY: I'm sorry I was so vehement just now, Aeney.

McPHEE: Don't be sorry, Jimmy — never make excuses or apologies: above all, not for speaking your mind.

JIMMY: I'm not sorry for what I said: it was an unnecessary time to say it.

McPHEE: Well — maybe you were right. Maybe we should just go somewhere nearer home — they're always looking for schoolmasters, even toothless old windbags like me: and Catriona's never out of a job. Maybe in Edinburgh: as a matter of fact, I always had a bit of a yen for Carlisle: Where the Picts and the Scots kept the Romans at bay. The Romans, I imagine, took one look at Scotland, decided they didn't *want* to go any further, anyway. Aye, maybe Carlisle . . .

CATRIONA: Now, dad, there's not much point in moving to Carlisle —

McPHEE: You find it a trifle whimsical: perhaps it is: perhaps I'm feeling old.

Pause.

JIMMY:	It's no more whimsical than Tennessee, Aeney, whatever way you look at it.
McPHEE:	(sighs). Aye. (He looks and feels very old and distant.)
CATRIONA:	(gently). You don't understand, Jimmy.
McPHEE:	What she means is, I've begun to hit the bottle — in veritate vino. If I don't get out quick, I'll be standing trembling outside the local distillery at four in the afternoon, begging for a tumbler of free raw malt to keep me going till opening time.
CATRIONA:	It's not as bad as that, dad.
McPHEE:	It will be. Today has not exactly helped.
JIMMY:	And pushing off to the Southern States is meant to be a cure, is it? I forecast cirrhosis of the liver on the train to Southampton: you must be kidding yourselves —
CATRIONA:	He's not exactly an alcoholic yet, Jimmy.
JIMMY:	Going to some bloody stupid slave-farm in a cultural desert is not going to stop him. It's driven many a better man to worse than drink.
McPHEE:	Aye, well. At least I can do it in private, out there, Jimmy, and not be forever peered at by the wee wifies, wondering when I'll get myself the sack from the school, and then when I'm going to fall into the burn on my way home and get drowned.
JIMMY:	That's the first time I've heard you want to *hide* something, Aeney: You disappoint me.
McPHEE:	Maybe it's part of the condition, Jimmy. (Goes very sad.) Maybe it's that.

JIMMY is embarrassed. CATRIONA gets very angry with JIMMY for saddening him like that, and flies into the attack.

CATRIONA:	Just who, in the name of creation, do you think you are, Jimmy Litherland, to tell him what's to be done and what's not. You come here from England for a year or two, then you're off again, back to Liverpool and Oxford and London and God knows where else besides, and you pop back here for a day or two for auld lang syne and *you're* the one who's telling *him* how great it is to live here and how

he's got to stay and dedicate himself to something you know nothing about whatsoever: he's only the schoolmaster, you know, not the abbott — this is Morna, not Iona, Mr Litherland. And the place is dying — dying every minute of every day. There's neither money here, nor work, nor young people, nor entertainment — they say they can't even get a decent picture on their televisions, let alone the sight of a real live film. All the bright young ones go off to school on the mainland when they're eleven or twelve and that's the end of them: they come back for their holidays and can't wait to get away again: in fact, the only ones who stay are either too old or too idle to get out. All there is here Jimmy, is cold ocean; hard rain; bare hills; hypocritical people; and a damp bed at the end of the day. Now, if you intend to get romantic over that, we'll need some evidence you've not taken leave of your senses.

McPHEE: We are to become like the Red Indians — a subject for advanced students to write theses on — worse than extinct: preserved. (Pause.) The time has come to get out.

CATRIONA: Just as you did. I don't see you rushing back.

JIMMY: Well I *am* back. And I've made up my mind. For better or worse, Aeney, I'm going to live here.

CATRIONA: My God, Jimmy, you *have* taken leave of your senses.

JIMMY: That's as may be. But I've made my decision.

JOHN JAMES has come round the outside and comes in through the door where he stands blinking at them.

JOHN JAMES: You're through with your Martinis, are you?

CATRIONA: Come in and sit down, John James — you look like something from outer space there at the door.

JOHN JAMES: (lumbering in). Stop peace-making: there's no war.

JIMMY: John James, could you do something for me?

JOHN JAMES: A-ha.

JIMMY: Can you get me a job on the boats?

Pause.

JOHN JAMES: For a couple of weeks, is it?

387

JIMMY:	Permanent.
CATRIONA:	Good God, Jimmy, you're more of a fool than I took you for.
JIMMY:	Do you know what I found myself doing — after four years at Liverpool and three at Oxford and two terms at the Sorbonne? Correcting spelling mistakes in Labour Party press handouts — what a way to overthrow capitalism . . .
CATRIONA:	But you've not given up politics, Jimmy?
JIMMY:	No. But *this* is where socialism has to start, here, where the people live and work. I'm back here, and back here to stay.

Silence.

CATRIONA:	Jimmy, would you not be better off teaching school — I mean, they *need* people here . . . particularly as dad's going soon — I'm sure you could step right into his job — there'd be no problem about that.
JIMMY:	If John James can't get me a job on the fishing boats, I'll shovel malt in the distillery — but I've a feeling they need people on the boats — is that not right, John James?
JOHN JAMES:	Aye. We can fix you up: heaving and pulling your guts out, scrubbing the fish hold, gutting and sorting, stinking of herring for the rest of your life . . .
JIMMY:	I'll take care of myself.
JOHN JAMES:	You wouldn't be thinking of starting your Socialism on board, would you, Jimmy? We'll have none of that stuff in Morna.
JIMMY:	I'll remember I'm not on the Battleship Potemkin, John James, for your sake . . . Can you fix me up?
JOHN JAMES:	(reluctantly). Aye, well, I suppose Andy Brown's a couple of hands short just now, and he's a decent enough man to work for, if you keep your nose clean. Where are you staying?
JIMMY:	Right here. I've a room for a month. Then maybe I'll find lodgings.

JOHN JAMES gets up.

JOHN JAMES:	Let's see your hands. (He goes over and looks at them, then laughs.) You'll not find it easy.

JIMMY: I didn't expect I would . . .

JOHN JAMES: I'll send for you tomorrow. Come away, now, Catriona, we'll get a bite to eat. I'm not much wanting to be hanging around this place today.

CATRIONA: Nor me. Are you coming up home, dad?

McPHEE: Go on, you two, I'll follow. I'll be glad to walk up on my own.

CATRIONA: Herself'll be waiting — Oh God . . .

She has suddenly realised where her mother is and breaks up. JOHN JAMES amazingly gently, puts his arm round her shoulders and leads her out. There is a tearful silence in the room. McPHEE is shaken by CATRIONA's tears, and feels close to them himself. JIMMY goes over to the bar and rings the bell on it. MARY appears at the door.

JIMMY: Will you take a half and a half pint to see you home?

McPHEE: No. I'll settle for a quick dram, Jimmy.

JIMMY: Two drams Mary.

MARY goes over to the bar, pours them and brings them over. JIMMY watches her.

Thank you, Mary. (She goes.)

McPHEE: Here is to you, then, Jimmy.

JIMMY: And here's to everything you taught me. (They drink.)

McPHEE: I'm glad you've come back here: I'm proud of that.

JIMMY: Aeney: don't go: this place needs you more than you need Tennessee. Without you, we'd all sink down into the bog without a trace.

McPHEE: I'm in mortal danger of sinking down myself, Jimmy.

JIMMY: I'll never let that happen, Aeney: trust me. I'll keep you on your toes.

McPHEE: Ah — Catriona's dead set on it.

JIMMY: Leave her to me: I've fought with Catriona through every grade and every classroom on the island. We have each other's measure. (Pause.) Perhaps I'll find the way to make her want to stay, too.

McPHEE gives him a shrewd look, not altogether disapproving.

McPHEE: She's a grand girl, Catriona — but a tough one.

JIMMY: She is one of the reasons I came back too. I tried to tell her, but she thought I was romancing.

McPHEE: A-ha. (Pause. Finishes drink. Gets up.)

JIMMY: Will I walk you home?

McPHEE: No. I'd prefer this one alone, Jimmy, if you don't mind. (He puts on his overcoat at the door, turns to JIMMY and laughs.) You always did ruin everybody's plans, Jimmy Litherland.

(JIMMY looks at him, not sure.)

                    It's good to have you back . . . (Laughs, and goes.)

MARY comes through, into the other bar, opens the door, and the IRISH WOMAN shuffles out without a word. MARY locks it. She comes back into the saloon, picks up McPHEE's glass . . . JIMMY drains his, hands it to her and catches her by the hand. They look at each other. He gets up, looks down on her, still holding her hand. She looks at him, wide-eyed, half mischievous, half romantic.

JIMMY: What time do you finish, Mary?

MARY: Oh, I'm free now for a couple of hours. (She looks up at him: they move close together and remain looking at each other, very close, as the lights go down.)

BLACKOUT

During the blackout, the sound of gulls screaming, the sea, and men arguing passionately.

Scene Three

April, 1964.

Opening time. The IRISH WOMAN waits outside. A few birds sing. MARY passes through the saloon to the bar, rustles the fire and opens the door. The IRISH WOMAN walks in and over to the bar. MARY pours her half pint.

IRISH WOMAN: They're meeting again. Arguing, shouting: bad cess to them: trouble-makers, villains.

MARY: Are you talking about Jimmy?

IRISH WOMAN: You need a few priests round here to keep the likes of him in order — (She gives MARY a look.)

MARY: We can manage well enough. You're no saint
               yourself.

IRISH WOMAN: Me? Aye, but what am I? Nothing. Dirt. Dung on
               the side of the road. I'm no lady. Them, they should
               know better.

(MARY looks at her.)

               Sorry I spoke. (She has unwillingly extracted the
               pennies for her half, and goes over to the fire, angry
               at herself.) *Shouldn't* speak. Tut, tut. (She settles
               down by the fire.)

The men come in: they are curiously silent and thoughtful, as if they
were afraid, or about to commit sacrilege. They almost all quietly
order drinks, and sit round in a group, pulling chairs round to make
a makeshift meeting. Some stand.

The IRISH WOMAN tries to make herself disappear.

JIMMY is there with CALUM, a young man of twenty-three from
JOHN JAMES' boat, who has become his unofficial lieutenant in his
campaigns.

The meeting is more or less called to order by ANDY, the oldest man
present — he was also at the funeral. He is clearly unhappy about
all this and makes a great effort to dissociate himself from the matter
in hand.

ANDY: We are all met here this morning to discuss the
               making of a union. As you know, we've never felt
               the need or call for such a thing: we're a small fleet,
               a small market, and the skippers of the boats are
               our friends and relations. To my way of looking
               at it, they've always treated us fair enough, but
               gentlemanly. However, there's a proposal to be put
               and discussed. First of all, we are very grateful to Mr
               Jimmy Litherland, who is at the moment working
               amongst us, for coming along to let us hear what
               he's got to say.

JIMMY does not stand. He pulls at his pint, then begins. He starts very
quietly, almost to himself, humbly and peaceably: but the intensity
and volume and power rise, step by step, until he has them where he
wants them.

JIMMY: Thank you, Andy. Well, there's not really a great
               deal that I can say to you on this subject. Of course,
               I haven't been long on the job, four or five months,
               not long, and of course many of you have families,

rent, I'm not underestimating the problems. One or two of us, as you say, find ourselves working for brothers, fathers, uncles, on the so-called family boats, naturally those people will not be so keen as their fellow- workers, who aren't going to inherit the boats, to get a fair deal from the owners.

And I am quite aware that every word I say will find its way back to Mr Andy Brown, and Mr John James McPhee and Mr Philip Donaldson and the others, and I expect I shall get the sack, and quite possibly not be able to work on this island again: such is the power of our lords and masters over our lives.

But I tell you this — and, by God, I'm amazed I should *have* to say it, in this day and age — conditions and wages on this fleet are a diabolical disgrace, a matter of shame, not only to the owners but also to *us* for standing around like half-witted loons *letting* it.

(Stands up.) There's not one boat that goes out from this harbour that's fit to be sailed in. Because the owner won't spend a penny-piece on it for fear of risking his profits . . . and yet, we have to go out there day in day out and risk our lives. Oh yes, I can see one or two shocked faces: nobody's ever dared to *say* those boats are death-traps before — because we don't want to know that, do we? And they use our silence, born of our fear, to increase their profits. And on board those rickety death traps, in the height of the gale as much as on a calm summer's day, we are obliged to work twelve, sixteen, eighteen hours a day even, hard, gut-wrenching labour, in the most squalid, filthy conditions unheard of since the worst moments of the nineteenth century. I tell you, here and now, no other worker in the rest of this country would allow himself to be used in this way for another man's profit. We are slaves, abject, exploited slaves. We must be out of our minds — expected to work sixteen hours a day in filthy hell-holes and on top of *that* to risk our lives, and our families' livelihoods, every minute of the day and night. And *why*? Because we're here, in this little island, cut off from the progress that's been forced through elsewhere. We're here, they know it, and there's nothing else for us to do except go away, and they know that too — and they treat us like serfs, like peasants in the middle ages; and like them we're not even allowed to get organised to protect ourselves . . . or are we? Don't let us forget that by *not* getting organised, by *not* joining forces with the other working men throughout the country, we are allowing them to get away with it, we are doing it to ourselves. Mr Chairman, I propose that we apply to the Transport and General Workers Union to send out an official to discuss the formation of a local shop on this island. Thank you.

He sits. There is silence.

ANDY: Is there a seconder for that motion? Seconded by Calum over there. Now then, what's to be said?

An OLDER MAN, MacDONALD gets up, awkwardly.

MacDONALD: Well, I just don't know. (He is deeply shocked.) We don't need any man from England to tell us the job's a hard one. Nor do we need them to divide us brother from brother, son from father. We're all in the same boat, here, in every way. We're all together. We don't want any class of a union saying you can do this, you can't do that —

At that moment, as MacDONALD shows signs of carrying the meeting JOHN JAMES bursts in, angry. He looks straight over at JIMMY. MacDONALD sits.

JOHN JAMES: So, ye're up to your tricks. (They eye each other.)

JIMMY: You're against us then?

JOHN JAMES: Aye. You can count on that.

JIMMY: You have no care what your crew's wages are like, what their boats are like, what conditions they live in and work in — do you have no thoughts about that?

JOHN JAMES: I have the same conditions, the same boats, and all but the same wages — what goes for me, goes for them.

JIMMY: And I suppose you like it the way it is?

JOHN JAMES: If I didn't, I'd not run snivelling to some sneaky Englishman to help me out, I'll tell you that.

JIMMY: The only way we can make you listen to us is to shout together —

JOHN JAMES:	Aye, and just that very minute you get yourselves teamed up for the eightsome, away I'll go with the boats — to Skye or to Barra or Stornoway — doesn't matter where — there's plenty of fish in the sea, and enough idle hands in these parts, by God.
JIMMY:	You'll not do that —
JOHN JAMES:	Oh yes I will — but you shouldn't be worrying about what I'm going to do —
JIMMY:	Why not — you're a bloody owner, aren't you?
JOHN JAMES:	Aye — just now. But you'd do well to enquire into the balance sheet before you go a lot further, Jimmy.
JIMMY:	Are you trying to tell us you'd sell up?
JOHN JAMES:	Aye — no doubt at all. And Fergusons are in a buying mood — they've bought every damn boat they can lay their hands on, and they have half a dozen more commissioned at Gateshead. They'd buy the entire fleet.
JIMMY:	By God, then we *would* have a decent fight on our hands. Ferguson Fisheries — (Rubs his hands.)
JOHN JAMES:	You'd have damn all on your hands, Jimmy. I've told you — they'd be away — and the whole lot of you'd be on the dole —
JIMMY:	Then we'd be after them. By God, you could shoot me down if I didn't sail away to Skye or to Barra or to Stornoway and to every port in the Highlands and form them up with us too, until we're all as one man.
JOHN JAMES:	(angry). You're a blethering, bloody maniac, and you ought to be locked away.

JIMMY is astounded.

	Do you know what it is you're saying?
JIMMY:	I'm not just talking about better conditions, you know, John James —
JOHN JAMES:	You don't realise what you *are* talking about. What the hell made you come back to these islands at all, Jimmy — go away and manipulate your manoeuvres somewhere that's already destroyed, don't come here bringing destruction with you.

JIMMY:	I suppose you'd like to keep the place as feudal as it always has been —
JOHN JAMES:	There's been fishing going on from that harbour for thousands of years, man — there's been boats going out into storms and getting swallowed up, there's been miserable conditions and miserable hours and miserable work, and there's always been a miserable living out of it, through century after century, and that's the way we're made here, don't you understand?
JIMMY:	I'm beginning to understand the way you're made. You're a reckless man John James, you couldn't care less what anybody else might suffer, what anybody's wife and children might have to do without, because *you* believe it's good for them ...
JOHN JAMES:	You'll hear me out, now, Jimmy. You'll listen and you'll strain your little mind to understand: because no fisherman will ever tell you this, and I'm going to.
JIMMY:	Don't tell me you do it for love?
JOHN JAMES:	(furious, he leaps up, picks JIMMY up by his lapels, talks into his face through clenched teeth). I'll tell you why we do it: because we don't want to spend our lives battling and arguing with men of mean spirit, with industrialists and trade unionists and pen pushers and productivity deals: we don't want to waste our spirits and our energies on clock watching and card punching and attending conveyor belts. We're looking for something that's bigger than these to pit ourselves against — and the men of these islands used to know what that is: and it's not just the sea and the wind and the rocks and the heaving nets and the flimsy boats — it's this: (He suddenly thrusts out his arms indicates his whole body, his whole self.) this is what we're battling against — ourselves — here is the battlefield, here, and here, and here (indicates head, hands and stomach) — and that's why you'll be a good little manny and run back to Liverpool or London, or wherever you got your pathetic little ideas from, and leave us some life to live, even if the rest of the world *is* slowly dying on its feet.
JIMMY:	You know where I got my ideas from, John James. Very well, if you want to fight against the sea,

against the world, against yourself, you do that but what your father taught me was that the real struggle was against man's inhumanity to man, against injustice and ignorance and suffering —

JOHN JAMES: Ach, the hell with that: he's a feeble minded old bletherer, with no more idea of living than you do . . .

JIMMY: You're a lonely, arrogant man, John James: and I feel sorry for you.

JOHN JAMES: And I'll tell you something: you are an ignorant man, with no more feeling in you than (Slams fist on table.) that, ready to turn an ancient way of life into an industrial dispute, to throw away the living of every man here, to depopulate the whole bloody island — and why? Just to show how mighty powerful you are . . .

JIMMY: We're going to win, John James.

JOHN JAMES: Win *what*?

JIMMY: To start with we're going to win some representation: there's nothing you can do will stop us. And then, piece by piece, we're going to win a decent, livable life for every man on that fleet. And as well as that, we're going to win these islands in the next election.

JOHN JAMES: Ha! So that's it — ? Once a politician, always a politician —

JIMMY: I have no ambitions in that direction myself.

JOHN JAMES: (cynically). Aye.

JIMMY: There's only one man should represent the people of these islands. I'm putting his name up to the Labour party selection committee tonight, if he'll accept — and if he will, he'll win.

JOHN JAMES: Are you talking about my father?

JIMMY: There'll be an election in the autumn: he'll be in Westminster before Christmas.

JOHN JAMES is stopped in his tracks. He sits down, pole axed.

JOHN JAMES: You're an astounding clever bastard.

JIMMY: He is going to be chosen, and he's going to win.

JOHN JAMES: (gets up). Right. It's you or me, Jimmy.

JIMMY: Now we're seeing your true colours, John James —

JOHN JAMES: I'll be having a word with Andy Brown. I've a feeling he'll not be needing so big a crew next time out — or *any* time out. And I'll be seeing my father — and Catriona. And if I don't get drunk tonight and pulp your head against a wall, I'll not know what stopped me.

A silence. They all look as if the matter was decided. Eventually one of the older men, MACBETH, looks up and speaks awkwardly.

MACBETH: Well now: we're not great speakers, Mr Litherland, Jimmy. I think I can safely say that the spirit of the meeting is — we're with you. Don't let's blether on about it. Let's do it. I propose Jimmy gets the job of looking into it.

ANDY: Is there a seconder for that motion . . . ?

Small chorus of Aye, hands lifted and flopped down, etc.

     Well now, we've got two motions before us, proposed and seconded: I think the only thing to do now is put them to the vote. To take the first motion first —

At that moment JOHN JAMES can contain himself no longer. He lets out a roar of anger, glowers around them, picks on CALUM.

JOHN JAMES: Calum — get down the job this minute.

CALUM instinctively stands up. JIMMY watches what is happening very carefully. CALUM hesitates, then stands still.

     Out!

CALUM still doesn't move. JOHN JAMES decides very simply to use force. It is not dramatic, merely practical. He shrugs his shoulders, wanders over to CALUM, and grabs him, swings him round and marches him to the door. He turns to the others at the door.

     You've all lost an hour's pay already — get back down the job before you lose more. Any man refusing can join the queue at the National Assistance tomorrow morning.

He holds the door open and waits. Nobody moves. ANDY continues.

ANDY: All those in favour of the first motion that application is made to the Transport and General Workers Union

397

to send out an official to discuss the formation of a local shop: raise your hands please.

(It is unanimous. CALUM votes from the door.)

Carried. All those in favour of the second motion that Jimmy here gets the job of looking into it: raise your hands please.

JOHN JAMES: (At the same time.) Voting, voting, voting. Get down the boats before I belt everyone of you . . .

Again unanimous.

ANDY: (to JOHN JAMES). We'll come down now, John James: the business is completed. (To ALL.) Right, then, there'll be another meeting in a month's time.

(They all get up and wander out past JOHN JAMES, who is standing over them at the door. Last but one is ANDY, who stops facing JOHN JAMES.)

You stupid fool . . .

He moves on. The last man is JIMMY. JOHN JAMES stops him, keeps him in the bar, and shuts the door after the others. He stands looking at JIMMY, trying to find the right words.

The IRISH WOMAN listens expectantly, but doesn't turn. MARY is at the bar. JOHN JAMES nods, turns and goes.

BLACKOUT

The sea again, and boats coming to harbour.

Scene Four

July, 1964

CATRIONA is sitting on the bench, reading, waiting.

JIMMY comes into the bar, alone, obviously out of work. MARY comes in to lock up, goes over to him.

MARY: I've just heard there's a job going in the distillery, Jimmy.

JIMMY: (turns away from her). Thank you, Mary . . .

MARY: It's near closing time.

But he is lost in thought. He realises what she said and turns to her.

JIMMY: Mary — I must go. I have things to do.

He stands there, brooding. She watches him, angry-eyed, feeling jilted, rejected. She goes to the door and rams home the bolts, vengefully.

              Mary — come here. Don't be upset. You mustn't get too serious about me, ever — I'm not worth it.

MARY: It's too late to tell me that, Jimmy.

JIMMY: Perhaps we should never have started . . .

MARY: Well now, that doesn't really matter: come on upstairs.

JIMMY: I can't any more, Mary.

MARY: You're chasing Catriona McPhee, is that what you're saying?

JIMMY: Aye, it is. I'm sorry.

MARY: I'll not go out in a boat and drown myself, or even end up talking to the owls, like some have done. You don't have to worry on that score, Jimmy. I'll manage just fine. (Pause.) Well — there's no more to be said. I'll take up knitting — until you change your mind.

She goes. JIMMY looks after her, amused at her confidence. He ducks under the bar, through into the saloon then goes out to CATRIONA. She looks up and smiles, as if she expected him. He holds out his hand to her, standing, as if waiting for her to get up and go with him. She pats the seat next to her.

CATRIONA: Hello.

JIMMY: Hello. Come on in, Catriona.

CATRIONA: I'm just fine out here.

JIMMY: (goes over to her, takes her hand). I meant every word I said to you last night — you know that, don't you?

CATRIONA: Well — it was very flattering, Jimmy.

JIMMY: And what do you think about it?

CATRIONA: (frowns). You'll need to give me time.

JIMMY: Catriona, come on inside, I can't talk to you properly out here. I feel all the island's peering at us through binoculars — I need to kiss you very much.

399

CATRIONA: (smiles). You mean you need very much to kiss me?

JIMMY: I mean I need very much to kiss you very much — Miss McPhee: and I can't very much out here.

CATRIONA: Calm down, Jimmy — it's not often we have a touch of sunlight this time of year. Sit down and enjoy it.

JIMMY: My desires are eternally foetid and internal with you, Catriona —

CATRIONA: Ach, don't be so doom-dungeon about everything.

JIMMY: I love you, Catriona. More than I've ever loved anyone else in the whole world.

CATRIONA: And perhaps I could love you, too, Jimmy, in my own peculiar way.

JIMMY: I need you. I'm terribly, terribly alone.

CATRIONA: (pause). Come on, let's walk along the cliff and see the fulmars — they're back this year in force: they're such neat little birds, neat and trim, not like gulls at all really.

(JIMMY holds his hands out. She gets up. He kisses her, and keeps on kissing her, trying to break her down into his own mood. She struggles free eventually.)

      They'll be enjoying those binoculars now, alright, getting their money's worth.

JIMMY: Do you care?

CATRIONA: (stung). I don't imagine they'll be interested in you and me getting up a bit of steam on a headland — it's not so exciting. But an ambitious young politician and a maid from the hotel — now that would be something to whisper about, eh?

JIMMY: Do you mean me and Mary Fraser?

CATRIONA: (laughing). It's the talk of the ladies' hairdressers, and already circulating to the furthest crofts with Miss Jeans in her travelling library-van.

JIMMY: I'm very fond of Mary, Catriona — but no more than that. Whatever was between us is now over.

CATRIONA: (darkening). Are you being straight with me? I'm

not sure that I can altogether trust you, you see.
That's what makes me dither a bit.

JIMMY: What can I say? I love you, I love no one else. I
want no one else, I'll have no one else but you —
and that's the finality of it.

CATRIONA: Is it? (He nods.)

She kisses him then turns away.

JIMMY: Is there anything else — making you dither?

CATRIONA: Aye, but I don't know what it is.

JIMMY: When you find out, will you tell me? I'll have
nothing come between us, Catriona: nothing in
the world.

He holds her again, strokes her hair, kisses her passionately, moans,
clenches his teeth.

CATRIONA: What is it?

JIMMY: When — when you've thought about it — if you
say yes — we'll be married soon, don't you think?

CATRIONA looks at him, grave with sympathy, bites her lip and nods.
He kisses her again, and again shows signs of going through some
internal agony.

CATRIONA: Was that all it was, Jimmy?

JIMMY: No. I — Ach, nothing.

CATRIONA: What? What is it?

JIMMY: I — the idea that one day I might — we might —
make love; perhaps it means too much to me.

CATRIONA: Don't be silly, Jimmy. You've had women before,
and I've had men — it's very nice, of course — but
it's only a part of it all.

JIMMY: With you it will be everything.

CATRIONA: (looks troubled). Stop it, Jimmy.

JIMMY: I *mean* it.

(She sits down and starts to cry away from him. He goes to comfort
her, turns her to him.)

Am I — blackmailing you, is that it?

(She shakes her head, cries some more.)

>Is it too overbearing, am I bullying you?

CATRIONA: (again shakes her head, pulls herself together).
No. What you say — it's quite natural. It makes
me proud.

JIMMY: Well — what?

CATRIONA: I can't tell you.

MARY appears from the far side of the hotel, buttoned up in a thick
shapeless overcoat. She stumps past them, nods curtly as JIMMY looks
up at her. CATRIONA has her face turned away, to hide her tears.
There is an awkward silence.

>Was that her?

JIMMY: (nods). Come up to my room — I can't talk to you
out here.

CATRIONA: (shrugs). I'm not going to bed with you, Jimmy.

JIMMY: (quietly). OK. (They get up, go to the door.) (Shouts.)
Are you all watching?

(Then they go in up to his room. As they go, JIMMY says:)

>Did you see that film 'The Blood of the Vampires?'

(He makes a vampire noise, and she screams and runs up into his
room, laughing. Once inside, he takes off her coat. CATRIONA sits on
a chair, by an electric fire that JIMMY switches on.)

>Would you like a wee dram?

(CATRIONA looks up.)

>Here — (Gets up, produces bottle and two glasses
from a drawer, pours.) I'm not tryin' to get you
drunk and incapacitated, you know. It might do us
both good, however.

(She takes the drink and holds it. She sips it later. He slips his back
right away, with relief.)

>I'm becoming an alcoholic on this island.

(She looks at him, thinking of her father, but obviously he has no
thought of that.)

>Do you know, I think our little scheme for a union

branch is going to work? We'd another grand meeting this morning — the whole thing's going through, nem con — in spite of the threats — and me getting the sack.

CATRIONA: John James?

JIMMY: Yes. I think there's something personal.

CATRIONA: Do you?

JIMMY: Your father, on the other hand, has been great — outstanding. He's massacred them in the public bar every night for three weeks. There's not one man on this island who doesn't know the difference between Rosa Luxembourg and the Social Democrats in detail, thanks to your father. There's no doubt about it in my mind — he's going to be our next MP.

CATRIONA: You might be destroying him, Jimmy. I really don't know if he's up to it.

JIMMY: He'll be a new man, you'll see.

CATRIONA: I don't know that you understand him.

JIMMY: I wish your mother was alive.

CATRIONA nods. JIMMY kneels in front of her. He puts his head on her knee, takes her hand and kisses it. He stays quite still, his arms around her.

              Do you love me?

CATRIONA: The fire's burning my leg.

He jumps up and laughs, then lays her down on the bed and gets a book.

JIMMY: I only want to read to you. I shan't rape you — unless you'd like me to.

She sits up, flustered.

CATRIONA: Let's go out, Jimmy.

JIMMY: I want to read you this — will you hear me?

CATRIONA: I — I'm sorry, I don't want to hurt you, Jimmy.

JIMMY: What is it?

CATRIONA: Oh . . . I just feel — well — I'd like to hear what it is, Jimmy.

(He kisses her hand and she takes his head and holds it to her, nursing him, and some inner grief that he cannot see. He puts his head up and kisses her again, but again, as soon as it becomes passionate, she draws gently away.)

Read to me.

JIMMY looks at her patiently, then reads to her. A poem by Sorley Maclean:

JIMMY: If it weren't for you, the Cuillin
would be a level wall of blue
encircling with its tight belt
my heart's barbarous retinue.

If it weren't for you, the numerous sand
that lies on Talisker's compact shore
would be the tablet of my wishes
without the sting of salt desire.

If it weren't for you, the huge seas
both in their motion and their rest
would raise the sea-foam of my mind
to a monument on a calm coast.

While the flat, brown and brindled moorland
and my clear intellect would be
drowsing together if it weren't
for the sovereign force of your decree.

And on the distant barren rock
there grew the harp of blossomed fire
and in its branches was your face,
my reason, semblance of a star.

At the end of this, CATRIONA smiles and looks at JIMMY. He again looks longingly at her.

CATRIONA: It's beautiful. Is it Sorley Maclean?

JIMMY: Come to bed, Catriona.

CATRIONA: I can't.

JIMMY: Do I mean so little to you?

CATRIONA: You mean a lot — more and more every day. It's not that, Jimmy.

JIMMY: What is it?

CATRIONA: I can't tell you. But if it's any consolation, I don't

404

think I could sleep with any man. (She thinks.) Jimmy, I might as well tell you now — I can't marry you. Neither you nor anyone.

JIMMY: (alarmed). But — do you have something physically wrong — I mean, we can soon get that sort of thing put right, er —

CATRIONA: It's nothing physical, Jimmy — now please don't ask me any more.

JIMMY: But Catriona, if it's something that's going to come between you and me, at least we should try to think about it together —

CATRIONA: Don't Jimmy. Now, come on, let's get away to the sunlight and the fulmars and the bright blue sky. I'm feeling claustrophobic in here.

JIMMY: No. You go if you must.

CATRIONA: Och come *on*, Jimmy.

JIMMY: I'm in no mood for striding along the top of cliffs — I might just chuck myself over.

CATRIONA: Oh now you don't have to do all that, Jimmy.

JIMMY: What's the matter with me then — tell me that? You've just rejected me, woman, don't you realise?

CATRIONA: Listen, Jimmy, I've not rejected you, don't you see?

JIMMY: No, I don't. Even if you won't marry me, you might at least trust me.

JIMMY: Stand up, Catriona. Come here.

CATRIONA: (afraid). No, Jimmy, no . . .

He draws the curtains, leaving only the glow from the fire. He goes to her and makes her stand up, facing him.

JIMMY: I will never judge you, nor condemn you, nor anything except try to love you, for the rest of my life. And one day you will hear me, and answer, and we'll have children and more children, beautiful children with your green eyes and your startled stare — and people will look at me and say — I don't see you in them — but I'll be there no bally fears — and they'll grow up and we'll grow old — but I'll be with you and you'll be with me, so stop all this guilt, Catriona.

He starts to touch her breasts. She stands, then throws herself on the bed, sobbing. He stands there watching her for a moment, then goes over and touches her to stand up again.

CATRIONA: You're going to win, aren't you?

JIMMY looks at her, then turns away. He picks up his coat, stands upright, sighs and heads for the door.

JIMMY: Goodbye, Catriona.

As he opens the door, she springs across the room and pummells his back, phrenetically. He stops, closes the door and turns round. She carries on beating him for a moment, then stops.

CATRIONA: (with a kind of gaiety and despair). Oh, come *on*, Jimmy, come on!

She throws her arms round his neck and begins kissing him in a sort of rage, dragging him backwards towards the bed. As they fall back on to it, her underneath, blackout.

BLACKOUT

Scene Five

October, 1964. Night.

Again the sound of the sea. The sky is heavy with storm clouds and the sea is thrashing against the rocks. As the far dim lights in the bar go up, JOHN JAMES puts down his last drop of whisky-pep and stands up.

The IRISH WOMAN, who is sitting with him, looks up apprehensively, as do the few others in the bar, but he doesn't fall over. He opens his mouth and sings, with tremendous conviction and pure feeling, in a kind of cross between a croon and a lilt, the American pop-song 'Scarlet Ribbons'. As he gets into the second verse a loudspeaker van can be heard getting nearer, pouring out a somewhat impassioned, repetitive political speech in favour of Labour Government.

JOHN JAMES glowers in its direction, but carries on. Eventually the van and the speech stop, leaving him the last verse in the clear. As soon as he finishes, the few people in the bar, led by the IRISH WOMAN, give him a clap and a cheer. While the singing is going on in the bar, JIMMY comes on, from the van, with McPHEE and CATRIONA in a big sheepskin coat and a balaclava helmet.

They stand for a moment, listening to JOHN JAMES, each with his own reaction. As the clapping and cheering break out, they smile at each other, and begin to move on towards the saloon door. McPHEE looks pre-occupied.

JIMMY: I have a feeling he'd like to slit my throat — in fact, I think he will, one dark night.

McPHEE: (nervous). Nothing so melodramatic, I'm sure.

JIMMY: He's not been entirely sober since the night we told him we were engaged . . . and he didn't exactly cherish me before that —

McPHEE: There's a lot of me in John James: don't forget that Jimmy.

JIMMY: You seem very gloomy tonight, Aeney — are you alright?

McPHEE: Ach — Jimmy, you know — I'm certain I'm never going to make it.

JIMMY: The election? No bother at all — there'll be a huge swing, and you're the man to grab every last Labour vote on this island . . . count yourself in Westminster, November 15.

CATRIONA: I don't think he was meaning votes, Jimmy.

JIMMY: What else is there, at the moment? We'll think of the rest of the problems once you're in, Aeneas McPhee.

McPHEE: (looks at JIMMY, sees there's not much point in going on). Aye. (He turns away to brood. CATRIONA is watching him with concern.) You were going to let me have something or other, Jimmy — press hand-outs, or whatever.

JIMMY: (now anxious himself). Ye-es, if you'd like to glance through them . . . (He doesn't though.)

McPHEE: (impatient). Go on, then, Jimmy, we can't stand here all night.

JIMMY: What . . . ? Is there something else?

McPHEE: (dismissive). Temporary lapse. Thinking of changing my name. The sheer bloody snobbery of these islands is stupendous — the fact that my name's McPhee, like the tinkers', stands to lose me 2,000 votes: now, out of 14,000 that's too many. You know that bloody Tory's got the word around Mingulay that I was never educated, have never left the islands in my life, and have difficulty reading — I hear half of the idiots believe him.

407

JIMMY: They're a lousy branch on Mingulay, I know that: we have a meeting there on the 20th; we'll sharpen them up a bit — maybe get young *Gordon* Mackenzie on the committee, eh?

McPHEE: (wearily). Aye — young Gordon's a good boy —

JIMMY: You have damn all to worry about, Aeney. They'll be proud to have a local man in parliament — they're just about ready to fire the Hon George Selkirk, back to wherever he came from, I can tell you that: you're safe as Merthyr Tydfil.

McPHEE: (under strain). You're a good boy, Jimmy.

JIMMY: Is there something else, Aeney?

McPHEE: (laughing). No, no, not at all — now away up and get my pieces of paper. I'm an old man and in need of my bed . . .

JIMMY: (Stands looking at him.) There is, isn't there?

They stand awkwardly, avoiding each other. At that moment, CALUM comes bursting out of the bar.

McPHEE: Hello there, Calum. (CALUM peers, can't make out who it is, and goes up close to him.)

CALUM: (to McPHEE). Oho — so it's the Socialist candidate. How's yourself?

McPHEE: Not so bad, considering.

JIMMY: I hope you've been down to the Committee rooms tonight, Calum.

There's a hell of a lot needs doing this week.

(CALUM looks him up and down with a certain drunken sheepishness.)

Ah — well, maybe you haven't. (Not at all put down.)

McPHEE: You're never going out tonight?

CALUM: (ironically). Oh, we don't let a bit of wind frighten us. We're not fair-weather sailors, like some we know. (Loses irony.) Ach, himself's a raving lunatic. I sometimes think he waits for the storm-cone to be hoisted for a signal to go out to sea.

JIMMY: How is he?

CALUM: John James? That's him now. (They listen to him quietly singing.) He's in great shape — but if he doesn't tear himself away from the Johnny Walker, we'll not get out of the harbour, let alone back in.

JIMMY: You know the union fixed the first meeting with the skippers for the 17th. Now we're organised we'll maybe bring him to his senses.

CALUM: I sometimes think he enjoys it, you know: he's punched every man in the island who'll stand up to him, now he's having a got at the poor bloody ocean.

(JOHN JAMES stops singing.)

McPHEE: Well good luck to you tonight, son. By Christ, if I had any authority over him, I'd tan his backside and put him to bed with a dummy-tit in his mouth, so I would. But he's beyond my controlling.

CALUM: Aye, well — he's not such a bad captain, when he's sober — Goodnight, Catriona, Jimmy, Mr McPhee.

JIMMY/McPHEE: Goodnight, Calum —

CATRIONA: Safe home —

McPHEE: We'll be looking out for you.

CALUM goes. They resume their awkwardness.

JIMMY: I — I'll get that stuff. Will you not step inside for five minutes?

McPHEE: Not at all, Jimmy — I'll just take the air.

JIMMY dallies. CATRIONA gestures to him to go and get the stuff. He goes. McPHEE walks away from her. Gently she follows him.

CATRIONA: Dad — stop thinking about her.

McPHEE: Oh now now, Catriona.

CATRIONA: You are, aren't you?

McPHEE: Aye. It does me no good, you're quite right. (Pause.) I'd a dream once or twice lately — about being up a tree, in the jungle, high high up, and getting ready to swing on this long, rather fragile, creeper: then I take in a deep breath, and plunge, you know, clinging tight, and I go skimming along over the undergrowth, and the snakes are looking up, and

409

the baboons and the crocodiles, for the second I let go — ach, what am I talking about, I'm no bloody Tarzan . . .

CATRIONA: Don't be afraid, father.

McPHEE: Hm. I wouldn't dignify it with the name of fear . . . it's something far less honourable. I'll just cling to whatever it is, as long as I'm able.

CATRIONA: I wish Jimmy understood these things . . .

McPHEE: He's not allowing himself to, just now: he has his priorities under control. He's a good boy.

CATRIONA: I suppose that's the way you win . . .

McPHEE: He'll win. (Smiles.)

CATRIONA looks at her father and smiles with him.

JIMMY comes out of the main door with some papers, sees CATRIONA and McPHEE, wonders, goes over to them.

JIMMY: This is just for the local rag next Friday. But this stuff I'm trying out on the London Times — though I doubt if the reactionary bastards will print a word of it.

McPHEE: I'll look it over. You're a stout support, Jimmy — I hope I don't disappoint you.

JIMMY: Aeney, even at the Bogden Women's Institute Hall tonight, you brought true socialism — and that's all we need to win. Now tomorrow night's not so easy — the Young Farmers need lining up against the wall and eliminating — but before we're allowed to do that, we must get them to vote for us. Here's the details of the subsidy they've been getting for the last seven or eight years, and here's the stuff on the Common Market. I'll pick you up about six thirty.

CATRIONA: Come on, father. I'm tired and you're tired, so we'll help each other along the rocky road . . . Goodnight Jimmy. (Kisses him.)

JIMMY: Aren't you coming in?

CATRIONA: (looks at her father). I'd better not.

Kisses him, sweeps up McPHEE and sets off with him. JIMMY goes in quite quickly. Before CATRIONA and McPHEE go, however, JOHN JAMES starts to sing again, a song from the islands this time, slow, throbbing, yearning, beautiful. CATRIONA and McPHEE stand and listen.

JIMMY has gone into the saloon. He sits down in an armchair, begins working on something. MARY comes in, goes over to him. He looks up at her, and she at him, and the song speaks for her. Eventually she says quietly:

MARY: Would you care for something, Mr Litherland?

JIMMY: I'll take a dram. Won't you take something yourself?

She goes off to get it, comes back, gives it to him. The song ends. An appreciative silence in the bar. Outside McPHEE turns to CATRIONA.

McPHEE: I'm going in for a dram, Catriona.

CATRIONA: Come on up home, father: you know what'll happen.

McPHEE: I want to hear. He's singing of his mother.

CATRIONA: Please, father.

McPHEE: (slow look at her). Are you going to tell me how
                   many votes I'll be losing?

CATRIONA: Oh, you're impossible.

McPHEE: Come on in with me.

CATRIONA: I couldn't. You know that too damn well.

McPHEE: Go you home. You're tired.

CATRIONA looks at him, shrugs and sighs.

CATRIONA: Try to get home in one piece.

McPHEE: I feel like a lamb jumping out of a lorry — wae hae!
                   (He kicks his heels in the air like a spring lamb.)
                   Baa-aa.

CATRIONA laughs and kisses him.

CATRIONA: Safe home.

She goes. McPHEE fishes in his pockets, checks how much money he has, and goes in.

In the bar there is a silence. JOHN JAMES resents McPHEE coming in, watches to see will he stay. McPHEE nods to him when he comes in. JOHN JAMES vaguely raises his drink. McPHEE goes over to the bar,

takes a pint from MARY and sits himself down in a corner with nods
right and left.

McPHEE: (to JOHN JAMES). Ah, well, Johnny — you'll do
                 yourself no good going out on a night like this:
                 will you?

At which, JOHN JAMES rather pointedly gets up, glaring at his father.
He goes to the piano and plays and sings 'Balls to Mr Banglestein'.

JOHN JAMES: Balls to Mr Banglestein, Banglestein, Banglestein,
                 Balls to Mr Banglestein, dirty old man —
                 For he keeps us waiting
                 While he's masturbating,
                 So balls to Mr Banglestein, dirty old man.

The IRISH WOMAN laughs, the others peer into their drinks. The
landlord MacALISTER leans anxiously over the counter. JOHN JAMES
finishes his song, slams down the lid of the piano, and looks at the
landlord.

                 Worried? (He gets up, goes to ROSITA.) I'm off.
                 One great stormy night I'll take you out with me,
                 you poor bloody whore.

IRISH WOMAN: (smiling). Manners, mister.

JOHN JAMES: (whispers, close to her). One great stormy night
                 I'll take you aboard and ride you through the gales
                 and drive you through the seas. Until the morning
                 comes and we slip out the nets into the oily waves.
                 Would you like that?

ROSITA: (frowning). Be careful with yourself. You're a mad
                 bugger.

JOHN JAMES: Come on outside.

ROSITA: Not at all. (Offended.) I'm not going under no hedge
                 with nobody, not even you.

JOHN JAMES: (a glance at McPHEE, then): Come up to the house.

ROSITA: (laughing, pleased again). Away to sea with you.
                 Come back with some valuable lobsters, and I'll
                 look at you with different eyes.

The other two men in his crew reluctantly leave the bar and go out
with JOHN JAMES, leaving the place empty but for MARY, McPHEE
and the IRISH WOMAN.

The IRISH WOMAN gets up and goes over to the bar with her glass.

IRISH WOMAN: (to MARY). By God, he's a good looking feller that John James McPhee. I could let him do some things to me, could not you, Mary Fraser?

(MARY looks at her.)

    You'll be thinking not many will be wanting a woman like me —

MARY: Not at all, not at all.

IRISH WOMAN: Aye well, a few men have, a few good men. Some of them used me, some of them abused me, but I've a quick brown body, Mary, and I know how to pleasure a man, so they've all of them come for more . . . (Whispers, quite loud to MARY.) I feel like a man tonight — don't you? (She turns her gaze wonderingly on McPHEE who says, looking at her:)

McPHEE: Two drams, Mary.

IRISH WOMAN: Can you sing like your son, mister?

McPHEE: Aye. I taught him that song he sung just now — it's one from Jura.

IRISH WOMAN: Well, sing us a song then . . .

McPHEE: I'm not in a mood, not now.

IRISH WOMAN: Go on, sing it out of yourself: you look as if you need a good cry, you poor man . . .

McPHEE: (looks kindly at her). Old schoolmasters with political ambitions are not meant to cry — not in public.

IRISH WOMAN: Well, sing then —

McPHEE shakes his head. Silence. She looks at him. Starts to hum the song JOHN JAMES sang. McPHEE gets up, drains his glass, goes to the bar.

McPHEE: Two more, Mary.

(McPHEE tips back his drink, and lurches across the room to the IRISH WOMAN with hers. As he sits beside her, he says despairingly and drunkenly:)

    I — can't sing *songs* — to *you*. (He looks at her aggressively. She makes up to him, stroking him.)

IRISH WOMAN: Oh, come on now, Mr McPhee, you've no call to be worrying: no call at all.

McPHEE:	(with self-loathing underneath). You're no more than an unwashed whore . . .
IRISH WOMAN:	(flaring up). I'm not that, mister — unwashed I may be, but I'm nobody's whore —

MARY goes out, embarrassed, to the saloon. McPHEE stands up and bellows

McPHEE:	You're a whore.
IRISH WOMAN:	Aye, and you're a wee bitty past it —
McPHEE:	Is that so? Is that so?
IRISH WOMAN:	Sit down, McPhee, you're enough to scare the crows standing there like that . . .
McPHEE:	Are you speaking to me?
IRISH WOMAN:	(quietly). You're a grand fellow, no doubt about it . . . you'll do better than your son, drunk as you are . . .
McPHEE:	(stopped in his tracks). Me, is it?
IRISH WOMAN:	What's on your mind, man, tell us and forget it . . .
McPHEE:	Will you come outside with me?
IRISH WOMAN:	It's a cold night.
McPHEE:	We'll think of a way to keep warm, no doubt.
IRISH WOMAN:	I'll drink up my drink . . .
McPHEE:	Come here — (He clutches her to him, body to body.) Aye — you're a warm one.

In the saloon, MARY whispers to JIMMY, who gets up, worried at what she has told him, but not sure whether to go into the bar and break it up, or quite what. MARY watches him, interested. Finally he turns to MARY.

JIMMY:	Ask him to come through for a minute.

She turns to go, but stops immediately, for McPhee has burst into song — 'Will ye go lassie, go.' At the end of the verse the IRISH WOMAN gives him a kiss on the cheek; MARY turns to JIMMY enquiringly, who nods. She goes through.

MARY:	Er, Mr McPhee — Jimmy would like to have a word with you — he says would you like to come through — ?

414

McPHEE: Tell him I'm pre-occupied . . .

MARY: But, Mr McPhee —

McPHEE: Tell him to leave me be. Tell him blood is thicker than socialism. Tell him I've had more joy from one moment with this woman here than I'll ever have from a lifetime of Westminsters . . .

JIMMY has by now got up and come through to the back of the bar, beside MARY. He is genuinely alarmed at all this.

JIMMY: Aeney, for Christ's sake — are you trying to fuck up the whole campaign — ? It only needs one word of this to get out —

McPHEE: (Now very drunk and wild.) Jimmy — I'm an old man — have I got to be the one to tell you? There's one kind of child runs round crying and throwing tantrums all day, and when he doesn't grow up we notice — but there's another trots about putting everything in its place and worrying if everybody's doing the right thing, and when he doesn't grow up — ach . . . *grow up* Jimmy, grow up.

JIMMY: Aeney, you can think what you like about my retarded development; there's a lot more at issue here than that — and don't forget it.

McPHEE: Aye — I'll tell you what's at issue — *me*; and don't I know it. Get out of here and leave me in peace.

JIMMY looks at him coldly and goes back into the saloon. MARY follows him. McPHEE remains glaring after him.

JIMMY: Och, maybe there's nothing to worry about . . .
You'll not go chattering, Mary?

MARY: No, not a word.

JIMMY: (sits). Am I such a fool, Mary?

She looks at him, goes and holds his head to her, consolingly.

In the bar:

McPHEE: I shouldn't have spoken like that to Jimmy. He was trying to look after me. I'm not fit to be looked after.

IRISH WOMAN: (laughs). I'll look after you — down there — (She lunges at his testicles. He takes her hand away.) Come on outside.

McPHEE: We'll keep the wind out, Rosita — come on round the back, there's a bothy full of straw MacAlaster keeps for his animals — (He stops — thinking.) I don't believe in it, you see: all my life I've told myself I believe in *socialism* — but I don't believe in all this they *tell* me is socialism — the technological revolution, the five per cent growth rate and the three per cent mortgage, the national plan and the old age pension increases — and I don't know what to do about it. I just want people to run their own lives and own their own land and to hell with capitalism. I don't believe in 'pragmatism'. (Turns to her.)

Will ye go, lassie, go
And we'll all go together
To pick wild mountain thyme
From among the blooming heather
Will ye go, lassie go?

(They start to move out, him still singing.)

Oh, the Summertime has come
And the leaves they are blooming, etc.

The song dies away around the corner. MARY stirs, looks at her watch.

MARY: Will I close the bar, Jimmy?

JIMMY: There's fifteen minutes to go —

MARY: Ach, there'll be nobody up here *now*. Shall I?

(He nods. She smiles and kisses him. She emerges flustered.)

I'll lock the door — I'll do the till later.

(She goes through and bolts the door, whistling. JIMMY picks up his papers and prepares to move out. She comes back, kisses him lightly — they go upstairs.)

(They don't put the light on in his room. She takes off her sweater. He sits on the edges of the bed, taking his shoes off. When he's done that he still sits.)

Do you want me to go, Jimmy? Am I keeping you up?

He reaches up and grabs her, dragging her down onto the bed with him. They more or less disappear into the bed, leaving the stage empty.

After a moment or two, CATRIONA comes back on, looking for her father.

She goes to the bar, tries the door, hesitantly, but finds it locked. She is surprised. She looks through a window, but can't make it. She goes round the front and tries the main door, which is open: she goes in and into the saloon. She looks through into the public bar, sees it is empty; begins to wonder a bit. She goes back into the saloon, and to the foot of the stairs, and listens.

As she does so, JOHN JAMES comes on stage and makes his way to the public bar. He is soaking wet and still drunk and stumbling. When he finds the door locked, he roars with rage, and hammers on it, bellowing.

JOHN JAMES: Open up. Open this bloody door. Give a man
                a drink!

As he hammers, CALUM and the two crewmen, also soaked, come on behind JOHN JAMES. He turns to them.

                What the hell time is this to bolt the door? You see
                what happens the minute we go to sea? The whole
                place falls in ruins . . .

He goes back to belting and rattling the door. CATRIONA, hearing all this, has come round the outside to them, amazed to hear JOHN JAMES' voice. JOHN JAMES stops banging when he sees her, and looks at her.

CATRIONA: John James — what — did you go out tonight — ?

JOHN JAMES: Aye. (He glowers at her for a minute, can't bring
                himself to explain, then goes back to hammering
                on the door.

Upstairs, MARY is frantically getting dressed, but already MacALASTER has been aroused from his fireside and is on his way through the bar to the door.

He now opens it, annoyed to find it locked.

JOHN JAMES: (charging in). If you're not wanting to serve
                customers, you'll not be needing your licence for
                long, MacAlaster —

MacALASTER: I do apologise — I've no idea what can have
                happened to Mary. I left her in charge here a wee
                minute ago, I —

JOHN JAMES: Well, make it a whisky-pep for me and my three
                men here, and (Sourly.) a martini for my sister —

CATRIONA: (as MacALASTER gets the whiskys). I'll take a
                brandy.

JOHN JAMES: You will so — a large brandy for herself —

417

At that moment, MARY appears, flustered but controlling herself.

MARY: I'm that sorry, Mr MacAlaster, I just slipped upstairs to the ladies and there was money in the till, so I locked the door — (Laughs.) I thought you were all away to the herrings . . . (Stops, realises they should be.) Why ever are you not?

JOHN JAMES: Excuses, excuses —

CATRIONA: And why are the four of you soaked to the skin?

An awkward silence. JOHN JAMES refuses to talk about it. During the silence, JIMMY appears at the back of the bar, looks around, takes in the scene.

JIMMY: (to CALUM). What was it?

CALUM: We — never quite made it out of the harbour . . . we got pushed on the Drummit rocks by the tide race, and the wind, of course. We should never have gone out.

JOHN JAMES: Hold your tongue, man. I say when we go out, and when we come back —

CALUM: We were lucky. We got a line ashore, and swung in.

(MacALASTER has got the drinks ready. He hands them round.)

Thanks. (Drinks) Another twenty yards and we'd have had to swim for it: and I don't know but we wouldn't all be dead.

CATRIONA: And the boat?

CALUM: She'll break her back as the tide goes out.

CATRIONA: Can we not — ?

CALUM: The tide's been running out for two hours already . . . she'll last maybe twenty minutes. She's stuck fast.

JOHN JAMES: (to CATRIONA). Perhaps you're thinking, the skipper would be better off to have gone down with her?

CATRIONA: (goes over to him gently, takes his hand). I'm sorry.

JOHN JAMES: Och, it's not the end — I'm a good skipper, and they know it.

JIMMY: You're a dangerous maniac who shouldn't be let

out with a rubber dinghy. You've risked the lives of your men and the happiness of their wives and children, and all for your he-man notions of yourself doing battle with the ocean — you can forget it, Captain — no man goes out with you again — ever.

JOHN JAMES: Now, you hear me, Jimmy Litherland —

JIMMY: You'll skipper empty boats from now on, John James, and no two ways about it — (To CALUM and the two men.) is that not so?

JOHN JAMES turns to them. They hang their heads and nod, muttering Aye, etc. JOHN JAMES turns back to JIMMY.

JOHN JAMES: Come out from behind that bar —

MacALASTER bangs on the counter.

MacALASTER: Stay where you are, both of you, I'll have no behaviour of this kind in this place —

JOHN JAMES: Come on, then, my wee jackanapes — outside . . .

JIMMY ducks under the bar. CATRIONA pushes him back, tries to stop him. JOHN JAMES waits at the door.

CATRIONA: No — no, stop it, Jimmy, you're like a couple of schoolboys —

JIMMY: If it's a fight he wants, by God, it's a fight he'll get.

JOHN JAMES: Come away, then —

CATRIONA: No, Jimmy — now if you set foot outside that door, you can keep on going, for I'll have none of you — etc.

While they are speaking, the IRISH WOMAN has come on from round the back, muttering and shaking her head, tugging her clothes together, irritated. At this point, McPHEE bellows after her:

McPHEE: (off.) Come here, you stupid woman, what's the matter with you?

IRISH WOMAN: (shouts back). You're a madman — a raving looney — I'll have none of you —

McPHEE: (off). Jesus, woman, I have it — Jesus woman, come back here — come back here!

Inside, the argument has stopped, and they all listen to this going on outside. The IRISH WOMAN makes a dismissing gesture and goes into the bar. When she gets in, she is taken aback by them all.

IRISH WOMAN:	What is this? What is it at all?
JOHN JAMES:	Come in, Rosita. (Closes the door behind her.)
IRISH WOMAN:	(sadly). He's an old man. A poor old man.
JOHN JAMES:	Did you —
IRISH WOMAN:	Nothing took place.

She goes over to the bar and sits.

McPHEE:	Come here, woman, can't you, I'm desperate —

McPHEE appears round the corner of the hotel, in a desperate state of impotent anguish. He is half undressed and looks awful. He slopes along to the door, goes in, sees them all, but only looks at the IRISH WOMAN. He looks at her longingly, sadly. He slowly looks around at them, clutches himself and curls up on the floor.

McPHEE:	Oh, Jesus, it's gone. Rosita, it's all gone.
JIMMY:	Aeney —
McPHEE:	Jimmy — it's no good. Do you know, ever since she died I've wanted only to be down there beside her. That's all I've wanted. Well —

He looks slowly at JIMMY, at JOHN JAMES, at CATRIONA, and at the IRISH WOMAN. CATRIONA runs to comfort him, but JOHN JAMES stops her.

JOHN JAMES:	Leave him.
McPHEE:	(nods). I've betrayed your mother, Johnny, or tried to: and you too.
JOHN JAMES:	Aye, and I could split your skull for it.
McPHEE:	Why don't you?
JOHN JAMES:	Stand up and I will.
JIMMY:	You're to take me first, John James: remember?
JOHN JAMES:	I'll deal with you in a minute.
JIMMY:	Come away from him.
JOHN JAMES:	Don't poke your nose where it's not wanted, do you hear? You've done enough of that since the minute you set foot here —
JIMMY:	Is that so?

JOHN JAMES: Who asked you to my mother's funeral — who
                asked you to organise your union, who asked you
                to drive him into the nuthouse — ?

JIMMY: I know what you want from me . . .

They stare at each other. MacALASTER gets nervous.

MacALASTER: Outside, gentlemen! Jimmy, will you get outside —

JIMMY: Come on, then —

He walks to the door, CATRIONA protesting. The two men and CALUM
follow JOHN JAMES. In the bar CATRIONA holds her father's hand,
anxious. The IRISH WOMAN sits thinking, glumly. MARY is desperately
anxious for JIMMY's fate and goes to the window to try and see.
MacALASTER glances at his watch.

The fight takes place. JOHN JAMES is heavy and crude and drunk.
JIMMY soon gets his measure, and has him falling all over the place.

Eventually, JIMMY wins, ending up putting the bot in and having to
be dragged off by the others. He is calmed down and led back into the
bar, the winner. He stands in the doorway, breathless, blood-covered,
waiting. JOHN JAMES is dragged in unconscious. One of the crewmen
gets water and a cloth to mop him up. CATRIONA can't bear to look
at JOHN JAMES. She looks at JIMMY.

CATRIONA: So you won again.

JIMMY: A-ha.

CATRIONA: Like you always do. (She goes out of the door. He
                runs after her.)

JIMMY: Catriona!

She turns briefly to say:

CATRIONA: That's the end, Jimmy.

Then she goes on. JIMMY believes it, is stunned. He goes back to
the bar.

McPHEE raises his glass to JIMMY, smiling wickedly.

McPHEE: Well, now, Jimmy — and here's to our next MP.
                (He drinks as the curtain falls.)

END ACT ONE

ACT TWO

Scene One

Night. Two thirty in the morning. The same hotel, subtly changed.

It is April 1966. Election Day.

Off stage, cheers and 'For He's a Jolly Good Fellow', etc. mingle with the sound of the sea.

The bar is dark. A light is on in a window of the hotel and MARY is looking out. She is joined by PAULINE, another younger girl, quite forward and pretty.

PAULINE:	What's going on?
MARY:	Somebody seems t'have won the election.
PAULINE:	. . . I wonder if it's Mr Litherland again — Oh I hope he's in again — (Listens, says:) — Oh, for he's a jolly good fellow!
MARY:	He is too, don't you think?
PAULINE:	(coy, hiding something). Oh, now, Mary. (Pause.) And how would I know?
MARY:	I should guess you'd have your ways of finding out, Pauline MacDonald.
PAULINE:	I should imagine he'd have a few ways about him, too. Oh, he's a lovely man.
MARY:	Will you listen to the sea.
PAULINE:	Shall I tell you something, Mary?
MARY:	I'll make no attempt to stop you.
PAULINE:	Will you promise not to tell?
MARY:	I can keep a secret as well as the next woman . . .
PAULINE:	Oh now, promise, or I'll be in terrible trouble with Calum.
MARY:	I'll swear my oath.
PAULINE:	Really?
MARY:	Come on. Cough it up. You're like a heifer with the croup.
PAULINE:	Well, I'll tell you. (Giggles.) Mr Litherland . . . (Fit of giggles.)

MARY: Oh, for any's sake, girl, you'll choke yourself. What's new about Jimmy Litherland?

PAULINE: He kissed me passionately.

MARY: I said, what's new? He kissed me passionately when I was at St Columba's Infants, and he's never missed an opportunity since. Did you not know about men like him? Were you born last Tuesday?

PAULINE: Ah. (Offended.) Ah, but that's not all.

MARY: (raising an eyebrow). In that case, you were born last Tuesday.

PAULINE: *I* don't care.

MARY: Don't care what?

PAULINE: If he came to see me. In my room.

MARY: You wouldn't mind if he would, you mean.

PAULINE: He *did*.

MARY: And?

PAULINE: He's lovely. He's the answer.

MARY: To a maiden's prayer.

PAULINE: I'm no maiden.

MARY: Pauline MacDonald.

PAULINE: But you promised not to tell, now, Mary.

MARY: I didn't promise not to give you a clip round the ears, now, did I?

PAULINE: Do you think I shouldn't have let him?

MARY: You're a silly wee heifer and you deserve all you get. I just hope for your sake, he's not been voted out.

PAULINE: I'm *sure* he'll get in.

MARY: He gets in most places. If he can enter half the virgins in the Hebrides, he shouldn't have much trouble entering Parliament. Here's a fellow — who's it?

PAULINE: It's Tom the barman, I can tell by his hat.

Enter below, MacKINNON the barman in mac and Robin Hood trilby, coming from the results.

MARY: (loud whisper). Hey, Tom!

MacKINNON: (startled). What in the name of . . . oh, it's you. I thought it was an apparition in the heavens.

MARY: What's the score?

MacKINNON: It's Jimmy Litherland the winner again. (Impressed.) By six thousand, five hundred majority this time.

PAULINE: (squeals). Wonderful, I *knew* he'd do it.

MARY: Thanks, Tom.

MacKINNON: I'm going to put out a drink in the resident's lounge. I think it's a triumph for the working man.

MARY: It's a triumph for Jimmy Litherland to get the bar open at three in the morning.

MacKINNON: He's a resident, isn't he?

MARY: As long as he doesn't bring that Frank Lockheed and *his* rabble with him.

MacKINNON: Not at all, just him and his missus, for a quiet brandy — to celebrate: they just want to be alone together — and they deserve it.

MARY: Good luck to them. Have they finished making a ceilidh over there?

MacKINNON: They're all away to their beds.

MARY: Well, so am I.

MacKINNON: Goodnight, then. (Goes off, across stage.)

MARY: You seem to have inspired your man, Pauline.

PAULINE: D'you think he'll need any more inspiration tonight?

MARY: Not if I know him. He'll try anything once: but I don't see him making any habits for himself. He has a wife.

PAULINE: Hm.

MARY: What does that mean?

PAULINE: Fat lot of good to him, she is.

MARY: Aha. Is that what he told you?

PAULINE: He did so.

MARY: Come away in, miss, till I tell you a thing or two.

PAULINE: Do you doubt his word?

MARY: (Whistles in amazement at PAULINE's credulity.) Are you wise?

PAULINE: But he says that they're not terribly well adjusted.

MARY: And I suppose jumping into bed with the likes of you's his way of squaring things up.

PAULINE: Oh, now, Mary, I couldn't resist him. Don't tell me I'm wicked or I'll cry.

MARY: (smiles). You're not so wicked. He's a beautiful man. I could go for him myself if I hadn't known him these fifteen years.

PAULINE: There you are, then . . .

MARY: Here's him and his maladjustment, get inside with you, quick.

PAULINE: Could we not give him a cheer?

MARY: Shift will you? I'm stuck.

PAULINE: Oh, he's lovely. Will we turn out the light and watch him? Oh, yes. Quick, or he'll be gone.

She goes in, MARY after her. The light goes off. PAULINE's face appears at the window, then bobs down.

JIMMY LITHERLAND comes on, his arm round RACHEL's shoulder, leaning heavily on her. They stop and listen to the sea. After a moment, he turns her to face him, and kisses her, gently, warmly. They hold each other tight.

JIMMY: Ma wee wee Hampstead lassie. We've made it again. 1964, 1966 —

RACHEL: Sh!

JIMMY: Can I say thank you, Rachel?

RACHEL: Come over here and watch the sea.

JIMMY: (as she leads him to the bench on the rocks). I've seen the sea, my beauty.

RACHEL: Come and look at it again with me. (They stand side by side.) I've been wanting just to stand and

> hold you, and watch the waves, and feel the wind
> blowing, ever since we came up here. It's good,
> isn't it? Say it's good.

PAULINE appears briefly, waves to JIMMY, and disappears.

JIMMY: It's evil, my broody hen.

RACHEL: But it's exciting and wild, and free.

JIMMY: You just don't know it like I do, ma wee wee
Hampstead lassie. You put yourself out in it in a
small boat, with a force ten gale in your face, and
then tell me if it's good.

RACHEL: It must be great to be out in a gale.

JIMMY: It's not when you're being paid twelve pounds five
shillings a week for it. This and every week. Hm?

RACHEL: (dutifully). Mm. But it's nice to stand here with
you, though, and watch it. It's very powerful.

JIMMY: Did MacKinnon not say he'd a few drinks laid
out for us?

RACHEL: Wasn't *that* a sign of success?

JIMMY: He's a keen Labour man is MacKinnon. One of the
old Catholics from Barra. They say the Reformation
never got through up there. Perhaps that's why
he's so generous with the brandy.

RACHEL: Mm. (Shows no sign of going in.)

JIMMY: Er — (Offers to go.)

RACHEL: Let's just sit a minute.

(They sit on the bench, JIMMY rather reluctant, but resigned. He
stretches determined now to make the most of it.)

That was a marvellous thank you speech, darling.
They really love you here.

JIMMY: Hm. I wonder how long for?

RACHEL: Oh, Jimmy, come off it. I don't see anything short
of an earthquake shifting you *now*.

JIMMY: I'm here until 1970, anyway —

RACHEL: The wireless reckons we're going to win by about

	forty-five seats. We can't fail, anyway, with things the way they are.
JIMMY:	Yes. It looks as if our leader's going to be scraping together a new Government.
RACHEL:	My father more or less made that man leader of the party.
JIMMY:	And no doubt will be suitably rewarded.
RACHEL:	I'm pretty sure you won't be forgotten either.
JIMMY:	Oh, why?
RACHEL:	Actually, he's more or less promised. You see, if he has a Left Wing Cabinet and a large majority, they'll push him into extreme Socialism.
JIMMY:	But *I'm* an extreme Socialist, didn't you know?
RACHEL:	(shaking her head). No, darling. You try to be. But you're not. You're too sensible.
JIMMY:	I see. So I'm in there by the kindness of my right-wing father-in-law . . . And the Hampstead old guard . . .
RACHEL:	No no no. Don't be ridiculous, Jimmy. Nobody's going to force you into the Government.
JIMMY:	(pause). You're a politician's daughter alright.
RACHEL:	Jimmy, it's a real opportunity —
JIMMY:	I feel very dangerous.
RACHEL:	Calm down, calm down.
JIMMY:	Don't talk to me like that.
RACHEL:	Alright. It's only an idea. My father didn't want me to tell you all this, anyway, so forget everything I've said.
JIMMY:	*He* said all that?
RACHEL:	Mm. I can easily ring him in the morning. Cancel it. (Pause.) He might be a bit upset.
JIMMY:	Hell!
RACHEL:	And it's not nepotism, if that's what you're worried about. He genuinely believes in you.

JIMMY:	(savagely). He believes in me because I'm the only politician under sixty he's clapped eyes on for the last twenty years.
RACHEL:	(shakes her head). No. Don't you trust his judgement?
JIMMY:	He's a very nice man. As a politician . . .
RACHEL:	Where do you draw the line?
JIMMY:	(Pause.) I'm tired. (Rubs his hand all over his face.) I haven't slept properly for six weeks. I need a rest.
RACHEL:	We should get back home by the morning plane.
JIMMY:	London, you mean? You'll be lucky.
RACHEL:	But we *must*.
JIMMY:	With this wind blowing? It'd blow the plane right out of the sky. No. There'll be no flight tomorrow.
RACHEL:	But we *can't* stay up here.
JIMMY:	(looking at her coolly). We'll stay up here a bit. Cool off.
RACHEL:	(Swallowing her arguments.) Mm. Well, I suppose it could be the cleverest move of all.
JIMMY:	(smiles at her affectionately). You're a fighter, aren't you? You never let up. I like you for that.
RACHEL:	Do you? (Softens.) I'm a hopeless female, really. I love you, that's all. I want everything for you. You deserve everything.
JIMMY:	Shall we go in?
RACHEL:	I'm so tired suddenly. Help me up. (He helps her up. She leans heavily on him.) I just want to sleep for a week.
JIMMY:	Do you?

As they turn to go in, he looks up. PAULINE has her face pressed against the window in the moonlight. She waves. He acknowledges, meaningfully.

RACHEL:	You don't mind if I take a sleeping pill, darling?
JIMMY:	No, not at all. Why don't you sleep in *your* room tonight. Have a good rest?

RACHEL: Mm. Will you tuck me in?

JIMMY: Of course I will. Come on. Then I'll slip down for
               my brandy, and listen to the results.

RACHEL: (laughing). Poor Tom! I hope he hasn't waited up.

JIMMY: He'll have gone to bed, don't worry.

RACHEL: (as they go off). I'm *so* proud of you, my darling.

PAULINE: (puts her head through the window). Me too.

As the lights fade, the window PAULINE was looking out of comes
down with a thump, as the sea swells up.

BLACKOUT

Scene Two

November 1968.

Upstairs, RACHEL is in the bedroom packing their suitcases.

Downstairs, a copy of *The Times*. Behind it JIMMY.

CATRIONA comes on, makes her way to the main door, goes in quietly.
She stands in the doorway of the saloon watching JIMMY for some
seconds before he senses someone is there, and turns round.

CATRIONA: Congratulations. I hear you've landed a good job
               down there.

JIMMY: Catriona!

CATRIONA: We wanted to tell you how pleased we are . . .
               Under-something at the Board of Trade, isn't it?
               (She comes in, easy, relaxed.)

JIMMY: It's a lowly rung on the ladder.

CATRIONA: Congratulations all the same.

JIMMY: Thank you.

Awkward pause.

CATRIONA: You haven't been round to see us, Jimmy.

JIMMY: I've been a wee bit — ach, Catriona, I can't look
               your father in the face any more, and you know
               that. To be honest, I find it hard to face you, too.

CATRIONA:	(laughs). Avoiding us, were you?
JIMMY:	Something like that: and the longer I stayed the more difficult it got . . .
CATRIONA:	Well, so I came to see you — and there's an end to it. (Pause.) Your wife's with you I believe. I'd hoped to meet her.
JIMMY:	(impatient). Catriona!
CATRIONA:	Well, why ever not?
JIMMY:	Look, what *is* this?
CATRIONA:	Surely you're not *so* ashamed of us . . .
JIMMY:	(fiercely). Of course I'm not ashamed of you.
CATRIONA:	Of hcr, then?
JIMMY:	(wearily). Oh, God!
CATRIONA:	You've not exactly rushed round to introduce her to us . . . you have been married a year or two . . . They say she's pretty.

PAULINE comes in. JIMMY orders a coffee. CATRIONA refuses to take anything. PAULINE looks at JIMMY. CATRIONA sees this and smiles. PAULINE goes.

JIMMY:	What have you come for?
CATRIONA:	Aha — the politician speaks: you suspect a darker motive?
JIMMY:	Come on now, Catriona: we know each other, don't we?
CATRIONA:	We're getting to know each other, as the years go by. (Pause.) You realise it's too late for him to leave the island now?
JIMMY:	It was too late then — Nashville, Tennessee — you were out of your nut to think of that one . . . You've not come to reproach me for stopping him?
CATRIONA:	He's in real trouble, Jimmy.
JIMMY:	I see. What? . . . Is there anything I can do?
CATRIONA:	You know he lost his job after that affair with Rosita? (JIMMY nods.) He's moved her into the

431

house now. She's turning him into an animal: I'm going to have to move out, I can't stand watching them. They're drunk nearly every hour of the day. They eat nothing at all. They live like a couple of stinking badgers in a sett, they never change their clothes, never wash, never so much as clean their teeth. Dad's gone into a kind of trance — he never speaks to me, just sniffs around the place, baleful, fish-eyed. The only thing that gets them out of the house, is to come down to the bar: and they're in such a bad way these days, they're even late for opening time. I can't get through to him any more. He seems to have sunk to as low as you can get. And there's nothing anybody can do about it. The woman's half mental — he'll be too, in a month or so.

JIMMY: Is he happy?

CATRIONA: He's desperate. I catch him every now and again reading the newspapers with a terrible glowing sort of intensity, scorching up the news as if he was on fire. Then he'll slump again into an old man's trance, grunt a lot, stagger up the hill and stand looking at the sea and the island for hours and hours. I can't do anything with that.

JIMMY: And John James?

CATRIONA: (smiles). He's gone to work for Ferguson's in Peterhead — something to do with marketing — fleets of lorries he has now under his thumb: I wouldn't say he was happy.

JIMMY: And you?

CATRIONA: I work. The public library would fall apart without me. I write a little bit — nothing serious.

JIMMY: I'd like to read something —

CATRIONA: I burn them.

JIMMY: Oh.

CATRIONA: For the rest, the rain, the sea, the hills, and a damp, empty bed at the end of the day: as ever. My life is not measured by anything, not disturbed. Finally, when the old man goes quite mad: that, I suppose, will be a landmark. I'm a very dull woman.

JIMMY: What can I say?

CATRIONA: (getting up). I've lost what I believed in. But my father is held together, if you can say he's held together at all, because he believes in *you*. He believes that you are going to do at last what he and his generation have given their *lives* trying to do.

JIMMY: What's that?

CATRIONA: I don't know what you call it, but he calls it Socialism.

JIMMY: He'll be wondering why we haven't chopped the Queen's head off.

CATRIONA: He'll be down in the bar in just a couple of minutes — will you have a drink with him?

JIMMY: But I can't promise him the Russian revolution, not this week. (CATRIONA makes a small gesture of impatience. JIMMY gets angry.) Now listen, Catriona, I'm not going to give him a pack of lies, just to cheer him up. I don't deal in fantasies any more.

CATRIONA: No. Good.

JIMMY: (looks at his watch). I hope he's quick — we're to catch the plane at 12.15.

CATRIONA: Ach, they'll hold it for you . . . I'll go and see if he is on his way . . .

She dashes out. JIMMY stands there, pulling at his lower lip. RACHEL comes staggering downstairs with two suitcases, banging her shins, manfully. JIMMY goes out and helps her.

JIMMY: Darling, we'll have to hang on just a couple of minutes — the old chap who once stood for Labour in this constituency wants to see me —

(She sighs with exasperation.)

No, I want to see him. We're not too badly off for time, are we?

RACHEL: Well — I suppose we can spare a minute or two, but no more, mind. Is this the one who got drunk and tried to rape somebody?

JIMMY: That's right.

RACHEL: He sounds amusing, anyway . . .

JIMMY: He was my teacher —

RACHEL: Was he the same man? God, a combination of Keir Hardie and Jack the Ripper. I can't wait . . .

JIMMY: Well, I'm afraid you're going to have to because I'm seeing him in the public bar, and you're definitely *not* encouraged —

RACHEL: Christ, the double standard rides again: why not?

JIMMY: Because that's the way we like it here, and you don't know what you're talking about . . .

RACHEL: Oh, God, the voice of the people: I thought you were meant to be a force for progress on these Victorian islands . . .

JIMMY: Well that's where you're wrong — I'm meant to be a force for the rights of the working man: and one of them is getting a moody drink away from the wife and kids: if that's what they want, that's what I'm here to make sure they get.

RACHEL: And what about these wives. Don't they get a chance for a drink with their husbands, for a change, away from the brats?

JIMMY: In one word — no. Because they don't want to. Because they're not so bloody stupid.

RACHEL: So these are the rights of the working man — Christ, you're a feudal bastard, Jimmy.

JIMMY: I don't want to discuss it with you: you're a pathetic London liberal with no clue about the way the rest of the country lives, and no bloody intention of finding out.

RACHEL: (angry, looks at her watch). Don't be stupid. Anyway, if he doesn't come quick, you won't have time for your man-to- man conversation at all. (She controls her anger, goes over to him.) Darling, I'm sorry, if I was stupid. I do love you.

JIMMY: What's wrong with me in bed, then?

RACHEL: (completely thrown). . . What? . . . Nothing —

JIMMY: Ah, forget it . . .

RACHEL: There's nothing wrong between us, is there?

JIMMY: No. Everything's just fine.

As he looks at her ruefully, CATRIONA comes in, stops when she sees RACHEL.

CATRIONA:	Oh — I'm sorry.
JIMMY:	Catriona, this is Rachel, my wife. Rachel, Catriona McPhee, Aeney McPhee's daughter.
CATRIONA:	How do you do?
RACHEL:	Catriona — what a lovely name — is it a Hebridean name?
CATRIONA:	Not exclusively — Jimmy, he'll be there in ten seconds. Now listen, don't go raking up the muck of the past — you're to concentrate on the future —
JIMMY:	Is she with him?
CATRIONA:	Thank God, no, she's sprained her ankle, or something unlikely, coming home flean one night — she's taken to her stall like a cow in winter.
JIMMY:	I'll go through the bar, then.
RACHEL:	You really can't be very long, darling —
JIMMY:	Have no fear —
RACHEL:	Oh, but I do — I'll come and fetch you if it gets out of hand.

JIMMY goes through the bar into the public, which is empty. He ducks under the bar and pings the bell to get some service, then sits at a table. CATRIONA and RACHEL sit very aware of each other.

RACHEL:	Don't you resent this men-only stuff?
CATRIONA:	Mm?
RACHEL:	All this segregated drinking?
CATRIONA:	Ach, they can keep it. I've no more desire to intrude on their privacy in the public bar than I would have in the public lavatory . . . It's pathetic, I dare say.
RACHEL:	I find it irritating, belittling.
CATRIONA:	(not in the least belittled). Oh, do you? (Pause.) I don't think you should feel that now.

At that moment, PAULINE goes through to the public bar, past them, and MARY comes in to RACHEL with the bill on a plate.

RACHEL:	Thank you, Mary.

She fishes in a busy way in her bag for a cheque book and pen, writes out a cheque, rips it off, vigorously, and dismisses MARY with a five shilling tip. CATRIONA watches quietly, amused.

In the bar, PAULINE has gone over to JIMMY to take his order. He holds her hand, stroking it, looking at her.

JIMMY: (whispers). I'll miss you in London, girl.

PAULINE: (whispers). You'll have to come back soon.

JIMMY: (nods, whispers). On my own, for a change.

(CATRIONA has come into the back of the bar and seen some of this. She smiles at JIMMY. He ostentatiously looks round, then says in a loud voice:)

                Fetch us a pint and a half pint, Pauline.

She goes off to get the drinks, a bit ashamed.

CATRIONA comes through to JIMMY, goes up to him very relaxed and familiar.

CARTIONA: Jimmy . . . !

He is looking up at her, ashamed and embarrassed. She looks over to PAULINE, who is busy with the drinks, bends down and kisses JIMMY fleetingly on the lips, then strokes his hair fondly, smiling at him. She is pleased to be able to forgive him.

JIMMY: Oh, God.

CATRIONA: Don't — I'm not your wife.

JIMMY: No. But you should be.

PAULINE comes over with the drinks, flustered.

PAULINE: One and a half pints.

JIMMY: Thank you, Pauline.

She goes, all worried and a bit angry.

CATRIONA: She *is* a bit young, Jimmy.

JIMMY: Why ever didn't you marry me?

CATRIONA: Mary still works here, doesn't she? Isn't that a bit inconvenient?

JIMMY: You know that nobody else has ever meant anything —

CATRIONA: Including . . . ? (She nods towards RACHEL.)

JIMMY: Aye, including.

CATRIONA: Who knows, Jimmy . . . I couldn't marry you, not then. You know why.

JIMMY: And now?

CATRIONA: I could still love you, I still do, in a way. But — I don't know if I respect you.

McPHEE comes in.

JIMMY: In what way?

CATRIONA: (seeing McPHEE through the window). Here's my father. In the way of constancy: as opposed to pragmatism.

The door opens, in comes McPHEE, in high spirits. Underneath, a terrible degeneration has taken place, in his clothes, his body, his whole humanity.

JIMMY: Aeney! Good to see you.

McPHEE: Good boy. Good boy.

JIMMY: There's a pint set up for you — will you take anything with it?

McPHEE: Not at all — Jimmy, Jimmy.

CATRIONA: If you'll excuse me, I've a job to do: we'll see you more often, Jimmy.

JIMMY: You will, rely on that.

CATRIONA: Goodbye now.

JIMMY: Catriona — I'll see you. (She goes.) I'm sorry I've not been up to you as much as I used, Aeney —

McPHEE: Don't! I know exactly how it must be . . . and how's the morale down there in Westminster — by God, the Tories must be scurrying to their holes like a field full of rabbits . . . I'm delighted at your triumph, Jimmy — your own personal one here, and the triumph of Socialism in the country. What's the first step, then?

JIMMY: Ah well, the first thing, Aeney, is to sort out the economy . . .

McPHEE: Dead right — nationalise the banks, get it all under

	control. You in the Board of Trade will have a big part —
JIMMY:	We-ell — not quite. We weren't put in to play at revolutionaries, you know . . . but, once we've got the economy on the right footing — you won't recognise the place.
McPHEE:	Aha. You're getting a grip on the Steel industry first, are you?
JIMMY:	It's not so easy, Aeney —
McPHEE:	You've got it in the bag. You've got the biggest majority any government's had for years, nothing can stop you —
JIMMY:	We're certainly going to get something done for the Hebrides, I can tell you. Tremendous incentive schemes to encourage private industry to come up here — everything possible.
McPHEE:	Can you not *direct* industry up here? Can you not take some *initiative*? That would be something. And what about the land? At long last you'll be able to get that out of the hands of those bloody absentee landlords, and back to the people it belongs to . . . and not before time.
JIMMY:	We're setting up a commission to go into that, we should have some results in time.
McPHEE:	Good, good — excellent. Press for that now, Jimmy, for that's where you can really hurt them — take their land. By God, when I think of how those bastards drove the people of these islands, out of their houses, herded them down the glens and into the boats, like so many cattle, and packed them off by the thousand to Canada — if they didn't die of cholera on the way there — when I think of *that*, Jimmy, I thank God or whoever's up there for the powers of a socialist government.
JIMMY:	It was a long time ago, Aeney.
McPHEE:	Aye, but it'll never be forgotten: nor forgiven: and they'd do the same thing again if it meant a penny more profit.
JIMMY:	At least we've got through a ten per cent wage claim for the men on the boats —

McPHEE:	They're the same old boats, and the same old owners, Jimmy. Don't let it rest there: they're as cunning as weasels, your capitalists — they'll get the better of you in the end, unless you take away the lot — every farthing they've got.
JIMMY:	I think we have them on the run . . .
McPHEE:	Good boy, Jimmy — I hope you have. Aye.
JIMMY:	How have you been yourself, Aeney?
McPHEE:	Pretty fair. Pretty fair. I'm not the old pedagogue I once was, of course — not that I'd go back to it. Pestilential profession: the powerless indoctrinating the mindless — what a way to live.
JIMMY:	What occupies you now?
McPHEE:	Oh — I'm trying to enter into the blessed state of mind of a clod of earth: preparing myself, you might say, to accept the penetration of the worms with impunity. It's not so easy. I once saw a ptarmigan, somewhere, way up there on the ben, and for some twenty minutes managed to obtain something of its mentality, or lack of it: but it passed. I keep trying, do you see.
JIMMY:	To become a ptarmigan?
McPHEE:	I have not altogether taken leave of my senses, Jimmy. You, of course, are too young, and your ambitions lie strictly in the world of men: a false world, transitory, full of shifts and calamities, nevertheless, one that has its urgencies. But what you learn up here, Jimmy, when you stop struggling with your poor, struggling fellow men, and walk around a bit — is that there's the rest of creation, lying there, heather and waves and clods of earth, moon and stars and milky way, just being, defiantly, regardless — am I talking a load of rubbish, do you think?
JIMMY:	Not at all, I just — tell me.
McPHEE:	Ach, I can never tell you. All I can say is, it's waiting here for you, and whether you like it or not, it'll have you. What I'm learning is how to make my peace with it. I've got as far down the ladder as the ptarmigan: when I break through to the soil, I'll tell you.
JIMMY:	Do you not find this — animal frame of mind a bit, well, boring?

McPHEE: You fight on inside the mesh, Jimmy. I'm not discounting that. The words I hear are for old men and lunatics. I have a woman, now. How's yours?

JIMMY: (looks at watch). She's well, but impatient, Aeney. I must go. The plane will be away without us. Will you come through and meet her?

McPHEE: Delighted. Never miss an opportunity to broaden my concept of the possible.

JIMMY: She's a wee bit English, you know.

McPHEE: Ah well, even the best of us have some affliction.

They go through the bar into the saloon. RACHEL is reading a magazine. She smiles warmly when McPHEE comes through, and stands up to greet him.

RACHEL: Mr McPhee — it's very nice to meet you.

McPHEE: I'm delighted to make your acquaintance, Mrs Litherland.

RACHEL: I've heard so much about you from Jimmy.

McPHEE: Your father's our new Minister of Health, I see. There'll be a lot of work for him on that front, of course. I'd like to see the faces of those Yankee medicine makers when he gets his hands on them — they've been bleeding our Health Service white — now he can't wait to be after their blood, I should imagine. We set the heather on fire up here when your husband was elected for the first time, Mrs Litherland — we set the whole bloody mountain on fire when he got in for the second, with that magnificent majority. We're in a mood for his sort, Mrs Litherland. I taught him the first principles of Socialism, you see; you can imagine what it means to me to see him now, a leading member of a Socialist Government, all set to revolutionise this ageing country? Jimmy, I mustn't keep you: it's been very good to converse with you and your wife. I can see you must go. Here, let me help you with that now . . .

JIMMY: Not at all, Aeney, I'll manage just fine. I'll see you next time — I'll be up before the end of the month, the twenty-seventh, I think it is, I'll see you then.

RACHEL: It's been very nice to meet you, Mr McPhee.

They make their way out, pursued to the door by McPHEE, who shouts after them:

McPHEE: Get hold of the banks first, Jimmy, and the rest'll be easy.

JIMMY turns at the door and waves, non-committed, but smiling. He and RACHEL walk round the front of the hotel and off towards the village, JIMMY carrying the suitcases. RACHEL is ahead of him. She stops and turns to him.

RACHEL: What on earth have you been saying to that poor old man, darling?

JIMMY: Oh — nothing at all, really: nothing at all.

They go off.

McPHEE gets back into the public bar, and goes for his drink. He sits and sips it, as the glassy-eyed stare comes back over him. He makes a low sound, like a bird — a ptarmigan maybe. Quite quietly, to himself.

McPHEE: Ee-ack ee-ack ee-ack ee-ack.

BLACKOUT

Scene Three

September 1970. Lunchtime.

The bar is empty, not even a barman in sight. CALUM enters, headed for the door of the bar. He enters, is staggered to see it empty, and goes over to the counter and fiendishly punches the bell, shouting:

CALUM: MacKinnon! MacKinnon! You priest-ridden Barra man! Stop! (He glares around him.) Where are they all? (Goes back to the bell.) Holy Holy Holy, Lord God of Hosts, Hosannah in the Highest.

MacKINNON comes on trying to look smart.

MacKINNON: Yis?

CALUM: Where are they all?

MacKINNON: Who?

CALUM: The people, who else? (Sees MacKINNON is not hearing him.) MacKinnon! How do you hear me, over?

MacKINNON: (yawns). Heavy interference, I'm afraid. Now — what can I do for you?

CALUM: Is the job too much for you, MacKinnon, or what is it?

MacKINNON: A whisky and peppermint, is it?

CALUM: Ah, so you recognise me! Well done, well done, well done.

MacKINNON: And a Mackieson for chaser.

CALUM: The Memory Man! And what came fourth in the Grand National in 1927?

MacKINNON: Here, you're back a bit soon.

CALUM: That's damned perspicacious.

MacKINNON: Where's the peppermint cordial?

CALUM: There in front of your eyes.

MacKINNON: Oh yes. Why are you back so soon?

CALUM: Because I've been laid off.

MacKINNON: Laid off? One whisky-pep.

CALUM: I've a good mind to prosecute. I've a strong case. It's victimisation run riot.

MacKINNON: One Mackieson. Five and a penny.

CALUM: What'll you take yourself?

MacKINNON: Not a drop.

CALUM: Come on man, set yourself up for the day with a Baccardi and gin.

MacKINNON: Five and a penny.

CALUM: Here. Keep the change for your collection at Mass.

MacKINNON: Why were you laid off?

CALUM: Because I'm the union secretary, I suppose. It may feel to you like 1970, MacKinnon, but this new Tory lot are trying to put us back to 1906. They say they're going to fine us for striking — prison too. I heard Jimmy Litherland got here last night. Is he up yet?

MacKINNON: (holding his head). He *was* here last night. He'll be down.

CALUM: Huh. I'll wait.

442

PAULINE comes cheerfully in, stops when she sees CALUM.

PAULINE: Hello, Calum . . . (CALUM nods curtly. She looks at him again.) What are you doing here?

CALUM: We may not be getting married quite as soon as we thought we were —

PAULINE: What do you mean — ?

CALUM turns away. The fishermen come into the bar in threes and fours, looking dejected and fed-up. One from each group goes up to the bar to order a half and a half pint or dram or a half of heavy. MacKINNON the barman serves them all, aided by PAULINE. CALUM stands when the first group comes in, then watches and understands that the whole lot of them have been laid off.

CALUM: Have the whole lot of you — ?

ANDY: We'll need your bloody union now, laddie. Fergusons have done a deal. The boats are away to Peterhead, and we've all been given a month's pay. (Pause.) It's the technological revolution.

CALUM: I'm not sure the union's going to allow the owners to sell up without proper consultations —

ANDY: Save your breath for your porridge, they've done it. And do you want to know who Ferguson's man is? John James McPhee. He was standing by with a dozen Norwegians — they're sailing on the tide, and they've a bus-load of police protecting them.

PETER FRASER: Well, Mr Secretary, what does your rule-book say about this?

At that moment, AENEY McPHEE, looking the ghost of his former self, comes on with the IRISH WOMAN, and they make their way, like a couple of old tramps, to the bar. They go in, are surprised to find so many there, and go on to the counter without speaking.

ANDY: Well, Aeney . . .

McPHEE: (clears his throat). In the shit, now, is it? (He laughs.) Don't be looking at me?

PETER FRASER: You lead us into this as much as the other fellow, Aeney. You were talkative enough then, were you not?

McPHEE: Aye. But it turned out I was not fit. Not fit to represent you in London, not fit even to teach your

children their ABC: it turned out I had something
between my legs, all the time — which no public
man is allowed to. Aach — (dismisses them — turns
back to the bar). Two halves of heavy and a nip.

IRISH WOMAN: What're you all doing in here, drinking and boozing
away — you'd think you had no work to go to . . .

McPHEE: Quiet woman.

ANDY: Aeney, for the love of God will you get her out of
here, we're about to have a serious meeting.

McPHEE: It's a public place.

IRISH WOMAN: I've heard it all before. I've heard every word.

McPHEE: She'll not speak.

They take their beers and wander in silence over to an empty table.

All eyes now turn to ANDY, standing at the bar. He looks around
him, sadly.

ANDY: Well — well, well, well, well. Seven years ago, you
asked me to be your chairman. I told you then I
didn't see any good coming out of it and now I'm
chairman of a lot of unemployed. Very well, we got
another thirty bob on the pay, very well we got two
weeks holiday: but now we've no boats. And you
cannot fish without boats, and there's an end. I say
the hell with the union, we were getting along just
fine, and nobody was exploiting nobody. There's
not much point in resigning from something that
no longer exists — but in case there is — I resign
from this bloody union right here right now.

He goes over and sits at a table, leaving CALUM at the bar. They all
turn to look at CALUM.

CALUM: I'm sorry to say so, Andy, but you're wrong — So it
was the union caused this, was it? Well I'm telling
you, with no union, this would have come sooner,
and a damn sight more brutal. I don't think the last
word's been said on this . . .

OTHERS: Away with you — Ach, away, etc . . .

CALUM: In fact, there's a hell of a lot more to be said: don't
forget, we've one ally, at least, in high places.

OTHERS: Ach that one — Jimmy Litherland . . . etc.

ANDY: Aye, and where is he — the fellow that got us all into it? — in London, nae bally fears.

CALUM: Andy, you're no comfort to us in our troubles, do you know that? (Silence. ANDY glares at him. He turns to PAULINE.) Pauline, would you go up and ask Jimmy to come down quickly on a matter of great urgency?

She goes off. He turns back to the others.

CALUM: There's no need to scuttle the ship before we've so much as manned the pumps, is there? We're not going to go under without a bit of a fight, are we? Jimmy Litherland, as I remember, got us into this. He'll not be wanting to leave us high and dry, do you think?

ANDY: I would not be so sure about that, wee Calum. There's one or two been left in the lurch by that same man — including one or two wee lassies on the island, or so I've heard tell . . .

CALUM: What're you muttering about, Andy? If you've anything to say, step forward.

ANDY: We'll leave it at that, Calum, and await the consequences . . . Anyway, she's big enough to look after herself.

The IRISH WOMAN cackles suddenly to herself.

CALUM catches on to what they're trying to tell him, and suddenly feels very unsure. At that moment, JIMMY and PAULINE come down the stairs, through the saloon and into the back of the bar. They stand together in the doorway for a minute. CALUM looks from JIMMY to PAULINE fiercely. PAULINE's face gives her away. CALUM takes a deep breath. JIMMY speaks.

JIMMY: A strike is it?

All are silent, waiting for CALUM, but he suddenly finds himself unable to say a word: he stands there, staring at PAULINE, then down into his beer.

JIMMY: Calum, what is it? Can you speak man?

CALUM points out behind him, still not looking at JIMMY.

CALUM: The boats — are away to Peterhead — excuse me.

He turns and walks out, having been humiliated before the entire fleet.

JIMMY looks after him, worried, then glances back at PAULINE, who is almost in tears. She turns and goes out through the main door and runs after CALUM.

JIMMY realises what has been going on, and realises that they all know it. However, he thinks it better to pretend he doesn't.

JIMMY:	Can nobody — Andy, what's going on here?
ANDY:	I'm none too sure what's going on here, Jimmy — but I'll tell you what's happened down there. Thanks to your bloody union and your extra four shillings, all the skippers on Morna have gone under: Fergusons have bought up the boats, and they're in the process of being rationalised to Peterhead: John James and a dozen Norwegians are taking possession —
JIMMY:	This is absolutely outrageous — we must stop them — who's for going down there and kicking them into the harbour? Who is with me?
ANDY:	Not so fast, Jimmy — they've thought of that one. There's a boatload of constables from Malaig standing, twiddling their thumbs under the harbour wall. They look murderously peaceful.
JIMMY:	We've got to keep those boats in the harbour. Once they're away, it will be impossible to get them back.
ANDY:	Well, ye'll not do it by force, I can tell you that.

Silence. They think.

PETER FRASER:	(MARY's young brother, a dour man, married and settled.) Could we never get out an interdict from the sheriff to stop them?
JIMMY:	You may have noticed — there's recently been a change of government. There's nothing in the law to help us, I'm afraid . . . not a word.
ANDY:	And why ever not — isn't that what you're there for, ah?
JIMMY:	Rome wasn't built in a day, Andy.
ANDY:	No, but it was sacked by the Huns in about twenty-five minutes —

JIMMY looks over to McPHEE who laughs.

McPHEE:	(his glass almost to his lips). In the shit, the lot of

you . . . (He drinks, puts his glass down, smacks his lips, and looks back at JIMMY.)

JIMMY: What time's the tide?

ANDY: The tide's at four, but they'll get out empty by two if they want to —

JIMMY: So we've an hour.

RACHEL has come downstairs and is standing in the saloon, wondering what is going on. JIMMY hears her and glances in her direction.

JIMMY: Give me a pint of beer, Tom — and a pint for every man who wants one with me. There must be a way to do this — Peter, will you go down and see what's happening, while we all have a think. I'll try and get a call in to Ferguson's Head Office in Newcastle while we're thinking — have a word with them. Thanks, Tom.

He takes the pint and goes into the saloon. RACHEL stops him.

RACHEL: What's happening?

JIMMY: The fleet's been sold up — they're all out of work, and I don't know what we're going to do about it.

RACHEL: Well you know it had to happen —

JIMMY: What the hell do you mean? You're talking like a Tory. Nothing *has* to happen.

RACHEL: It was an old, inefficient way of acquiring fish. What on earth is the point of landing your fish on an island stuck out in the Atlantic when all you've got to do is sail the boats to the markets on the mainland. Any fool could see that.

JIMMY: It's what has kept the whole community together for centuries, woman — made it what it is . . .

RACHEL: Then maybe it's got to change.

JIMMY: Don't be so bloody stupid.

RACHEL: It's not struck me as being so bloody marvellous . . .

JIMMY: Oh hasn't it? Well, I like it the way it is —

RACHEL: Who's talking like a conservative now? You're getting absurdly sentimental about this place, Jimmy. The world's changing, faster than it ever has — is there

447

any reason why your little childhood acre should
be preserved in aspic?

JIMMY: It's not because I'm sentimental about it, Rachel
— you don't understand — I owe everything I've
got to those men out there, every damn thing —

RACHEL: They'll manage extremely well, I should think. We've
invented severance pay, redundancy payments,
haven't we? They'll not starve, and they know it.

JIMMY: That's not the point. What I'm talking about is a
whole race of men.

RACHEL: Those men out there don't know they're born. Can
you imagine what would become of them if this
happened in India — or Venezuela — or Greece —
they'd starve.

JIMMY: That's no excuse for it to happen here —

RACHEL: Oh, isn't it? Well, do they know why unemployment
benefits can be so high in this country? Do they
think it has nothing to do with hungry Indians,
or starving Africans? We're still living off the fat
of two hundred years of exploiting the last penny
out of every African, Asian, Chinaman and South
American we could lay our hands on — and don't
let them forget that.

JIMMY: You really hate them, don't you?

RACHEL: (pause.) I just don't want you to go sacrificing
yourself on their altar, that's all. You're worth a hell
of a lot to the party, Jimmy, and you've great things
ahead of you — if only you'd be what you are . . .

JIMMY: What's that?

RACHEL: A politician for goodness' sake: stop pussy-footing
about as if you were the young Shelley, and get on
with your job.

JIMMY: And what might that be?

RACHEL: Getting back into power.

JIMMY: You're a cynical bitch.

RACHEL: Of course I'm not cynical — listen, if you want to
achieve anything, you've got to be in power —
without it you can make lovely noises and have

lovely demonstrations and shout great emotional slogans, but you'll never *do* anything: there's something in you that responds to all that phoney ballyhooing and romantic posturing, isn't there? You seem afraid to just get down to work, to do the things you *can* do, in the real world, the things you're good at doing: don't listen to that other part of you, Jimmy — it will ruin you.

JIMMY: And if I do listen to it?

RACHEL: I leave you. I don't want to watch you declining into a sentimental old failure.

JIMMY: In that case you can start packing:

RACHEL: What are you talking about?

JIMMY: I'm going to ring Moynihan and ask him to make an order restraining the sale to Fergusons —

RACHEL: How?

JIMMY: Monopolies Act, Companies Act — I don't know. Moynihan can think of something: if he doesn't, I'm going to lead those men down to the harbour and occupy the boats. If it comes to it, we'll fight until every last one of us is arrested. I'm looking forward to it.

RACHEL: You're completely out of your mind. I shall leave you.

JIMMY: I may well be — and you may well leave me. Excuse me.

He goes into the hallway and out to make his call. RACHEL wonders how she can out-manoeuvre him.

CATRIONA comes on, and in through the main door to the saloon. She stops when she sees RACHEL.

CATRIONA: Oh — excuse me: I was looking for — er — Jimmy.

RACHEL: Can I help?

CATRIONA: Do you know has he heard about the boats?

RACHEL: I'm afraid he has. He's on the phone to the President of the Board of Trade.

CATRIONA: Will he do any good, do you think?

RACHEL: Not a snowball in Hell's chance. He's just making himself look rather impetuous.

CATRIONA:	Oh.
RACHEL:	He's offering to punch the local bobby if the boats aren't stopped.
CATRIONA:	(pleased). Is he now. That's more like it —
RACHEL:	More like what?
CATRIONA:	The Jimmy I used to know, Mrs Litherland.
RACHEL:	It's more like political suicide, if you want to know the truth. Jimmy's been Under Secretary at the Board of Trade himself and he knows damn well there's no law, rule, or regulation to stop the boat-owners selling up.
CATRIONA:	Is that so?
RACHEL:	They're just shutting up shop because they're losing money. If Jimmy thinks that the Board of Trade can order a man to carry on losing money, he's got another think coming. I know old Moynihan, and so does Jimmy — he'll listen patiently for two minutes, then he'll bite Jimmy's head off . . .
CATRIONA:	But the people on these islands want the boats to stay, Mrs Litherland, and Jimmy's just letting them know about it. Our democracy is supposed to express the will of the majority . . . is that not so?
RACHEL:	I wish it were so simple.
CATRIONA:	Do you know, I think it probably is. It's just — there's something come between what people want and what they get . . .

JIMMY comes in, darkly scowling.

JIMMY:	Aye, and maybe it's me. But I'll not be in the way for long — hello Catriona, my dear. (He kisses her and holds her at arm's length.) Shall we make a fight of it do you think?
CATRIONA:	You'll need to.
RACHEL:	What happened on the phone?
JIMMY:	They'll ring me back when they're through to him . . .

PETER FRASER runs into the bar and spreads a word. The others look up.

RACHEL: You know, we *were* going to call on Mrs Johnson
at the distillery at one-thirty —

JIMMY: Ach, all that'll have to wait a wee while . . . Ssh,
what's happening?

Meanwhile, JOHN JAMES has appeared, and gone to the door of the
public bar. He opens it and stands there, smiling round at all of them.
He's dressed very well now, and has a more well fed, tamed look about
him. The men are eyeing him with a mixture of curiosity, caution and
bitterness.

JOHN JAMES: And where's your MP?

ANDY stands up, quaking with anger, and points at JOHN JAMES.

ANDY: John James McPhee. I don't know how you can
stand there — unless you've come for a pint of beer
in your face.

JOHN JAMES: A dram for me barman.

JIMMY has heard and reacts. He comes in behind the bar and looks at
JOHN JAMES.

JIMMY: John James, there's an embargo about to be placed
on those boats being moved out today — you'll be
hearing from Ferguson's Head Office within the
hour . . . you'll kindly stay by the phone here.

JOHN JAMES: Is that so? (Sharper.) I said I'll take a dram, barman.

FRASER: You'll not serve him, MacKinnon.

JOHN JAMES: Now then, Peter Fraser, now then: I'm here to
try to help the likes of you. You're married now,
aren't you?

FRASER: Does that concern you then, McPhee junior? I hear
you're not, nor ever likely to be.

JOHN JAMES: That's enough of bitterness, Peter. I'm here to tell
you, one and all, that when these boats join the big
fleet at Peterhead, Fergusons will have vacancies
for a dozen or so men: you here are to have first
choice. You'll be working a regular week, Monday
to Friday — You can either move to Peterhead, or
travel home here for weekends like some of the
others do to Aberdeen or Fort William. The pay's
the same as you're getting, the pace a bit faster.
Fergusons are an American financed group; they'll
not be doing with Trade Unions, so you can forget

451

that for a start and add your union subs to your
beer money. If you want work, the address is left
with the unemployment office — you can write.
No trouble makers need apply. That's all I have to
say. Now — do I get my drink, or don't I?

Nobody dares to speak against him. MacKINNON gets the spirit of the
meeting, and pours him one. JOHN JAMES comes over to get it. JIMMY
is behind the bar. CATRIONA comes in behind him and RACHEL listens
keenly in the saloon.

JIMMY:	Who's idea was it to buy up all the boats in the first place?
JOHN JAMES:	The board at Fergusons — on behalf of their seventeen thousand shareholders.
JIMMY:	And who put it into their heads?
JOHN JAMES:	I can't imagine.
JIMMY:	And who thought of this latest piece of 'rationalisation'?
JOHN JAMES:	I work for them. I do as I'm told.
JIMMY:	You know damn fine what's going to happen to this town if those boats sail away?
JOHN JAMES:	I imagine it won't be so full of Labour voters . . .
JIMMY:	In three years it will be empty.
JOHN JAMES:	I don't think any man here will blame Fergusons for that — or even me, though you seem to think I did it single-handed. We don't need very long memories to remember who brought the unions in to the island, do we? And there is even one or two of us can figure out why.
JIMMY:	You know damn well, why, John James — I said to you then, and I'll say it again to you now: if Fergusons want a fight, by God, we'll give them one. I'm ready to sail to every island in the west, every port in the north, to organise their victims against those bloody vultures.
JOHN JAMES:	(laughs). I'd like to see you try.
JIMMY:	I'll do more than try — I'll break Fergusons if it's the last thing I do.
JOHN JAMES:	It will be. Just let me tell you a thing or two,

Mr Honourable Member, that maybe you don't know. Fishing's changed. We're in the age of the freezer. Fergusons is not just Calum's uncle on a bigger scale, you know. It's just one of a massive international group, owned by 17,000 ordinary Americans and controlled from New York. They own boats, markets and lorries in Norway, Sweden, Denmark, Greenland, Iceland, Ireland, Holland, France and Germany, apart from seven or eight harbours they control here. And they're organised just like General Motors or United Fruit: they manufacture their product wherever it's cheapest and easiest. So if *you*, Mr Litherland, make it too difficult for them in Morna, they'll up sticks and away to Peterhead, where they've a freezer, and if you make it too tight for them there, if you organise the whole of Scotland — they'll just sail their boats away to Spitzbergen until you make it easy for them to come back. These boys weren't born yesterday Jimmy, they're not your old-fashioned, small-time bosses — they're men of the future — and you don't stand a chance.

JIMMY:

Very well — if their exploitation is scientific and international, our defences must be scientific and international . . .

McPHEE:

(Stands) And how the hell are you going to arrange *that*, Jimmy? Your party, *my* party, *our* party has been in power for six years; they've had their chance — and they never for one minute showed the first inclination of putting into action one word, one thought, of socialist theory. You let yourselves be told what you could and what you could not do, internally and externally, by the controllers of international capital, and by the punters in the City. You kowtowed to every reactionary instinct in the British people — on race, and students and drugs and God knows what else besides. You put your foreign policy in the pockets of American businessmen, and you've even tried to smash the unions themselves. You tell me how *you* are going to fight an American financed, international cartel on behalf of these men sitting here — just tell me, Jimmy. The first two years you were in were like a bad dream — the last four were sheer bloody torture, to me, and to millions like me. And we want to know what you intend to do about it, because you speak for us.

JIMMY stands as they all look at him, and thinks about what McPHEE has said.

JIMMY: I could argue with everything you've said, Aeney — you've exaggerated greatly, even been a little hysterical.

(The phone rings off. RACHEL goes through and gets it as JIMMY continues.)

               We found ourselves in a tricky situation, and we tried to fight our way out of it constitutionally and in accordance with what we take to be the wishes of the majority. However, (He sighs.) when I look at you, and I look at them, and I look at him —

RACHEL comes in as he shakes his head sadly.

RACHEL: Moynihan for you, Jimmy.

JIMMY: Excuse me. I'll be right back.

He goes back into the saloon. CATRIONA watches as RACHEL catches him and says urgently:

RACHEL: Now, Jimmy — no rash threats. If you say anything stupid I'll leave you, and that's flat.

JIMMY turns to her, coolly, looks at her. Then he looks up and notices CATRIONA watching. He smiles.

JIMMY: Will you? Is that a promise?

RACHEL swings round and sees CATRIONA, is very angry.

RACHEL: Yes, indeed it is.

They look at each other. Moynihan is waiting. JIMMY goes to the phone. RACHEL turns to CATRIONA.

               I hope you and your father realise what you are doing to him.

CATRIONA: Aha.

Pause.

RACHEL: This wouldn't be some obscure form of revenge, would it, Miss McPhee — I gather you both have cause . . . ?

CATRIONA: Do you know, Mrs Litherland, I honestly don't think it is. No.

454

RACHEL: Then what *are* you trying to do?

CATRIONA: Have you noticed a peculiar thing about these islands,
            Mrs Litherland? No trees. Scarcely one to be seen for
            miles and miles. Except around the country seats,
            the hunting lodges, the rich farms, — and the manses
            suddenly profusion — rhododendrons, beech and
            birch, pine and oak, and a sturdy undergrowth —
            they always seem to us to serve as a kind of cloak
            for what goes on inside — and inside the minds
            of their owners. We bumpkins — crofters and
            fishermen, and distillery men, and, God knows,
            country teachers — don't have the comfort of woods
            around us: no windbrakes or coverings. We tend to
            be hit in the teeth by the elements without let or
            hindrance every day of the year, and — unpleasant
            as it might be — it does give a certain sense of the
            realities of life. It has seemed to us lately — to me
            and my father, and our few friends at least, as if
            the minds of the people of England, and most of
            Scotland too, had got themselves surrounded by
            thickets, hidden themselves away from the elements
            round a cosy fire in a chintzy room, were somehow
            protecting themselves. Jimmy's not from these
            islands, neither's my father — but they both know
            the blast of a cold north wind, and the feel of a
            grave on a stony hillside. You won't know what
            I'm talking about, but Jimmy will, and if you think
            you can stop him seeing and hearing and feeling, to
            make him a proper politician, that's up to you. But
            we know that lie and cheat and deceive himself as
            hard as he may, there's a part of Jimmy that's out
            there on the bare moor, knowing what's happening:
            and it's that part of him that we're interested in.

RACHEL: It's the part of him that will make him a great
            politician.

CATRIONA: Aye. If he sells it.

RACHEL: (shrugs). It's his own choice. It's out of my hands.
            Unlike Jimmy, I never threaten to do something
            unless I intend to do it. If he mucks up his career
            for the sake of a few fishing boats, as far as I'm
            concerned he's finished — and that goes for my
            father and the rest of the party, I can assure you.
            And whether he'd have his head in a bag or a
            bramble bush, he'd be a bloody fool.

JIMMY comes back from the phone, shaken.

JIMMY: He told me not to interfere with the liberty of the individual to buy and sell as he pleases. I intend to get myself arrested for a wide and enjoyable variety of crimes —

RACHEL marches straight out, upstairs, and begins packing.

CATRIONA and JIMMY are alone: JIMMY looks after RACHEL with a certain amount of regret. Then he turns to CATRIONA. He is very shaken, shivering with fright at the step he has taken. He goes over to CATRIONA and takes her hand.

I'll need help

CATRIONA: Yes.

JIMMY: Don't go away. (He kisses her hand, then goes through into the bar.) I've spoken to the President of the Board of Trade. He refuses to help. He says there's no law against it.

JOHN JAMES laughs.

McPHEE: Great God. The almighty dollar has spoken . . .

JIMMY: So we're going to have to fight —

ANDY: Fight: What with? (JIMMY holds up his fist.)

JIMMY: This! They can put me inside for ten years —

PETER FRASER: They probably will —

A general reaction of surprise and incomprehension.

McPHEE: (stunned, then overcome with joy). Well done, Jimmy, well done, well done — do you know, those are the first words of spirit I've heard for five years —

PETER FRASER stands up. Silence.

FRASER: There is, er, just one thing. Now I think it's all very fine for Mr Litherland to fight for his principles — but where does all this leave us?

JIMMY: Well I'm still your MP of course: I can still fight, even from prison.

JOHN JAMES: Poor Jimmy. (They all look at him.) Talk. Fight You're too late . . . (Looks at watch.) Your boats have gone.

They all stand up, ready to move. CATRIONA comes through. JOHN JAMES does not see her.

Sit down, sit down. You'll need to swim after them if you want them back: your MP has spent too long talking about it — and saved himself a few months in prison, bye the bye, though you might as well have gone, for you're going to lose your seat in a year or two.

JIMMY: Is that so, John James?

JOHN JAMES: It is. (JOHN JAMES goes to the door, about to leave.)

McPHEE: Away to hell out of here, boy —

JOHN JAMES closes door again, turns to McPHEE.

JOHN JAMES: Father —

CATRIONA now steps forward out of the bar.

CATRIONA: Haven't you done enough to him —

JOHN JAMES turns and sees her for the first time.

JOHN JAMES: Catriona . . .

JIMMY: (meaning CATRIONA). I've gained one thing you'll never have.

JOHN JAMES: (looking at them). You'll never make it. (He turns away) Good-bye, Catriona. I wish you joy — sister.

CATRIONA: You'd better go, John James —

McPHEE: Away, you Yankee's lackey —

JOHN JAMES: Father — if I may still call you father — in case I never see you alive again (Takes a grubby press-cutting from his wallet.) — I have guarded this for you, carefully — (Gives it him.) Take it. Read it. (He turns to the men, opens the door.) Why don't you all go down and see the boats off, now. It's an historic sight — never to be repeated. (JOHN JAMES goes out. A silence.)

IRISH WOMAN: Bad cess to that one: he's never forgiven his mother for dying on him.

ANDY: I never thought to see the day.

McPHEE is looking very shaky. CATRIONA goes over to him. He crumples up the piece of paper and throws it away. She picks it up.

CATRIONA: (reading it). Dad, what is it?

457

FRASER: (turns to JIMMY). Jimmy, what did you say you'd be doing for us?

JIMMY: It's clearly too late to occupy the boats. We should have done that in 1966. At the moment, all I can do is fight from the back-benches.

FRASER: In parliament, ah?

JIMMY: Aye. That's how democracy works . . .

FRASER: Then I'm sorry to say this to your face, Jimmy, after you've made such a gesture — but if that's how it works, democracy's a bloody farce.

JIMMY shakes his head, doesn't say anything.

McPHEE has gone ashen pale, and is still staring at the piece of paper. CATRIONA speaks to him gently.

CATRIONA: Dad, it's not even true . . . it's only a *theory*. And even if it was, it only happened in some cases, not all . . . Dad, you musn't let him do this to you.

IRISH WOMAN: What is it, what is it? (She snatches at the piece of paper. McPHEE snatches it away from her.)

McPHEE: (to IRISH WOMAN). Will you go away from me?

IRISH WOMAN: Tut. Tut. Fancy throwing a lady out — come on sailor —

McPHEE: Go away from me, woman: and don't let me see you again.

IRISH WOMAN: You'll not get rid of me as easy as that, you know!

CATRIONA: (gently). Rosita, could you just leave him for a while — could you?

IRISH WOMAN: It's a public place.

McPHEE: Then I'll go myself. Jimmy, you've shown courage today. I'm proud to know you.

JIMMY: (wondering what's wrong with McPHEE). What? Aeney, are you alright? You're looking terribly pale.

McPHEE: My son has just given me a piece of paper from a pseudo-scientific journal. It reports the researches of an American medical team in Omaha. They claim to have isolated a virus responsible for cervical cancer, the one that Bessie — they say it is transmitted to the womb by an unclean male —

458

JIMMY: That's not true, Aeney — it's rubbish — pseudo-scientific rubbish.

McPHEE: I know. But my son has just tried to kill me, do you see?

CATRIONA: Don't let him —

McPHEE: No, no, of course not. Excuse me. You'll find me at the house. Kindly keep that harridan at bay.

He turns and goes. The IRISH WOMAN sulks into her beer. JIMMY and CATRIONA look at each other, this time very much closer together than ever before.

As they stand looking at each other, RACHEL comes downstairs, with her suitcase and through into the public bar.

RACHEL: (seeing them). Touching sight. So you're not in a cell, then . . .

JIMMY: The boats had gone before we could do anything — we spent too long talking about it.

RACHEL laughs, but she is very unhappy. She knows she has to leave him.

RACHEL: Pity, you missed an opportunity. (She turns to MacKINNON.) Mr MacKinnon, would you find the taxi?

MacKINNON: Aye, I'll do that.

She goes through to the saloon. JIMMY follows.

JIMMY: What can I *say*?

RACHEL: What's happening to you?

JIMMY: I don't know. It's got something to do with the law of the land. I spent six years trying to make it. Now I've lost any respect for it.

RACHEL: You can't go on like that.

JIMMY: I know. It's got something to do with this island too, no doubt. I want to sink back into it. (Smiles.) You'd better go. I don't see you as the wife of a failure.

RACHEL: I'm going to get married to Colin Peel. I've been having an affair with him for eighteen months: I shall never forgive you for not noticing — Goodbye, Jimmy.

JIMMY: Er — Yes. Goodbye.

She turns and goes. He gazes after her. The door closes. CATRIONA looks over. JIMMY goes to the hatch and calls her through. She sits amongst the fishermen who have been sitting still and silent thinking about their future. She goes to him. They stand in the saloon, looking at each other.

Shall we go and look at the fulmars?

CATRIONA: (nods). And the seals. And the gannets plunging into the cold sea. And the razor-bills and the cormorants and the guillemots. And the rain on the back of the waves — and the loneliness of the empty places.

JIMMY: And the drift to the south-east, and the drift into Europe, and the drift into profitability, and away from humanity —

CATRIONA: Come on: the ptarmigans will be changing colour for the winter, if we hang about much longer.

JIMMY: You know, I don't think I'm going to stand the humiliation of (Points to bar.) all that — much longer. *We're* romantics. (Indicating the men.) *They* are the ones who should be — (He makes a violent gesture of revolution.)

CATRIONA: Come on, Jimmy. You did what you could, I suppose.

JIMMY: Did I?

She puts a hand on his arm, neither agreeing nor disagreeing. They go off. The MEN are left alone in the bar. The lights come up strongly on to them. They stir quietly. PETER FRASER gets up and knocks on the counter.

PETER FRASER: MacKinnon!

(He then hammers, angrily, impatiently, violently on the bar.)

MacKinnon!

<u>END</u>

2

Six-pack:
Plays for Scotland